Eastern Europe in the 1980s

Also of Interest

† *The Domestic Context of Soviet Foreign Policy*, edited by Seweryn Bialer

† *The Soviet Union in the Third World: Successes and Failures*, edited by Robert H. Donaldson

† *The Soviet Union in World Politics*, edited by Kurt L. London

Arms Control and Defense Postures in the 1980s, edited by Richard Burt

† Available in hardcover and paperback.

About the Book and Editor

Eastern Europe in the 1980s
edited by Stephen Fischer-Galati

The death of Josip Broz Tito and the recent workers' strikes in Poland were, for many, harbingers of change in Eastern Europe's political landscape; Stephen Fischer-Galati, for one, remains unconvinced that any real change can occur. Minor improvements in the *condition humaine*, an easing here and there, a few small concessions—yes—but no major reshuffling or political and social departures. The contributors to this volume are convinced that the Soviet Union will not relax its stranglehold and will in fact continue to dominate Eastern Europe's cultural, social, and economic policies. In their view, although broadly based libertarian movements such as the strike-supported drive for independent unions in Poland might actually topple sections of government and bureaucracy and even result in greater freedom, such attempts cannot march beyond the limits of Soviet convenience, military power, and the rigid contours of the current Soviet aims and policies, internal and external.

This book assesses the contemporary state of affairs in Eastern Europe from an historical perspective and in terms of continuity and change under Communist rule. The assessment is on an areawide rather than a country-by-country basis inasmuch as the authors feel that the "bloc" concept cannot be abandoned in favor of polycentric or sum-of-the-individual-developments approaches that have been advocated from time to time.

Stephen Fischer-Galati is professor of history and director of the Center for Slavic and Eastern European Studies at the University of Colorado. He is also editor of the *East European Quarterly*.

Eastern Europe in the 1980s

edited by
Stephen Fischer-Galati

Westview Press • Boulder, Colorado

Croom Helm • London, England

Copyright © 1981 by Westview Press, Inc.

Published in 1981 in the United States of America by
  Westview Press, Inc.
  5500 Central Avenue
  Boulder, Colorado 80301
  Frederick A. Praeger, Publisher

Second printing, 1982

Published in 1981 in Great Britain by
  Croom Helm Ltd.
  2-10 St. John's Road
  London, S.W. 11

Library of Congress Catalog Card Number: 80-28765
ISBN (U.S.): 0-89158-198-7; 0-86531-122-6 pb.
ISBN (U.K.): 0-7099-1005-3

Printed and bound in the United States of America

Contents

Tables and Figures

Chapter 5

Chapter 7

Chapter 8

Figures

Chapter 5

The Contributors

ELEFTHERIOS N. BOTSAS is professor of economics and management at Oakland University. He has published extensively in the area of East European trade.

GEORGE R. FEIWEL is Alumni Distinguished Service Professor at the University of Tennessee. He is the author of numerous books including *Economics of Socialist Enterprise, Soviet Quest for Economic Efficiency, New Economic Patterns in Czechoslovakia, Industrialization and Planning Under Polish Socialism,* and *Growth and Reforms in Centrally Planned Economies.*

LEWIS A. FISCHER is research associate in agricultural economics at Macdonald College of McGill University. He is the author of four books, the coauthor of three others, and has published numerous articles on agricultural policy and agricultural economics.

STEPHEN FISCHER-GALATI is professor of history at the University of Colorado and editor of the *East European Quarterly* and of *East European Monographs.* He is the author or coauthor of numerous books on East European history and politics including *Eastern Europe in the Sixties, The New Rumania: From People's Democracy to Socialist Republic, Twentieth Century Rumania,* and *The Communist Parties of Eastern Europe.*

TROND GILBERG is professor of political science and associate director of the Slavic and Soviet Area Center at the Pennsylvania State University. He is author of *The Soviet Communist Party and Scandinavian Communism* and *Modernization in Romania Since World War II.*

ROY E. HEATH received his doctorate from the University of Wisconsin and is a specialist on East European education.

JOSEPH HELD is currently associate dean of University College, Camden,

Rutgers University. He has published in a wide range of areas in East European history. His latest work is *The Modernization of Agriculture: Rural Transformation in Hungary, 1848–1975,* which he edited.

DANIEL N. NELSON is associate professor of political science at the University of Kentucky. He is the author of *Democratic Centralism in Romania,* editor of *Local Politics in Communist Countries* and several other books, and has published numerous articles on Communist politics.

ROBIN ALISON REMINGTON is professor of political science at the University of Missouri at Columbia and a research affiliate of the Massachusetts Institute of Technology Center for International Studies. Her publications include *Winter in Prague: Documents on Czechoslovak Communism in Crisis* and *The Warsaw Pact: Case Studies in Communist Conflict Resolution.*

WAYNE S. VUCINICH is Robert and Florence McDonnell Professor of East European Studies at Stanford University. He is the author or editor of numerous books on East European history including *Eastern Europe, Contemporary Yugoslavia, The Ottoman Empire: Its Record and Legacy,* and *Serbia Between East and West.*

Introduction

The 1980s began with an event that was for a long time focal to the attention of individuals concerned with international affairs and to the prognosticating instincts of Kremlinologists—the death of Josip Broz Tito. The question so often asked, What will happen after Tito? is symbolic of concern over the future of Eastern Europe in the face of the ever-present possibility of Soviet military intervention for one reason or another related to Soviet imperialism. The fact that only a few months before Tito's death the Kremlin ordered the invasion of Afghanistan merely exacerbated the fears of those who remain convinced that the Kremlin, under certain "objective conditions" of its own definition, is likely to restore Soviet control over all of Eastern Europe. Yet, it is also true that the very same observers and analysts who have repeatedly asked the question regarding Tito's death have developed theories supporting the existence of a new order in the Soviet bloc, an order that ostensibly is different from that of the monolithic 1950s and early 1960s. After all, they argue, Yugoslavia is pursuing its own road to socialism; so are Romania, at least in the field of foreign affairs, and Hungary, in internal economic development. And, they add, even Bulgaria and Czechoslovakia display variations of the Soviet model and both the German Democratic Republic and particularly Poland have evolved in ways not always to the Kremlin's liking. Albania is, of course, a shining symbol of defied Stalinism.

Then why this grave concern over the possible intentions of Moscow vis-à-vis post-Titoist Yugoslavia? Does Yugoslavia indeed pose a danger to the security and interests of the Soviet empire? If it does, some thirty years after Tito's defiance of Stalin's threats, then little has changed in the essential relationship between the USSR and the socialist countries of Eastern Europe, and we may well conclude that in essence Eastern Europe in the 1980s is remarkably similar to Eastern Europe in the 1960s. If it does not, and the question is either rhetorical or a reflection of ill-founded apprehensions, we would have to take at face value the statements and assurances uttered by Leonid Brezhnev and other Soviet spokesmen regarding the inviolability of the Yugoslav socialist state and political system.

The contributors to this volume provide data and interpretations that essentially deny the credibility of Brezhnev's assurances. The data and analyses are themselves subject to varying interpretations but, in general, tend to substantiate the editor's view that the course of Eastern Europe in the 1980s will remain a function of Soviet interests and concerns. Since the 1980s do not promise any improvement in the present global status quo and, in fact, are more likely to be fraught with economic and political uncertainties and crises, the future of Eastern Europe during this decade is likely to be bleaker than at any time since 1968. Disengagement from Soviet tutelage and commands in political matters seems implausible; rather, greater coordination of economic and military positions is likely to occur in the 1980s, barring, of course, a major succession crisis in the Kremlin following Brezhnev's inevitable retirement. Whether Yugoslavia will be able to maintain its present policies and order is a matter of conjecture and, again, a function of events in the USSR. Thus, more relevant to any possible assessment of developments in Eastern Europe in the 1980s is not the answer to the question What will happen after Tito? but to that of What will happen after Brezhnev?

Offhand, the answer to that question would seem to be "nothing drastic." In other words, the socialist countries of Eastern Europe will remain socialist, politically and economically insecure, and ultimately dependent on Russia's power for their continuing existence as Communist states. And their continuing existence as Communist states will always be a sine qua non of Russian foreign policy no matter who succeeds Brezhnev.

*   *   *

These pessimistic views merely reflect a long-term assessment of the historical processes that have governed Russian foreign affairs since the nineteenth century. We are, of course, not concerned with Eastern Europe in the nineteenth century in this volume; but the elements of continuity in Russian imperialism are self-evident and were emphasized, albeit primarily with reference to the sixth and seventh decades of the twentieth century, in our previous volume, *Eastern Europe in the Sixties*, which appeared nearly twenty years ago in 1963. In a sense, then, *Eastern Europe in the 1980s* is an updated version of the earlier volume. Just as in the case of Dumas's *Vingt ans après*, the elements of continuity are paramount. This is not to say that elements of change are not present, for indeed they are. Continuity, however, has the upper hand and thus the old adage *plus ça change plus c'est la même chose* remains as valid in the 1980s as in the days of Dumas.

It is noteworthy, too, that these considerations apply also to the editor and publisher of the present volume. The continuity is evident in both cases, and I am grateful to Frederick A. Praeger for having encouraged the publication of this 1980s volume. Whether we will join efforts in the publication, some twenty years from now, of *Eastern Europe in the Twenty-First Century* remains to be seen.

Stephen Fischer-Galati

Wayne S. Vucinich

1

Major Trends
In Eastern Europe

The 1970s did not witness any major doctrinal political conflicts in the East European Communist world. By periodic purges of the leadership and ranks, reissuance of party cards, and organizational changes, the Communist parties sought to strengthen their position. These changes, however, were hardly sufficient to keep pace with the many problems that continue to plague each country's political and economic life. Throughout the 1970s the leaders of all the Communist countries in Eastern Europe continued to complain about the lack of dedication, discipline, and vigilance on the part of the Communists and Communist party organizations. The situation seemed particularly delicate in Poland, where the ability of the Polish Communist party to govern the country "in a rational and efficient fashion was significantly eroded."[1]

Even Yugoslavia, a non-bloc country, had its problems. In the early 1970s, the Yugoslav leaders cited opportunism, liberalism, and techno-cratism, as well as factionalism and counter-revolutionary activities as some of the problems facing the League of Communists of Yugoslavia (LCY). The regime was particularly disturbed by the Croatian nationalist agitation and similar manifestations among other ethnic groups. President Tito was bent on achieving ideological unity in the country and tighter control over the LCY. The official measures resulted in purges and resignations of several prominent party and government leaders. The new LCY statute adopted in 1974 emphasized democratic centralism, strengthened the executive organs of the LCY, and abandoned the "federalization" of the party.[2] By the time the Eleventh Congress of the League of the Communists of Yugoslavia met in June 1978, Tito could

The author wishes to express his gratitude for assistance to a number of his colleagues, especially to Ann Halsted, Vera Henzl, Wojciech Zalewski, Laszlo Citron, Laszlo Horvat, Marc Truit, Eric Terzuolo, and Nicholas Pappas.

1

speak with certainty about Yugoslavia's stability over the past thirty years and the continued advance of socialism as "capitalism" slipped into "ever deeper crisis." He recognized different roads to socialism, demanded respect for independence and equality of states, and regretted the fact that conflicts persisted among the nonaligned countries. The Yugoslav leaders stressed the importance of the teachings of Marx and reiterated Marx's belief in the necessity of democratic centralism. But Tito was not without critics, Marxist and non-Marxist, less for his problems in maneuvering Yugoslavia through difficult times than for his "great vanity and the monotheistic cult he has permitted to be built around himself, and for equating his personal interests with those of his country." The critics also resented his "proclivity for pomp and other trappings of power," and his extravagant personal habits.[3]

The questions of Marxism, socialism, and ideology have remained uppermost in the minds of the Communist leaders in Eastern Europe. From time to time they have sponsored conferences, national and international, to reaffirm loyalty to the Marxist tenets and doctrines. One of the more important gatherings was the Yugoslav-sponsored conference at Cavtat on the Dalmatian coast, October 1-5, 1979, at which 113 Marxists from 57 countries met to discuss the problems of Communist parties ("The Subjective Force of Socialism"). The speakers noted that capitalism had survived despite prophecies about its "imminent death." The Soviet and Yugoslav Marxists engaged in heated polemics over whether the "Leninist type of Communist party" was valid any longer, and the Polish and Yugoslav delegates clashed over the problem of self-management. Yugoslavia's Aleksandar Grličkov denied the existence of any "leading center" of the international Communist movement, insisting that there should be "various roads to socialism."[4]

On December 12-17, 1978, the Bulgarian Communist party and the Soviet journal *Problemy mira i sotsializma* sponsored an international conference in Sofia on "Construction of Socialism and Communism and World Progress." Seventy-four Communist parties sent their representatives to this conference. The purpose of this gathering was made clear by the host, Todor Zhivkov, who observed that world Communism could progress only through the solidarity of all Communist movements with the Soviet Union, and by recognition of the Soviet hegemony over the Communist world.[5] As it turned out, except for confirmation of existing Soviet policies, no important decisions were made at this meeting. Zhivkov's blind obedience to the Soviet Union has stood him well. He is the undisputed master of Bulgaria. Like Ceaușescu of Romania, the seventy-year-old Zhivkov, the first party secretary since 1954, has also encouraged the development of a "personality cult," and in doing so he has eliminated his potential enemies. Since her mother's death (1971), Ludmilla Zhivkov, the Bulgarian leader's daughter, has been designated the chairman of the Committee on Culture and has been playing the role of Bulgaria's "First Lady."

Largely isolated from the main currents of Communist thought, Albania organized its own "National Conference on the Problems of Socialist Construction" (November 22–23, 1979), when it celebrated the hundredth anniversary of Stalin's birth, using the occasion to denounce the revisionists and to proclaim that "all true Marxist-Leninists are loyal to the teachings of Stalin."[6] Albania has continued to have its own special problems. It went through a period of "thaw" from 1970 to 1974, characterized by a measure of tolerance and permissiveness. Since then, Albania's party has tightened its controls and purged some potentially dissenting military and civil personnel. Professing loyalty to Stalinism, Albanian leaders took steps to prevent the emergence of a "new class" of the kind that existed in the Soviet Union and other "revisionist countries." In this connection, the People's Assembly adopted a law that prohibited the ratio between the average wage of workers and the highest wage of functionaries from being greater than 1 : 2.[7]

Romania has not relented in its oppressive domestic policy, although it has conceded in allowing a slight degree of freedom in matters of culture and intellectual activity. Ceaușescu criticized the domestic and foreign enemies of Romania, calling for improved ideological and propaganda activity. Romania's domestic problems also stem from a mismanaged economy and low standard of living. Despite enormous investments, it now appears that Romania will not become a middle-developed state by 1985, as Ceaușescu had envisioned. The Romanian Communist leaders have complained of the complacency of the party membership with its lack of ideological conviction. Consequently, in September 1977, Romania's party drew up an "Ideological Action Program," the purpose of which was to bring ideology and education in line with the principle of "permanent revolution."[8]

Growing criticism is being made of the Nicolae Ceaușescu personality cult. The critics object to the increasing identification of the Romanian leader with the Communist party and the Romanian nation and to his portrayal as the greatest figure in Romanian history and a source of universal truth. The critics also charge Ceaușescu with nepotism for having designated his wife Elena as the Communist party's foremost decision-making woman, and for putting his son in charge of the Communist Youth Organization. Ceaușescu's "personality cult" has also been extended to his wife, whom he portrays as an ideal human being, a model wife and mother. But one thing in Ceaușescu's favor is that he has succeeded in establishing the self-identification of Romania within the Communist bloc, and his defense of Romanian independence from Soviet domination by means of the Warsaw Pact and COMECON has won a degree of institutionalization. He considers his country a part of the Third World, and as a result Romania participated in the Havana conference of nonaligned powers in 1979.

The instability of the Communist states is also attested to by frequent constitutional changes and administrative reorganization. In the 1970s, several Communist states have either adopted new constitutions or amended existing ones. Constitutional reform in October 1968 made Czechoslovakia a federal state comprising the Czech Socialist Republic and the Slovak Socialist Republic. This was the only measure that survived Alexander Dubcek's abortive attempt to liberalize Czechoslovakia. The Hungarian constitution of 1972 recognized the Hungarian Socialist Workers' party (HSWP) as the "Marxist-Leninist party of the working class" and "the leading force in society." After much debate the Polish parliament (*sejm*) approved a number of amendments in 1976 to the Polish constitution of 1952. The proposed amendments provoked a great deal of discussion inside and outside official circles. Strong protests were voiced against the amendments because they threatened to curtail the abridged civil rights further and to commit Poland to lasting dependence on the Soviet Union. The amendments were modified in their final adoption. Poland was transformed from a "people's democratic state" to a "socialist state," and the Polish United Workers' Party (PUWP) was recognized for the first time as "the leading political force in the country." Instead of proclaiming Poland's dependence on the Soviet Union, as originally intended, the modified amendment merely speaks of Poland's intention to strengthen "its friendship and cooperation with the Soviet Union and other socialist forces."

In 1974 Yugoslavia adopted its fourth fundamental law (others were adopted in 1946, 1953, and 1963) since the end of the war. This document was unlike any other in the Communist world. It introduced a new representational system and provided that the federal parliament—the Assembly of the Socialist Federal Republic of Yugoslavia—be made up of an equal number of delegates from each of the republics. The assembly was reduced from five to two chambers—the Federal Chamber with 220 delegates (30 for each of the six republics and 20 each for the two autonomous provinces) and the Chamber of the Republics and Autonomous Provinces with 88 delegates (12 from each republic and 8 from each province). The local assemblies, from communes to republics, were divided into three chambers—a chamber of associate labor, a chamber of local communities, and a sociopolitical chamber. The "producers" at the local level selected delegates to assemblies of the republics, which in turn selected delegates to the federal parliament. This system was devised to assure full worker participation in the representative bodies and to give the party greater control over the elected representatives—the delegates. Each republic, from the largest to the smallest, had the same voice in legislative affairs.

Of the major changes in the Communist systems, certainly Yugoslav self-managing socialism remains the most innovative. Introduced in the 1950s and the 1960s, Yugoslav self-managing socialism has matured in the 1970s. Under self-managing socialism, the worker "manages" the means of production and "decides" on the distribution of the fruits of his labor, thus placing him at the focus of all socialist affairs.[9] Within Yugoslavia, self-management provides the foundation for "the democratization of social life" and "the construction of a political system" that expresses the plurality of interests in society and allows contradictions inherent in such a society "to be resolved democratically by dialogue and consultations." Internationally, self-management stresses Yugoslavia's national independence by emphasizing a nonalignment policy. The Yugoslav theorists caution that "Socialism cannot create a world of its own that can exist in isolation from the rest of the world." Self-management affects almost every facet of Yugoslav life. Its application to the government and administration is reflected in the 1974 Constitution.[10]

The Yugoslavs contend that their social and economic system shows a realistic appreciation of objective economic laws, which have not ceased to operate as a result of the socialization of the means of production. For them, for example, development plans are not seen as supreme and infallible laws that provide all the details for the activity of every working organization and every individual. The Yugoslavs treat such laws merely as instruments that assist the working people in gradually reaching mastery over the economic and social processes and their contradictions.[11]

Self-management and nonalignment prompted opening to the West and encouraged the adoption of an economic reform that introduced a certain amount of market economy into Yugoslavia's socialist planning, bringing with it serious problems such as a revival of regional nationalism and the development of a technocratic and managerial elite.[12] The foundation of the nonalignment policy on which Yugoslav foreign policy rests may also be seen as the application of self-management to international affairs—the right of each nation to pursue the foreign policy that best serves its interests. In the ideological sphere the same concept can serve to justify the doctrine of separate paths to socialism.

Two additional changes in the Yugoslav Communist system are unique: the all-people's defense system and the collective presidency. After the Soviet invasion of Czechoslovakia in 1968, in view of uncertainty caused by Tito's advanced age, the Yugoslav leaders gave a great deal of thought to the country's defense. In 1970, they announced a concept of nationwide defense, which they term "all-people's defense." As an integral part of the self-management system, the all-people's defense would tap the memory of the partisan struggle and make use of the experience gained in the national liberation struggle. Under this system every citizen and organization would be obliged to fight any enemy of the country. The local armed units would be locally provisioned by communal governments and local enterprises and by voluntary contributions of individual citizens. Their organization would rely heavily on self-management organizations for an infrastructural base. What this means is that some of the national defense expenditures have been shifted from the central government to the local governments. Courses on "all-people's defense" have been introduced in the universities and lower-level educational institutions.

To prevent a possible succession crisis after Tito's death, in 1970 the Presidium of the League of Yugoslav Communists established a collective presidency called the "Presidency of the Yugoslav Republic." This body would function as the president and exercise some functions of the Federal Executive Council; it would be made up of representatives of the various republics and provinces and the principal social and political organizations. It is believed that a collective presidency, made up of representatives of all the nationalities and principal interest groups, was intended to prevent possible conflict between nationalities and reduce other kinds of political strife that might give the Soviet Union an excuse to invade Yugoslavia after Tito's death. The Constitution of 1974 reduced the membership of the collective presidency from twenty-three to nine and designated the workers' self-management system as the infrastructure of social power in Yugoslavia.[13] Prior to Tito's recent death the collective leadership proved effective and it is likely to continue to be so.

Albania's new constitution, adopted in 1976, proclaims Marxism-Leninism as the nation's official ideology, reaffirms the building of socialism on the principle of "self-reliance," exempts citizens from taxes, promises state support for the development of literature and art ("in accordance with the tenets of socialist realism"), and requires the government to pursue an atheist policy and inculcate the people with a "scientific materialistic world outlook."[14] The Albanian Party of Labor (Communist) is described as the only legal political party in the country.

Some Communist countries in Eastern Europe continued a pretense of democracy by including token representatives of non-Communist parties in the government. There are indications that these non-Communist parties have gained in strength, particularly in Poland, where the ruling Polish United Workers' party consults with them on occasion. As a result of the 1976 elections, of the total 460 seats in the Polish parliament, the Communists received 261 seats, the United Peasant party 113, and the Democratic party received 37. Forty-nine seats went to smaller organizations, 13 of them to various Catholic groups. In theory the Bulgarian Agrarian National Union (BANU) of about 120,000 members, once the country's largest party, continues to participate in the government of Bulgaria, although it recognizes Communist control and leadership. The Agrarians hold three ministries and head a number of local administrations, including that of Plovdiv. The union's leader, Petur Tanchev, is the first president of the State Council.

In the German Democratic Republic, the National Front government is controlled by the Socialist Unity party of Germany (SED). However, in order to appeal to specific segments of the population in building a socialist society, the government also includes four middle-class parties—the Christian Democratic Union, the Liberal Democratic party, the Democratic Peasant party, and the National Democratic party.

A number of East European countries, for purposes of administrative efficiency and economy, have merged smaller bureaucracies into larger administrative units. Measures introduced in Poland between 1973 and 1975 reduced 4,300 rural administrative units into 3,350, which later were consolidated into 1,900 large units. The purpose of these measures was to simplify administrative operations and eliminate bottlenecks that previously had hampered dealings between the regional *voivodships* and the rural communities. As a result of an administrative reform in 1978, Bulgaria merged the existing 1,399 municipalities into 283 larger ones.

The party congresses of the East European countries, which convene every five years to ratify decisions of the Central Committee and other principal party bodies, were held with regularity. During 1978, all the Yugoslav republics and the two autonomous provinces convened their congresses, and finally, in June, the Eleventh Congress of the League of Communists was held.[15] The Twelfth Congress of the Communist party of Romania met on November 19–23, 1979, and adopted a Five-Year Economic Plan (1981–1985), a Nine-Year Plan for Scientific Research (1981–1990), a Nine-Year Plan for Technological Development (1981–1990), and an Energy Program (1981–1990). In Poland the Eighth Congress of the PUWP took place in February 1980; in Hungary the Twelfth Party Congress was held in March 1980; Czechoslovakia is now preparing for its Sixteenth Party Congress in 1981.

Ethnic and Confessional Friction

Mounting dissent, open and clandestine, has become a particularly disturbing factor in nearly all East European countries. The dissent stems not only from political and economic conditions, but also from ethnic and confessional grievances. Three Communist countries in Eastern Europe (Albania, Poland, and Hungary) are ethnically homogeneous. Others are beset with ethnic problems of varying intensity. Albania has the potential for a Gheg-Tosk linguistic conflict and Muslim-Christian religious conflict. The main question is Albanian ethnic claims against Greece and, particularly, Yugoslavia. Despite Greek xenophobic pretensions to southern Albania (Northern Epirus), this conflict has been reduced to minor significance. The ethnic claim against Yugoslavia, although usually cloaked in ideological verbiage, has been a major obstacle to normalization of relations between Albania and Yugoslavia. The question has been complicated for Albania because its large minority in Yugoslavia is somewhat better off than the Albanians in Albania proper.

Hungary, similarly, with no serious ethnic problems at home, does have ethnic grievances against neighboring Czechoslovakia and Romania and has not hesitated to vent its grievances openly. During the 1970s its relations with Romania were strained because of the latter's alleged oppression and "deculturization" of the Hungarian minority in Romania. Particularly articulate in this regard has been Gyula Illyés, Hungary's eminent writer, who on several occasions spoke on behalf of his conationals in Romania and Czechoslovakia.[16] Historians of Hungary and Romania continue to disagree on the interpretation of Transylvania's past. This is an old controversy that has once again flared up. Romanian scholars assert the continuity of the Romanian state with its Dacian and Roman antecedents, and Hungarian historians maintain that the Hungarians settled an unpopulated Transylvania in the tenth century.[17] A group of Romanian historians criticized a recently published Hungarian ethnographic dictionary for failing to give due attention to Romanian history during the first millennium.[18] The tension between the two countries became so great that on June 15–16, 1977, Ceauşescu and Kadar (the Hungarian leader) found it necessary to meet at Oradea (Romania) and Debrecen (Hungary) in order to discuss improving the relations between the two countries. The Romanian leader agreed to satisfy the cultural needs of the Hungarian minority in Romania. Very little concrete resulted from this conference, however, and on November 9, 1978, a Hungarian delegation visited Romania to discuss delays in the implementation of the Kadar-Ceauşescu agreements.

Bulgaria has Turkish Muslim and Macedonian minority problems, and a simmering territorial dispute over Dobrudja with Romania. Despite the expulsion of a large number of Turks and Muslim gypsies to Turkey in the 1950s, a substantial Muslim minority has remained in Bulgaria, consisting of the Pomaks (Islamicized Slavs), Turks, and Muslim gypsies. By virtue of their Muslim religion, the Pomaks and Muslim gypsies empathize with the Turks and Muslims at home and abroad. The Pomaks are officially classed as ethnic Bulgarians, although most, like the Muslims of Bosnia and Hercegovina, would prefer to be Muslims. For Bulgaria, the Macedonian minority is a special problem. Most Bulgarians, whether Communist or not, believe that Macedonian Slavs are Bulgarians and reject the official doctrine of Tito's Yugoslavia that the Macedonians are a distinct nation. The Bulgarians want the Macedonians to unite with Bulgaria.[19]

In Czechoslovakia bickering between the Czechs and Slovaks has continued. The Czech-Slovak state dualism did not satisfy all the Czechs and Slovaks because the federalization of the state into two autonomous Czech and Slovak republics has not been matched by decentralization of the Communist party of Czechoslovakia. What currently exists is the Communist party of Czechoslovakia and its "territorial organization" in Slovakia, the Communist party of Slovakia. The state had been federalized but the party remained "unified." Czechoslovakia also has minority problems. The Hungarian minority (backed by Hungarians abroad) and a small Ukrainian group have complained of denial of their human rights.

Romanian Russophobia "is second only to that of the Poles."[20] After World War II the Soviet Union attempted to de-Latinize and denationalize Romania culturally and politically and to inculcate a love of Russia, Communism, and the Soviet regime. Among other things, the Soviet political leaders and writers developed theories of the ethnic and linguistic exclusiveness of the Moldavians, when in reality these people consider themselves Romanians. The Romanians grew resentful over the Soviet policies, which in turn unleashed latent hostility toward the Russians. Problems that had been suppressed surfaced, such as the controversy over Bessarabia. Both the Soviet Union and Romania claimed this province on historical and ethnic grounds and Romania has never forgiven the Soviet Union for annexing Bessarabia. Since 1975, Soviet and Romanian historians have engaged in a debate over the history of Bessarabia and the ethnicity of its inhabitants.[21]

For some time the Romanian leaders have vigorously opposed the Soviet plan for economic specialization within the socialist camp because it assigned Romania's economy to agriculture and the production of raw materials. The literary men began to "re-Latinize the language, and the historians rectified the rewriting of history." The Romanian leaders, Ghorghe Gheorghiu-Dej and his successor, Nicolae Ceauşescu, gained unprecedented popular backing, which encouraged them to continue national policies. The first major act of military-political defiance was Romania's refusal to participate, in 1968, in the Soviet invasion of Czechoslovakia.

Romania also has minority problems, the most serious of which is the Hungarian minority of about two million inhabitants. Immediately after the Communists came to power, the Hungarian minority was favored while the Germans, some of whom collaborated with the Nazis, were discriminated against. In the wake of the Hungarian unrest in 1956, the privileges of the Hungarian minority in Romania were reduced. Later, under Ceaușescu a more conciliatory minority policy was introduced, but the Hungarians remained restricted.[22] Despite constitutional guarantees of equality under law of all citizens regardless of nationality, of the free use of native languages and native language books and magazines, and of education at all levels in native languages, a number of laws and decrees impinge on the cultural and religious heritage of the Hungarian minority. In response to Soviet, Hungarian, and Bulgarian writings on the history of the territories that Romania either possesses (Transylvania, Northern Dobrogea) or hopes to regain (Bessarabia, Northern Bukovina), in 1977 Walter Roman, the party ideologist, published an article justifying the Hungarian Revolution of 1956 as a response to Stalinist excesses. He also condemned the Soviet invasion of Czechoslovakia in 1968.[23]

Yet, the excitement of Romanian nationalism in the 1960s was wearing off in the 1970s, even though Ceaușescu is still able to rouse it from time to time with considerable success. Internal weakness and the recognition of superior Soviet power have compelled Romania to maintain acceptable relations with the Soviet Union. These relations, however, are so fragile that they can break at any moment.

A special kind of conflict exists between Yugoslavia and Albania because Albania hopes someday to extend its control over Yugoslavia's Kosovo region, inhabited overwhelmingly by Albanians and organized into an autonomous province. When the Cominform expelled Yugoslavia in June 1948, Albania's leader, Enver Hoxha, welcomed the opportunity to free Albania from Yugoslav political and economic control and sided with the Soviet Union. At the time, Albania was confident that the Soviet Union would prevail over Yugoslavia. But when, in 1955, the Soviet Union and Yugoslavia normalized relations, Albania found a backer in China. In the late 1970s Albania severed relations with China and adopted an independent national policy, one that opposes all "revisionist" states, including China, the Soviet Union, and Yugoslavia. To weaken the appeal of Albania's irredentism, Yugoslavia has made steady concessions to its Albanian minority. In fact, Yugoslavia has done remarkably well in uplifting the quality of Albanian economic, social, cultural, and political life. The progress in Kosovo has been particularly pronounced since the removal of Rankovich, the head of internal security, and the purges of his entourage in 1966. It is no secret that the Albanians of the Autonomous Province of Kosmet are better off politically, economically, and culturally than their conationals in Albania. For example, steps are being taken to raise Kosovo's Society of Science to the level of an Academy of Science.[24]

But the progress thus far achieved in Kosovo does not satisfy the national desideratum of the Albanian minority, which, incited by Albanian propaganda from the Albanian capital, Tirana, and nationalistic elements in Yugoslavia, particularly in Croatia, demands that its province be elevated to the rank of a republic and given a status equal to that of the South Slav nations in Yugoslavia.

For Yugoslavia, the Hungarian minority is not currently a problem although it could become one. The Hungarian minority appears to be satisfied with its place in the Autonomous Province of Vojvodina and, therefore, has not been a factor in Yugoslavia's relations with Hungary. Hungarian studies at the University of Novi Sad and in general have received full support. It was announced in 1979 that Srpska Matica, the principal society of learning in Vojvodina established in the nineteenth century, will be transformed into the Academy of Sciences and Arts as further recognition of the importance of Vojvodina, an ethnically heterogeneous province.[25]

Although it appears that most Macedonians accept the Socialist Republic of Macedonia in Yugoslavia, organized on the premise that the Macedonians are a distinct nationality with a distinct language, some Macedonians would prefer to be annexed to Bulgaria. To provide the Socialist Republic of Macedonia with all the trappings of a nation-state, in 1967 the Macedonian Orthodox community was awarded an autocephalous ecclesiastical administration headed by a metropolitan, independent of the Serbian patriarch who has his seat in Belgrade. Macedonia remains an obstacle to harmonious relations between Bulgaria and Yugoslavia. Bulgaria uses every occasion (e.g., the anniversary celebration commemorating the founding of San Stefano Bulgaria in 1878 and—according to announcement—the pending celebration of the 1300th anniversary of the foundation of the first Bulgarian state in 681) to emphasize with oral and written word Macedonia's historical and cultural ties with Bulgaria, always equating Macedonians with Bulgarians. When the Macedonians of Yugoslavia announced plans to celebrate on December 7, 1972, the seventieth anniversary of Nikola Vaptsarov, a prominent Macedonian poet, the Bulgarians attacked the idea on the grounds that Vaptsarov was one of "the jewels" of Bulgarian culture.[26]

The Yugoslavs continue to refute Bulgarian claims and to issue their own. The Eleventh Congress of the LCY (1978) adopted a resolution that attacked Bulgaria for refusing to recognize its Macedonian citizens as a "national minority" and charged Bulgaria with being in violation of the United Nations Charter and the Helsinki Agreement. Significantly, Tito interpreted the Bulgarian refusal to recognize the existence of a separate Macedonian nationality as tantamount to denial of "the legitimacy of one of the [Yugoslav] sovereign republics."[27] The Bulgarians held to their position, insisting that "there has never been and there is not at present a Macedonian national minority." In her memoirs, Tsola Dragoicheva, the well-known Bulgarian Communist revolutionary, writes that the Macedonians are Bulgarians and criticizes the Yugoslav policy as anti-Bulgarian.[28] Mihailo Apostolski, the president of the Macedonian Academy of Sciences and a prominent wartime Yugoslav Macedonian partisan leader, responded with sharp condemnation of Dragoicheva's contentions.

Both Bulgaria and Yugoslavia have published materials, books and articles, in support of their respective positions on the Macedonian question. In 1978, Bulgaria's Academy of Sciences released a selection of documents translated into English, the purpose of which was to prove that, unlike the Yugoslav Communist party, the Bulgarian Communist party never advocated the annexation of Macedonia to Bulgaria, but only sought autonomy or independence for it.[29] In recent years the Bulgarian party leaders have on several occasions repeated that they have had no intention of annexing Macedonia. As the war of words over Macedonia continued, other charges and countercharges emerged. The Bulgarians, for example, allege that after World War II the Yugoslav Communist party treated the Bulgarian Communist party with disdain.

Yugoslavia has never trusted Soviet-backed Bulgaria's designs on Macedonia. The Soviet Union has with some exception favored Bulgaria's claims to Macedonia. To allay Yugoslav suspicion, on April 27, 1979, Zhivkov declared that Bulgaria had no territorial claim against Yugoslavia (Macedonia and parts of Serbia), and that it would not relinquish any of its territory (presumably the Macedonian-inhabited Petrich district) to Yugoslavia. He renewed his invitation to Tito for discussions, which the Yugoslav leader refused to accept until Bulgaria acknowledged the existence of a "Macedonian minority" in Bulgaria.

Even Yugoslavia's nation-states have grievances. The federalist principle, generally accepted in Yugoslavia, has not resolved the ethnic and national problems to the satisfaction of every group. In Croatia, relative freedom of discussion and individual initiative, the product of the

Yugoslav policy of devolution of power and economic decentralization, has led to the revival of nationalism. The ferment there reached dangerous proportions in the early 1970s. Realizing that things had gone too far, and that the Croatian Communist leadership itself had begun to succumb to nationalist pressure, Tito decided to purge the party and adopt a policy of repression. Subsequently, this repressive policy was extended to Serbia, Macedonia, and other Yugoslav republics. One author thinks that Tito's action "was directed not so much at nationalism as at liberalism."[30] It seemed that the Yugoslav leader might return to a more rigid form of government, but the repression has since relaxed somewhat.

The Croat nationalist outburst in 1971, though suppressed, has had lasting reverberations. In 1978, a Croatian party leader warned against "the continued, very aggressive activities of certain nationalist elements." Among the Croats there are groups that continue to fear Serbian hegemony. At the same time, the Serbs complain of what appears to them to be an anti-Serbian regime. The Slovenes and Croats suggest that too much of their wealth is siphoned by the central government for investments in the developing areas of Yugoslavia. Incidentally, in 1979, Yugoslavia's federal government was expected to contribute a substantial part of the country's national revenues to the developing republics of Bosnia-Hercegovina, Macedonia, and Montenegro, and the Province of Kosovo. That allocations to the developing regions are formidable can be seen from the 1978 figure, which amounted to about 700 million dollars. The Slovene and Croat nationalists believe that their nationalities would do better if Yugoslavia were transformed into a confederation, within which each nation-republic would enjoy full independence and could dispose of its human and material resources as it saw fit. That this sort of confederation would be tantamount to breaking up Yugoslavia may or may not occur to them.

Montenegro is a special problem. It was constituted as a separate republic primarily because of a long historical tradition of separatism. For various reasons, more and more Montenegrins are claiming that they belong to a separate nation with its own attributes and language. In recent years, the republic's Society of Learning was transformed into a fullfledged Academy of Sciences. Yet, despite a determined official effort to make Montenegro a separate nation and to prove "scientifically" that it has all the attributes of a separate nation, a high percentage of Montenegrins continue to identify themselves as Serbs—Montenegrin Serbs.

Yugoslavia's policy of "diversity in unity" has in some ways been harmful because the government has given more attention to "diversity" than "unity," which has encouraged exclusive nationalisms and slowed down the process of South Slav integration. Nonetheless, many South Slavs continue to identify themselves as "Yugoslavs," even though this concept has been rejected as ethnographically unscientific and politically reactionary. In 1978, 90,732 members of the League of Communists of Yugoslavia (5.59 percent of the total) continued to describe themselves as "Yugoslavs," and the government now appears to acquiesce when its citizens use this identification.[31]

Yugoslavia has another special, if not unique, problem. It concerns the Muslims of Bosnia and Hercegovina. Even before World War II the Communist party recognized the Muslims as a separate group, neither Croat nor Serb. The Communists repeated this distinction regarding Muslims during World War II in official pronouncements and declarations. Their decision to recognize Muslims as a separate category was not implemented until the early 1970s. Before then, the Muslims of Bosnia and Hercegovina were recorded in the census as Croats, Serbs, Yugoslavs, or as "Muslims-unspecified" and "Yugoslavs-unspecified." Consequently, for political and numerical advantage the Croats and Serbs continue to compete in claiming the Muslims as their respective conationals.

In the 1971 census, for the first time, the Muslims (Islamicized Slavs) were allowed and, in fact, pressured to declare themselves as Muslims, even though this is a religious rather than an ethnic concept. (When Yugoslavs indicate the religious group they write "muslim" and for the ethnic group, "Muslim.") As a result more than 1.7 million inhabitants of Bosnia and Hercegovina declared themselves "Muslims by nationality."[32] Of this number, 88 percent were Muslims of Bosnia-Hercegovina (1.5 million, or 5.8 percent of the total Yugoslav population). The figure showed that the Muslims had become the largest demographic element of the population of the Socialist Republic of Bosnia and Hercegovina. (In Yugoslavia there are four principal Muslim groups—the Muslims of Bosnia and Hercegovina who are Islamicized Slavs, the Muslim Albanians, the Turks, and the Muslim gypsies.) The Muslims for the first time surpassed the size of the Serbian population. This is partly due to the heavier losses of Serbian population during World War II, greater Serbian emigration to other Yugoslav republics since the war, and probably also to higher Muslim natural increase.

After World War II, as a minority group, the Muslims closed ranks, regardless of their past and present ideologies. Both the Communist and non-Communist Muslims became identified by their common historical and cultural tradition. Once the Communist party recognized the Muslims as a separate "ethnic" group, it became necessary to prove this "scientifically" through research and writing. A number of books, collective works, and many articles have been published discussing the character of Muslim culture and demonstrating Muslim historical exclusiveness. Much energy has been spent toward establishing the ethnic origin of the Muslims, linking them to the oldest South Slavic element of the population and to the medieval Bogomils. The Croatian and Serbian nationalists, who claim Muslims as their respective conationals, and the Muslims who identify as Croats, Serbs, or Yugoslavs reject the concept of Muslim ethnic exclusiveness.

The recognition of separateness has given the Muslims not only a sense of pride, but, what is more important, it has given them a sense of power. This has precipitated an unprecedented cultural and spiritual revival of the Yugoslav Muslims, and it has also regenerated their Islamic beliefs, a development that has been stimulated by the spread of Muslim fundamentalism abroad. The recognition of the Muslims as a separate ethnic entity bore consequences not foreseen by Yugoslavia's Communist leaders. The Muslims began to relate to their coreligionists abroad, and to identify with Islamic ecumenicity. The ideas of Pan-Islamism found supporters among the Yugoslav Muslims.

In the postwar years, Yugoslavia established close relations with Muslim countries, sent technical personnel and diplomats of Muslim background to those countries, and exchanged official visits with them. Over the years dozens of students attended theological and other schools in Muslim countries. In turn, the Muslim countries exchanged their students as well as diplomatic and other missions with Yugoslavia. Muslim dignitaries visited Yugoslavia and often toured Sarajevo and other Muslim communities. They left gifts at mosques. These inter-Muslim contacts no doubt helped arouse the Islamic sentiments of the Yugoslav Muslims, who identified with their coreligionists on the international issues involving Muslims (such as the Arab-Israeli conflict). The head of the Yugoslav Muslims, Ahmed Smajlović, considered by some as the country's spiritual leader, while criticizing Ayatollah Khomeini for his anti-Western stand and his attitude toward women, lauded "the Muslim victory" in Iran and the "rejection of Marxism-Leninism."[33] Another Muslim leader, Muhamed Filipović, was reprimanded by the government for discovering in the Islamic unrest abroad "a clear revival of the revolutionary role of Islam."[34]

Caught in an unexpected dilemma, the Yugoslav government in 1979 launched a campaign against Pan-Islamism and those sympathizing with it. The official press criticized "the divisive and ideologically harmful" influence of Pan-Islamism. The critics were themselves mostly of Muslim background. The most outspoken critic of Pan-Islamic ideas and activities was Hamdija Pozderac, a Muslim representative in the Central

Committee of the Presidium of the League of Communists of Yugoslavia. Pozderac criticized the attempts by Muslim religious leaders to persuade the Muslims of the republic of Bosnia-Hercegovina to equate the idea of Islamic religion with the idea of nation and to harbor the idea of Pan-Islamism.[35]

Although scarred, the church as an institution survives throughout Eastern Europe, except in Albania, which has outlawed religion. Where it exists the church has been allowed to have a certain amount of property and a limited number of religious schools and publications. In some countries there are university-level religious institutions and theological faculties (Yugoslavia), and in one country a Catholic university (Lublin in Poland). Most countries allow seminaries for training priests and religious instruction on the elementary-school level. The Catholic church, aided mainly by its better organization and international affiliation, has been more successful in resisting Communist antireligious measures than other churches. So powerful is the Catholic church in Eastern Europe that in the 1970s all the Communist governments, except that of Albania, have been obliged to seek accommodations with it.

Yet, there is no doubt that religion everywhere in Eastern Europe is on the decline, more markedly in the Orthodox than the Catholic areas of Eastern Europe. Nonetheless, the Catholic and Orthodox churches continue to derive strength from close ties to nationalism and traditional culture. Participation in religious rites, such as baptism, confirmation, communion, and wedding services, is so deeply rooted in the culture of the people that sometimes even Communists and their children participate in them. Modernization, however, has proven to be as great an enemy of the church as Communist legislation. The attraction of materialism and urban civilization has weaned away from the church many young and old persons, especially the former. Many religious customs and practices (fasting, roasting of animals, burning of yule logs) as products of rural culture are discarded in the urban centers, if for no other reason than impracticality. Finally, it should be added that all churches must exist on limited revenues and meager private donations. Almost everywhere, the state maintains only those religious buildings that are proclaimed to be historical or artistic monuments.

In no East European country does the church command such power as in Poland. The Roman Catholic church in Poland is healthy and dynamic. This is attested to by large church attendance, the number of priests, which has reached an all-time high, and the full seminaries.[36] No Catholic country can compare with Poland in attracting young priests. The great majority of Poland's 35 million people are practicing Roman Catholics and they pose a major problem to the Polish Communist party and government. The Polish church has many grievances against the state. The educational reform of 1972 was resented by the Polish Catholic church because it closed small rural schools, making regular religious instruction difficult or inaccessible.[37] The church sought authority for publication of its literature free of censorship and the right to debate public issues.[38] It was in the interest of both the state and the church to find a way that would enable the "believers and non-believers" to coexist.

In the 1970s, the Polish government began to abandon the rigid anti-church policy of the 1960s, when the government had attempted to deprive the church of its leadership, economic resources, and ties with the population.[39] A relaxed policy is in conformity with the Gierek government's New Realism program. The party and the government finally recognized the strength of the Catholic church and, in 1977, decided to come to terms with the church. Gierek needed the support of the church in attempting to solve the nation's economic woes. Several anti-church measures were dropped, such as state support for minor denominations, support of the so-called patriot priests who cooperated with the state, taxes on churches and clergy, and the imprisonment of clergy for "tax evasion." New churches, built illegally, have been allowed to stand, sometimes after perfunctory persecution.

In Poland, the notion that the church could be used for the good of a socialist society has come to prevail. Some of the lands in the western territories were finally turned over to the Polish church free of cost and of rent previously paid by the church. The church's debts to the state (such as the 57 million złoty debt of the Catholic University in Lublin) were cancelled.[40] Today, the religious instruction of children on a regular basis has become widely accessible. Excursions and pilgrimages (e.g., to Czestochowa), guided by priests, are permitted. The Polish official tourist agency, Orbis, organizes excursions to Rome with priests as unofficial guides.

The church and state, however, remain suspicious of one another, and a genuine reconciliation between them does not seem likely. The church has continued to protest against repressive and discriminatory measures. Stefan Cardinal Wyszynski has demanded that the government "pension off" its censors and allow discussion of religious views over the air and in the press.[41]

The election of a Polish pope marked one of the most momentous developments in the history of Polish Catholicism. The election was an astute political move that deeply stirred the religious and patriotic sensitivities of the Poles. That the pope was Polish was of particular importance in restraining the power of Communism. The Polish Communist party had no choice but to accept the election. Even to the Communist Poles it meant something real—"for the first time, a Pole had become head of the Church." The entire nation was in a state of ecstasy, an eloquent testimonial to the closeness between Polish Catholicism and Polish nationalism.

During his visit to Poland, the pope spoke cautiously but critically of Communism. He advocated reconciliation and accommodation between church and state. It is difficult to assess what the results of this simultaneous "confrontation and coexistence" with Communism will be. As for the immediate impact, the pope's policy has given an unprecedented lift to all the religious communities in the East European Communist world, although criticism has been voiced that the pope did not do enough for ecumenical relations, and that the pope's contact with non-Catholic leaders was nominal.[42] On the whole, it seems doubtful that church dialogue with the Marxists will bring détente or rapprochement with the Communists.[43]

In 1968, Czechoslovakia began exerting tighter control over religion and culture. The church-state conflict involves several specific issues, such as restrictions imposed on the training of priests and appointment of bishops, and the persecution of and discrimination against the clergy. The government-sponsored union of clergy, the Pacem in Terris, which serves as the instrument of the Communist antichurch policies, has been encouraged to hold periodic congresses. For failing to conform, many priests were forced to take up other professions. In 1977, only two sees had resident bishops. Four bishops were barred from office. Out of 4,600 parishes, 1,600 were vacant. In more recent years, however, the state has begun to seek an agreement with the Vatican, especially in regard to the appointment of bishops to vacant dioceses.

The religious policy of Hungary has been characterized as one of relative tolerance. A prominent Hungarian clergyman who visited the United States in 1979 stated that there was more freedom of religion in Hungary today than in the past.[44] In June 1977, Kadar visited Rome and was received by the pope. The visit is said to have normalized state-church relations. Kadar observed on the occasion that Hungary had no human rights problems, adding that "We are not afraid of the views of the people." The visit had a profound impact in Hungary, where the Catholic church retains a strong influence. As a result of negotiations with the Vatican, four new bishops were appointed in April 1979. Leniency has also been shown in the matter of theological schools and travel abroad by Catholic bishops. The state has abrogated its right to confirm the appointment of priests. The American evangelist, Billy Graham, on his visit to Hungary on September 3–10, 1978, observed that he found no signs of religious oppression in Hungary.

The Yugoslavs distinguish religion from clericalism, which they look upon as the "political arsenal" behind the church. Yugoslavs believe that after the war church leaders were for the most part opposed to the Communist "revolution" and "the liberation struggle," and they still see "a small part of the Church" fighting the established order in the name of nationalism and patriotism. For the Yugoslav Communists religious freedom is a part of freedom as a whole.[45] To them, conditions for dialogue in Yugoslavia between the state and the church have always been available; under Yugoslavia's self-management system the clergyman is a citizen just like any other person and the system is not antichurch, but, in reality, benefits the church. In December 1979, a high official stated that cooperation between the "social community and the church" has been good thus far and is expected to be better.[46]

Small religious communities, such as the Baptists in Poland and Romania and the Adventists in Yugoslavia, have their own specific grievances and have periodically protested against infringement of their religious and human rights. Judaism in Eastern Europe fares no better than other religions. In Hungary, Jews enjoy considerable tolerance and Romania allows Jewish emigration almost on request. The Polish government has given increasing attention to its Jewish community.

Political Dissidents

In every East European country one hears criticism of the government for its undemocratic practices, monopoly of power, violation of human rights, and economic exploitation. This opposition is most vocal and best organized in Poland and Czechoslovakia. While Czechoslovakia has taken harsh measures to stamp out dissidents, Poland has been less punitive. In Poland, unauthorized gatherings on the street are allowed and critics of the government (including those associated with the Catholic *Tygodnik Powszechny*) are permitted to travel, teach, and publish in the West. Official leniency has been manifested also toward historical and literary work. Today, it is possible to write more freely on the interwar history of Poland, the Home Army, and the uprising in Warsaw in 1944, and to vent officially unacceptable views. Scholarly inquiry into sociology and economics (both heavily ideological) has gained wide recognition in the West for its high quality. The authorities have not taken serious reprisals against the so-called flying universities, groups that meet in private homes and are organized by university professors. Such groups discuss subjects not covered in official curricula. Polish dissidents have been circulating leaflets and organizing public rallies, which usually commemorate prominent events in recent Polish history.

The Polish dissidents are principally concerned with thought control and censorship.[47] They have organized a thriving underground press, including a periodical (Robotnik) that appears in thousands of copies. Many manuscripts have been published abroad. Some Polish dissidents publish in Kultura, an emigré anti-Communist journal published in Paris. The prominent writers who have published abroad and written for the underground press have not been persecuted, but the less prominent ones have not been so fortunate. The harassment of dissidents continues. In early 1980, the police broke up a meeting of dissidents at the home of Jacek Kuron, one of the leading critics of the Polish political order.

The most active among the oppostion groups are the Movement for the Defense of Human and Civil Rights (ROPCO) and the Committee for the Defense of Workers (KOR), both organized by intellectuals who have ties with workers. Initially, the latter organization offered legal, financial, and moral support to workers victimized by the 1976 protests. KOR protested against the government's policies during the food riots in 1976 and established contact with Western Communist parties. It objected to "the imposition of the Soviet system," which, it believed, had devastated Poland's "social and moral life." The committee, headed by prominent members of the country's intellectual elite, publicizes, often through emigré media, violations of human rights in Poland and criticizes official reports on the state of the economy by pointing out discrepancies.

The Polish dissidents have maintained contact with their counterparts in Czechoslovakia. In one instance, sixteen Polish students scuffled with Warsaw policemen while attempting to protest in front of the Czechoslovak Cultural Center. Shortly after that, a dozen Polish activists withdrew into a church and held a week-long hunger strike to express solidarity with their friends in Prague.[48] A planned meeting between the representatives of Charter '77, a Czechoslovak dissident organization, and their Polish supporters on the borders was broken up by the police.

Since 1972, the activities of Czechoslovak dissidents have received a great deal of publicity. The protest movement in Czechoslovakia culminated in the formation of the Charter '77 group of about one thousand signatories. Organized in 1977, Charter '77 stands for human and civil rights as expressed in the Charter of the United Nations and the Helsinki Agreement (1975), both signed by Czechoslovakia. The purpose of the group is to draw attention to violations of civil and human rights, to submit petitions and proposals, and to act as a mediator in disputes between citizens and the state. The spokesman for the group, Jiři Hajek, contends that the Charter '77 movement is "fully within the framework" of Czechoslovakia's constitution and laws. Other prominent leaders of the movement are the well-known playwright Vaclav Havel and the philosopher Jan Patočka. The Chartists lack an organization, registered membership, a statute, or permanent news organs.

In 1977, the Chartists protested to Gustav Husak about violations of human rights, accusing the government of denying admission to the university of persons whose parents had taken part in the 1968 reform government. As early as in April 1975, the police undertook a series of house searches throughout the country. An unpublished manuscript of the philosopher Kavel Kosik was confiscated and later returned. Despite repressive measures against them, the Chartists continue their work and their denunciations of police intimidation and harassment. They continue to distribute within Czechoslovakia statements critical of Czechoslovak political and social life and to distribute in the West their clandestine publications—especially the "Padlock Editions" (Edice-Petlice) of manuscripts turned down by official publishing houses. Another underground publication, the periodical *Čtverec* (The square), carries reports critical of the Czechoslovak government.

In October 1979, six members of the Charter '77 group, who had organized the Committee for the Defense of the Unjustly Persecuted, were tried on charges of subversion against the state and given heavy prison terms. Among those sentenced were Vaclav Havel and the economist Peter Uhl. The trial was condemned by the Communist parties in Italy, France, and Spain. The treatment of the dissidents has complicated relations between the Czechoslovak party and the Communist parties of Western Europe.[49] The United States, Amnesty International in New York, and Senator Robert Dole protested against the treatment of dissidents in Czechoslovakia.

The Czechoslovak authorities also have been intolerant of those who deviate from official norms of art and literature. Steps were taken to curb undesirable Western music. Two popular rock groups were brought to trial in Prague for "inciting youth to rebellion" and "singing obscene lyrics."

Dissent in Romania had been mild until it suddenly boiled over. It is neither as organized nor as extensive as in Poland, Czechoslovakia, and Hungary. A small group, led by the author Paul Goma, sent a letter to the signatories of the Helsinki Agreement bringing to their attention violations of human rights in Romania. Romania's leader, Ceauşescu, condemned the protesters as "traitors" and offered them passports to leave the country. The regime was determined to stamp out dissenters through trials and expatriation. Several dissidents were given short-term prison sentences, and some have emigrated. Opposition to the regime is particularly extensive among those of Hungarian national- ity. Refusing to recognize the problem, Ceauşescu has insisted that the Hungarian minority is incited from abroad. He threatened those who were "serving foreigners" with dire consequences and criticized foreign religious groups for interfering in Romanian domestic affairs and creating confusion in regard to the human rights problem in Romania. There are indications that a certain amount of dissent over Romanian human rights also exists within the Romanian Communist party.

Romania accepted the provisions of the Jackson-Vanik Amendment and promised to allow any Jews who so wished to emigrate. Since 1971, about 20,000 Jews have emigrated, leaving behind approximately 30,000. Complaints have been made, however, that the emigrés are sub- jected to various bureaucratic delays and to economic retaliation. The United States has protested against such delays. In May 1979, represen- tatives of the United States discussed with Romanian officials issues covered under the Helsinki Agreement, such as religious freedom, equal- ity before the law, the right to bilingual education, and cultural freedom for ethnic Hungarians and other nationalities. Among other things, Romanians promised to cooperate in reuniting divided families.[50]

The problem of the Hungarian minority in Romania—the largest minority in Eastern Europe—is a serious one. The Hungarian minority has protested against the violation of its rights. In letters of protest since 1968, the Hungarians have accused the Romanian leadership of a perver- sion of socialism. Should the Hungarian minority resort to violence, the Soviet Union and Hungary may intervene to "save" socialism in the name of the Brezhnev Doctrine.

In Hungary, the dissident movement is confined to a small group of in- tellectuals. About thirty intellectuals issued a statement in support of the Charter '77 group. Among them were several intellectuals known for earlier acts of protest. More than two hundred critics of the government have received minor sentences. Some dissent in Hungary also comes from within the Marxist ranks. A publicized example of this was the criticism of the regime by Miklos Haraszti, from an ultra-Marxist point of view.

Although no organized group of dissidents has been reported in Bul- garia, there are signs of discontent. One Western author observes that the Bulgarians have an "inborn capacity" to conceal their thoughts; "it would be unwise to write off Bulgaria as forever a Soviet satrapy."[51]

The State Department's report on human rights in 1978 stated that Yugoslav citizens, unlike those in other East European countries, enjoyed broad freedom of movement and access to foreign publications and broadcasts. It added that restrictions on freedom of speech did exist, but that apart from some allegations, there was no indication that torture and degrading punishment were used.[52] Nonetheless, dissent does exist in Yugoslavia. In 1978, on various occasions, the Yugoslav leaders attacked "hostile forces." The secretary of the Central Committee of the League of Communists of Croatia complained of "the continued, very aggressive activities of certain nationalist elements." Milovan Djilas has been accused of meeting with Croatian "nationalist protagonists," and of conspiring with them against the Yugoslav government. He was warned to refrain from "criminal activities" and forced to pay a fine for issuing a mimeographed periodical, *Časovnik* (The clock).[53] The prominent Serbian novelist, Dobrica Ćosić, was accused of "great Serbian nationalism" and bourgeois influence in his portrayal of the partisan-Chetnik conflict during World War II.[54] In 1979, it appeared that the Yugoslav regime was determined to curb the activities of the dissidents, and to stop anti-Communist activity cloaked as "the struggle for human rights."[55] A number of individuals have been sent to prison for nationalistic activity.[56]

Workers' Strikes

Although strikes are prohibited in East European countries, there have been both strikes (in Romania and Yugoslavia) and workers' insurrections (Poland). Yugoslavia is the only Communist country where workers' strikes are neither forbidden nor permitted, but are tolerated. There were several hundred strikes in Yugoslavia largely due to low wages, violations of self-management, and the decrease of "workers' influence" at all levels from workers' councils to trade unions. In August 1977, a large-scale organized strike broke out among the Romanian miners in the Jiu Valley of Romania over the new pension law, which was highly unfavorable to the workers in general and to the miners in particular.[57] Later, in 1979, a group called the Free Trade Union of Romanian Workers protested against the low standard of living, unemployment, forced retirements, low wages, excessive work norms, and involuntary political activity.

Increases in food prices in December 1970 prompted shipyard workers in Gdańsk, Poland, to go out on strike. The strike escalated to violence, with looting and burning of buildings, including the party headquarters at Gdańsk. The strike spread to neighboring cities, including Sopot and Gdynia. The government refused to meet any of the workers' demands, and on December 17, 1970, a state of national emergency was declared. Premier Cyrankiewicz stressed that price increases were necessary if Poland was to advance technologically and economically.[58]

After workers' insurrections in both Szczecin and Gdańsk,

Wladyslaw Gomulka was forced to resign as head of the party in January 1971. He was succeeded by Edward Gierek, whose first years of tenure proved quite successful. He broadened relations with the West and obtained large credits there. Living conditions improved and intellectual freedom increased. The situation, however, grew worse after 1976, partly due to political measures but mostly due to the country's serious economic problems—high inflation, increased food prices, and heavy debt to Western creditors. After the announcement of price increases on food and other items in June 1976, there were widespread strikes and work stoppages across the country. The most serious violence occurred in Ursus, a suburb of Warsaw, where workers ripped up rails and derailed the Paris-Moscow express, and in Radom, also a suburb of Warsaw, where widespread vandalism occurred and shops were burned. But there were protests and violence elsewhere as well. After the June riots there were mass arrrests of Polish workers. The party leadership momentarily lost complete support, and Premier Jaroszewicz was compelled to withdraw the price proposals. Soon after, the sentences of workers sent to prisons were suspended.

Significantly, the Polish army ignored commands from the government (i.e., the party) to use repressive force in putting down the disturbances. Actually, the armed forces failed to support the party in subduing worker unrest in Poznań (1956), in Gdańsk (1970), in Lodz and Warsaw (1976), and again during the major strikes of 1980. "The Polish soldiers," the minister of defense said, "could not fire on Polish workers." The armed forces are primarily staffed by conscripts and tend to reflect national consciousness.[59]

A Concluding Word

The events of the 1970s made it increasingly obvious that the objectives of Communist countries of Eastern Europe, as originally conceived, are not likely to be realized. Continuing political and economic problems have been exacerbated by growing ethnic and confessional unrest, lack of raw materials, agricultural failures, an unfavorable balance of trade, the energy crisis, and the ever-expanding civil and military establishments. A problem of immediate concern is the uncertain line of succession in the Communist leaderships, particularly in the Soviet Union, Yugoslavia, and Albania. Whatever happens in the Soviet Union will invariably affect the East European Communist states. Tito's successors have been able to maintain stability but the Soviet Union might still attempt to capitalize on possible unrest in Yugoslavia. The Soviet-organized emigré Yugoslavian Communist party, which has a negligible following in Yugoslavia, appears to have been in contact (directly or through Soviet intelligence) with some Croatian political refugees in Germany, who are anxious to participate in the dismemberment of Yugoslavia. In Albania, both the seventy-three-year-old Enver Hoxha and the sixty-eight-year-old Premier Mehmet Shehu have been ailing. Here the situation is somewhat more stable than in Yugoslavia, and most observers believe that Hoxha has made arrangements for his succession.

The Yugoslav defection in 1948, Albania's political meanderings, and the Romanian estrangement from the Soviet bloc, coupled with uprisings against Soviet domination in Poland, Hungary, and Czechoslovakia, long ago shattered ideological solidarity among the Communist countries of Eastern Europe. The presence of the Yugoslav socialist alternative and Romania's independent foreign policy have had a profound effect on both the leaders and the populace of the other Communist countries. Marxist-Leninist ideology has been made the servant of realpolitik and thereby reduced to the level of theoretical discussion. To be sure, discussion continues as to the relevance and irrelevance of ideology in Eastern Europe, and various views have been expressed by men of prominence (Solzhenytsin, Sakharov, among others). But in general, ideology appears to consist of little more than the observance of formalities. It has been reduced to hollow ritualism, and the revitalization of Marxist-Leninism as a viable ideology is not likely.

The Soviet bloc countries continue to face the identity crisis imposed upon them by the end of the Stalinist era and the unfulfilled promises of the Twentieth Congress of the Communist Party of the Soviet Union. In appeals to their countrymen, Communist leaders employ slogans little related to Communist ideology (often even hostile to it) in order to secure support. The criticism of Stalin's approach to socialist construction still reverberates in the consciences of these countries, which were first compelled to accommodate to the rigors of Stalinism and now are told that a more direct route to socialism is through the market economy. Frequent changes in policies and directions have confused and disillusioned even the strongest supporters of Communism. In a recent lecture, Adam Ulam observed that the people of Eastern Europe remain imprisoned, but "not their minds or spirits."

Everywhere in Eastern Europe, Communist revolutionary élan has faded despite strenuous efforts to regenerate it. A long period of peace, steady improvements in living conditions, the absence of great causes, and disappointments in Communism and the Soviet Union (including widespread indignation over the Soviet occupation of Afghanistan), have produced apathy and indifference. Though they are by temperament pro-Western, and particularly pro-American, most East European countries are forced by considerations of pragmatism to accept Soviet hegemony. They grudgingly subscribe to both COMECON and the Warsaw Pact. That Western powers would not come to their assistance was made amply clear by the Soviet aggression in Hungary (1956) and Czechoslovakia (1968). Yugoslavia remains the exception: it alone can count on Western aid should it be attacked by the Soviet Union or its proxies. However friendly they may be toward the United States and the West, the East European countries do not want another world war even though they know that only through a Soviet military setback could their position improve.

Although the armies of the Warsaw Pact countries have been effectively integrated into the Soviet military system, not all of them are of equal reliability or quality. Apart from the Yugoslav armed forces, the only other significant military force in Eastern Europe outside of the Soviet Union is that of Poland. While it is obviously no match for the far superior Soviet force, it is strong enough to have its voice heard. This is important since traditional Polish-Soviet animosity, aggravated during and since World War II, has not disappeared. Polish officers in the Military Staff and Joint Command of the Warsaw Pact are probably in a position to exert some pressure on the Soviet Union, especially since Poland has the largest and the most modern of all non-Soviet Warsaw Pact forces. Polish armed forces participated in the International Control Commission in Vietnam and in the United Nations peace-keeping force in the Middle East, participation that may have given the Polish army a degree of independence from Soviet-dominated military policy.

The Communist parties of Eastern Europe watch closely for "deformity" in their ranks, weeding out undesirable members and recruiting acceptable ones, preferably of working-class origins. All of them have had difficulty in attracting young members. Greater concern is caused by the fact that the Communist parties are characterized by internal factionalism. Because of faltering economies, seething social ferment, and widespread discontent, the regimes have wooed the support of people by playing on their patriotism. One vehicle for building support has been the commemorative celebration of historically prominent individuals and events. Celebrations honoring recent revolutionary events and leaders have been even more common.

Thus, the Communist governments and parties are seeking ways to cope with their domestic problems, many of which are not unlike those in the West. It would be a mistake to attribute all of the many problems that plague the Communist countries of Eastern Europe to the failings of Communist policies and to Soviet economic and political hegemony. Many of the extant problems are products not of failure but of success, for example, rapid industrialization and the accompanying rise in the standard of living.

Notes

1. Andrzej Korbonski, "Poland," in Teresa Rakowska-Harmstone and Andrew Gyorgy, eds., *Communism in Eastern Europe* (Bloomington: Indiana University Press, 1979), p. 54.

2. *Politika,* November 4, 1974. Supplement.

3. Dusko Doder, *The Yugoslavs* (New York, 1979), pp. 119–120.

4. *Borba,* October 6, 1979; *Socijalizam,* October 1979.

5. "Stroitel'stvo sotsializma i kommunizma i mirovoe razvitie. Mezhdunarodnaia teoreticheskaia konferentsiia," *Problemy mira i sotsializma,* February 1979, pp. 3–19; March 1979, pp. 3–59; and April 1979, pp. 3–41.

6. *Bashkimi,* April 27, 1979.

7. *Gazeta zyrtare,* March 1979.

8. *Yearbook of International Communist Affairs (YICA)* (1977), pp. 63–69.

9. Kino Gligorov, "Concepts of the Yugoslav Socio-Economic System," *Yugoslav Life* 23, nos. 10–11 (October–November 1978):4.

10. For an excellent discussion of self-management socialism, see Duncan Wilson, *Tito's Yugoslavia* (Cambridge, England: Cambridge University Press, 1979).

11. Gligorov, "Concepts," p. 4.

12. Stephen Clissold in *Times Literary Supplement,* January 11, 1980, p. 31.

13. *NIN,* October 28, 1979.

14. *Zëri i popullit,* January 5, 1979.

15. *YICA* (1975), p. 95; *Borba,* June 21, 1978.

16. *New York Times (NYT),* August 26, 1979.

17. *Magyar Hirlap,* December 25, 1977; *Contemporanul,* February 10, 1977.

18. Florin Constantiniu, Hadrian Daicoviciu, and Radu Popa, "Historical Considerations on a Book of Unhistorical Ethnography," *Romania: Pages of History,* nos. 3–4 (Bucharest, 1977), pp. 155–169.

19. Hugh Seton-Watson, *The Imperial Revolutionaries* (Stanford, Calif.: Hoover Institution Press, 1978), p. 105.

20. Seton-Watson, *Imperial Revolutionaries,* p. 103.

21. *YICA* (1977), pp. 63–69.

22. Robert R. King, "Romania," in Rakowska-Harmstone and Gyorgy, *Communism in Eastern Europe,* p. 16.

23. *Anale de Istorie,* May–June 1977.

24. *Yugoslav Life* 23, nos. 10–11 (October–November 1978):10.

25. Ibid.

26. *Rabotnichesko delo,* August 3, 1979.

27. *Tanjug,* April 19, 1979.

28. Tsola Dragoicheva, *Iz moite spomeni* (Sofia, 1979).

29. Bulgarian Academy of Sciences, *Macedonia. Documents and Material* (Sofia, 1978). For Yugoslav response, see Momčilo Stefanović and Milislav Krstić, *Mihailo Apostolski: Velikobugarske pretenzije od San Stefana do danas* (Belgrade, 1978); and Lazar Mojsov, *The Macedonian Historical Themes* (Belgrade, Medjunarodna politika, 1979).

30. Seton-Watson, *Imperial Revolutionaries*, p. 118.

31. *Yugoslav Life* 23, nos. 10–11 (October–November 1978):9.

32. *Yugoslav Survey*, no. 1, February 1971.

33. *Frankfurter Allgemeine Zeitung*, May 22 and June 7, 1979.

34. *Komunist*, October 26, 1979.

35. *Komunist*, November 23, 1979.

36. Thadeusz Cieplak, "Church and State in People's Poland," *Polish American Studies* 26, no. 2 (1969):27.

37. Trevor Beeson, "Polish Catholic-Communist Confrontation," *Christian Century* 90, no. 47 (1973):1276–1277.

38. *U.S. News and World Report*, October 30, 1978, p. 26.

39. Eugene F. Keefe, *Area Handbook of Poland* (Washington, D.C.: American University, 1973), p. 76.

40. Stanislaus Staron, "The State and the Church," *Canadian Slavonic Papers* 15, no. 1/2 (1973):165.

41. *NYT*, November 19, 1978, p. 17.

42. *NYT*, November 4, 1979, p. 50.

43. *Wall Street Journal*, December 6, 1979, p. 6.

44. *NYT*, November 4, 1979, p. 50. On Kadar's visit to Rome and his audience with the pope, see *Népszabadság*, June 10, 1977.

45. Todo Kurtović, "Religion and Self-Management," *Yugoslav Life* 23, nos. 10–11 (October–November 1978):6–7; by the same author, *Crkva i religija u socijalističkom samoupravnom društvu* (Belgrade, 1978).

46. "Religion and Self-Management," *Yugoslav Life* 23, nos. 10–11 (October–November 1978):6–7.

47. *NYT*, October 28, 1979, p. 9.

48. Ibid.

49. Ibid., p. E2.

50. U.S. Department of State, Bureau of Public Affairs, "U.S.-Romanian Relations," October 1979.

51. Seton-Watson, *Imperial Revolutionaries*, p. 106.

52. *NYT*, February 10, 1978.

53. *NYT*, April 8, 1979, and October 16, 1979; *Večernje novosti*, October 16, 1979; *Politika*, October 16, 1979.

54. *Politika*, November 12, 1978.

55. *Borba*, January 5, 1979.

56. *Politika ekspress*, February 28, 1979; *Tanjug*, August 8, 1979.

57. *YICA* (1978), p. 60.

58. *YICA*, p. 63.

59. Michael Costellans, "The Party and the Military Poland," Radio Free Europe Research Paper, Poland/12, April 26, 1971, pp. 2–3.

Lewis A. Fischer

2

Agriculture and Rural Development

State-owned farm units, Marxist-Leninist cooperatives, and private farm enterprises coexist in East European agriculture. This conglomerate can be characterized as a jungle of laws, national price supports, production-control programs, and state-supported storage systems. In the international marketplace, tariffs, quotas, and export subsidies govern the trade in goods of agricultural origin. After the inception of a socialist planning system in the late 1940s, agriculture was given a "special status." In the first twenty years it was practically neglected, as à tout prix industrialization was the prime goal of economic and political planning.

This chapter concentrates on the development of agriculture as affected by reforms in the second half of the 1960s, reforms that shaped the farm industry of the 1970s. Attention is paid to the trends toward integration on both the domestic and the international scene. It is assumed that these movements are likely to form the nature and the scope of East European agriculture for the rest of the century. In the final section these trends are examined as they have influenced the changing rural landscape in socialist Eastern Europe.

The Reform and the Farm

Ten years after Stalin's death, in the wake of Khrushchev's elimination from the political arena, a spirit of reform permeated the socialist orbit of Eastern Europe. In March 1965, only five months after Khrushchev's dismissal, the Central Committee of the Soviet Communist Party's Plenary Session approved the first important alteration of agricultural policy planning by substantially increasing the decision-making power of sovchos and kolchos leadership. Subsequently all socialist countries—including Yugoslavia—have introduced economic reforms. National differences in economic systems called for variations in the structure and application of these reforms. However, one common feature was the trend toward decentralization of the orthodox model of economic planning. Another common feature was the shift of priorities in setting growth goals and allocating investments. These leading principles paved the way for agricultural reforms, and a plethora of economic and political reasons urged their application. In the past, centrally directed planning systems assigned only inadequate investment to consumer-oriented industries. Thus, agriculture suffered from a lack of incentive for the producer. General stagnation, low productivity, and poor remuneration of labor characterized the farm industry. Furthermore, the difference between real production costs and artificially depressed retail prices distorted the domestic market. Consumers often encountered bottlenecks in food supply. The interrelationship between such economic irregularities and ever-present political issues created an atmosphere of internal pressure that—time and time again—caused overt rebellion.

Agricultural reforms in the late 1960s have relaxed the detailed central control of enterprises, encouraged specialization in production, and paid greater attention to the profit position of individual operations. The reforms were given their widest application in Hungary, while their narrowest application was in Poland. In Poland, reform affected only the state farms, which incorporate no more than 13 percent of the total agricultural land. What follows is a brief review of the specific nature of the reforms applied in individual countries.

Czechoslovakia and the German Democratic Republic

Czechoslovakia (CSSR) and the German Democratic Republic (GDR) have been and still are the industrially most advanced countries in the COMECON. There are proportionately fewer people engaged in agriculture in these two countries than in any of the others.[1] The constant decline of per capita output demonstrates the stagnation of prereform agriculture. Per capita index dropped in the period 1960–1965 from 113 to 103 in the GDR, and from 102 to 94 in the CSSR (per capita index for 1957–1959 = 100). (8:160) In Czechoslovakia, the reform—officially introduced on January 1, 1967—gave the management of state farms and collectives more power to make decisions, authorizing them to determine their own production targets. Still, decisions about the production of "essential" commodities (for example, bread grains and meat) remained under the control of the Central Planning Office. A new price regulation system freed some 15 percent of commodities while "essential products," which accounted for the remaining 85 percent, were held in the fixed-price sector. Other impacts of the reform were not as clearly positive. For instance, a sharp decline in net investment, especially of machinery purchases in 1967–1969, occurred as a result of the perceptible price increases of industrial inputs as a whole, and of machinery in particular, as a consequence of the general price reform. (1:3) However, the remuneration of agricultural labor has steadily improved under the impact of the reform. Nevertheless, the invasion of COMECON troops in 1968 had a detrimental effect on the national economy and on the positive aspects of the cautious a priori reform. The supply potential of both industry and agriculture diminished. On the domestic market, the demand for food was scarcely met, while heavy grain imports from Russia and the West upset the balance of payments.

From the outset, the GDR government has exempted agriculture from the framework of its economic reform. In 1969/70, however, a Council for Agricultural Production and Food Economy (RLN) was finally created. Its primary aim was to revitalize agriculture and to integrate the various branches of the council into the national economy. The RLN freed the enterprises from the pressure of compulsory deliveries, but replaced the compulsory deliveries with the almost equally heavy burden of a "contract" system. The contracts issued by the RLN determined both the quality and the quantity of commodities to be produced by the individual farm unit. Very soon it became evident that the system did not work, and in 1969/70 centrally planned compulsory figures were reestablished for sugarbeets, milk, and eggs. (14:303) Another salient feature of agricultural reform was the promotion of the association of collective farms. The idea was to create closer collaboration between the farm industry and the consumer, whereby the latter was supposed to influence the mix and scope of production. However, the rigid Marxist ideology did not allow for an exemption of the directives on production from the authority of central planning. Hence, the movement toward economic integration gradually lost momentum. In brief, agriculture in the GDR entered the 1970s as a highly regimented and isolated component of the national economy.

Hungary

The Hungarian reform measures were embodied in the New Economic Mechanism (NEM), formally instituted in January 1968. In the words of its leading architects, "the concept of [reform] was to provide new criteria for planning the economy of the people. It has been decided that instead of dogmatic and quantifying norms a new system of indicators must be established and made obligatory to the socialist society." (2:364) Pre-reform agriculture suffered under political and economic constraints;

production volume in 1950 represented a mere 89 percent of what it had been in prewar years. The period after Stalin's death marked the advent of slow recovery, but the Revolution of 1956 brought about substantial setbacks. Several collective enterprises were disbanded, and in the atmosphere of repression a great many agricultural experts left the country. Collectivization was resumed and completed by 1962. (5:306)

The changes imposed by the reform were both institutional and structural in nature. The major institutional change was the merger of the ministries of agriculture and food into one unit, demonstrating the interdependence between consumer and producer. Furthermore, the isolation of the enterprise from international markets was ended with the introduction of incentives for the production of exportable commodities. The most striking feature of these structural changes was the consolidation of farm units. Specialization and integration took priority in the new agricultural development program. According to a leading agricultural economist, "this process is connected with the technological revolution taking place in agriculture, with rapid scientific and technical advance and with growing demand for processed food." (19:19) The "technological revolution" resulted in a shrinkage of the labor force and accelerated mechanization. To counteract migration from the farms, many types of so-called auxiliary enterprises were established under the auspices of farm cooperatives. Industrial and service activities performed by the cooperatives increased between 1966 and 1970 by 335 percent. Along with subsequent developments, cooperatives became involved in processing, marketing, industrial, and construction operations often surpassing the concept of "auxiliary" or "subsidiary" enterprises. In some cases, cooperatives entered into contracts that came close to "capitalist" speculation. In many such instances agriculture was greatly neglected. Guidelines issued at the end of 1971 laid down limits and rules to administrative control of auxiliary activities.

The positive and negative results of NEM in agriculture were recognized by the early 1970s. The increased production and income level of the agricultural population resulted from the price policy that provided incentives to the producer and from the adjustment of wages to those earned in other sectors of the national economy. However, the prevailing tax system made technological progress very expensive and labor cheap. National income revenue remained excessively centralized, hindering the self-financing greatly desired by the planners and the profit-seeking of farm enterprises. While emphasizing the various positive results of the reform, J. Márton aptly states: "these results, however, are bearing several contradictions and imperfections in the particularities. . . . Extension achieved in the production, is not incarnated in the same assortment as scheduled in national economic plans or required by inland and foreign markets . . . and investments more particularly exceeded the planned level." (17:22)

Romania

Ethnic features and natural conditions in Romania create regional differences that affect all sectors of the national economy. A surprising variety exists among the regions in soil and climatic conditions, particularly among regions shaping the performance of the farm industry. A lack of competent farm managers and technicians for modernized agricultural enterprises still prevails in many areas. In view of such human and natural divergencies it is difficult to assess agricultural achievements. Discrepancies in detailed statistics are yet another impediment. National averages are misleading and aggravate the difficulty of analyzing economic development. In the mid-1960s some 56 percent of the labor force was engaged in agriculture, yet low yields put Romania among the lowest-ranking COMECON member countries.

The 1966–1970 plan calling for a 26 to 45 percent raise in production was the first effort to resolve the serious problems of collectivized agriculture. Investment funds allotted to agriculture were augmented by 66 percent over the previous five-year plan. Some 3,200 specialized model farms with nearly independent management were set up to improve production and productivity in the socialized farm industry. These farms were to operate on the basis of new principles: concentration and specialization of production, territorial delimitation and stability, the provision of permanent means of production, and the setting up of separate income and expenditure plans in each farm. The national plan gave the National Union of the Agricultural Production of Cooperatives sole responsibility for restructuring agriculture in order to improve both productivity and rural living conditions. Years of unsatisfactory results followed. The average annual output lagged behind plan targets, as did living conditions both on farms and in nonfarm rural areas. In 1972, T. Stanciu, deputy minister of agriculture, reviewed in an extremely objective article the economic performance of the agricultural cooperatives during the 1966–1970 plan period. (23) His criticism overwhelmingly blamed management for setbacks, maintaining that increased investment in mechanization, fertilization, and irrigation had not improved yields in either crop or livestock production. In summary, after a widely publicized "reform" in the second half of the 1960s Romanian agriculture entered the 1970s as a continued drag on the national economy.

Bulgaria

In 1967, Bulgaria drafted new statutes for a model collective farm and for the Union of Collective Farms. The former included management and organizational changes and introduced a five-year contract program for the state purchase of commodities. This is particularly important because compulsory delivery prices were originally set at very low levels. Following the Soviet price and procurement system, Bulgarian planners had previously adopted the feature of double—or triple—prices for identical farm products. The new system tried to eliminate the confusion prevailing in those price and delivery quotas by reorganizing the structure of the whole marketing system. Some (basic) commodity prices were still set according to the "cost of production" principle of Marxist-Leninist theory; other prices were adjusted in a much more pragmatic manner.

There has been a steady decline in the agricultural labor force in Bulgaria. In the postwar period 81,000 high-school- and college-educated agricultural experts have been produced, of which only 37,000 were still active in agriculture in 1970. The demand for skilled labor grew constantly, a demand generated by the expansion of both the industrial and service sector on the one hand and by the planned industrialization of agriculture on the other. The planned technological improvement of agriculture depends upon the availability of skilled labor, and the limited supply inhibits progress toward modernization.

By attracting industrial enterprises to rural areas through construction activity and trade expansion, the Bulgarian government hopes to retain people who might otherwise search for work in the towns. Agricultural planners consider structural reorganization of the rural population a sine qua non for the establishment of an "industrialized" farm industry, which is the final goal of farm policy. Accordingly, the crucial feature of Bulgarian economic reform was the concentration of agricultural production and management, resulting in the construction of huge agro-industrial enterprises.

Yugoslavia and Poland

Yugoslavia and Poland had painful experiments with total collectivization in the 1940s and 1950s. By the 1960s an average of 85 to 90 percent of farm industry was privately owned and 10 to 15 percent publicly owned. The socialization of agriculture remains the final goal, but the struggle for implementation differs according to the dominant political and economic conditions at any one time. In Yugoslavia, prior to the economic reform of 1965, the emphasis was on extending the area of socialist agriculture at all cost, irrespective of economic effects. After the inception of the reform, however, emphasis shifted toward increasing the output of the socialist sector and directing the private sector toward closer cooperation with socialist farm enterprises. The salient feature of the Yugoslav reform model was the termination of the fixed-price system. The new pricing method was based on world-market prices in commodities subject to export or import. Products predominantly sold on the domestic market—dairy, pork, vegetable, etc.—received price subsidies so as to raise the income of the producer without putting too great a burden on the consumer. Investment allocated to agriculture was raised to 14 percent of the total. The reform plan called for an annual growth rate of 11 percent in the socialist sector and 3 percent in the private sector. However, the actual average annual growth rates for the period 1965–1970 reached only 4.9 and 2.3 percent respectively. (14:307) The status of the farmer deteriorated as prices of productive inputs soared rapidly. The wholesale prices for farm machinery were 70 percent higher in 1967 than in 1964, and those for chemical products went up by 105 percent. Land prices between 1963 and 1967 skyrocketed an average of 369 percent. (14:309) At the outset, the reform brought about some improvement in the entire farm industry. However, improvement of the economic situation of the socialist and private sectors has been obstructed by the ever-prevailing bureaucracy; the consumer's purchasing power has gradually declined and the lack of efficient market organization has generated an incompetent approach to external markets.

There was virtually no agricultural reform in Poland, although some decentralization of management was introduced after Gomulka's return to power in 1956. But new policies were limited to the areas of socialized farms and aimed at the increase of production, regardless of return on investment. Shortages in the supply of input items and the lack of professional skill in management offset cautious attempts at decentralization. The trend toward transforming privately operated farms into socialist systems eliminated incentives, if, in fact, any ever existed. The creation of Russian-type "combinates," another step toward socialist agriculture, was unable to resolve the prevailing agro-economic problems. Indeed, according to official statistics, the quantities of grain imported between 1965 and 1973 totalled 21,850,000 tons, or an average of more than 2.4 million tons a year. (11:4)

Integration: The Search for the Future

Since the inauguration of COMECON, the economic and political power of the Soviet Union has governed the planning process in individual member states. Accordingly, the Marxist-Leninist concept of public ownership of production factors is the central pillar of the system. The predominance of private farms in Poland is an exception, the elimination of which is the prime target of Polish economic policy. The reforms of the 1960s in Eastern Europe have been constantly revised and modified, with particular attention paid to avoiding any deviation from socialist dogmas and principles. The Communist parties drew the limits to the extent of the reform. When in early 1974 the NEM appeared to go too far in Hungary, some of the leading architects and founders of the reform were replaced. Subsequently, regulative intervention by state authorities in Hungary reduced the impact of measures that admitted some private entrepreneurs into such areas as the handicraft, construction, and manufacturing industries. Despite persistent struggles for modernization, East European agriculture at the beginning of the 1970s was undercapitalized and characterized by low productivity and management inhibited by centralization. To overcome these shortcomings and to pave the way for a modern, unified system of agriculture and food, the planners encouraged integration of the production, processing, and marketing of agricultural commodities.

In the context of socialist agriculture a distinction must be made between internal and international integration. The former refers to consolidation and concentration of economic units within the border of an individual state, while international integration denotes the collaboration and cooperation of the countries within COMECON.

Integration on the Domestic Scene

Both vertical and horizontal integration have been growing in importance in Eastern Europe. Interfarm cooperation through horizontal integration has substantially reduced the number, and increased the size of, farm enterprises. In turn it has promoted specialization and concentration by establishing new, specialized production units. Due to this movement in Hungary between 1961 and 1974, the average size of a state farm increased 1.7 times, and that of a cooperative 2.4 times, to reach an average size of 6,607 and 2,559 hectares respectively. (3:662.)

Vertical integration is a contractual arrangement between the agricultural and industrial sector. In the words of one of its leading advocates, "vertical integration contributes to the unity and continuity of reproduction and technological process to better utilization of economic resources and the establishment of new specialized production units." (19:10) The final aim of internal agricultural integration is to secure a constant supply of adequate quality food for the customer, simultaneously securing the producer an adequate return on his labor and investment. There is a valuable body of literature on socialist-type integration in agriculture. Scholars from both socialist and nonsocialist camps have analyzed the nature, scope, and potential impact of this integration on the farm industry. (17;18;19;25;26) Perusal of these contributions and empirical evidence in the areas concerned indicates that two basic forms of internal integration emerged in the 1970s in East European agriculture. One is the Hungarian model constructed under the influence of West European and North American experience; the other is the Bulgarian model, which is a replica of integration in USSR agriculture. The rest of the COMECON members and Yugoslavia have adapted integration formulas that are modifications, transformations, or combinations of these two basic models.

The Hungarian model grew out of experts' perceptions that neither the traditional peasant agricultural system of Western Europe nor the fundamentally different pattern of Soviet agriculture would be likely to improve production and marketing efficiency in the Hungarian farm industry. Thus, experts began to study North American large-scale farming methods. Consequently, the state farm Babolna made a joint venture with a Chicago firm to establish a closed production system (CPS) in hybrid maize production. This marked the beginning of integration on a large scale. The main criterion of CPS is fully mechanized production, processing, and marketing of one given product. Up to 1974, four production systems were introduced. Each system encompassed the cultivation, processing, and storage of the crop. The essence of each system is cooperation with other enterprises—state farms and collectives—in order to ensure the utilization of the aggregate machinery investment. Thus, the system embraces both vertical and horizontal integration, i.e., spatial expansion on the one hand and sequential linkage in the stages of production, processing, and marketing on the other. An important feature of the contractual arrangement is the time element, allowing the termination of the linkage if desired. This secures the independence of the partners. Integrated systems expanded rapidly; crop-growing areas under the production system accounted for 38,900 hectares in 1971 and for 909,847 by 1975. Of the latter, 587,370 hectares were devoted to maize and 11,000 to wheat. (19:26) Yields increased markedly on farms in production systems: official statistics indicate that average yield on these farms increased by 41.5 percent in corn and 19.7 percent in sugarbeet between 1971 and 1974. (16:52-53)

Three types of agricultural integration eventually emerged: (1) vertical economic associations that incorporated medium-sized production-processing-marketing units, predominantly in the grape and wine sector; (2) merger—a form of organizational arrangement among legally independent firms. The final aim of this kind of concentration is strict coordination of the whole operation, which may eventually lead to total conversion into one large unit. This pattern is still in an early stage and unlikely to expand; (3) combinate—a big firm incorporating different producing, processing, and marketing operations. By the end of 1974 there were 520 such intersectoral associations involving state farms, cooperatives, and food processing, machinery manufacturing, and construction firms. Still, the majority of nonagricultural firms that entered into contracts belonged to the construction industry, while the goal of the movement was to integrate the food processing and distributing sector. Though only a few have been established, most combinates shifted their emphasis toward semi-industrial animal breeding of poultry, pigs, and sheep. The reluctance of the food industry to enter into contractual arrangements with agricultural firms has been attributed to a lack of disposable funds and/or the risk involved in such an association. As long as this situation prevails, progress in the desired vertical arrangement will be limited and integration restricted to crop production. There are already real and satisfactory results in that area. However, the livestock sector lags far behind and needs thorough reconstruction in production, processing, and marketing before any real progress can be made.

Since its incorporation into the Communist orbit, Bulgaria has been the closest follower of the Soviet Union, both in ideology and economic policy. As far as agriculture is concerned, Bulgaria refrained from reforms that implied any modification of orthodox Marxist-Leninist dogma. A marked feature of Soviet state farming is the huge farm unit, supposedly embodying the Marxist principle of the superiority of large-scale agricultural production. While the prewar policy in the USSR was to discourage gigantism, to some extent because of the painful experience of the early collectivization period, the reverse tendency prevailed after World War II. Accordingly, the key feature of the Bulgarian agricultural integration model is the construction of huge agro-industrial complexes (AICs). These powerful organizations are aimed at the construction of large enterprises in which agricultural production is "industrialized." While cooperatives and state farms integrated into AICs may in principle preserve their economic and managerial independence, the AICs are subordinated to the central planning body, i.e, the Council of Ministers.

Obviously there are inherent conflicts in the AIC statute, the final draft of which was outlined in the Decree of 5 August 1976. In 1971/72 there were already 170 AICs in operation. According to a Hungarian report of 1971 (10:17), areas under AIC management varied from 197,000 to 1,200,000 hectares. More recent reports indicate, however, that some reorganization took place in the 1973/74 period. By the end of

1974 there were 153 AICs, two scientific-productional associations, and nine industrial-agricultural complexes (IACs). In all, membership of the AICs and IACs amounted to 462 cooperative farms, 130 state farms, and 427 specialized enterprises. Some complexes are much larger than average (100,000 hectares and more), but some are considerably smaller. (9:343) Most of the agricultural land and about two-thirds of the labor force have been incorporated into the AICs or IACs. The prime goal of the AIC is concentration of, and specialization in, production. Further, it is assumed that close collaboration of enterprises fosters even distribution of labor, thereby allowing intra-enterprise exchange of labor. Intra-enterprise specialization within the framework of the global AIC plan has priority and has resulted in the birth of special units within the complexes. In 1975 there were 703 such specialized units, indicating an average of 5 such units to one AIC. As a prominent expert stated, this development may well lead to perfect vertical integration. (26:54)

The AIC faces two structural problems: the first is the future of household plots and the second is the preservation of territorial and managerial independence of incorporated farm units. In view of these difficulties, it seems that in the long run the final model of the AIC will be completely amalgamated into large-scale organizations governed by sophisticated central management, where all the fringe characteristics of the cooperative system will disappear. New economic problems may also emerge over time. The system is in its infancy; consequently any final judgement would be premature. Yet, evidence from the Soviet Union points to the difficulties inherent in gigantism. Diversity in resources, in natural conditions, and in composition of the labor force are the major impediments. Also, the new approach to modernization has greatly and rapidly increased capital requirements, as most mechanical and other technical inputs must be imported.

Another pattern of concentration involves the integration of agriculture and industry. The first IAC was founded at the beginning of 1973. In the intersectoral organization, industry is the dominant element. Sugarbeet-producing farm units and sugar factories have been transformed into gigantic enterprises to improve productivity and profitability. After only a few years of operation it is as yet impossible to judge the impact of IACs on agriculture. The IAC system continues to struggle with constraints such as lack of storage facilities, lack of capital, and particularly lack of managerial skill.

Senior Bulgarian officials like to characterize their country as an "agro-industrial" state. This concept refers to the transfer of economic emphasis in Bulgaria from agriculture to industry. It also refers to the reorganization of the food economy, and to the desire to achieve a completely integrated structure of relatively few agro-industrial or industrial-agricultural giants. Along with the stronger centralization this implies, a centrally directed bureaucracy may arise, bringing increased political interference in managerial decisions. Theoretically, the concept of economics of scale points in the direction of larger production units. Yet, the experience of the socialist economy in the Soviet Union and of the market economies in the United States and South America warns that agricultural particularities may place severe limits on the level of concentration.

The crucial feature of integration in the GDR is specialization. In 1976 there were 168 cooperatives (LPGs) and twelve state farms (VEGs) specializing in plant production. (Seven LPGs and twelve VEGs specialized in livestock production.) Furthermore, 1,570 farms were classified as "transition units" (KAPs). These units grew out of the consolidation of former independent socialist farms and represented about one-third of the total number of LPGs and VEGs. The size of the specialized units averages between 20 and 25 thousand hectares. At the Ninth Congress of the Communist party (1976) a new model, the agricultural-industrial-union (AIV), was introduced. This model seems to follow the Bulgarian pattern of horizontal and vertical integration, except that the sizes of the first two units organized were not larger than 32 and 35 thousand hectares respectively. Briefly, the situation in the GDR is still a fluid one, and progress is very slow indeed.

By and large, integration in the Czechoslovak farm industry is modeled after GDR principles. The goal is to eliminate inefficient small units and introduce some kind of specialization. Along these lines, during the period 1960-1974 the number of farms declined from 10,816 to 3,619, while agricultural land in farms increased from 421 to 1,150 hectares. (1:27) Concurrently, a rather cautious tendency toward integration generated the construction of large units aimed at improved productivity and higher efficiency. Between 1961 and 1975 ten such enterprises emerged; their size varies between 19 and 81 thousand hectares. (1:32) Interestingly, most of these enterprises are located in areas bordering the GDR, and, not surprisingly, their structure and performance are almost a replica of those in the GDR. However, in view of contradictory reports and changing managerial approaches since the inception of these enterprises, it is unrealistic to assess the economic value and efficiency of the enterprises at this stage.

Cooperation between the social and private sectors of Yugoslav agriculture is a unique method of coexistence for mutual benefit. At first this cooperation was restricted to an individual producer's contract with a cooperative, but since the 1965-1967 reform several other schemes have been introduced. In the center of the cooperation stands the combinate, which is a vertically integrated socialist unit combining production of primary farm commodities with product processing capacity for the market. Although the combinates are socialist enterprises, they may enter into contractual arrangements with private farmers, cooperatives, or commercial firms. There is ample evidence that this kind of cooperation has increased both crop yield and livestock output on the farms involved and has improved the income situation of the participants. Cooperation, however, is seen as a transitory economic relationship and thus there are no statistics on its extent.

There has been very little cooperation in Polish agriculture. The government promotes agricultural circles (ACs), which occupy a central position in the organization of agriculture. The idea behind the AC concept is to create useful cooperation among the private farms and then to involve the socialist sector as well. Amalgamation of state farms was first initiated in 1973, but this process remains at an experimental stage.

In Romania, agriculture stands rather isolated from the other components of the national economy. The main emphasis is on the improvement of gross output, and the directives of the latest five-year plan (1976–1980) provide for a 25 to 40 percent average annual increase of yield. There is reasonable Western skepticism concerning the achievement of these targets. Under the impact of the integration movement in other COMECON countries the tendency toward amalgamation of socialist farm units has been limited. In 1973, statistics reported 413 large, horizontally integrated units specializing in livestock, fruit and vegetable production, and technical repairs. (24:691) At the end of 1976 an Inter-Cooperative Council was established to function as an umbrella over the local councils set up in rural centers. These local councils design the plans for the farm units, monitor their implementation, and control the operation. They are designed to foster the merger of small or medium-sized units, whether they are cooperatives or state farms. In the initial stage there is a great deal of confusion on the part of the local councils regarding decision-making power, the selection of units to be incorporated, etc. Nonetheless, government sources predict that the present strictly horizontal integration will achieve more agro-industrial vertical cooperation and may well evolve as a crossbreed of the Hungarian and Bulgarian models.

International Integration

There is no common agricultural policy in COMECON. Basic divergencies in the structure, technological progress, and economic targets of the member countries precluded the formation of such a common policy. However, after more than two decades, COMECON leaders are now seeking to integrate farm policies. The principle of Marxist-Leninist planning is to coordinate the components of the national economy with general socialist interests. Consequently, the decision concerning priorities in the socialist distribution of labor is influenced first by general socialist interests and then by particular interests of individual national economies. The twenty-fifth council meeting of COMECON in 1971 adopted a Comprehensive Program that included COMECON integration. According to this document, economic integration should be based on respect for state sovereignty, state independence, and national interest. Thus the role of agriculture in integration is functionally related to its position in and its effect on national economies. The coordination of agriculture with the food industry was considered a means of further improving the integrated system of marketing. The program also stressed the prominent function of integrated planning to promote continued progress and cooperation in economics and scientific-industrial relations. Integrated planning was seen to include the development of a uniform methodology to prepare prognoses concerning supply and demand in agriculture and in the food industry. The methodology that was adopted enabled experts to project a strategy for the long-term future (fifteen to twenty years). The agricultural economists Márton and Ujhelyi provide detailed information about the elements of and the consequences of agricultural prognoses, both at a national and COMECON level. (20:252–261) These findings are of paramount importance not only for the countries involved, but for the West, as the major supplier of the commodities incorporated in the prognoses. The essentials of the projections for 1985 are as follows.[2]

Plant production will expand by 60 to 80 percent, of which the grains' share will account for 300 million metric tons, i.e., 50 percent more than the 1973 crop. If implemented, bread grain requirements will be met in Bulgaria, Hungary, and the Soviet Union, while Czechoslovakia, Poland, and the GDR will be dependent on imports. In the feed grain sector there will be a considerable gap between supply and demand for protein-content feed in all member countries.

Aggregate fruit production is to increase by 150 percent. Hungary, Romania, and Bulgaria remain fruit surplus countries but their exports cannot meet the import demand of the Soviet Union, Poland, and Czechoslovakia.[3] The part of consumption covered by domestic production will account for 40–50 percent in the Soviet Union, 50 percent in the GDR, 20 percent in Poland, and 15 percent in Czechoslovakia. As far as vegetables (fresh and canned) are concerned, it is likely that the intra-COMECON deficit—which might be rather insignificant—could be met by farsighted cooperation.

Due to international obligations and in order to meet the constant need of its Far East regions, the Soviet Union is likely to continue sugar imports. Hungary, Czechoslovakia, and the GDR are to be self-sufficient, and Poland may have some exportable surplus.

The livestock sector remains a problem area. The prognoses assume that measures introduced to improve efficiency will allow targets to be reached, thus increasing productivity as planned. If so, an average of 25 to 50 percent improvement of yields can be expected in the dairy sector, and the domestic demand for dairy products will be met in all member countries.

Meat supply should increase by 70 percent. However, demand is likely to grow by 80 percent. In view of the expected aggregate meat deficit the need for augmented intra-COMECON trade is obvious. The prognoses predict an average annual meat import in the magnitude of 2.5–3.0 million metric tons for the Soviet Union. Czechoslovakia and the GDR may reach self-sufficiency. Hungary will export 25 to 30 percent of its production, Poland and Bulgaria 2.5 and 5 percent respectively. The prognosis signals an overall expansion of intra-COMECON trade in agricultural and food products. A growing volume of trade will have comprehensive implications and will be adjusted to international requirements. Such increased trade calls for specialization and integration at an individual enterprise level. Thus internal and international integration are closely related.

Since its inception, COMECON has had a Standing Commission for agriculture, and a consultive body for coordinating better cooperation among the member countries. During the first two decades of economic stagnation the activities of these organizations were restricted to exchanges of experiences and the dissemination of knowledge originating from Soviet sources. In 1969, however, N. Palagatschev, chairman of the Standing Commission, restated the main task of his organization as one of coordinating agricultural plans in member states. (22:10–14) This statement may be regarded as the beginning of a new trend toward integration, instead of the sometimes loose, sometimes intensive, cooperation under the umbrella of Soviet research. As mentioned earlier, the Comprehensive Program of 1971 included the key provisions of economic integration among member countries. The program stressed that agricultural integration meant better use of each country's natural resources. This implies greater regional specialization, which the commission seeks to achieve through bilateral and multilateral long-term agreements on the supply of products and machinery. Interestingly enough, there is no mention of the free movement of or integrated utilization of labor that would seem to be essential to the long-term success of the program. Another Standing Commission was established to expand production and provide the necessary input items for agriculture.

Recognition of the importance of international cooperation accelerated the drive toward integration in the COMECON. Three major pressure points fostered this development. In somewhat simplified form they are:

1. The accelerated need for unified struggle to create preconditions for the socialist division of labor on the international level as set out in the Comprehensive Program.
2. Increased scope of horizontal and vertical integration in both industry and agriculture of member countries.
3. The apparent success of the European Economic Community (EEC) during a period of change in the structure of the world economy, especially with respect to the problems of fluctuating supply and demand in basic raw materials.

It is expected that various forms of cooperation among the socialist countries will expand and may eventually provide the basis for a common agricultural policy in the COMECON. Obviously any common agricultural policy will be adjusted to long-term plan coordination, in accordance with the principles of the Comprehensive Program. B. Csikos-Nagy, an agricultural economist, emphasized that in the process of integration "the new element is the method of approach to international integration. This approach will not be determined any more in the sphere of microeconomics but it will be organized on the macroeconomic level." (2:251) Along these lines the economist G. Fülöp has outlined the tentative design of a common agricultural policy for the COMECON. It would include: 1) the structural coordination of "modern nutritional proportions"; 2) the structural coordination of the productive branches of agriculture and the food industry, based on prevailing conditions in individual member countries; and 3) concern for extra-COMECON relations. This agricultural policy would also serve to improve the effectiveness of long-term export-imports as a safeguard. (7:216) Within such a model, individual countries would concentrate on the production and processing of products in which they have a comparative advantage.

In the first years of the Comprehensive Program (1971 and 1972) member countries signed multilateral agreements in ten production sectors, including the production of trucks, farm machinery, and farm chemicals. Subsequently, a multilateral organization to coordinate the production of machinery for vegetable, fruit, and wine production—AGROMASCH—was established. Partners in this organization are Bulgaria, Hungary, East Germany, and the Soviet Union. The aim was not restricted to coordination as it also focused on resolving problems of technology in the production of fruits and vegetables. The Standing Commission completed plans for economic cooperation on a multilateral basis. The expansion of production and the securing of requirements in the most important sectors, including agriculture, the food industry, and the chemical industry, occupy a central role in the work. In the long term the plan for science and technology will become the most important component of all the coordinated economic plans.

Following the events discussed above, collaboration among COMECON member countries has assumed a multilateral character. Politicians and economists in the Soviet Union have advocated—albeit cautiously—setting up "international economic complexes," the leadership of which would be an "appropriate center." As expected, the other members, always concerned about independence, have rejected this idea. Therefore, the proposals submitted to and accepted by the 1975 COMECON Conference in Budapest avoided clarification of these matters. For the period 1976–1980 the conference approved ten joint-enterprise projects, predominantly on Soviet territory, involving investments of up to 9 and 10 billion rubles. Stimulation of agricultural cooperation is included as a goal in the projects concerned with energy and raw materials.

The introduction of a COMECON budget was a new feature, although it was not made clear in detail just how it would be used. Further, the conference failed to resolve three major problems: 1) the establishment of COMECON-wide labor mobility; 2) currency convertibility; and 3) the question of international socialist ownership. The latter is particularly important in relation to the intra-COMECON integration of agriculture. The current trend toward international integration of agriculture and food production presupposes the creation of joint enterprises. Their capacity and location may well go beyond national borders. It is in this connection that the concept of socialist ownership or socialist property became a frequently discussed subject in the economic literature of the socialist orbit. (21:17) Some workers recommend the establishment of forms and methods enabling countries with a joint enterprise to interfere directly in its operation, regardless of the location of the enterprise. "International socialist ownership" would be the concept that would provide the legal and practical means for such a system. Evidently, the implementation of this concept would result in the "internationalization" of productive resources throughout COMECON. For the agriculture and food industry of non-Soviet member countries this could mean the renunciation of autonomous rights in several aspects of planning, production, processing, and marketing. Therefore, it is a fair assumption that countries such as Romania, Hungary, and Poland will not accept the idea in the foreseeable future.

The Budapest conference devoted the major part of its discussion to the establishment of a new price policy, considered the most important feature of integrational measures for the short-term plan period—1975 to 1980. Romania, Bulgaria, and Hungary insisted on a more favorable price system for farm products in bilateral trade with the Soviet Union. Since the Soviet Union was greatly interested in price increases for exported crude oil and petroleum products, it could hardly refuse this demand of its partners. The core of the agreement is that, in the future, prices—at least in the Soviet-Hungarian agreement—will be determined on the basis of a three-year average. The new price structure is supposed to eliminate the discrepancy between domestic prices and prices obtained on the world market, i.e., from Western buyers. It is expected that the new price structure may foster intra-COMECON agricultural trade, and of course the final goal of the COMECON planning system is to cement a strong integration of "fraternal nations" within the framework of COMECON. This should be achieved by the creation of a modern specialized economic structure within the integrated area and by the gradual equalization of levels of development in the member countries. Agriculture and the food industry occupy a central role in COMECON's economic policy and their accentuated integration is likely to stimulate the trend toward integration in all other sectors.

Economic and other impediments outlined in this study will always prevent the complete removal of trade barriers. Moreover, the disproportionate power of the Soviet economy may be expected to continue to inhibit integration in the socialist bloc. Despite all these negative elements, however, it is probable that fruitful cooperation will develop if the principles laid down in the Comprehensive Program are pursued. If members can avoid excessive rivalry and the trend toward à tout prix self-sufficiency in agriculture and food, then improvements in living standards in rural areas may well be realized.

Rural Development

Changes in the institutional setting, in administration, in land tenure, and in agricultural technology have brought about parallel changes in the social structure of rural communities in Eastern Europe. Political and economic transformation caused profound changes in the way of life in both agricultural and nonagricultural rural settlements. The interaction between the rapidity of change and the extent of government intervention shaped the new landscape in COMECON countries. The developments of the past twenty-five years or so reflect the attempts of governments to establish distinctive social and economic systems in a new environment. The impact of the mid-1960s reform is the product of a growing concern of planners with the living conditions of the rural population and the need to minimize income disparities between the rural and urban professions.

The common feature of rural transformation is the migration of labor from agriculture. By the end of World War II, Yugoslavia's population was 84 percent rural and 67 percent agricultural. By 1971 these figures had declined to 65 and 35 percent respectively. (27:3) The reform accelerated this trend but was unable to provide jobs for the predominantly young people leaving the farms. Under pressure of constantly growing unemployment in the early 1970s, the government enacted strict legislation regulating off-farm movement of young people. Although 200,000 new jobs were created in both 1974 and 1975, by 1975 the rate of unemployment had reached ten percent. (28:172–174) At the same time, 1.1 million Yugoslavs were working abroad. As recession hit the West a great many *Gastarbeiter* (guest workers) lost their jobs and had to return home. The Yugoslav government provided significant subsidies and tax benefits for those who resettled in rural areas. This might create a new situation in terms of cooperation between the rural population and the government. The need for such cooperation is recognized and has been outlined by a distinguished Yugoslav sociologist who stated that "the common denominator of many problems in practice is the fact that we are dealing with a contradictory, transitional situation: farmers are still basically disorganized and government is withdrawing from the scene." (27: 233)

Polish private farming is extremely labor intensive. It produces its own draft power. Accordingly, most of the villages are primarily agricultural settlements and social restratification is taking place very slowly. The government introduced legislation in the first half of the 1970s within the framework of various land consolidation programs that stipulated the transfer of unprofitable small units to the socialist sector. In the years 1968–1972 alone, 1.6 million hectares were consolidated. (29:27) The result of this changing situation is the distortion of the sex and age composition of the farm population. This is expected to be accentuated even more seriously in the future. To counteract this trend, legislation has offered an opportunity to elderly farmers to surrender their farms to state organizations. These new socialist farms will be less labor intensive; and together with the relative shortage of nonagricultural jobs in rural areas this is likely to further stimulate the transfer of human resources from rural to urban areas. According to the economist Z. Fallenbuchl, "it is expected that at least 2.2 million people will have to be shifted from agriculture during the period 1971–1990 to meet nonagricultural labor requirements. An additional 1.3 to 1.6 million are expected to leave agriculture in the years 1991–2000." (30:776) The demographic transition will be manifest then in a fundamentally different rural landscape, presenting a plethora of social, economic, and political problems to the planners of Poland's future.

A shortage of manpower was a constant problem in the prereform agriculture of Czechoslovakia. The reforms brought about a better wage structure, a social insurance scheme, and some improvement in the quality of life in rural areas. In turn, these generated a markedly positive development in the age, sex, and educational structure of the labor force on the farms. Subsequently, in the early 1970s off-farm migration lost momentum. By the mid-1970s material and other advantages were being offered to people opting for farm jobs, particularly at a managerial level, and it seems that a major reorganization of the rural infrastructure, including recreational facilities, will receive further priority in the plans of the late 1970s and the 1980s. However, as farm mechanization continues to replace unqualified and elderly manual workers, there will be a continued but slower rate of decline in permanent agricultural employment. It has been estimated that by 1980 farm labor will account for 11 percent of total employment. (1:36–41)

In the densely populated and industrialized regions of Bohemia and Moravia the quality of rural life is likely to improve rapidly if the reorganization of agriculture proceeds, and the results develop along the lines described above. The problem area is Slovakia where the difficulties of modernizing agriculture are aggravated by environmental, economic, and human conditions. Here, a large segment of the population is reluctant to go along with the new policy trends and this attitude hinders the transformation of the low economic structure of the rural society.

As mentioned earlier, agriculture in the GDR is now in a stage of gradual modernization. The salient feature of government policy is the reduction of the economic and social gap between the agricultural and industrial worker. The traditionally close relationship between the rural and small-town populations has fostered the implementation of the plans of the party. The first step was toward the equalization of wages. In 1955, farm wages were only 70 percent as high as industrial earnings. By 1973 this disparity had been reduced to 2 percent and now, according to the GDR government, it has been wiped out completely. (31:201) Restructuring of rural education and improvement of social and health services are expected to follow. The new farm policy emphasizing specialization and integration accelerates the amalgamation of the rural and urban demographic strata. This special kind of transformation may create a new landscape in most of the GDR.

The radical conversion of Hungarian agriculture by means of land reform and subsequent collectivization created a disorganized entanglement of the rural population. In the period between the completion of collectivization (1962) and the Act of Parliament on Collective Farms (1967) about one-half of the active earners on the cooperatives consisted of members below the age of sixty, the other half were family members or pensioners doing auxiliary work, or employees. Since 1961, the number of cooperative members below the age of twenty has decreased by 5,000 to 6,000 (annually). (32:70) The lack of a regulated wage system, uncertain income distribution, long working hours, almost no recreation facilities, and poor health service all discouraged the younger generation from remaining in or entering into cooperative farming. This continual exodus of young people seriously affected the cooperatives and forced the cooperatives to establish basically new labor relations as permitted by the Act on Collective Farms. Consequently, since the late 1960s, cooperatives have offered the same terms of employment as offered by the state farms, which are roughly comparable to those in the industrial sector. Furthermore, the development of auxiliary industries in the cooperative farms has provided incentives and opportunities for skilled young people to leave the cities for the countryside. The present tendency toward the elimination of the material differences between state farms and cooperatives may further reduce the rate of off-farm migration. On the other hand, the economic geographer G. Enyedi maintains that the decline will continue since 40 percent of the agrarian population had already reached retirement age by 1973. Accordingly, it is expected that by 1985 only 15 percent of the active population will be employed in agriculture. (4:12) Hungarian experts seem to agree that with this development the population of the villages may increase over time. The reasons for this are seen to be growing job availability, the better quality of rural life, and the improving rural infrastructure vis-à-vis the ever-decreasing attraction of large cities.

The scarcity of recent and reliable data prevents any useful discussion of rural development in Bulgaria and Romania. As indicated in an earlier section of this chapter, agriculture in these countries is still in a formative period and it would be premature to assess the impact of probable structural changes on rural areas.

Off-farm movement is a demographic phenomenon of the post–World War II period throughout the world. In Eastern Europe it is the direct product of regionally varying political and economic forces; thus, its imprint on the rural landscape varies accordingly. Both in the German Democratic Republic and in the industrialized parts of Czechoslovakia

(Bohemia and Moravia) the modifications that the agricultural sector is undergoing have accelerated the equalization process, which began even prior to the establishment of a socialist system. Income equalization, family ties, uniform educational schemes, and improved infrastructures have paved the way for the convergence of rural farm and nonfarm communities.

Interregional disparities notwithstanding, the transformation of rural societies in Hungary, Poland, Slovakia, and Yugoslavia reflect a common trend. Obviously, this is somewhat of an oversimplification, due to the space limitation of this study. In particular, however, interregional discrepancies within Yugoslavia must be considered. Conditions in Bosnia, Macedonia, Montenegro, and other southern parts of the federation differ substantially from those in Vojvodina, Croatia, and Slovenia. The following discussion applies to the latter areas including most of Serbia proper.

The socioeconomic changes inherent in the increased mobility of labor outlined above have decisively affected the living conditions of the rural population. In spite of those changes, however, certain cultural traditions still exist today. Thus in Hungary there are 45,000 independent peasants who are not members of some type of collective and who work on 25,000 small farms of their own. (4:16) While they account for less than 2 percent of the 2.6 million active agricultural farmers, their influence on the social pattern of rural communities is great. This influence is even greater in Poland and Yugoslavia where private farmers greatly outnumber their "socialized" brethren. Indeed visiting a family farm in Slovenia, I was proudly told by the farmer that the property had been in his family's possession since 1746 and "will remain so." On the other hand the interdependence among individuals—peasant or nonpeasant—in the villages and the collective farms is growing rapidly. As F. Erdei, one of the founders of Hungarian socialist agriculture, stated, "the peasant is a small commodity producer, linked in peculiar way to co-operative farming. . . . No longer the former independent small-commodity producer, he is a peculiar formation of our co-operative agriculture, and the whole stratum forms a part of the co-operative agrarian society." (33:19) Also in Yugoslavia and Poland mutual dependence is an unavoidable consequence of agro-industrial development. While many of the older and middle-aged peasants retain certain characteristics of their former way of life, "the goals which motivated their efforts in the old days—the acquisition of land and fine animals and the founding of a self-sufficient farm for one's successors—have lost meaning. This is true not only in the material sphere, but also in other aspects." (34:383)

Throughout the developed world the rural way of life is turning toward the imitation of modern urban living. Young people of peasant origin seek to learn a skill that will enable them to enter the modern production system, whether in agriculture or industry. Further, in Eastern Europe the service sector is now growing, offering attractive new jobs to adequately trained young people.

One of the ultimate goals of current policy planning in the more advanced East European countries is to achieve a steady rise in the living standard of the rural population. Urbanization and industrialization are likely to end the isolation of villages. Traditional village values are dying out.[4] The change in the social stratification of society is immense, particularly in Hungary and Yugoslavia, and is rapidly expanding in Poland and Slovakia. The characteristics of the transformation are similar to those in other developed European countries: however, the transfer of ownership in agriculture and industry added tremendous impetus to that development in the socialist orbit. Yugoslav scholars emphasize the rapid expansion of part-time farming, and E. Csizmadia, an agricultural economist, also reports that "nowadays only 17 percent of the families living in Hungarian villages have all members engaged in agriculture. At the same time, 24 percent of families have only one member engaged in agriculture, with the other members of the family, particularly the young skilled workers, employed in the non-agricultural sectors." (35:360) The economist E. Kenéz projects that the distribution of the Hungarian population, which in 1970 accounted for 4.6 million in towns versus 5.7 million in villages, will change by 1985 to 5.9 million and 5.0 million respectively. (36:17) One has to remember, however, that the housing problems in the large cities, the misery of commuting from suburban homes to work, and the recently introduced fixed wages with fixed hours in both farming and rural industries, have motivated a great many people, particularly the young, to move back to rural areas. By supporting rural industries, the East European governments further promote this new demographic trend.

Rural development in Eastern Europe has been shaped by conflicting trends toward conflicting goals, set partly by ideology and partly by the economic and technological realities of the modern world. Regional disparities emerging from environmental and human characteristics interfere with the tendency toward uniformity in the structure of the rural landscape. There is, however, a uniformity of physical expression in the rising socialist rural landscape, in contrast to development elsewhere. The presently amorphous situation stimulates the efforts of policymakers to understand particular aspects of reality that may or may not suggest the preservation of values and perceptions of historical legacy. The future is likely to emerge as the result of the impact of the factors outlined, whereby the interaction of regional forces and governmental interference will form the definitive image of the rural scene.

Notes

1. Average proportion in the GDR for the period 1966-1970 was 14 percent. This declined to 12 percent by 1973. The corresponding figures for the CSSR were 19 and 16 percent respectively. (1:122)

2. Romania has been in many instances omitted from the prognoses. Apparently the lack of reliable information forced the workers to refrain from predictions on agricultural development there.

3. There is a tendency in surplus countries to export as much as possible to countries with convertible currencies.

4. Vojislav Duric presented the following observation: "If I wanted to sum up in one sentence what is happening to the complex of values in the old Yugoslav village, I would say: it is losing its old values and accepting new ones (often of doubtful humanity) with more or less skepticism, and it is still in a cultural vacuum, disoriented and left on its own." (27:185)

References

1. Bajaja, V., "The Organization of Czechoslovak Agriculture." Mimeographed. University of Glasgow, 1976.
2. Csikós-Nagy, B., *Magyar gazdaságpolitika* [Hungarian economic policy]. Budapest: Kossuth Konyvkiado, 1971.
3. Donáth, F., "A kollektivizalt mezogazdasg iparosodasa Magyarorszagon" [The industrialization of collective agriculture in Hungary]. *Kozgazdasagi Szemle* (Budapest), no. 6 (1976).
4. Enyedi, Gy., *Rural Transformation in Hungary.* Budapest: Akademiai Kiado, 1976.
5. Fischer, L. A., "Efficiency in Hungarian Agriculture after Six Years of Economic Reform." In Z. M. Fallenbuchl, ed., *Economic Development in the Soviet Union and Eastern Europe.* Vol. 2. New York: Praeger Publishers, 1976.
6. Fischer, L. A. and P. E. Uren, *The New Hungarian Agriculture.* Montreal: McGill-Queen's University Press, 1973.
7. Fülöp, G., *Gazdaságunk és a KGST* [Our economy and the Comecon], Budapest: Kossuth Konyvkiado, 1974.
8. Gamarnikov, M., *Economic Reforms in Eastern Europe.* Detroit: Wayne State University Press, 1968.
9. Jacobs, E. J., "Recent Development in Organization and Management of

Agriculture in Eastern Europe." In U.S., Congress, Joint Economic Committee, *East-European Economics Post-Helsinki.* Washington, D.C., 1977.

10. Kovács, S., "Agrar-Ipari Komplexumok Bulgariaban" [Agro-industrial complexes in Bulgaria]. University of Keszthely, 1971.

11. Kozlowski, Z., "The Organizational Framework of Polish Agriculture." Mimeographed. University of Glasgow, 1976.

12. Krebs, C., "Die wirtschaftlichen und sozialen Zielsetzungen für die Landwirtschaft der DDR und deren Realizierung" [The economic and social goals for agriculture of the DDR and their implementation], *Forschungsstelle fur Gesamtdeutsche Wirtschaftliche und Soziale Fragen,* 1976.

13. Kurjo, A., *Agrarproduction in den Mitgliedslandern des Rates fur Gegenseitige Wirtschaftshilfe* (GWR) [Agricultural production in the Comecon countries]. Duncker & Humboldt, 1975.

14. Loncarevic, I. et al., eds., *Reformen in der Osteuropaischen Landwirtschaft* [Reforms in East European agriculture]. Wirtschaftsordnungen Osteuropas im Wandel Ergebnisse und Probleme der Wirtschaftsreformen. Munich: Verlag Rombach, 1976.

15. Loncarevic, I. and D. J. Matko, "The Organization of Yugoslav Agriculture." Mimeographed. University of Glasgow, 1976.

16. Magyarváry, L., "Production System/Hungarian Agriculture." Research Institute for Agricultural Economics, *Bulletin* (Budapest), no. 38 (1976).

17. Márton, J., "The Vertical Integration of the Hungarian Food Economy." *Acta Oeconomica* (Budapest) 11, no. 1 (1973).

18. _____, "Economic Regulations—The Interest of the Enterprises." Research Institute for Agricultural Economics, *Bulletin,* no. 33 (1973).

19. Márton, J., and J. Németh, "Horizontal and Vertical Integration of Hungarian Agriculture." Research Institute for Agricultural Economics, *Bulletin,* no. 38 (1976).

20. Márton, J., and T. Ujhelyi, *Elelmiszergazdasagunk jovoje es a nemzetkozi munkamegosztas* [Future of our food economy and international division of labor]. Budapest: Kozgazdasgi es jogi Konyvkiado, 1976.

21. Mirocha, L., "Internationales Sozialistisches Eigentum" [International socialist property]. *Neue Zürcher Zeitung* (Zurich), August 17, 1974.

22. Palagatschev, N., "Uber die Zusammenarbeit der Mitgliedlander des RGW auf dem Gebiet der Landwirtschaft" [Cooperation of Comecon member countries in agriculture]. *Internationale Zeitschrift der Landwirtschaft* (Berlin), no. 1 (1969).

23. Stanciu, T., "The Increase in and Efficiency of Cooperative Agriculture." *Lupta de Clasa* (Bucharest), no. 4 (1972).

24. Wädekin, K. E., "Industrialisierung der Landwirtschaft" [Industrialization of agriculture]. *Osteuropa* (Stuttgart) 24 (1974):8.

25. _____, "Die 'agro-industrielle' Integration in der Soviet-union und Osteuropa" [The agro-industrial integration in the Soviet Union]. *Osteuropa* 24 (1974).

26. _____, "Agro-industrielle Integration in Bulgarien" [Agro-industrial integration in Bulgaria]. *Agrarwirtschaft* (Hannover, W. Germany) 26 (1977):2.
27. Bethlen, Graf S., ed., *Osthandel in der Krise* [Eastern trade in crisis]. Munich: G. Olzog, 1976.
28. Csizmadia, E., "New Features in Hungarian Agriculture in the 1970's." *Acta Oeconomica*, nos. 3-4 (1974).
29. Department of Rural Sociology, *The Yugoslav Village*. Belgrade University, 1972.
30. Erdei, F., "Social Problems of Co-operative Farms." Research Institute for Agricultural Economics, *Bulletin*, no. 25 (1969).
31. Fallenbuchl, Z., *Poland in the Last Quarter of the Twentieth Century: The Economy*. Reprint Series Serial no. 95. University of Windsor, 1976.
32. Fel, E. and T. Hofer, *Proper Peasants*. Chicago: Aldine Publishing Co., 1977.
33. Francisco, R.A., "The Future of East German Agriculture: The Feasibility of the 1976–80 Plan." In R. D. Laird et al., eds., *The Future of Agriculture in the Soviet Union and Eastern Europe*. Boulder: Westview Press, 1977.
34. Kenéz, E., "Rural Households, Rural Families." Research Institute for Agricultural Economics, *Bulletin*, no. 30 (1971).
35. Orolin, Z., "Hungarian Agriculture and the Problem with the Supply of Labour." In I. Benet and J. Gyenis, eds. *Economic Studies of Hungary's Agriculture*. Budapest: Akademiai Kiado, 1977.

George R. Feiwel **3**

Industrialization

Is Growth a Maximand?

Whatever the stress on the international growth-rate race, it seems that at present the fundamental problems of the economies that adopted the Soviet pattern—which are grouped under the inadequate umbrella "Soviet-type economies" (STE's)[1]—are not those of quantity, but of quality, of output composition, of production and distribution efficiency, of technical dynamism, and of creative adaptation of world knowledge. It is evident that if a particular national economy outdistances another in the growth race, this by itself cannot be taken as a demonstration of long-term economic success and of satisfactory advance of the living standards of its population. Increasingly the cardinal questions are: Growth for what and for whom and at what costs?

The classical economists identified the growth of a nation's physical production with the growth of public welfare, but modern economists go to great lengths to emphasize that GNP—or its variants measuring overall economic performance—is an index of production, not one of economic welfare, of the standard of living, or of consumption. Economists continue to concentrate on the dynamics of the quantity of economic goods and services because of the refractory nature of the qualitative dimensions of economic life. But national economic progress cannot be identified with the velocity of the index of traditional GNP.

Recently a pioneering attempt was made by William Nordhaus and James Tobin to develop a welfare-oriented measure of economic activity and to correct the statistical GNP of the United States so as to gauge the quality of economic life. Not suprisingly, the very tentative estimates for 1929–1965 have shown that "net economic welfare" has been growing at a considerably lower rate than net national product.[2] It would appear that if—on top of other complex recalculations of STEs' GNP required for comparisons with the West—one were to undertake the Herculean task of recalculating to reflect economic welfare, one would probably find that the gap between the rates of growth of traditional measures of production and those of economic welfare would be even larger than in the West. Some of the reasons contributing to this state of affairs are: unfavorable allocation of inputs to consumption in both quantitative and qualitative terms; production of much wasteful, plan-satisfying, inferior-quality output; substitution of "unwanted" goods, forced on the buyer by the insensitivity of the producer to demand and by all sorts of shortages and maldistribution; dearth and poor quality of services; shopping frustrations; and waste of time in dealing with an overgrown bureaucracy.

Clearly maximization of output growth is not a sensible aim of economic activity. It might be advantageous, for instance, to forfeit higher growth rates for the sake of raising the consumption standards of the masses in the immediate future, of improving the quality of life, and of a more balanced and sustained "noninflationary" full employment growth. Identical growth rates can be achieved in different ways, with varied consumption and employment paths and with more or less desirable or adverse noneconomic consequences. Certain measures are very expedient in terms of producing transitory high growth rates, but they might be particularly destructive to the performance of economic actors and to their environment.

All this is not an accolade to those who argue that higher growth rates of GNP result in "gross national pollution," that such growth rates are achieved at the price of irreparable decay of environment and welfare, and that *ipso facto* a smaller GNP would result in "greater national pleasure." This is not the place to resolve the controversy about the possibility, desirability, and necessity of economic growth. Whatever the pros and cons are, growth does matter, particularly to those who have not yet experienced its delights and banes.

Growth and Planning

One of the distinguishing characteristics of different social systems is how they generate and utilize economic surplus. A centrally planned economy provides significant opportunities for simultaneously solving the problems of capital accumulation, aggregate demand, and income distribution. One of the key problems is how much economic surplus should be extracted and how to accomplish this. But a no less important question for the system's dynamic efficiency is that of the uses made of the accumulation fund collected. Roughly, the relationship of the value of consumer goods and services made available on the market to the total wage fund should be set so as to achieve the necessary surplus. In principle, by setting an appropriate price-wage ratio so as to achieve full utilization of resources (both in the long and short period), the central planner (c.p.) of a socialist economy determines the division of national income into accumulation and consumption and solves the financing of accumulation. The crucial decision about the size of accumulation is largely political.

The intertemporal choice problem is customarily presented as a resolution of the conflict between present and future consumption, but the future can be interpreted as a time interval of various lengths. A higher growth rate might impinge on the level of consumption over a certain period and enhance it thereafter. Hence the relative advantages of raising the growth rate become greater, the longer the time span considered. The question is not only one of choice between the present and future generations, but also of the shape of the time paths in the life span of a given generation.

The c.p. should compare the benefits of raising the growth rate (and hence the accumulation rate) with the inroads into consumption resulting in possible consumers' resistance. A conflict arises between the c.p.'s desire to step up capital accumulation and the workers' refusal to accept the level of real wages compatible with the postulated accumulation. Generally, the higher the accumulation rate, the stronger is the consumers' opposition. Real wages can only be reduced up to a certain point (or perhaps a maneuverable range) without provoking pressures to restore the previous level. Reduction of real wages below a certain level encounters the frustration barrier (defined as the lower limit below which real wages cannot be reduced without provoking political and social disturbances and damaging labor productivity, morale, and social consciousness).[3] Such a barrier generally arises at the level of real wages to which the workers have become accustomed or at the "normal" increase that they have come to expect, frustrating the c.p.'s attempt to increase the rate of capital formation.

The traditional STE growth strategy featured, *inter alia*, stress on rapid industrialization; priority of investment and other resources for heavy industry, and discriminatory allocation within heavy industry, with relative neglect of light industry and agriculture; faster growth of investment than of national income (and *ipso facto* of consumption); autarkic tendencies; and the nationalization of industry and forced collectivization of agriculture. Progress was identified not only with maximization of the short-term growth rate of industrial output, but also with the rate of growth of specific key industries—"leading links." Such a growth strategy gave rise to striking imbalances and disproportions between the development of agriculture and industry; among branches of industry, broadly, heavy versus light; between the new processing capacity and the supply of raw materials; among the sheer quantitative growth of output and quality, production techniques, and costs; between

the investments in new factories and the obsolescence of the under-
privileged branches; and between the productive and nonproductive activities, with appalling neglect of the service sector. Already at the planning stage consumption was largely treated as a residue; it suffered further during implementation when it was treated as a shock absorber for
planning blunders, unforeseen developments in unplannable activities
(e.g., foreign trade and agriculture), and interim shifts in priorities.

The traditional growth strategy relied largely on quantitative or "extensive" growth, propelled by huge investment and employment, as con-
trasted with predominantly "intensive" development characterized by
improved quality and composition, cost reduction, and increased productivity, spurred, *inter alia*, by the diffusion of technical and organizational progress and incentives to produce.

The growth speed-up maneuvers were usually accompanied by a
growing disparity between the rapidly expanding wage fund and the
sluggish supply of consumer goods. While increased investment leads to
enhanced purchasing power, it also means cuts in the production of consumer goods. The latter can be procured by imports, but increased
investment strains the balance of payments by generating greater
requirements for imports of producer goods. In the end, not only can industrial consumer goods not be imported, but imports of raw materials
for consumer goods production are also constrained, while some consumer goods are being exported to pay for the additional imports of producer goods to sustain the investment momentum.

A rise in the rate of investment is accompanied by a growth of employment in the investment sector. In construction the average wage rate is
usually above that in the economy as a whole, so that even without a rise
in overall wage rates, the reallocation of labor from lower to higher-
than-average wage sectors boosts the wage fund. Intensified industrialization is supported by material inducements for speeding it up and by
the use of the allocative function of earnings to lure labor to priority activities. Interestingly, the propensity to expand employment is not sufficiently counteracted by command and monetary restrictions on enterprise liquidity.

During plan implementation the increase of purchasing power exceeds
the increase in production of consumer goods. The real test for the c.p.
comes when he is confronted with the need to reshuffle resources in favor
of consumption. The investment drive increasingly absorbs resources
originally destined for current consumption, resulting in underfulfillment
of the plan for consumer goods, and in a deficiency of producer goods
for the consumer sector.

To reduce these inflationary pressures, the c.p. endeavors to contain
the rise in wages and employment. However, in this he is severely con-

strained by his own mechanism of plan construction and implementation, which not only does not oppose households' pressures to raise their living standards by means of increasing the number of gainfully employed, but also provides its own pressures for expanding employment, giving rise to the phenomenon of disguised unemployment in industry.[4]

The c.p. tends to accelerate the tempo of economic growth by setting as a target an immediate growth rate at the "highest possible" level. Aside from the adverse time distribution of consumption, such a decision encounters various technical and organizational barriers, ceilings, and rigidities. The c.p. tends to underrate the barriers and to overrate his ability to overcome them. This gives rise to optimistic plans resulting in misallocation of resources and in more extreme cases of breakdowns and costly shifts.[5] In general, the periodic fluctuations in activity lead to underutilization of resources and depress long-term performance. The postulation of overambitious growth rates results in a *de facto* lower long-term rate than that which could have been achieved had more modest goals been planned at the outset.

The traditional plan construction method starts out by assuming target rates of expansion of various activities and is thus incompatible with complex plan coordination. Such a method leads to shortages and surpluses in various activities. The c.p. often attempts to eliminate the shortages by achieving only a spurious accounting balance, by manipulating input-output coefficients, by relying on output of capacities that are not likely to be commissioned during that period, by imprudent projections of foreign trade and agricultural targets , by expecting plan overfulfillment without providing the necessary inputs, and by anticipating gains in efficiency from postulated reforms without creating conditions for their implementation. These attempts are often accompanied by an equally dangerous tendency to maintain the high indexes of "surplus" branches, especially those identified with progress. This approach tends to swell the inputs appropriated for such products and/or to classify the surplus as a reserve, which is wasteful both at the planning and execution stages. Such an ambitious and unrealistic plan contains the seeds of frequent revisions or even of breakdown, entailing losses and costs of change. Hence the result is worse than that which could have been achieved had a more cautious plan been adopted. This raises questions of plan stability and impact on executants. While the plan is supposed to be regarded as law by the executant, the same does not apply to the c.p. The plan is often adopted after the beginning of the period, the annual five-year plan (FYP) excerpts do not correspond to the actual annual plan, and even the annual and quarterly plans are manipulated and often retailored to fit reports—debunking the proclaimed and desired plan stability.

Internal consistency and feasibility are indispensable for practical plan implementation. The plan should be constructed so as to avoid both shortages and useless surpluses. The iterative process of plan construction *should* start out by assuming a certain growth rate of national income. Then assumptions can be made about the future structure of consumption and its relationship to nonproductive investments. These assumptions will roughly determine the distribution of national income into productive and nonproductive investment, the increase in stocks, and consumption. Essentially the branch structure is determined by the growth rate of national income, the structure of consumption in relation to nonproductive investments, and efficiency analyses of alternative production techniques and foreign trade variants. A realistic plan has to be set so as to minimize the risks of its unfulfillment. There is an extensive list of growth barriers and ceilings, but one should pay particular attention to the balancing of foreign trade, the lag of construction capacity behind investment and of raw materials behind the processing industries, the emerging general or specific labor shortages, and the frustration barrier.[6]

The Pace of Growth

In a dynamic process, present events are the result of preceding developments and present events, in turn, contribute to the future development of the system. The rate of economic growth at a given time is a phenomenon deeply rooted in the preceding economic, social, technical, and cultural developments, rather than determined fully by recent macroeconomic policy and arrangements for resource utilization. It is not only the pace but the character of the development process that matters. A dynamic process is marked by the difficulty of isolating the interaction of quantitative and qualitative changes.

Roughly the rate of economic growth depends on 1) the share of and uses made of accumulation in national income and 2) the non-investment sources of growth. The strategic decisions include, *inter alia*, 1) the size of accumulation in GNP; 2) the real composition of accumulation and of direct and indirect production (the distribution of investment between productive and nonproductive—that is, human capital—endeavors; sectoral and branch allocation of investment; absorption, adaptation, and diffusion of world knowledge; and choice of techniques) and the scrapping policy; 3) the internal and external financing of accumulation; and 4) the economic mechanism for allocating and utilizing resources and for fostering the system's dynamic efficiency (technical dynamism and institutional innovations).

Comparison of the relative levels of development is a very tricky task

TABLE 1

INDEXES OF PER CAPITA NATIONAL INCOME, INDUSTRIAL OUTPUT,
AND AGRICULTURAL OUTPUT, 1950-1973 (USSR = 100)

Countries	National Income		Industrial Output		Agricultural Output	
	1950	1973	1950	1973	1950	1973
Bulgaria	66	101	43	88	97	112
Czechoslovakia	157	107	151	111	110	94
GDR	112	137	131	157	99	111
Hungary	114	83	77	71	138	143
Poland	103	89	68	79	185	130
Rumania	56	80	33	67	77	94

Source: R. Constantinescu, Era Socialista 24(1974), p. 24.

even if it is restricted to a specific social system.[7] Generally, the most commonly used comparison indicator of relative levels of development is the per capita national product.[8] This and various other indicators suffer from vexing problems of definition and interpretation; they must be viewed with great circumspection. To trace the history of the STEs is a task beyond the scope of this paper. It may be noted, however, that when they embarked on Soviet-type development, these countries were at disparate stages of industrialization and could be classified in three groups: 1) most developed (Czechoslovakia and East Germany—GDR), 2) intermediate (Hungary and Poland), and 3) least developed (Bulgaria and Romania).

Generally in all STEs in the early 1950s the productive potential apparently regained or exceeded prewar levels, with industrial output above and agricultural output below prewar levels.[9] According to the estimates made by the Research Project on National Income in East Central Europe (hereafter referred to as the Alton-Project), by 1950 Bulgaria surpassed by 3 percent its 1939 level of per capita GNP, Poland by about 40 percent its 1937 level, Czechoslovakia by over 20 percent its 1937 level, whereas Hungary was 7 percent below its 1938 level, and in Romania and the GDR (for which data are particularly treacherous) the prewar level was not quite reached in the first and was almost 25 percent below in the second.[10]

From 1950 to 1973 the relative positions of Bulgaria and Romania have improved substantially; those of the GDR and USSR only slightly; Poland and Hungary lost ground; and Czechoslovakia came out as the remarkable loser (as shown in Table 1)—when one considers that Bulgaria and Romania were the most backward and Czechoslovakia the most advanced countries at the time Soviet-type development began. According to Alton-Project recalculations (illustrated in Table 2), by 1975 Romania and Bulgaria came close to bridging the gap between them and

TABLE 2

ALTON-PROJECT RECALCULATIONS OF PER CAPITA GNP, 1965-1975

Countries	1965[a]	1970[a]	1970 Index[b]	1975[a]	1975 Index[b]	1975 Index[c]
Bulgaria	1,129	1,404	124	1,662	147	29.9
Czechoslovakia	2,154	2,525	117	2,902	135	52.2
GDR	2,063	2,388	115	2,816	136	50.7
Hungary	1,412	1,611	114	1,898	134	34.2
Poland	1,235	1,448	117	1,975	160	35.6
Rumania	1,102	1,310	119	1,731	157	31.2

Notes: a - in constant 1972 dollars; b - 1965 = 100; c - USA = 100.

Source: T. P. Alton et al., Economic Growth in Eastern Europe 1965-1975,
          OP-50 (New York, 1976), p. 14.

Hungary and Poland in per capita GNP (slightly over one-third of the
U.S. GNP), with Czechoslovakia and the GDR still way ahead (slightly
over one-half of the U.S. GNP).

According to projections of the Czechoslovak Research Institute for
Planning and Management, per capita GNP in 1965 prices (dollars)
would grow as follows from 1970 to 1990: Czechoslovakia from 1,932 to
4,251 (by 120 percent); the GDR from 1,825 to 4,309 (by 136 percent);
the USSR from 1,431 to 3,294 (by 130 percent); Hungary from 1,358 to
2,985 (by 120 percent); Poland from 1,252 to 3,117 (by 149 percent);
Bulgaria from 1,201 to 3,195 (by 166 percent); and Romania from 943 to
2,547 (by 170 percent).[11] By 1990 the GDR would displace Czechoslovakia as the country with the highest per capita GNP; Bulgaria would
come up from sixth to fourth place; Poland and Romania would retain
their fifth and seventh places respectively; and Hungary would slide
down from fourth to sixth place. In terms of Czechoslovak per capita
GNP equaling 100, the respective figures for 1970 and 1990 would be:
GDR, 94.46 and 101.36: USSR, 74.06 and 77.48; Hungary, 70.28 and
70.22; Poland, 64.80 and 73.32; Bulgaria, 62.16 and 75.15; and
Romania, 48.8 and 59.72.   Again, the fastest rates of growth were
predicted for Romania and Bulgaria, with Poland, the GDR, and the
USSR making a relatively good showing, and Czechoslovakia and
Hungary trailing considerably behind.

STEs have recorded relatively high but unstable growth rates in the
postwar period. However, one should stress the refractory nature of the
statistics and the tentativeness and limited comparability of the growth
measures. During the period 1951-1967 the countries could be ranked as
follows in descending order of the average growth rates: Romania,
Bulgaria, USSR, GDR, Poland, Czechoslovakia, and Hungary. Ob-

TABLE 3

AVERAGE ANNUAL GROWTH RATES OF NATIONAL INCOME (1)
AND INDUSTRIAL OUTPUT (2), 1951-1975

Countries		1951-67	1961-72	1951-55	1956-60	1961-65	1966-70	1971-75
Bulgaria	1	9.6	7.6	12.2	9.6	6.6	8.7	7.9
	2	13.6	10.9	13.7	15.9	11.7	10.9	9.0
Czechoslovakia	1	6.0	4.5	8.1	7.0	1.9	6.9	5.6
	2	8.6	6.1	10.9	10.5	5.2	6.7	6.7
GDR	1	7.7	4.5	13.2	7.4	3.4	5.2	5.4
	2	9.1	6.1	13.8	9.2	6.0	6.5	6.3
Hungary	1	5.7	5.5	5.7	6.0	4.1	6.8	6.2
	2	9.2	6.8	13.2	7.6	7.5	6.2	6.3
Poland	1	7.1	6.6	8.6	6.6	6.2	6.0	9.9
	2	11.0	8.5	16.2	9.9	8.5	8.3	10.5
Rumania	1	9.8	8.9	14.2	6.6	9.2	7.6	11.3
	2	13.2	12.6	15.1	10.9	13.8	11.9	13.0
USSR	1	8.8	6.7	11.3	9.2	6.5	7.8	5.7
	2	10.5	8.3	13.2	10.4	8.6	8.5	7.4

Sources: Rozwoj gospodarczy krajow RWPG 1950-1968 (Warsaw: 1968), pp. 44 and 47;
Rocznik statystyki miedzynarodowej 1973 (Warsaw: 1973), pp. 97 and 118;
Kraje RWPG 1960-1975 (Warsaw: 1976), pp. 39 and 48.

viously the ranking differs depending on the period considered, but in almost all cases Romania and Bulgaria have recorded the highest growth rates, as indicated in Table 3. The differences in growth rates are fairly large. There have been other exceptions, but Hungary appears to have been the major deviator from the observed rough pattern of an inverse relation between the growth speed and level of development. These growth rates are quite impressive compared to those of the same period in Western countries, but they do not fare quite as well in comparison with those of Western countries at similar levels of development.[12]

Major structural transformations occurred in the USSR before the East European countries adopted the Soviet pattern. These countries were at disparate levels of development and were lopsidedly endowed with natural resources, but they imitated the Soviet model mechanically without understanding that the Soviet economic structure could not be transplanted at will.[13] The structural shifts were very rapid. Industrial output grew at an accelerated rate, with widely disparate rates of sectoral advance and priority of heavy industry.

Again, the most backward countries registered the highest increases in the share of industry in national income as shown in Table 4. Among the most advanced countries, the share of industry rose in the GDR and declined or was barely maintained in Czechoslovakia. There were changes in prices, and the data for the 1970s are not quite comparable, particularly in the case of Hungary. Industry exhibited the highest or second highest (after construction) growth rates for most of the postwar

TABLE 4

SHARES OF INDUSTRY (1), CONSTRUCTION (2), AND AGRICULTURE (3)
IN NATIONAL INCOME PRODUCED, SELECTED YEARS, 1950-1975

Countries		1950	1955	1960	1965	1970	1972	1975
Bulgaria	1	36.8	34.3	45.6	45.0	49.1	50.8	51.0
	2	6.6	8.0	7.1	7.3	8.7	8.8	8.8
	3	42.1	29.2	31.5	32.5	21.9	23.5	22.0
Czechoslovakia	1	62.5	63.3	63.4	66.4	62.1	62.0	64.4
	2	8.7	10.4	10.7	9.3	11.4	12.3	12.1
	3	16.2	14.7	14.7	12.0	10.1	10.5	8.3
GDR	1	47.0	52.1	56.4	59.2	60.9	61.1	62.2
	2	6.1	5.8	7.0	7.4	8.2	8.2	8.0
	3	28.4	20.2	16.4	13.8	11.7	11.1	10.0
Hungary	1	48.6	54.2	60.1	61.3	43.6	41.2	47.0
	2	6.8	5.9	10.4	9.0	12.0	12.5	12.9
	3	24.9	32.8	22.5	19.9	18.2	18.3	16.3
Poland	1	37.1	43.6	47.0	53.4	57.5	50.1	52.1
	2	7.9	8.9	9.3	9.0	9.8	9.1	13.3
	3	40.1	28.2	23.3	19.2	13.1	16.4	9.7
Rumania	1	43.4	39.3	42.1	48.6	60.1	57.6	57.1
	2	6.2	5.8	8.9	8.4	10.8	9.1	8.4
	3	27.3	36.8	34.8	28.2	20.1	22.6	16.6
USSR	1	57.5	54.1	52.3	51.7	51.2	52.0	52.7
	2	6.1	8.5	10.0	9.3	10.3	11.4	11.4
	3	21.8	22.8	20.5	22.5	21.8	18.8	16.8

Sources: Statisticheski Yezhegodnik Stran-Chlenov Soveta Ekonomicheskoy Vzaimopomoshchi
1971 (Moscow: 1971), p. 46; Statisticheski Yezhegodnik Stran-Chlenov Soveta
Ekonomicheskoy Vzaimopomoshchi 1973 (Moscow: 1973), p. 48; Kraje RWPG 1977
(Warsaw, 1977), p. 45.

period in almost every country. With some notable exceptions, construction recorded high rates, and welfare-oriented activities tended to trail behind. Agricultural output grew at a slower rate than nonfarm sectors.[14] Since industry and agriculture are the principal sectoral determinants of the size of national output, their relative rates of growth tend to have a commanding influence over the velocity of the aggregate rate. *Cateris paribus*, the higher the level of industrialization in the base period, the heavier the weight of industry's performance in the overall growth rate, and the smaller the depressing effect of lagging agricultural performance. *Ipso facto*, a country with a weighty but sluggish agriculture (like Bulgaria) must outpace others in industrial growth in order to produce the same aggregate rate.

The findings of the Alton-Project generally corroborate the official picture of the growth pattern.[15] The differences pertain mainly to the varied assessments of the speed of the sectoral rates and of their impact on the shifting structure of production. By their very approach the Alton-Project estimates imply the upward bias of the official measure of industry's contribution.[16] Toward the end of the 1960s the Alton-Project's ranking with reference to contribution of industry to GNP was: GDR, 41.2 percent; Czechoslovakia, 39.7 percent; Poland, 35.3 percent; Hungary, 33.7 percent; Bulgaria, 33.3 percent; and Romania, 30.6 percent. The ranking according to agriculture was:

Romania, 37.3 percent; Bulgaria, 29.2 percent; Hungary, 25.6 percent; Poland, 23.9 percent; Czechoslovakia, 19.3 percent; and GDR, 15.8 percent.[17]

The shifting sectoral contributions to national output reflect an economy's structure at the start of accelerated industrialization; the strength of the industrialization push and the stormy drives to sustain and accelerate it, followed by periods of consolidation and retrenchment; the discriminatory and shifting allocation policies; the specific economy's limited absorption capacity; and a certain system-made proclivity to perpetuate the existing structure of production. In this respect, not only are the conspicuous shifts remarkable, but also the technical and institutional obstacles of a planned economy, which depart sharply from the established structural patterns. Despite the center's power and command over resources it is very difficult to correct "wrong" decisions or developed imbalances.

In conformity with the adopted strategy, the growth rates of industrial output are the pulse of economic performance. According to Table 3, the ranking of STEs in descending order of average annual growth rates of industrial output in 1951–1967 was: Bulgaria, Romania, Poland, USSR, Hungary, GDR, and Czechoslovakia. This ranking differs somewhat from that of national-income growth rates due primarily to the performance in agriculture and other sectors. But once again the most backward countries exhibited the highest growth rates, with Czechoslovakia trailing considerably behind. This general pattern holds whether measured by official or recalculated data.[18] According to the Alton-Project estimates in the 1960s, the growth rates of industrial output in Czechoslovakia and the GDR compared unfavorably with the European Economic Community (EEC), whereas those of Poland and Hungary were slightly above the EEC, and Bulgaria and Romania maintained their leading positions.[19]

Growth rates of producer goods (A) tended to exceed those of consumer goods (B), with the notable exceptions in Bulgaria in 1951, 1953, 1955, 1957, and 1961; Czechoslovakia in 1954, 1955, 1957, 1961, and 1965; Poland in 1955, 1957, 1958, 1971, and 1972; Romania in 1954, 1955, 1960, and 1972; and the USSR in 1953 and 1971. In Hungary there was a sharp reversal of this policy during the New Course, the economic policy adopted after Stalin's death. Also during the 1960s and 1970s, B grew at a slightly higher rate than A. Moreover, in all countries since the mid-1960s the discrepancy between the growth rates of A and B was less pronounced.[20]

The progress of industrialization in STEs is often reckoned by the relative share of A in total industrial output, but the ambiguous nature of this measure of priority accorded to heavy industry is well recognized.[21]

TABLE 5

ALTON-PROJECT ESTIMATES OF TOTAL GNP (1) AND GNP
ORIGINATING IN INDUSTRY (2) AT ADJUSTED FACTOR COST, 1965-1975

Years		Bulgaria	Czecho-slovakia	GDR	Hungary	Poland	Rumania
1966	1	108.0	103.8	103.4	106.2	106.4	111.3
	2	110.7	101.5	103.0	105.0	105.3	111.7
1967	1	113.9	107.8	106.6	112.3	110.6	116.2
	2	121.6	105.5	106.5	110.0	112.6	124.1
1968	1	116.2	112.9	110.7	113.8	117.4	118.6
	2	133.1	109.8	110.5	114.9	121.0	136.2
1969	1	121.9	114.5	113.3	117.5	116.6	124.4
	2	143.0	111.7	115.3	116.9	129.5	152.6
1970	1	128.8	116.1	116.0	116.2	121.1	126.6
	2	150.5	116.8	119.5	122.5	133.3	167.9
1971	1	133.3	119.5	118.3	121.9	131.6	144.3
	2	160.7	118.7	122.5	124.9	147.9	182.6
1972	1	139.9	123.1	123.3	124.9	141.3	153.4
	2	166.1	122.4	126.3	127.0	160.1	197.2
1973	1	145.3	126.7	127.4	131.6	152.2	158.1
	2	173.7	125.8	130.8	133.3	173.2	216.4
1974	1	148.9	130.5	132.7	135.8	162.3	166.2
	2	180.8	128.2	136.0	138.9	189.9	239.1
1975	1	156.9	133.1	135.2	139.6	172.8	175.5
	2	189.8	131.8	140.8	142.4	209.3	259.9

Source: Alton et al., Economic Growth in Eastern Europe 1965-1975 (New York, 1976), p. 12 and errata.

In 1950 Bulgaria and Czechoslovakia were the only countries whose share of A was below 50 percent (38.2 and 48.6 percent respectively). By 1970 this distinction disappeared; but whereas in Bulgaria the share of A was somewhat over 50 percent, it was well over 60-70 percent in other countries, indicating the greater importance of consumer goods production in Bulgaria than in other STEs.[22] But this picture is not complete without the relative dynamics of A and B output. The priority accorded to production of A was more pronounced in Bulgaria and Romania than in other countries. Taking 1950 as 100, by 1970 A grew 18 and 15 times respectively and B was 806 and 719, whereas in Poland A and B grew to 957 and 548 respectively, in Czechoslovakia to 608 and 373, and in the USSR to 781 and 538.[23] According to the Alton-Project estimates, during the period 1950-1965 the ratios of growth of heavy industry (excluding mining) to all industry were: in Bulgaria, 1.9; Romania, 1.5; Poland, 1.4; and about 1.2 in Hungary, Czechoslovakia, and the GDR. The ratio of the two indexes in the EEC was about 1.3, which put the first three countries above and the last three below.[24] But the West European ratio cannot be taken as a yardstick.

The Alton-Project estimates of GNP and industrial growth in Eastern Europe, shown in Table 5, confirm that for intercountry comparisons the last decade should be divided into two periods, 1965-1970 and

TABLE 6

DISTRIBUTION OF NATIONAL INCOME INTO CONSUMPTION (1)
AND ACCUMULATION (2), 1950-1974 (IN "CONSTANT" PRICES)

Years	Bulgaria		Czecho-slovakia		GDR[a]		Hungary		Poland	
	1	2	1	2	1	2	1	2	1	2
1950	n.a.	n.a.	94.1[b]	5.9[b]	90.4	9.6	77.0	23.0	78.9	21.1
1951	n.a.	n.a.	88.2	11.8	89.3	10.7	70.4	29.6	79.3	20.7
1952	76.2[c]	23.8[c]	85.1	14.9	87.6	12.4	74.7	25.3	76.8	23.2
1953	69.7	30.3	83.3	16.7	86.6	13.4	71.9	28.1	71.5	28.5
1954	79.7	20.3	90.6	9.4	89.7	10.3	78.5	21.5	76.4	23.6
1955[d]	79.3	20.7	85.6	14.4	88.3	11.7	77.0	23.0	77.3	22.7
1956	85.7	14.3	86.9	13.1	85.5	14.5	91.2	8.8	79.2	20.8
1957	79.9	20.1	85.1	14.9	84.3	15.7	85.6	14.4	77.3	22.7
1958	80.5	19.4	80.9	19.1	81.4	18.6	80.2	19.8	77.4	22.6
1959	69.9	30.1	79.7	20.3	81.0	19.0	78.3	21.7	76.9	23.1
1960[e]	72.5	27.5	80.5	19.5	82.9	17.1	75.0	25.0	75.8	24.2
1961	77.7	22.3	78.2	21.8	83.4	16.6	74.4	25.6	75.0	25.0
1962	74.6	25.4	79.8	20.1	80.6	19.4	73.0	27.0	75.7	24.3
1963	71.0	29.0	84.8	15.2	81.3	18.7	72.1	27.9	74.5	25.5
1964[f]	69.0	31.0	85.9	14.1	80.9	19.1	72.0	28.0	74.3	25.7
1965[g]	71.7	28.3	86.5	13.5	79.8	20.2	75.6	24.4	72.9	27.1
1966	65.8	34.2	83.7	16.3	79.6	20.4	74.9	25.1	72.0	28.0
1967[h]	66.9	33.1	78.2	21.8	75.7	24.3	75.0	25.0	72.5	27.5
1968[i]	67.8	32.2	77.4	22.6	80.3	19.7	76.0	24.0	71.2	28.8
1969	68.6	31.4	74.0	26.0	78.4	21.6	76.2	23.8	72.3	27.7
1970	70.8	29.2	72.9	27.1	77.2	22.8	72.8	27.2	74.7	25.3
1971	76.0	24.0	74.0	26.0	78.0	22.0	69.0	31.0	71.0	29.0
1972	73.0	27.0	75.0	25.0	78.0	22.0	74.0	26.0	68.0	32.0
1973	72.0	28.0	73.0	27.0	78.0	22.0	74.0	26.0	65.0	35.0
1974[j]	69.2	30.8	71.4	28.6	77.2	22.8	74.6	25.4	62.0	38.0
1975[k]	67.5	32.5	70.7	29.3	78.1	21.9	74.8	25.2	62.8	37.2

Notes: a - 1950-54 in current prices; b - in 1955 prices; c - in 1957 prices;
d - for Bulgaria 1955 in current prices, for Czechoslovakia 1955 in 1962
prices; e - all in current prices, except Poland in 1961 prices; f - for
Bulgaria 1964 in 1962 prices, for Czechoslovakia 1964 in 1960 prices;
g - for Bulgaria 1965 at current prices, for Czechoslovakia 1965 in 1960
prices; h - all in current prices, except Poland in 1961 prices; i - for
Bulgaria 1968 in 1962 prices, for Czechoslovakia 1968 in 1967 prices,
for Hungary 1968 in 1967 prices; j - in current prices for Bulgaria,
estimates for Hungary; k - in current prices for Bulgaria.

Sources: Rozwoj gospodarczy krajow RWPG 1950-1968, p. 62; Polska wsrod krajow
europejskich 1950-1970 (Warsaw: 1971), p. 34; Rocznik statystyczny
1967 (Warsaw: 1967), p. 630; Rocznik statystyczny 1970 (Warsaw: 1970),
p. 600; Rocznik statystyczny 1971 (Warsaw: 1971), p. 660; Rocznik
statystyczny 1972 (Warsaw: 1972), p. 626; Rocznik statystyczny 1973
(Warsaw: 1973), p. 653; Rocznik statystyczny 1974 (Warsaw, 1974), p. 652;
Rocznik statystyczny 1975 (Warsaw: 1975), p. 566; Statistical Yearbook
of Bulgaria 1971 (Sofia: 1971), p. 58; Kraje RWPG 1960-1975, p. 40;
Kraje RWPG 1977 (Warsaw: 1977), p. 53.

1971-1975. During the first period, Romania and Bulgaria recorded the
highest rates in both national income and industrial output, followed
closely by Poland, and only trailed by Hungary, the GDR, and Czechoslovakia. In the second period, Bulgaria was considerably outdistanced
by both Romania and Poland, with Hungary, the GDR, and Czechoslovakia following Bulgaria. This was primarily due to a remarkable up-
surge of investment activity in this period in Poland (as indicated in

Table 6)—reminiscent of the waves of investments in the 1950s and early 1960s—which once again gave rise to the frustration barrier so pointedly demonstrated by the workers in the summer of 1976.

Investment and Fluctuations

Measures of comparative "investment effort" in various countries tend to be unreliable. The available evidence seems to point to significantly higher investment rates among the STEs, but the quantitative differences can only be interpreted with great circumspection. Even comparisons confined within the Council on Mutual Economic Assistance (CMEA) or intertemporally to one country suffer from distortions. The shares calculated in current prices tend to differ markedly from those in constant prices, particularly if substantial changes in relative prices of investment and consumer goods took place. The bulk of turnover tax is levied on consumer goods, whereas investment goods tend to be exempt and benefit from various subsidies. The prices of the latter were greatly understated, particularly in the earlier period. Thus the share of consumption was inflated and that of accumulation understated. Throughout the postwar period Bulgaria exhibited extraordinarily high rates of capital formation, considerably above the very rapid rates of output expansion. Moreover, for most years, the variances between these rates were higher in Bulgaria and Romania than in most other STEs.

Table 6 shows that distribution of national income in STEs featured an upward trend in the share of accumulation and, *ipso facto*, a downward trend in that of consumption, and considerable annual and periodic fluctuations of the shares. The CMEA investment rates generally surpassed those of the Organization of Economic Cooperation and Development (OECD) countries by a wide margin and were only occasionally equaled in the West.[25] The data on relative movements of investment outlays and fixed capital put into operation are inaccurate and sometimes conflicting. Roughly, the greater the acceleration of investment outlays, the slower the additions to the stock of fixed capital, and the greater the accumulation of unfinished construction. While many factors are at work (including the arbitrary cutoffs of FYPs, planners' desires to start as many projects as possible at the beginning of the period and to finish as many as possible before the start of the new period, time lags, etc.), the strategic factor in speeding the process of putting capital stock into operation is the slowdown in the investment push (reduction of the number of projects started).

The data on the shares of productive and nonproductive investments

TABLE 7

INVESTMENT DYNAMICS IN THE ECONOMY (1) AND IN INDUSTRY (2),
SELECTED YEARS, 1950-1974 (INDEX 1960 = 100)

Countries	1950		1970		1972		1974	
	1	2	1	2	1	2	1	2
Bulgaria	25	25	263	349	295	356	339	390
Czechoslovakia	34	37	157	152	179	163	214	202
GDR	22	21	204	213	214	234	241	253
Hungary	51	n.a.	219	189	241	219	269	232
Poland	39	37	205	212	272	316	418	488
Rumania	23	23	290	314	354	406	435	508
USSR	30	33	195	194	222	217	252	248

Sources: Kraje RWPG 1950-1973 (Warsaw: 1974), pp. 29-30; Kraje RWPG 1960-1975,
pp. 41-42.

in STEs are of limited comparability. In ranking the countries in ascending order of the share of nonproductive investments, significantly the least developed countries (which place the greatest stress on investment as a growth-forcing factor) have the lowest share of nonproductive investments: Romania, Bulgaria, Hungary, Poland, Czechoslovakia, and the USSR.[26]

From 1960 to 1970 the STEs could be classified as follows according to their investment dynamics in industry: Bulgaria, Romania, the GDR, Poland, the USSR, Hungary, and Czechoslovakia. In the 1970s, Poland and Romania displaced Bulgaria to third place, followed by the GDR, the USSR, Hungary, and Czechoslovakia, as illustrated in Table 7. Table 7 also indicates that until 1970 the dynamics of investment in industry considerably exceeded those in the economy as a whole in most STEs, with the exception of Hungary (and to some extent Czechoslovakia and the USSR). In the 1970s the growth of investment in industry continued to outpace total investment in Poland, Bulgaria, Romania, and the GDR, whereas the opposite occurred in Hungary, and the rates in Czechoslovakia and the USSR were quite close.

Alton-Project estimates of industrial fixed-capital expansion suggest that during 1952-1967 Bulgaria's average rate of growth was nearly 12 percent, or almost double that of Czechoslovakia during 1948-1967 (6.3 percent) and one and one-half times as large as Hungary during 1949-1967 (7.7 percent). This limited intra-CMEA comparison was extended for the period 1960-1967, indicating a top rank for Bulgaria (14.3 percent), followed by Romania (10.7 percent), Hungary (7.5 percent), Poland (6.9 percent), and Czechoslovakia (6.7 percent).[27] Despite the retardation of the growth rate of industrial output in the 1960s, there was no corresponding decline in the rate of increase of capital inputs in industry. Contrariwise, except for Hungary, the average rate of growth of capital rose, indicating declining returns. Also, average growth rates tend to blur the considerable fluctuations of investment outlays in industry, which not only correspond to the fluctuations of investment per se, but also reflect periodic relative priorities and the large swings of the pendulum of priorities.

Socialist critics had good reasons to point to the pronounced output, employment, and price instabilities of laissez-faire market economies. On this score the postwar record until the late 1960s has been remarkably good, but business fluctuations—often of a milder and quite different nature than in the prewar period—are not dead. Surprisingly, however, the centrally planned STEs have manifested appreciable fluctuations in the rates of economic activity, which in large measure seem to be system-made.

Aside from the high growth rates, the two basic features of postwar development in STEs were fluctuating and declining rates of activity. The relatively lower rates of activity in the 1960s (compared with the 1950s) were generally accompanied by relatively less pronounced fluctuations. *Prima facie* it would appear that the STEs could be ranked as follows in descending order according to their experience of fluctuations in economic activity: Bulgaria, Romania, Hungary, Czechoslovakia, the GDR, Poland, and the USSR.[28] The fluctuations were particularly pronounced in the first four countries and especially in terms of the most volatile macrovariable considered (investment). In almost all cases the fluctuations in the growth rates of investment were more striking than those of national income, which, in turn, were more marked than those of industrial output (partly because of the "unplannable" agricultural component). In the boom periods growth rates of investment far exceeded both industrial output and national income, and in the downturns investment grew at much slower rates than either industrial output or national income. Czechoslovakia and the GDR followed the general pattern, but fluctuations in national income and industrial output evinced roughly similar amplitudes, partly due to the relatively lesser weight of agriculture. While both Bulgaria and Romania exhibited appreciable fluctuations of industrial output their amplitudes seem to have been less sharp than those in Czechoslovakia, especially in view of the deceleration from 1960 to 1963 and the absolute decline in 1963, which (with the exception of the tragic 1956 events in Hungary) was unprecedented in postwar CMEA.[29] Fluctuations of industrial output appear to have been weakest in the USSR and Poland.

In countries that rely predominantly on the domestic supply of capital goods (Czechoslovakia and the GDR), the wide amplitudes in fluctuations of investment affect significantly the fluctuations of industrial output. In countries that rely primarily on imports of capital goods (Bulgaria and Romania), the balance of payments tensions and the offsetting effect of aid are crucial factors affecting fluctuations. Other factors are the erratic supply of imported and domestic machinery, the supply of raw materials, the absorptive capacity of construction, and the availability of building materials.

Poor harvests—whether attributable to nature or mismanagement—contributed to amplifying fluctuations in national income. Their influence on industrial output was similar, especially in the less developed countries, where a weighty share of industrial output is derived from agricultural raw materials. Both Romania and Bulgaria suffered from ample fluctuations in agricultural output, with sharper fluctuations evident in Romania. In both countries the fluctuations were less pronounced in the 1960s than in the 1950s. Hence in the later period the impact of agriculture on fluctuations of overall production was weaker, also due to the relatively lower share of agriculture in total output.

It is difficult to judge to what extent the booms and downturns in activity coincided among the countries. With the exception of the USSR, and allowing for certain variations in time span and considerable differences in amplitudes, it would appear that from 1950 until 1965 in most STEs the periods of booms and downturns were more or less synchronized, with the booms occurring in ca. 1951–1953 and 1958–1960 and the downturns in ca. 1954–1956 and 1961–1963. Thereafter the fluctuations became less pronounced and less synchronized.

Productive Efficiency

In general, the STEs have been falling behind the West in productivity gains. A. Bergson's research led him to conclude that in the USSR productive efficiency "may well be low by Western standards."[30] For CMEA countries productivity increases "have always been distinctly more costly" than for OECD countries.[31] The c.p. is particularly concerned with the relative position of his country within CMEA and drastic measures are usually called for if the relative productivity deteriorates.

The growth rates of output per employee are considered as rough indicators of the growth of productivity. Estimates differ, but in terms of GDP (gross domestic product) per employee in 1950 (index CMEA = 100), the levels in Romania (49) and Bulgaria (59) were the lowest. The USSR and Poland were about 100, Hungary was 109, the GDR, 139, and Czechoslovakia, 161. By 1967 (CMEA = 100), Romania's and Bulgaria's

relative positions (62 and 77 respectively) improved, Czechoslovakia
deteriorated sharply to 132, the GDR only slightly to 134, Hungary fell
to 87 and Poland to 82, and the USSR improved slightly to 103.[32]

Despite their wide divergencies, both official and recalculated data
place Bulgaria and Romania at the top in terms of average growth rates
of aggregate output per employee during 1952–1967. Both these countries seem to have done better in the 1960s than in the 1950s. With the exception of Hungary (with its depressed performance in the 1950s), all
other STEs registered lower growth rates in the 1960s. In comparing the
growth rates of labor productivity for the same period, it appears that
Bulgaria (6.4 percent) and Romania (6.2 percent) have done better than
the Western countries at roughly comparable levels of development
(Greece, 5 percent; Spain, 5.3 percent; and Yugoslavia, 5.4 percent).
However, the record looks less impressive if recalculated data are applied
(Romania, 5 percent). The comparison of STEs at higher levels of
development with their Western counterparts indicates lower growth
rates of labor productivity in the former, with far worse performance if
recalculated data are used.[33]

Throughout the 1960s, the c.p. in most STEs was anxious about the
deterioration of the incremental-capital output ratios (ICORs).[34] From
the second quinquennium of the 1950s to the first of the 1960s this coefficient increased 4.5 times in Czechoslovakia, about twice in Bulgaria and
Hungary, by 50 percent in the USSR, and by 25 percent in Poland.[35]
Tentative Alton-Project estimates suggest that in Eastern Europe, investment costs tended to exceed those in the West. On the average the East
European countries required about 25 percent more gross fixed investments to achieve one unit increase of GNP (at factor cost) during
1951–1964. The sectoral differentials were substantially higher: 45 percent more in industry, considerably more in agriculture, but about the
same in services. Czechoslovakia exhibited the highest ICORs, followed
by the GDR, Hungary, Bulgaria, and Poland. The coefficient in the GDR
was way higher than in the German Federal Republic (GFR);
Czechoslovakia was above France; and in Bulgaria it was some 70
percent above Greece. The differences are even more striking if investment costs in industry are compared. Not only did the East European
countries show worse yields on investment, but the differences between
them and the closest comparable Western countries were growing in the
1960s.[36]

Attribution of yields to productive factors is a controversial theoretical question, beset with grave measurement problems.[37] Tenuous as
the estimates are, in the 1950s the rates of increase of industrial output
per unit of fixed capital were positive in Bulgaria, Czechoslovakia, and

TABLE 8

DYNAMICS OF LABOR (1)^a AND CAPITAL (2)^b PRODUCTIVITY
IN INDUSTRY, 1965-1975 (INDEX 1970 = 100)

Countries		1965	1971	1972	1973	1974	1974^c	1975
Bulgaria	1	72	107	113	120	128	-	136
	2	113	101	102	102	98	77	n.a.
Czechoslovakia	1	77	106	111	116	122	-	129
	2	89	102	103	104	105	118	n.a.
GDR	1	75	105	106	111	119	-	125
	2	94	100	99	100	100	104	n.a.
Hungary	1	83	108	113	119	127	-	133
	2	99	100	99	98	98	94	n.a.
Poland	1	79	105	111	121	132	-	144
	2	101	101	103	105	106	115	n.a.
Rumania	1	70	105	112	119	127	-	136
	2	106	99	100	102	103	116	n.a.
USSR	1	76	107	112	118	125	-	132
	2	100	99	97	96	96	85	n.a.

Notes: a - gross output per employee; b - gross output per unit of fixed
assets; c - index 1960 = 100.

Source: Kraje RWPG 1960-1975, p. 51.

Hungary. But for the 1961-1967 period these rates became negative for all East European countries, with wide discrepancies in the intensity of change.[38] The negative changes of capital productivity were particularly striking in heavy industry, mining, and electric power in Czechoslovakia, the GDR, and Hungary and in Bulgaria in mining, ferrous metallurgy, building materials, woodworking, paper, glass, and textiles.[39] Also GNP per unit of capital indicated negative growth rates in all East European countries during 1960-1972.[40]

In the last ten years most STEs registered a relatively positive advance in the dynamics of labor productivity, as shown in Table 8. Although the variations were relatively small, by 1975 the classification of these countries in order of the highest growth rates was as follows: Poland, with Romania and Bulgaria tieing for second place, Hungary, the USSR, Czechoslovakia, and the GDR. But a substantially altered picture emerges in the dynamics of capital productivity: In 1965 this index was substantially higher than in 1970 in Bulgaria and Romania and about the same in Poland, the USSR, and Hungary. Only the GDR and Czechoslovakia significantly improved this index from 1965 to 1970. By 1974 this index was somewhat lower than in 1970 in the USSR, Bulgaria, and Hungary. The situation in Bulgaria and the USSR—where capital productivity declined by 23 and 15 percent respectively from 1960 to 1974—was particularly alarming. But the other STEs had no reason to rejoice either. From 1960 to 1974 capital productivity also declined in

TABLE 9

AVERAGE ANNUAL PERCENTAGE GROWTH OF NATIONAL INCOME
FOR EACH PERCENTAGE POINT INCREMENT OF INDUSTRIAL OUTPUT (1),
INVESTMENT (2), AND EXPORT (3), 1951-1975

Countries		1951-55	1956-60	1961-65	1966-70	1971-75
Bulgaria	1	0.9	0.6	0.6	0.8	0.9
	2	1.0	0.5	0.8	0.7	1.2
	3	0.8	0.5	0.4	0.8	0.6
Czechoslovakia	1	0.7	0.7	0.4	1.0	0.8
	2	0.8	0.5	1.0	0.9	0.7
	3	0.9	0.7	0.3	1.0	0.5
GDR	1	1.0	0.8	0.6	0.8	0.9
	2	0.7	0.5	0.7	0.5	1.3
	3	0.5	0.6	0.5	0.6	0.4
Hungary	1	0.4	0.8	0.5	1.1	1.0
	2	4.8	0.5	0.8	0.6	0.9
	3	0.4	0.8	0.4	0.8	0.4
Poland	1	0.6	0.7	0.7	0.7	0.9
	2	0.8	0.7	0.9	0.7	0.6
	3	1.1	0.9	0.6	0.6	0.5
Romania	1	0.9	0.6	0.7	0.6	0.9
	2	0.8	0.5	0.8	0.7	1.0
	3	1.0	0.6	1.0	0.7	0.6
USSR	1	0.9	0.9	0.8	0.9	0.8
	2	0.9	0.7	1.0	1.0	0.8
	3	0.8	0.9	0.8	0.8	0.4

Source: Kraje RWPG 1960-1975, pp. 40-41.

Hungary by 6 percent, and increased in the GDR by only 4 percent and
in Poland, Romania, and Czechoslovakia by 15, 16, and 18 percent
respectively. This was yet another indication that in the 1970s Romania
and Poland were overtaking Bulgaria as the CMEA growth leaders.
Another indication of the decreasing productivity of capital is the steadily growing share of accumulation in national income, especially apparent from the 1960s on, as illustrated in Table 6. But this is not an
altogether unambiguous indicator. The successive price revisions in STEs
have tended to raise the very understated prices of investment goods
(bridging the gap between prices of A and B goods), thus partly mitigat-
ing the statistical distortion of the distribution of national income in
favor of consumption.

During the last quarter century, the incremental national income–industrial output ratio was below 1.0 in all CMEA countries, as shown in
Table 9. This ratio was particularly low during 1951-1955 in Hungary
and Poland, where the industrialization push at the expense of agriculture
was most severe. From 1956 to 1970 the ratio recovered somewhat in
Hungary, but remained quite low in Poland, which was by then joined

by Romania and Bulgaria, where in both countries a considerable industrialization effort was made. In the last quinquennium this ratio was the
lowest in Czechoslovakia and the USSR (0.8) and the highest in Hungary
(1.0). During this period the incremental national income–investment
ratio was more varied. In the first quinquennium it reached never-to-be-
equaled highs in Hungary and was 1.0 only in Bulgaria; it was slightly
below that in the USSR, Romania, Poland, Czechoslovakia, and the
GDR. In the next quinquennium this ratio was very low; it only reached
0.7 in the USSR and Poland and was 0.5 in all other countries, probably
due to their exceedingly high investment activity during 1958–1960.
During 1961–1970 this ratio improved somewhat in all countries, particularly in the USSR. In the last quinquennium this ratio improved particularly in the GDR, Bulgaria, Romania, and Hungary, but fell sharply
in Poland and Czechoslovakia, in the former because of the high rate of
investment and in the latter because of the relatively low growth rate of
national income. Throughout these twenty-five years there appears to
have been, in almost all countries, a steady decline of the incremental national income–export ratio, indicating that an increasing amount of export was required to produce a given increment of national income and
hence the decreasing efficiency of exports.

Consumption, Institutional Arrangements, and Growth Strategy

Theoretically a centrally planned economy affords a considerable
degree of freedom for the c.p. to choose the direction, pace, and pattern
of economic development and the working arrangements for resource
allocation. Yet a plethora of political, ideological, and institutional
obstacles and legacies of the past constrain this freedom. All too often
the c.p. fails to recognize that such questions as volume, structure, and
techniques of production, the pattern of foreign trade, and working
arrangements should be treated simultaneously as part of an interde-
pendent and complex problem. The incongruity among various components of the economic process reduces the long-term growth rate and
accentuates or creates instabilities.

During the last quarter century the STEs have recorded respectable but
unstable growth rates, with conspicuous signs of retrogression in the
long-term growth momentum. Naturally movements of macrovariables
differed at various times and among the different countries that adopted
a similar growth strategy and functioning system. These differences are
largely traceable to disparities in the initial levels of development and to
endowment in resources. Of course, high priority was accorded not to

growth as such, but to a particular kind of lopsided and forced industrialization, without really considering the ends of production. Official
promulgations often stressed the goal of production to be the growth of
living standards, but in practice the strategy pursued was largely incon-
sistent with the enunciated objective.

The statistics on the consumer's lot are often treacherous, making it
very difficult to arrive at plausible recalculations. For instance, consumer
prices tend to be inflated due to the incidence of the turnover tax; there
are many price-fixing irregularities, and some "nonwelfare-oriented" activities (such as military spending) are sometimes included in public consumption. Moreover the index of the rise in living standards would have
to be adjusted for such imponderables as loss of welfare due to inferior
quality of goods and services, restricted choice, forced substitution, and
all sorts of shopping frustrations.

Prima facie evidence indicates that the rates of improvement of living
standards are lower than those that could have been achieved had
development policy consistently respected improvement of consumption, had planner's tensions been removed and a buyer's market instituted, had the distribution system been streamlined, and generally had a
more efficient functioning system, responsive to consumer wants, been
introduced. Moreover, the official statistics tend to stress the fairly rapid
dynamics of consumption; only occasionally are the structual disproportions within the aggregate pointed out. It is not only the key *ex ante*
macroeconomic allocation, but the mode of the planner's behavior during plan implementation that matters. The system "bamboozled" the consumer in the microcomposition of the total, and this is not dictated by
the growth strategy but is a result of the traditional functioning system,
and in final analysis the system encroaches on the growth momentum.

Improvement in living standards can be evaluated in comparison with
the past, with other countries, and with shifts within the structure of consumption. There has been increasing, justified dissatisfaction with the
first two criteria. Moreover, to measure relative standards of living it is
insufficient to compare flow of current consumer outlays. Stocks of consumer durables are an important yardstick. One could argue that
housing and automobiles are probably the main determinants of welfare
improvement, as evaluated by the consumer.

What really matters is that rightly or wrongly the consumers tend to
underrate the achievements in raising consumption standards and are not
overly impressed with the high dynamics of aggregate per capita consumption. In a high-pressure economy even the real attempts of the government to raise living standards have a reduced impact on the consumer, partly because he is forced to substitute goods he can obtain for

the unavailable goods he wants—thus the frustration of unfulfilled shopping aspirations. Moreover, distribution is discriminatory. The best or better goods are appropriated by the privileged groups who also get preferential access to services.

Naturally the worker is simultaneously a producer and consumer. His disillusionment with progress in living standards affects not only his well-being but also his work performance. It appears that some c.p.s do not realize that a sustained improvement in living standards is a condition for really successful planning for long-term growth. One of the most adverse consequences of traditional industrialization policy and the planning system is their depressing effect on performance and the erosion of morality at all levels of public life.

The future path and structure of consumption ought to justify a given rate and composition of investment and the possible privations imposed at a given time.[41] This entails a profoundly different approach to plan construction, where the volume and structure of investment are determined by a growth rate of national income set to take into account the given growth and structure of consumption and the technical and organizational barriers. Calculations of investment efficiency should indicate the minimum investment compatible with the constrained growth rate, with full utilization of labor resources, and with the requisites of the external balance. A plan that provides for a lower level of investment than that consistent with full employment would be unrealistic for it would entail unemployment, and one that provides for a higher level of investment would be wasteful for it would entail idle capacity and would adversely affect consumption.

Of course, investment calculus by itself cannot fully determine production techniques or patterns of foreign trade. For instance, choice of the most effective structure of exports is constrained on the demand side by the limited absorptive capacity of foreign markets for different exportables (the export pattern tends to be most effective when the rate of expansion is low). On the supply side various technical and organizational barriers limit the rate of expansion of production of specific branches and activities.[42] Working arrangements also affect the efficiency of investment at the implementation stage (not to speak of influencing the type and the reliability of projects proposed). Some countries force exports of machinery because this index is often identified with the level of industrialization. Whatever the considerations, the machinery seller has to compete in demanding foreign markets and he has to be flexible and adaptable in a microeconomic sense—and here the STEs suffer from considerable system-made obstacles.

Soviet-type development cannot be considered a success story not only because of the slowdown in the long-term growth rate (appreciable fluctuations of rates), the deleteriously unbalanced structure of production, and the inferior living standards, but also because of the high—and rising—costs of achieving such development. In the industrialized market economies modern economic growth has been characterized by high productivity growth rates,[43] owing primarily to accretion of useful knowledge and innovations in institutional arrangements, rather than to an increase of inputs (labor and investment). Thus a high rate of technical progress, improvements in the quality of inputs, and better arrangements account partly for the relatively lower rates of capital accumulation and higher rates of consumption. If, as is usually the case in STEs, a smaller share of growth of output is attributable to gains in productivity, larger employment is required to achieve the same results, and—in case of an emerging labor barrier—more investments are needed to substitute capital for labor. At present the major problem of STEs is to shift from investment to noninvestment sources of growth and to instill in the system the badly needed technical and economic dynamism, the innovative spirit, and the motivation to work and to create.

Diffusion of foreign-generated innovations appears to be at present the most important agent of technical change and a key factor in productivity growth. The growth rate of diffusion varies over time and is affected by the embodied type (import of investment goods, incorporating new foreign techniques) and the disembodied type (licenses, patents, industrial espionage, international exchanges of research and personnel).[44] In STEs the fundamental problem is the rate at which new techniques are adopted, incorporated into production, and spread throughout the system. There seems to be a major difference between the technical change in priority areas—which benefit not only from discriminatory allocation of best resources but also from removal of some of the obstacles to new technology—and the rest of the economy.

The diffusion of technical progress cannot be accomplished by propaganda and by political mobilization alone, as the record so pointedly demonstrates. Nor can it be accomplished by partial modifications of the economic mechanism or shifts in foreign trade. The obstacles to such diffusion in various sectors in STEs and the problem of redirecting foreign trade cannot be pursued here.[45] Aside from the defective institutional arrangements and reward system, one needs to emphasize that an overheated economy is hardly conducive to qualitative improvements. The persisting insistence on high output growth rates in most sectors affects the ways of achieving them. The official rhetoric notwithstanding, a quantity-oriented system overrates the benefits of expansion in volume and underrates the disadvantages in terms of output content, of the system's dynamic efficiency, and of the welfare of its subjects.

The burdens of the industrialization rush could have been significantly lightened without impinging on the objectives of the system's directors. There is a striking divergence between the system's potential for designing an appropriate growth strategy and working arrangements, and the practical resistance to major innovations in economic policy, planning methodology, and institutional arrangements. It takes drastic shocks (serious imbalances, popular protests, strikes, etc.) to make major changes and even then there persists a tendency to preserve the existing structure as much as possible and to resort to half or transitory measures (the most recent example of this is the poor economic performance of Poland under the Gierek government). Even without changes in macropolicy considerable improvements can be achieved by removing dissonant elements from the system. Indeed, the problem is not so much one of deficiency of resources, or even of recognizing the anomaly of the economic situation, but one of unwillingness to take bold and comprehensive corrective action. The student of impediments to economic change and progress in any system would have no difficulty in recognizing that these economic problems require political solutions.

Notes

1. This umbrella covers Bulgaria, Czechoslovakia, the GDR (East Germany), Hungary, Poland, Romania, and the USSR. In this chapter we will also refer to them as CMEA (Council for Mutual Economic Assistance) countries, and for our purposes we disregard such CMEA members as Mongolia and Albania (which has never formally withdrawn but does not actively participate in CMEA) and such associate (or observer) members as Yugoslavia and Cuba.

2. W. Nordhaus and J. Tobin, *Economic Growth* (New York, 1972).

3. For Joan Robinson's treatment of the inflation barrier see *The Accumulation of Capital* (New York, 1966), pp. 48 and passim.

4. Cf. G. R. Feiwel, "Causes and Consequences of Disguised Industrial Unemployment in a Socialized Economy," *Soviet Studies* 126, no. 3 (July 1974): 344–362.

5. Cf. G. R. Feiwel, *Problems in Polish Economic Planning,* vol. II, *Industrialization and Planning Under Polish Socialism* (New York, 1971), pp. 293ff.

6. For a discussion of realistic plan construction based on his experience as architect of the 1961–1975 perspective plan that was never approved or adopted by the Polish government, but is to this day the most comprehensive and coherent attempt at long-term planning in Eastern Europe see M. Kalecki, *Nowe Drogi,* no. 8 (1958), pp. 27–45; *Nauka Polska,* no. 1 (1959), pp. 53–58; *Polish Perspectives,* no. 3 (1959), pp. 3–19; and *Z zagadnien gospodarczo-spolecznych Polski Ludowej* (Warsaw, 1964).

7. Cf. E. Denison, *Why Growth Rates Differ* (Washington, 1967), pp. 11ff; United Nations, *Economic Survey of Europe in 1959* (Geneva, 1960), p. 8.

8. S. Kuznets, *Population, Capital and Growth* (New York, 1973), p. 263.

9. United Nations, *Economic Survey Since the War* (New York, 1953), Chapters 3 and 4.

10. U.S., Congress, Joint Economic Committee, *Economic Developments in Countries of Eastern Europe* (Washington, 1970), p. 47; G. R. Feiwel, ed., *New Currents in Soviet-Type Economies* (Scranton, 1968), p. 82.

11. *Der Spiegel*, January 20, 1975, p. 59.

12. Cf. S. Kuznets, *Modern Economic Growth* (New Haven, 1966).

13. Cf. G. R. Feiwel, *Poland's Industrialization Policy*, vol. I, *Industrialization and Planning*, Chapter 3.

14. *Rozwoj gospodarczy krajow RWPG 1950-1968* (Warsaw, 1969), p. 44.

15. T. P. Alton et al., *Statistics on East European Economic Structure and Growth*, OP-48 (New York, 1975), pp. 52-57; E. Bass, *Bulgarian GNP by Sectors of Origin, 1950-1974*, OP-44 (New York, 1975), p. 2.

16. Cf. G. R. Feiwel, *American Economic Review* 55, no. 5 (December 1966): 1300-1302.

17. Alton, *Statistics*, pp. 8-57.

18. U.S., Congress, *Economic Developments*, p. 243; Alton, *Statistics*, p. 67.

19. U.S., Congress, *Economic Developments*, p. 437.

20. *Rozwoj gospodarczy*, pp. 14-41; M. Golebiowski and B. Zielinska, *Gospodarka planowa*, no. 4 (1973), p. 238; United Nations, *Economic Survey of Europe in 1973* (New York, 1974), p. 108.

21. Cf. G. R. Feiwel, *The Soviet Quest for Economic Efficiency* (New York, 1972), pp. 516ff.

22. *Rozwoj gospodarczy*, p. 66; *Statisticheski Yezhegodnik Stran-Chlenov Soveta Ekonomicheskoy Vzaimopomoshchi 1971* (Moscow, 1971), pp. 59-60; *Statisticheski Yezhegodnik Stran-Chlenov Soveta Ekonomicheskoy Vzaimopomoshchi 1973* (Moscow, 1973), pp. 67-68.

23. *Statisticheski Yezhegodnik, 1971*, p. 58.

24. U.S., Congress, *Economic Developments*, p. 244.

25. Cf. Feiwel, *New Currents*, p. 93; Denison, *Why Growth Rates Differ*, p. 118.

26. *Statisticheski Yezhegodnik, 1971*, p. 141; *Statisticheski Yezhegodnik, 1973*, p. 157; United Nations, *Economic Bulletin for Europe* 28, no. 1 (Nov. 1966):41.

27. U.S., Congress, *Economic Developments*, p. 438.

28. For statistical data, graphic presentation, and analysis of fluctuations in STEs see G. R. Feiwel, *Growth and Reforms in Centrally Planned Economies* (New York, 1977), pp. 38-49.

29. For an analysis of the Czechoslovak developments see Feiwel, *New Currents*, pp. 112-122; J. Goldmann and K. Kouba, *Economic Growth in Czechoslovakia* (White Plains, N.Y., 1969); and G. R. Feiwel, *New Economic Patterns in Czechoslovakia* (New York, 1968), Chapter 1. For fluctuations of industrial output in Romania see J. M. Montias, *Economic Development in Communist Rumania* (Cambridge, Mass., 1967), p. 16. For the record of fluctuations in Yugoslavia see B. Horvat, *Business Cycles in Yugoslavia* (White Plains, N. Y., 1971) and *Ekonomist* (Belgrade), no. 1-2 (1974). For a comparative study of

Yugoslavia and STEs see A. Bajt, "Investment Cycles in European Socialist Economies," *Journal of Economic Literature* 9, no. 1 (March 1971):56–59. For comparisons of fluctuations East and West see G. J. Staller, "Fluctuations in Economic Activity," *American Economic Review* 54, no. 4 (June 1964):385–395.

30. J. Tinbergen et al., *Optimum Social Welfare and Productivity* (New York, 1972), p. 92.

31. A. Bergson, "Development Under Two Systems," *World Politics* 23, no. 4 (July 1971):599; Cf. U.S., Congress, *Economic Developments*, p. 63.

32. United Nations, *Economic Survey of Europe in 1969*, Part I (New York, 1970), p. 10.

33. United Nations, *Economic Survey of Europe in 1971*, Part I (New York, 1972), p. 6; U.S., Congress, *Economic Developments*, p. 62.

34. The ICOR plays a prominent role in development planning, but the ambiguity of the coefficient and the pitfalls of measurement have long been recognized. Feiwel, *Poland's Industrialization*, p. 48; United Nations, *Economic Survey of Europe in 1968* (New York, 1969), p. 146. As with many other measures, it is probably more important to warn what ICOR is not saying (e.g., it is not a meaningful indicator of capital productivity; it neglects labor's contribution and tends to underrate that of technical progress), on what assumptions the available estimates are based, and what are the irksome problems of identifying and associating the increment in capital with that of output.

35. United Nations, *Economic Survey of Europe 1966* (New York, 1967), Chapter 2, p. 45; United Nations, *Economic Survey of Europe in 1973*, pp. 122–123. Other estimates indicate a relatively sharper increase in Bulgaria. U.S., Congress, *Economic Developments*, p. 64. Moreover, the United Nations estimates of the ratio of productive investment to increase in income show a similar (slightly higher) tendency to increase. United Nations, *Economic Bulletin for Europe*, p. 39; cf. *Problemy ekonomiczne* (Cracow), no. 3 (1971), p. 10.

36. Feiwel, *New Currents*, pp. 95–96; cf. U.S., Congress, *Economic Developments*, pp. 268–270.

37. Cf. Feiwel, *Poland's Industrialization*, p. 47.

38. U.S., Congress, *Economic Developments*, p. 438.

39. Ibid., pp. 456–458.

40. U.S., Congress, Joint Economic Committee, *Reorientation and Commercial Relations of the Economies of Eastern Europe* (Washington, 1974), p. 281.

41. The choice of the planner's maximand for a given period has been the subject of considerable controversy. If growth of national income is chosen, it has to be constrained by a minimum consumption growth and other side conditions. If growth of consumption is chosen it then has to be constrained by a minimum growth rate of national income together with other side conditions. For the literature on the subject see O. Lange, *Decyzje optymalne* (Warsaw, 1964), Ch. 6; Feiwel, *Poland's Industrialization*, pp. 40–41 and references therein.

42. M. Kalecki, *Problemy teorii gospodarki socjalistycznej* (Warsaw, 1970), pp. 111–116.

43. Kuznets, *Population, Capital and Growth*, p. 167.

44. For a discussion and quantitative assessment of the components of

technical change in various countries and an interesting analysis of Soviet growth determinants see S. Gomulka, *Inventive Activity, Diffusion and the Stages of Economic Growth* (Arhus, Denmark, 1971).

45. One of the key features of CMEA foreign trade is that by far the largest share of trade remains within the bloc, leaving these countries' industrial output rather insensitive to the more sophisticated technology and higher quality of goods imported from the West or to the more stringent requirements of Western buyers. With the exception of Romania, more than two-thirds of foreign trade of CMEA countries in the past has been with the socialist countries. Moreover, with the exceptions of Romania and Czechoslovakia, the geographical trade orientation of CMEA countries did not change drastically, except for a modest increase in the share of trade with nonsocialist countries that began in the mid-1960s. *Rozwoj gospodarczy*, pp. 115–118; *Statisticheski Yezhegodnik, 1973*, p. 353. By 1974 a significant reduction of trade with socialist countries occurred in Romania, Poland, the USSR, and Hungary where the percentages of trade with other socialist countries (total trade = 100) were as follows:

	Imports		Exports	
	1960	1974	1960	1974
Bulgaria	83.9	70.1	84.0	76.0
Czechoslovakia	71.3	65.0	72.3	67.4
GDR	73.8	60.2	75.7	68.4
Hungary	70.9	57.6	71.5	67.1
Poland	63.5	44.4	62.6	55.7
Romania	73.1	39.2	73.0	43.3
USSR	70.7	54.7	75.7	53.5

Source: *Kraje RWPG 1960–1975*, pp. 117–118.

With the exception of the USSR, in the other three countries imports from socialist countries dropped more sharply than did exports. Also imports from the developed market economies increased to a larger extent than did exports to these countries.

Eleftherios N. Botsas

4

Patterns of Trade

Overview

Karl Marx was interested in the theory of the growth and collapse of capitalism, not in the theory of socialism or trade among socialist countries and their capitalist counterparts. Therefore, he left no prescriptions on international trade policies. Marxist theoreticians and practitioners had to develop their own perceptions of the role of international trade, but while theoreticians are always free to develop intellectual frameworks, practitioners have to deal with plans and targets that may be destabilized by international trade. Thus, antitrade biases among bureaucrats of the centrally planned economies (CPEs) should be expected.[1] Accurate information about the availabilities of inputs in amounts no larger and no smaller than those required for overall planning commands a premium in the planning process, especially when prices are not free to fluctuate according to relative scarcities.

The antitrade biases in the CPEs have been attributed by Western economists to 1) the drive for autarky, 2) planning, 3) the existence of state monopolies, and 4) "price irrationality" and inconvertibility.

Autarky, or economic self-sufficiency, is not an attribute limited to the CPEs; it is present in all nations. However, autarky comes at a price, and trade dependence is an index of a nation's unwillingness to pay such a price. Moreover, dependence on any specific country or commodity can be avoided through geographic or commodity diversification for both imports and exports. Because central planning originated in the Soviet Union, a country vast enough to be potentially self-sufficient, autarky became a good in itself. It was the Stalinist, not the Marxist model, that assigned low priorities to international trade. The Soviet *Textbook of Political Economy* asserts that foreign trade is "a supplementary source of aid for the development of production."[2] When the East European economies came under Soviet hegemony at the end of World War II, they inherited, among other things, the Soviet drive toward autarky.

In response to the Marshall Plan and the creation of the Organization for European Economic Cooperation (OEEC), the Soviet Union and the other East European countries (Albania, Bulgaria, Czechoslovakia, Hungary, Poland, and Romania) formed the Council for Mutual Economic Assistance (CMEA)—also known as CEMA and COMECON—in 1949. (The German Democratic Republic—GDR—entered the bloc in 1950.) By the time of the formation of CMEA, East European economies had already been diverted from the West to the Soviet Union and, to a lesser extent, to each other. "The most important result of the Second World War, and its economic consequences," Stalin wrote in 1952, "must be recognized to be the collapse of the unified, all-embracing world market. This circumstance has induced a further deepening of the general crisis of the world capitalist system."[3] The creation of the "second parallel market" was supposed to surpass trade of the Western countries.

The drive for autarky in the East was assisted by so-called Western economic warfare.[4] The U.S. Export Control Act of 1949 provided the overall framework for the embargo on exports of "strategic" items to the Communist countries, while the Battle Act of 1951 attempted to widen the application of export controls beyond the national limits of the United States by declaring "that no military, economic, or financial assistance shall be supplied to any nation unless it applies an embargo" on strategic items. The NATO countries (with the exception of Iceland) and Japan formed a Coordinating Committee (Cocom) to coordinate the export controls. The effects of the controls on the Communist countries are debatable. However, they did succeed in the creation of short-run bottlenecks and in raising the costs to the East European economies.

CMEA's policy to achieve maximum economic independence from the West would lead to bloc autarky, but not necessarily to autarky for each country. Although Eastern rhetoric dismissed comparative advantage as a "pseudoscientific tool of capitalistic exploitation," in principle the CMEA countries could specialize in production and integrate their economies. CMEA's first communiqué stated that "the conference noted considerable success in the development of the economic relations among the countries concerned and above all the great rise in the turnover of trade."[5] Increased intra-CMEA trade would require, however, supranational economic planning or convertibility of intra-CMEA currencies. However, the East European economy was geared more toward the duplication of Soviet plans than toward specialization.

Foreign trade is an integral part of economic planning, and under the Stalinist model the quantities to be imported were stated in terms of plan fulfillments. Planning per se is not antitrade. Indeed, Eastern rhetoric has argued that planning is superior to market anarchy because it provides for agreements of long duration (usually three years or longer) and it prespecifies quantities, commodities, and prices, thus reducing uncertainties and instability. Empirical studies of trade behavior have shown, however, there has not been a reduction of uncertainties and instability.[6] The ministries of foreign trade, in cooperation with other ministries and the foreign trade enterprises, work out the plans for foreign trade. As Josef Wilczynski has stated, "whereas in the developed market economies the emphasis appears to be on exports, in the centrally planned economies it is imports that occupy the focus of attention. Imports are the starting side in the planning process, since they are considered as indispensable to meet development targets."[7] As we shall see later on, the appetite of the CMEA countries for imports from the developed West seems to be insatiable.

International fluctuations in income and prices are transmitted to the domestic economy through imports and exports. It is a fundamental assumption of Marxist doctrine that market economies are highly unstable. Therefore, central planners, desiring to insulate themselves against the whims of the market and to reduce the range of error in their domestic plans, develop a tendency to underestimate the importance of trade as a means of raising welfare standards. The greater the dependence on foreign trade, the greater the impact of trade on economic planning. However, international trade increases the range of substitutable techniques of productions, thus permitting a more efficient utilization of resources.

After Stalin's death and the uprisings in Poland and Hungary, the interest of the central planners in Eastern Europe changed from autarky to a search for economic efficiency. Between 1950 and 1962, trade turnover (imports plus exports) between Western and Eastern Europe increased by 270 percent (see Table 7). The drive to develop a second "parallel world market" could not materialize under the Stalinist model of planning. Thus, in 1965, Vneshniaia Torgovlia stated the role of trade as follows:

> From an economic point of view, autarchy is disadvantageous, because it tends to slow down the development of the productive forces, to brake the growth of labor productivity. . . . The Soviet Union and the other Socialistic countries are not secluding themselves within the bounds of their national markets or of the world Socialist market, but are striving to utilize the advantages of the international division of labor on a world wide scale.[8]

When planning depends on direct allocation of resources, foreign trade cannot be decentralized. The existence of state monopolies for foreign trade coupled with the frequent pronouncements of East European officials that trade is a legitimate tool in the struggle to overthrow capitalism gave rise to the opinion that the USSR and her satellites used trade for political purposes only. Such an opinion was easily accepted among Western commentators. Moreover, in the West, monopoly is associated with "badness," with a power to distribute gains in its favor. Economists argue that monopoly power depends on the relative dominance of the market and the price elasticities, themselves being functions of alternative substitutes. To the extent that state monopolies affect the volume of trade, they affect it through their bureaucratic and inflexible procedures rather than their market power.

Price irrationality refers to the fact that prices prevailing in the CPEs reflect the preferences of the central planners rather than the preference of consumers as expressed through their interactions with the producing units. Therefore, domestic prices do not reflect opportunity costs. For example, in order to encourage enterprises to use an intermediate or capital good A, central planners may assign to good A a price that is low in comparison with another good B or with its cost of production. In addition, turnover and other taxes further distort the relative prices of the commodities. In such cases, the CPEs cannot let foreign holders of their currencies shop around, because if they did, CPEs would experience the wrong trade mix, in the sense that they would become exporters of the commodities they need most.[9]

Irrational prices and inconvertibility have led to bilateralism. Bilateralism always reduces the potential volume of trade because it requires the partners to trade equal values. If country A exports goods and services to country B worth more than A's imports from B, A is extending credit to B. In the late 1940s, bilateral agreements existed almost exclusively between the USSR and the CMEA countries, but not among the six East European countries. Bilateralism spread later on to cover both intra-CMEA trade and East-West trade. At the end of 1968, Josef Wilczynski counted 350 bilateral agreements among European CMEA countries and Western developed and developing countries.[10]

Growth and Direction of Trade

The previous section summarized the impediments to trade of CPEs either among themselves or between the bloc and the non-Communist world. Because of the impediments, especially those introduced by planning, one would expect the volume of CPE international trade to be below its optimum. To be sure, all governments introduce varying degrees of impediments to the international flow of goods and services, but the impediments that are unique to the CPEs have been presumed to have a greater negative impact on trade than the impediments of market economies. For example, Frederic L. Pryor estimated that "in 1955, no

TABLE 1

GEOGRAPHIC DISTRIBUTION OF CMEA-EUROPE TRADE
(PERCENTAGE OF VALUE OF IMPORTS AND EXPORTS)

Year	Intra-bloc	Developed MES	Rest of World
1938	10	73	17
1948	44	40	16
1953	64	15	21
1954	63	16	21
1955	60	19	21
1956	59	20	21
1957	62	20	18
1958	61	19	20
1959	62	18	20
1960	60	19	21
1961	64	19	17
1962	63	18	19
1963	66	17	17
1964	64	19	17
1965	62	21	17
1966	62	22	16
1967	63	22	16
1968	64	21	15
1969	63	21	16
1970	63	22	15
1971	63	23	14
1972	63	23	15
1973	58	28	14
1974	53	32	15
1975	55	30	15
1976	54	31	15
1977	55	29	16

Note: Trade between the two Germanies is excluded.

Source: Calculated from United Nations, *Yearbook of International Trade Statistics*.

CEMA bloc nation realized over 50 percent of its 'potential' trade per capita,"[11] and many Western economists agree that the foreign trade of CPEs is below their potential.[12] However, comparisons with some kind of optimum imply comparisons with the classical model of comparative advantage, which is based on assumptions that differ dramatically from those governing the trade behavior of the CPEs.

In 1938, the share of the European CMEA countries in world trade was about 4 percent; in the 1940s, their share declined and then increased to reach the rate of about 9 percent in the 1960s. The period 1948-1953 was one of reorientation in both ideology and trade, of power consolidation, of peak Cold War antagonism, and of imitation of the Stalinist model of material planning. As Table 1 shows, intra-CMEA trade (measured as a percentage of the value of exports plus imports) reached its peak in 1953, and then started its gradual decline. At least one Western author has credited the CMEA with trade-creation dynamics. Michael Kaser wrote, "the expansion of commerce within Comecon can fairly be attributed to the existence of the agency itself."[13] However, to the extent that CMEA was fairly inactive and failed to provide for specialization during the Stalin years, trade-creation effects are post-Stalin phenomena.

The second period of intra-CMEA trade, as well as trade with the rest of the world, covers the post-Stalin era. Recently intra-CMEA shares of trade declined. Therefore, trade with the rest of the world increased faster than trade among partners, although overall trade increased rapidly. Table 2 shows the rates of growth in net material product (NMP), and the value of imports and exports of the European countries of the bloc. Their average rates of growth in both imports and exports exceeded the annual rates of growth in NMP in every case, indicating the increasing dependence of the CMEA countries on foreign trade. Of course, the reader must keep in mind that values are affected by the price levels of imports and exports. Indeed, the Economic Commission for Europe (ECE) concluded that:

> Intra–east European trade is conducted in almost complete isolation from the rest of the world market, and investigations—whether conducted in eastern or western Europe—indicate that price levels ruling in that trade sector are significantly above those in east-west and intra-west trade. This suggests that trade data used here for east European countries have an upward bias, but by how much cannot be ascertained.[14]

Nevertheless, actual rates of growth in trade exceeded, between 1959-1965, planned rates in all countries except Czechoslovakia. Between 1971 and 1975, all countries had growth rates of trade in excess of growth of NMP.[15]

One of the measures economists use to estimate the dependence of a given economy on international trade is the ratio of exports and imports to GDP (gross domestic product). This measure has many shortcomings but it is the best index of the average dependence of a society's domestic production on the foreign trade sector. However, when the ratio is applied to CPEs, it loses precision. The loss in precision is caused by the dual price mechanism that prevails throughout the CPEs. As we have seen, domestic prices are divorced from market forces (even after the reforms adopted in the East European economies), while foreign trade prices attempt to approximate the international market prices. This price dichotomy tends to overestimate the trade dependence of the CPEs. However, even if one were to allow for such overestimates, the general

TABLE 2

ANNUAL GROWTH RATES IN THE VOLUME OF NMP
AND
THE VALUE OF IMPORTS AND EXPORTS IN EUROPEAN CPEs, 1953-1967

Country	NMP growth				Import growth				Export growth			
	A	B	C	D	A	B	C	D	A	B	C	D
Bulgaria	8.8	7.9	8.3	8.9	19.6	15.5	17.6	18.2	16.1	15.1	15.6	16.2
Czechoslovakia	6.9	3.1	5.0	4.2	10.3	7.4	8.8	8.5	9.7	7.5	8.6	8.0
G.D.R.	7.8	3.6	5.7	4.8	13.6	6.3	9.9	9.0	14.1	7.1	10.6	9.9
Hungary	6.2	5.6	5.9	6.2	10.8	10.9	10.9	13.0	11.4	10.6	11.0	11.4
Poland	6.6	6.0	6.3	6.4	9.6	8.4	9.0	9.0	7.0	10.3	9.1	9.6
Romania	8.2	9.3	8.8	9.4	10.3	12.2	11.2	13.1	13.9	11.0	12.4	11.9
U.S.S.R.	9.2	6.6	7.9	7.1	10.5	7.5	9.0	8.8	9.9	8.0	9.0	9.0

A: average 1953-1957 to average 1958-1962
B: average 1958-1962 to average 1963-1967
C: average 1953-1957 to average 1963-1967
D: Least squares trend rate (G.D.R. 1960-1968, Romania 1959-1967, and rest 1955-1967)

Source: U.N. Economic Commission for Europe, *Economic Bulletin for Europe*, Vol. 21, No. 1 (New York: 1970), p.44.

TABLE 3

GROWTH OF FOREIGN TRADE AND TRADE DEPENDENCE
OF THE EUROPEAN CPEs, 1966-1975

Country & Period	Average Annual Rate of Growth		Trade as a Percentage of GMP at	
	GMP	Trade Turnover	Domestic Prices	Foreign Prices
Bulgaria				
1966-1970	8.7	10.3	33.0	20.0
1971-1975	7.8	12.0	40.0	25.0
Czechoslovakia				
1966-1970	6.9	6.9	27.0	15.0
1971-1975	5.7	6.4	28.0	16.0
G.D.R.				
1966-1970	5.2	9.9	19.0	16.0
1971-1975	5.4	9.1	25.0	19.0
Hungary				
1966-1970	6.8	9.7	30.0	20.0
1971-1975	6.3	8.3	34.0	23.0
Poland				
1966-1970	6.0	9.4	23.0	10.0
1971-1975	9.8	13.0	27.0	12.0
Romania				
1966-1970	7.7	9.4	23.0	11.0
1971-1975	11.3	13.0	27.0	13.0
U.S.S.R.				
1966-1970	7.8	8.6	4.4	3.9
1971-1975	5.7	9.8	5.3	4.7

Source: UNECE, *Economic Survey of Europe in 1976*, Part II (New York: 1977), p. 120.

trend is of increasing dependence of the East European economies on foreign trade. Table 3 shows the ECE estimates of such dependence based on volume data. Whether one views the estimates from the point of domestic prices of gross material product (GMP) or from corrected estimates, one cannot escape the conclusion that trade dependence is increasing for all countries in the bloc. Moreover, as one would expect, the least industrialized country, Bulgaria, has the highest rates of growth and the highest dependence.

CMEA's first communiqué of January 1949 emphasized two aspects: 1) economic cooperation among the participants, and 2) national sovereignty. The second aspect was mainly for propaganda purposes, since Soviet control over the governments of Eastern Europe was indisputable. The CMEA was a direct Soviet response to the "Marshallization" of Western Europe, and the Soviet Union needed the additional propaganda. Also, CMEA's steps toward fulfilling the first aspect were limited during the Stalin period. However, the emphasis on national sovereignty has come to be the greatest obstacle to economic integration in Eastern Europe. The well-publicized objections of Romania to supranational planning and specialization are based on the principle of national sovereignty. The founders of the CMEA did not foresee the possibility of common action being frustrated by individual countries, other than the USSR, yet the Romanians have declared their strong opposition to supranational plans and division of labor. The Romania declaration of 1964 argued that:

> the idea of a single planning body for all CMEA countries has the most serious economic and political implications. The planned management of the national economy is one of the fundamental, essential, and inalienable attributes of the sovereignty of the socialist state—the state plan being the chief means through which the socialist state achieves its political and socioeconomic objectives.[16]

Yet, Brezhnev argued a year later that "it would be incorrect—more than that, it would be inadmissible—to oppose the interests of the economic development of the whole system of socialism to the interest of the development of individual socialist countries."[17] What is at stake here, beyond the issue of national sovereignty, is that industrialization would proceed at unequal rates if the Soviet proposal for areawide balanced development with specialization along existing lines of activity was adopted. Such a policy would provide the impetus for faster industrialization of Czechoslovakia and the GDR, while the least industrialized countries, Romania and Bulgaria, would specialize more in food production and low-technology manufacturing.[18]

Basically, Romania appealed to two traditional arguments against specialization: 1) the infant industry argument, and 2) the balance-of-payments argument. Not wishing to increase trade dependence on the rest of the bloc, Romania pursued policies that were nationalistic because it perceived a conflict of interest between national objectives and global objectives of the bloc. Therefore, starting in 1960, Romania gradually reduced her relative trade turnover with the bloc. Since Romania substituted trade with the West for trade with the East, overall trade dependence did not decline.

While in 1962 and 1963 summit meetings of CMEA failed to support Khrushchev's drive for subordination of national planning to supranational planning, CMEA did succeed in moving in the direction of multilateralism and limited division of labor through: 1) the creation of the International Bank for Economic Cooperation (IBEC), 2) the adoption of the "transferable ruble" system, 3) the provision for long-term planning and coordination, and 4) cooperation and specialization.

Up to January 1964, trade and payments among the CMEA countries were based on bilateral clearing. Bilateral clearing restricts trade because it requires the value of exports of any country to be balanced with imports from each country individually. This handicap was corrected at times by trilateral agreements, but trilateral agreements cannot provide multilateralism. Thus, for example, if country A wants to import from country B, but B has no demand for A's goods, A will have to produce the potential imports or find another country, C, that is willing to buy A's goods and sell its own goods to B. This cumbersome process is time consuming and costly. As a way out, CMEA engaged in a process of import substitution that duplicated production and increased the cost of products. For example, "five of the six satellites . . . were producing their own tractors, with annual output split as follows: Czechoslovakia, 32,000; Romania, 22,000; Poland, 15,000; East Germany, 14,000; Hungary 3,000."[19] It was against such a background that CMEA established IBEC and the transferable ruble, the latter being a unit of account, not a convertible currency. For convertible currencies, the bank had to borrow in the Euro-money markets.

Although the primary function of IBEC was to facilitate intra-CMEA trade through the provision of clearing facilities, it has become more known in the West through its borrowing in the Western money markets. Operations in the West have increased from about 9 percent of the bank's volume of operations in 1966 to 40 percent in 1975. The reasons for the increased activity of the bank in hard currencies (Western convertible currencies) are to be found in the increased volume of East-West trade (to be discussed below) and in the increased trade in hard-currency commodities—commodities that command a higher price in the world markets than within CMEA—among the CMEA countries. In addition, CMEA established the International Investment Bank (IIB) in 1971 for the purpose of financing CMEA projects that increase the "international Socialist division of labor." The two banks act in the West as specialized agencies of CMEA rather than as representatives of governments, and thus they acquire some of the characteristics of supranational bodies. By 1977, IIB had advanced $4 billion to various enterprises in the bloc.

Unlike plan coordination that requires subordination of national interest to the interest of the bloc, "cooperation and specialization" are limited to project and trade agreements. Since almost all countries developed parallel industries, specialization is achieved in components of the industrial branches. For example, of Czechoslovakia's imports from the CMEA countries during the period 1971–1975, 40 percent were machinery, and "this figure is planned to rise to 50 percent during the 1976–1980 period."[20] Bulgaria is another example, promoting its machinery exports from almost nothing to "40 percent of total exports of CMEA countries in 1975, and the figure may go up to more than 50 percent by 1980."[21] Overall, "trade based on these *cooperation agreements* has been the most dynamic trade flow within the region: its value rose from $2.6 billion in 1973 to some $5 billion in 1975."[22] One has to be careful, of course, to distinguish between overall trade and changes in trade. Trade based on these agreements represents about 6 percent of the bloc's trade turnover. Yet it is the most promising force of trade growth within the bloc.

Cooperation agreements of the 1960s and the first half of the 1970s were concentrated on the traditional sectors of automobiles, textiles, shipbuilding, tools, etc. The energy crisis of the mid-1970s and the world shortage of raw materials shifted the emphasis to energy production and raw materials production. Such economic activities are capital intensive and the CMEA countries are known for their lack of capital. Therefore the projects represent a pooling of funds for joint exploitation of energy and raw materials. "The value of projects scheduled for implementation . . . during the period 1976–1980 is estimated at 7 billion transferable roubles (almost 12 billion 1976 dollars)."[23] The participating countries will receive the output according to their contribution of capital, skills, and resources, thus providing a further stimulus to trade. Since energy and raw materials are located in the Soviet Union, the bulk of the investment is located in the Soviet Union. This further increases the Soviet Union's dominance in the bloc.

Other cooperation agreements that have a great promise for future trade are joint projects in engineering and scientific cooperation. Cooperation agreements in manufacturing sectors accounted for "24 percent of the total intra-CMEA trade in machinery in 1975."[24] The number of multilateral specialization agreements signed in 1975 alone covered 2150 items. Thus an attempt is being made toward meeting the goals of tighter integration within the bloc without resorting to supranational planning.

TABLE 4

TRADE TURNOVER OF EASTERN EUROPE
AND THE SOVIET UNION, 1966-1977

(MILLIONS OF CURRENT DOLLARS)

Year	Bulgaria	Czecho-slovakia	G.D.R.	Hungary	Poland	Romania	U.S.S.R.
1966	2,783	5,481	6,420	3,160	4,766	2,399	16,754
1967	3,030	5,544	6,735	3,478	5,173	2,491	18,186
1968	3,397	6,120	7,364	3,593	5,711	3,078	20,044
1969	3,550	6,614	8,258	4,012	6,354	3,374	21,982
1970	3,835	7,487	9,428	4,823	7,155	3,811	24,539
1971	4,302	8,190	10,057	5,491	7,911	4,217	25,864
1972	5,394	9,577	12,088	6,446	10,267	5,219	31,415
1973	6,567	12,172	15,375	8,352	14,187	7,147	42,571
1974	8,202	14,585	18,394	11,306	18,797	10,014	52,384
1975	10,099	17,433	21,378	13,267	22,818	10,683	70,287
1976	11,008	18,741	24,557	10,460	24,884	12,233	75,277
1977	12,658	21,967	26,358	12,354	27,010	14,423	85,978
Rates of Growth	15.79	14.66	15.13	15.43	19.38	18.61	17.35

Sources: 1966-1970, International Monetary Fund, *Directions of Trade*; 1971-1976, United Nations, *Yearbook of International Trade Statistics*; 1977, United Nations, *Monthly Bulletin of Statistics*. Rates of growth estimated according to text equation.

The shares of imports originating in and exports destined to CMEA vary from country to country. In the first half of the 1970s, Romania had the lowest share of trade (about 40 percent of exports and 35 percent of imports) with CMEA, followed by the Soviet Union (about 42 percent of trade turnover). On the other extreme, Bulgaria had over 70 percent of its trade with the bloc (over 50 percent with the Soviet Union alone).

The trade turnover (exports to, plus imports from, the world) of the seven countries for the recent past is given in Table 4, while the intrabloc trade is given in Table 5. Rates of growth were estimated by least-squares estimates of the form:

log T = a + bt
where T = trade turnover
t = time in years
and a, b are the intercept and parameter to be estimated.

For the bloc as a whole, trade turnover increased at an average rate of 16.7 percent per year. The imports amd exports (not shown here) of individual countries grew at approximately the same rates. There seems to be enough evidence that the old policy of achieving overall balance in the trade accounts is still present in the CMEA countries. The exception is in 1974-1975 when prices were changed for intrabloc trade.

TABLE 5

INTRA-CMEA (EUROPE) TRADE TURNOVER

(MILLIONS OF CURRENT DOLLARS)

Year	Bulgaria	Czecho-slovakia	G.D.R.	Hungary	Poland	Romania	U.S.S.R.
1967	2,193	3,685	4,659	2,237	3,154	1,391	10,131
1968	2,509	4,004	5,125	2,395	3,500	1,403	11,280
1969	2,701	4,292	5,663	2,573	3,946	1,646	12,209
1970	2,847	4,798	6,331	2,974	4,510	1,872	12,392
1971	3,223	5,240	6,749	3,507	4,885	1,978	14,500
1972	3,993	6,431	8,114	4,144	6,073	2,416	17,405
1973	4,968	7,809	10,027	5,259	7,523	3,059	21,017
1974	5,582	8,759	11,019	6,239	8,803	3,409	22,869
1975	7,233	11,400	13,960	8,646	11,302	4,021	32,129
1976	8,241	12,541	15,449	5,543	12,473	4,769	33,605
1977	9,728	14,377	16,247	6,391	14,247	5,853	39,517

Note: Exports f.o.b.; imports f.o.b. for all except Hungary, for which imports are valued C.I.F.

Sources: United Nations, *Yearbook of International Trade Statistics*, and *Monthly Bulletin of Statistics*, June 1978 and June 1979.

The problem of prices at which bloc countries trade among themselves fascinated Western economists because relative prices distribute the gains from specialization and trade. In the case of market economies, prices are determined by the interaction of consumer preferences and relative scarcities, but in the case of the CPEs the prices are set by administrative authority. The terms of trade, Px/pm (the ratio of the prices of exports over the prices of imports), give us the purchasing power of a country's exports in terms of imports. There are two basic comparisons: one involves comparing the Px/pm ratio of the bloc countries with those of the world markets and the other involves movements of Px/pm through time. It is the first comparison that is of importance here.

In the early 1960s, some Western economists argued that the satellite economies were paying prices for imports from the USSR higher than those prevailing in the world markets and they were receiving prices of exports to the USSR lower than they could receive in the world markets.[25] If this were the case, then income was being transferred through the terms of trade from the satellites to the Soviet Union. However, because of lack of complete data, studies on price discrimination have been inconclusive. Moreover, since the East European economies are net exporters of manufactured goods and net importers of raw materials and energy in their trade with the Soviet Union, it is extremely difficult to compare the prices of their manufactures with those prevailing in the West. The qualitative differences of similar products were very high. Frederic Pryor concluded that "from 1952 through 1959 every CMEA nation in almost every year received more favorable terms of trade with Bloc than with Western partners."[26]

Nevertheless, in their search for optimum price in intra-CMEA trade, the CMEA countries agreed to use *lagged* average world prices, "corrected" for seasonal and cyclical fluctuations, speculation, cost of transportation, etc. The policy of using world prices for intra-CMEA trade is sound since the CMEA countries are small buyers and sellers in world markets. They are what economists call "price takers." However, if substantial qualitative differences exist between the commodities the CMEA countries trade among themselves and the commodities traded in world markets, prices of the latter are poor indices of the prices that should prevail in the former. Moreover, the use of lagged prices smooths out fluctuations, but it does not respond to relative scarcities. Price stability is achieved at the expense of economic rationality. However, as the trade of the CMEA countries with the West increased in the 1970s, more flexibility has been introduced to the price formula.

Intra-CMEA trade of the first half of the 1970s was supposed to be governed by the average world prices prevailing in the second half of the

1960s. Such a time lag was not unusual for intra-CMEA trade. However, the early 1970s—especially the second half of 1973 and the first half of 1974—experienced dramatic price increases in raw materials and fuel. Maintenance of the price formula would mean that the Soviet Union would be selling oil to her East European partners in 1974–1975 at the average price prevailing in the late 1960s. This would be not only a massive deterioration of the Soviet terms of trade but also an uneconomical use of a scarce commodity.[27] Moreover, given the demand of the Soviet Union for Western commodities and the high price of oil in Western markets, the Soviet Union would be taking a substantial loss if the agreed price formula were retained. Therefore, CMEA agreed to revamp the price formula for raising the prices of the traded commodities. There was an agreement to use a five-year moving average, but, in order to avoid detrimental effects on the East European economies—which could recreate the upheavals of the 1950s—the 1973–1974 increases were spread over many years. The Economic Commission for Europe summarized the new changes as follows:

> So far three rounds of adjustment have been made: in January 1975 average prices for the region were raised by 20 percent (those of oil by 130 percent); in January 1976 the rise was more moderate (8 percent for oil), as it was in January 1977 (20 percent for oil, the price of which reached some $10 per barrel). The amplitude of price fluctuation on the world market also narrowed considerably in 1975 and 1976. Throughout this period the terms of trade have been moving in favour of the Soviet Union. This is because the price adjustments have favoured fuels and raw materials which figure prominently in Soviet exports, but little in its imports.[28]

Even after revamping, the price of oil exported to Eastern Europe is still below the world price. Martin J. Kohn and Nicholas R. Lang found, in their research of the new prices, that "the immediate effect of the rises in CMEA prices was to improve the USSR's terms of trade substantially but still by much less than would have been the case if world prices had been applied."[29] Part of the explanation of why the Soviet Union did not extract from its CMEA trading partners the maximum price for fuels and raw materials may be due to the fact that, as we have seen under agreements of cooperation, exploitation of fuels and raw materials in the USSR is done with capital and labor from the other CMEA countries. Moreover, the terms of trade are affected by prices of both exports and imports, and the evidence that the USSR does not charge world prices for her exports is still inconclusive. The USSR may be charging prices lower than those prevailing in world markets, but she may also be paying prices for imports below world-market prices.

TABLE 6

THE TERMS OF TRADE OF EASTERN EUROPE

(1970 = 100)

Country	1963	1968	1969	1971	1972	1973	1974	1975	1976
Bulgaria	103	97	97	99	100	99	98	96	91
Czechoslovakia	101	101	97	99	97	96	96	91	88
G.D.R.	101	100	100	100	99	95	90	86	87
Hungary	99	98	99	99	98	97	89	82	85
Poland	100	98	98	104	106	104	102	102	104
U.S.S.R.	115	106	102	104	102	109	108	102	109

Source: United Nations, *Yearbook of International Trade Statistics*.

The 1975 change in intra-CMEA prices caused a sudden surge in the value of intra-CMEA trade; the value increased by about 30 percent over the 1974 level. However, "roughly two-thirds of the increase was due to the price increases, implying a volume growth of 10 percent."[30] The value of intra-CMEA trade for recent years is shown in Table 5.

In the first half of the 1970s the terms of trade with respect to exports to and imports from the world deteriorated for all CMEA countries, except the USSR and Poland. Table 6 shows the relative prices (Px/pm) for selected years. Since our data stop at 1975, the movement in Soviet terms of trade is not reflected accurately. Looking at the bloc as a unit, the terms of trade improved by 1.5 percent in 1973 over 1972; they declined by 2.3 percent and 4.1 percent in 1974 and 1975 and then improved by 2.9 percent in 1976.[31] The greater the proportion of price-sensitive commodities, like manufactures, in total exports and the higher the proportion of raw materials and especially energy in imports, the greater the deterioration in the terms of trade is likely to be.

Trade With the West

East-West trade became interwoven with the ideological and political differences between the CPEs and the market economies (MEs) during the Cold War and its aftermath. As Josef Wilczynski has observed, "trade between the two camps can be viewed as a barometer reflecting ups and downs in the East-West political scene."[32] Drastic trade disruptions as those of the 1950s, as well as the growth of trade in the 1970s, cannot be explained by economic forces alone. The politics of confrontation, coexistence, and détente have affected both the volume and direction of East-West trade.

Although the West has been singled out as the practitioner of economic warfare, the East is not blameless. Khrushchev's declaration that the CPEs "value trade least for economic reasons and most for political reasons"[33] is not an isolated pronouncement or practice. The Western belief that the East was using trade as a tool of destabilization of Western economies could be substantiated easily by the declarations of Eastern leaders. As Table 7 shows, trade between the two parts of Europe reached its minimum in 1953. Then, with the introduction of the policy of peaceful coexistence, trade started its hesitant rise.

Trade turnover between Eastern and Western Europe accounted for 5.9 percent of world trade in 1938; in 1953, it was only 1.2 percent of world trade (trade between the two Germanies is excluded from all calculations of East-West trade). However, the policy of peaceful coexistence left its imprint on trade relations between Eastern and Western Europe. Table 7 shows the continuous increase in trade between the European CPEs and MEs. However, the high rates of growth that characterized trade between the two blocs are functions of both the low level of trade in the early 1950s and the relaxation of restrictions in the late 1950s. Insignificant as it was in terms of total trade of both the CPEs and MEs, trade between them was helpful at least in removing some of the Cold War legacies. The reader should note the growth of USSR trade in particular.

The data in Table 7 has been separated from data on more recent years (Table 8) for three basic reasons: 1) the low level of trade in the early years would add an upward bias in the rates of growth, 2) it was the mid-1960s when the European CPEs moved from extensive to intensive growth, and 3) East-West trade during the earlier period was basically trade between the two parts of Europe. Neither Japan nor the United States were significant participants. Even today, about 80 percent of European CMEA trade with the developed market economies is with Western Europe. Unlike Table 7 that shows only European trade (Yugoslavia and Finland are included in Western Europe), Table 8 shows CMEA trade with all developed market economies, as well as Western Europe.

By the mid-1960s it had become obvious that the rhetoric of the 1950s was allowing for substantial commercial intercourse between East and West. There were, however, many doubts about the extent to which economic interdependence between MEs and CPEs could proceed. Thus the *Background Study on East-West Trade* argued that:

The prospects for expanded trade with the bloc are chiefly a function of bloc industrialization plans. . . . However, looking beyond the near term, there is no indication that for most countries of the free world the Soviet

TABLE 7

WESTERN EUROPE'S* IMPORTS FROM AND EXPORTS TO
EASTERN EUROPE AND THE SOVIET UNION, 1950-1962

(IN MILLIONS OF CURRENT U.S. DOLLARS; IMPORTS C.I.F., EXPORTS F.O.B.)

Year	Eastern Europe Imports	Eastern Europe Exports	U.S.S.R. Imports	U.S.S.R. Exports	Total Imports	Total Exports
1950	625.6	502.6	175.3	139.8	800.9	642.4
1951	697.9	570.0	315.6	177.5	1013.5	747.5
1952	610.6	483.5	384.0	255.1	994.6	738.6
1953	575.8	478.1	334.0	311.3	909.8	789.4
1954	619.2	580.0	415.1	392.4	1034.3	972.4
1955	826.0	701.6	536.4	400.4	1362.4	1102.0
1956	965.2	786.8	668.4	536.4	1633.6	1323.2
1957	964.4	908.0	839.3	622.8	1803.7†	1530.8†
1958	1063.2	955.0	770.1	566.0	1837.3†	1521.2†
1959	1117.2	1057.6	944.4	651.2	2061.6†	1708.8†
1960	1322.4	1249.2	1057.2	866.8	2379.6†	2116.0†
1961	1420.4	1413.2	1100.0	896.4	2520.4†	2309.6†
1962	1510.8	1458.8	1203.6	1070.8	2714.4†	2529.6†
Rates of Growth†	8.69	10.62	15.77	17.01	11.16	12.61

*Yugoslavia is included in Western Europe.

†Includes trade with Albania.

†Estimated as log Y = a + bT.

Source: U.N., Economic Commission for Europe, *Economic Bulletin for Europe*, Vol. 16, No. 2 (1964), pp. 74-77.

TABLE 8

CMEA-EUROPE EXPORTS TO AND IMPORTS FROM
DEVELOPED MARKET ECONOMIES

(MILLIONS OF CURRENT DOLLARS)

Year	Exports (f.o.b.) Total	Europe	Imports (f.o.b.) Total	Europe
1965	4,080	3,650	4,040	3,260
1966	4,770	4,220	4,620	3,660
1967	5,170	4,470	4,970	4,280
1968	5,500	4,760	5,320	4,620
1969	6,210	5,460	5,890	5,150
1970	6,290	6,120	6,940	5,840
1971	7,840	6,980	7,610	6,340
1972	8,750	7,720	10,170	8,040
1973	13,392	11,651	15,039	11,572
1974	19,878	17,476	21,038	17,264
1975	20,199	18,204	27,861	21,698
1976	24,275	21,950	29,676	21,728
Rates of Growth	18.16	18.31	21.26	20.21

Source: United Nations, *Yearbook of International Trade Statistics.*

bloc market should be regarded as anything but marginal. Rumania not-withstanding, bloc imports of needed machinery and equipment from the West, rather than constituting the beginnings of a fruitful international division of labor presaging substantial increases in the level of trade, may make the bloc more independent of the need for such imports in the future.[34]

Rapprochement on trade was expected to continue between the smaller CPEs and the MEs, but the volume of trade experienced in the 1970s was unthinkable in the late 1960s. After all, the entire CMEA accounted for almost 30 percent of the world industrial output but for only 10 percent of its trade. There was no doubt that the East needed trade with the West, but the demand was not perceived as being reciprocal. "On the whole, the Soviet bloc is less important to the West [than the reverse] as a source of imports."[35] An asymmetry was recognized by almost every writer in the field.

Many forces contributed to the changing conditions that gave a surge to East-West trade, the most significant of which were: 1) the East's movement from extensive to intensive growth, 2) the coalescence of polit-

TABLE 9

PLANNED AND REALIZED GROWTH OF OUTPUT AND TRADE, 1959-1965

	Planned		Realized	
	NMP	Trade turnover	NMP	Trade turnover
Bulgaria	9.9	13.2	6.2	14.3
Czechoslovakia	8.0	9.7	3.5	11.7
Eastern Germany	7.9	9.8	5.9	8.9
Hungary	7.0	7.6	6.5	15.2
Poland	7.5	6.5	7.4	12.8
Romania	---	---	8.0	9.9
Soviet Union	8.6	8.3	7.8	11.3

Source: U.N. Economic Commission for Europe, *Economic Bulletin for Europe*, Vol. 21, No. 1 (New York: 1970), p. 47.

ical relations, and 3) the rise of neomercantilism in the West.

Economic growth and industrialization in the CPEs proceeded at high rates in the 1950s due to the extensive use of inputs. That is, growth was due to high rates of increased inputs rather than input productivity. For the period 1950-1967, Abram Bergson found that labor productivity in the European CPEs increased at the same rate as labor productivity in the OECD (Organization for Economic Cooperation and Development) countries, but in terms of capital growth, production was more expensive in the East than it was in OECD.[36] This type of criticism is found among both Eastern and Western specialists. For example, referring to Czechoslovakia's economic performance in 1965, President Novotny said: "for the time being . . . we have not succeeded in achieving a basic change in the development of our economy. We still build expensively, we produce expensively."[37] Thad P. Alton found that "the performance of Eastern Europe as measured by the rates of growth in labor productivity has been below that of such countries as Austria, West Germany, Italy, and Japan."[38]

No one could expect the high rates of growth experienced in the 1950s to continue indefinitely. Such growth is not possible. As the level of full employment of resources is achieved and reallocation of agriculture and services to higher productivity sectors is completed, growth requires technological change. However, capital productivity in all European CPEs except Romania turned from positive to negative in the early 1960s. The negative productivity of capital has been verified by other researchers[39] and, therefore, it will not be dealt with here except to say that it signaled the relative stagnation of the CPEs in the early 1960s. As Table 9 shows, realized rates of growth of output fell short of planned, while realized rates of growth of trade turnover exceeded planned rates during the medium-plan period 1959–1965.

Given the planners' preoccupation with high rates of growth of output, the performance of the CPEs was a disappointment. It was realized that reforms were needed to bring the shadow prices closer to the market. Within the bloc, the countries with the lowest rates of growth experienced the strongest pressures for reforms. However, decentralization and price reforms could not be of great assistance as long as the foreign trade monopoly was decentralized through the creation of foreign trade enterprises (FTEs), which enjoy some degree of autonomy and have direct access to foreign markets but not unlimited rights to intervene as they see fit. It must be remembered that foreign trade is still subordinate to the goals of the state.

Overall, the rates of growth were low because production of the inputs was low, and productivity was low because the rate of technological change was low. Technology can be either developed indigenously or imported. The CPEs realized the significance of imported technology, and the gradual dismantling of the embargo permitted them a higher level of imports of manufactured goods, especially engineering technology. Table 10 shows the increasing CMEA imbalance of imports of those goods from Western Europe.

The most important reforms that affected East-West trade were enterprise to enterprise and government to government agreements of cooperation. By the end of 1973, over one thousand interfirm agreements on industrial cooperation were in force. In 1974 and the first half of 1975, only a few new agreements were signed, but "between July 1975 and July 1976, 298 new contracts were signed, and the new contracts were reported as favouring high types of cooperation."[40] In the 1970s, Hungary, Poland, and Romania occupied the leading position in terms of the number of agreements signed.[41] However, the impact of the agreements on East-West trade will be most significant in the 1980s.

The form that industrial cooperation agreements take varies from industry to industry and country to country. The Soviet Union prefers the so-called turnkey agreements—the sale by a Western firm of a complete production system—for its chemical and metallurgical industries. In terms of industries, engineering and transport equipment occupy the dominant position (about 60 percent of all agreements signed). Other common forms of agreements are licensing, coproduction, joint research, joint marketing, and countertrade, which is a form of partial payment for the value of the exports of the Western firm.

Countertrade, or counterpurchase,[42] is actually an instrument of control of Eastern deficits that will be discussed under balances below. Its importance is, and will continue to be in the future, its stimulation of

TABLE 10

IMPORTS OF MANUFACTURES INTO WESTERN EUROPE (C.I.F.) FROM EAST
EUROPEAN COUNTRIES, AS A PERCENTAGE OF EXPORTS (F.O.B.) TO THEM[a]

A = All manufactures
B = Engineering products

Country	Total western Europe					
	1955		1960		1968	
	A	B	A	B	A	B
Eastern Germany	235	1162	147	217	123	86
Czechoslovakia	189	256	136	90	79	50
Hungary	42	64	63	71	43	27
Poland	41	6	38	9	35	19
Bulgaria	(40)	6	(15)	5	17	9
Romania	(14)	---	(8)	1	15	3
Soviet Union	11	1	13	7	13	11
Total Eastern Europe	48	36	43	25	32	19

SITC Divisions

1955} West European imports 32
      West European exports 32, 33, 34, 35

1960}
1968} Imports and exports 37, 38, 39

[a]Percentages based on any one trade flow below $10 million are in
parentheses.

Source: U.N. Economic Commission for Europe, *Economic Bulletin for
Europe*, Vol. 21, No. 1 (New York: 1970), p. 75.

East-West trade since it provides for future deliveries to the West for current Western exports to the East. For example, the biggest deal between
the Soviet Union and the West in the field of industrial cooperation at the
present concerns gas. "At the present," said the ECE in 1977, "the Soviet
Union imports large-diameter tubes . . . and other equipment . . . to be
repaid by future counterpart deliveries of gas—23 billion cu. m. per year
by 1980."[43] Moreover, imports from the West frequently become the
contribution of East European countries to intra-CMEA cooperation
projects, thus increasing intra-CMEA trade.

Détente has affected, and has been affected by, East-West trade. East-
West politics cannot leave the volume of trade unaffected. Moreover, the
U.S. policy of tying business deals to political considerations provided

TABLE 11

U.S. EXPORTS TO, AND IMPORTS
(C.I.F.) FROM, EASTERN EUROPE AND THE U.S.S.R.

(MILLIONS OF DOLLARS)

	1971	1972	1973	1974	1975	1976	1977	1978
Bulgaria								
Exports		4	7	22	30	43	24	48
Imports	3	3	5	9	21	28	19	20
Czechoslovakia								
Exports	39	50	72	49	53	149	75	105
Imports	25	30	37	51	38	40	41	65
G.D.R.								
Exports	25	18	28	21	17	65	36	170
Imports	11	11	12	15	12	15	18	38
Hungary								
Exports	28	23	33	56	76	63	80	98
Imports	9	13	18	79	38	53	50	74
Poland								
Exports	73	114	350	396	583	623	439	679
Imports	61	101	233	375	280	339	355	479
Romania								
Exports	53	69	117	278	191	250	260	319
Imports	14	34	60	139	147	218	254	376
U.S.S.R.								
Exports	162	542	1195	609	1836	2308	1627	2252
Imports	61	101	233	375	280	239	469	561

Source: International Monetary Fund, *Direction of Trade 1971-77* and *1972-78*.

many opportunities for (non-U.S.) Western firms to explore the East European markets. In a sense, the political distance between the two leaders of the blocs provided for profitable opportunities among the smaller powers. Once détente became the common policy of the two leaders, the Soviet Union took a more euphoric attitude with respect to East-West trade by emphasizing the irreversibility of détente. Soviet policy has been one of creating a vested interest of U.S. firms in trade expansion. President (then Party Chairman) Brezhnev told the U.S.-USSR Trade and Economic Council in 1976 that "U.S. businessmen have lost $2 billion in export orders to the USSR because of restrictions in the Trade Act of 1974."[44] Trade between the United States and the CPEs is shown in Table 11.

Unlike U.S. exports to the USSR and the other Communist countries, imports to the United States from the CPEs were restricted mainly through tariff discrimination, that is, denial of most favored nation (MFN) treatment. The U.S. Trade Agreements Extension Act of 1951 provided that the president "suspend, withdraw or prevent the application of any reduction in rate of duty . . . to imports from the Soviet Socialist Republics and to imports from any nation . . . dominated or controlled by . . . the world Communist movement." Yugoslavia was granted MFN treatment under the assumption that Yugoslavia was not controlled by the world Communist movement. Poland was reaccorded MFN treatment in 1960, but the 1962 Trade Expansion Act made it impossible to grant MFN treatment to additional Communist countries without legislative action. Therefore, Soviet efforts in the mid-1970s were directed toward removing import restrictions in the United States, while Congress wanted to link MFN treatment to the issue of free emigration, SALT, and other political matters.

Given that exports were prohibited and imports were only taxed, it was, at least in theory, possible for the CPEs to have an export surplus with the United States. That was the case up to 1957, when the first relaxation of export controls was applied. However, the surpluses were insignificant. There are three plausible explanations for this phenomenon: 1) U.S. tariffs were so discriminatory as to make CPEs' exports to the U.S. market noncompetitive, 2) the CPEs themselves applied some kind of export controls, and 3) the CPEs lacked the products demanded in the United States.

The U.S. Tariff Commission found that the bulk of Soviet exports to the United States was not subject to substantial tariff discrimination (see Table 12). The range of products that the USSR exported to the United States was limited to duty-free items. As the rate of industrialization accelerated in the CPEs, the percentage of exports subject to tariff discrimination increased for all countries, but especially for Romania. (Romania was granted MFN treatment in 1975.) The Soviet Union has indicated again and again that it considers the restrictions "intolerable." Thus, in May 1977 "the Soviet Foreign Trade Minister, N. Patolichev . . . announced his country's intention to slash non-agricultural imports from the United States because of these restrictions."[45]

"Politics—not the structure of the economic goals of centrally planned economies—have dictated the pattern and level of economic cooperation," wrote Franklyn D. Holzman and Robert Legvold in 1975.[46] Although we are far removed from the economic warfare of the 1950s, U.S. policy has been one of linkages—linking trade to emigration, to Soviet expansionism in the Middle East and Africa, and to human rights violations. However, the increased trade between the two superpowers is an index of the success of the Soviet strategy to break détente into its components and to separate economic from political considerations.

Neomercantilism—the trend to develop export surpluses in the balance

TABLE 12

PERCENTAGE OF U.S. IMPORTS FROM EASTERN EUROPE
THAT WERE SUBJECT TO SUBSTANTIAL
DISCRIMINATION, SELECTED YEARS

(BASED ON VALUE)

Country	1951	1966	1970	1972
Bulgaria	84	32	17	34
Czechoslovakia	70	66	73	87
G.D.R.	53	30	85	76
Hungary	57	44 [*]	43	51
Poland	37	MFN	--	--
Romania	2	41	42	73
U.S.S.R.	24	4	10	25

[*] Since 1960

Source:
John E. Jelacic, *The Impact of Granting Most Favored Nation Treatment to the Countries of Eastern Europe and the People's Republic of China* (U.S. Tariff Commission Staff Research Studies, No. 6, 1974), p. 12.

of trade without a rise in average import duties—has also contributed to the expansion of East-West trade. In the 1960s, West European firms could compete among themselves in exports to the CPEs but not with U.S. firms. Moreover, the United States had a surplus—though insignificant—in her trade with the CPEs. When the overall trade account of the United States ran into deficits, pressures within the United States for a change in policy were intensified.

Free trade among Common Market (European Economic Community—EEC) and EFTA (European Free Trade Association) members, as well as tariff reduction agreements between the two Western groups, have been viewed as discriminatory in the East. Yet trade concessions have been granted to all CPEs by Western Europe. Moreover, in an effort to increase their exports to the CPEs, Western governments have provided, directly or indirectly, credits to the CPEs. The bulk of the credits is export oriented. For Western Europe, as one author put it,

there is little doubt that official credit support (OCS) has played a relatively important role in exporting to the socialist countries. Between 1963 and 1970, for example, while only 3.5 percent of French exports went to CMEA countries, 28.9 percent of French OCS for export credits of more than five years supported exports to the region. In 1972, the proportion of the five major Western grantors (of credit to the East) of worldwide authorizations to the CMEA was 3.3 times the proportion of these countries' total exports directed to the CMEA region.[47]

Competition among Western firms and governments for a share of the CPEs' market has created a kind of credit "explosion." As of 1976, Soviet-Japanese projects in energy and timber amounted to credits of $4.6 billion; and Italian credits to the Soviet Union amounted to $1.9 billion.[48] Competition from the United States is expected to further increase credits for CPE purchases in the West. As the Economic Commission for Europe put it, "a system of financing and guaranteeing exports exists in all western countries. In recent years, their resources have been increasingly directed towards promoting east-west trade."[49] The mild recessions of 1974 and 1976 provided additional pressures in the West to seek exports to the East through officially guaranteed credits.

Balances

Although the CPEs strive for overall balances in their trade accounts, their appetite for Western products has created serious deficits in their trade with the West. The United States, West Germany, France, and Canada remain the strongest creditor countries in East-West trade in the 1970s. The imbalances have forced the CPEs to borrow heavily in order to finance their imports. Between 1965 and 1976, imports of the seven CMEA countries from the developed MEs increased at an annual rate of 21.26 percent, while their exports to the same MEs increased at a rate of 18.16 percent per year (estimated from Table 8). This imbalance forced the CPEs to borrow from the MEs, and this increased borrowing became a controversial issue in the West.

There is no agreement as to the magnitude of the CPEs' debt. Richard Portes estimated it to be $46 billion at the end of 1976.[50] This figure is at variance with the ECE estimates (Table 13). However, the ECE estimates refer to the net position of the banks. Total debt seems to be somewhere between $35 billion and $46 billion. About 30 percent of the total debt represents Western governments' guaranteed credits that have long maturities. In terms of total indebtedness, the USSR and Poland are the biggest borrowers, while France, West Germany, the United Kingdom, and Italy are the most important grantors of official credits. From the point of view of distribution, the bulk of French credits has been extended to Bulgaria and the USSR; West German to the GDR and the USSR; United

TABLE 13

EAST EUROPEAN DEBT TO THE WEST

(MILLIONS OF U.S. DOLLARS)

| Country | End of 1976 | Net Position of Western Banks | | | |
		1975	1976	1977	March 1978
Albania		45	-78	-59	14
Bulgaria	2,800	1,318	1,618	1,900	2,487
Czechoslovakia	2,100	38	510	815	1,245
G.D.R.	5,800	2,019	2,959	438	4,287
Hungary	3,500	1,446	2,152	3,347	4,215
Poland	10,400	3,362	4,799	6,404	9,311
Romania	2,800	506	437	991	1,474
U.S.S.R.	14,400	4,743	6,621	6,332	7,033
CMEA Bank	3,500	--			
Residual	--	1,811	2,289	1,952	2,223
Total	45,300	15,288	21,307	25,123	32,289

Sources: Column 1, Richard Portes, "East Europe's Debt to the West," *Foreign Affairs* (July 1977), p. 757; rest, Economic Commission for Europe, *Economic Bulletin for Europe*, Vol. 30, No. 1 (New York: United Nations, 1979), p. 78.

Kingdom to Hungary and Poland; and Italian to Hungary and Romania.[51]

There is nothing wrong with external debt when the debt is used to increase future productivity that will reduce imports and/or increase exports. Ability to pay debt servicing depends on the economies' ability to save from domestic output and to earn hard currencies through exports of goods and services. The former is not a problem in the CPEs where saving is a function of planning. The latter has been viewed with growing concern among Western commentators. As Portes put it:

> The common arguments which initially made lenders eager to accept East European business, and which they still use to bolster the market's confidence, appear extremely dubious. . . . The excellent repayment record of East European countries before the recent explosion of their debts can be viewed skeptically as merely a conscious, careful preparation for a major foray into Western credit markets—or at least as irrelevant to the totally transformed current situation.[52]

The burden of debt can be measured only if we know the debt-service ratio, which we do not. Speculation that the smaller CPEs such as Bulgaria, Poland, and Hungary may default or request rescheduling is premature. The debt of a CPE differs from the debt of an ME. In the former case, the state and the economy are one and the same thing. The

TABLE 14

TRADE OF THE EUROPEAN CMEA WITH THE INDUSTRIAL WEST, 1970-1978*

(MILLIONS OF CURRENT DOLLARS)

	1970	1971	1972	1973	1974	1975	1976	1977	1978
Bulgaria									
Exports	189.8	202.8	221.3	299.4	321.3	290.1	344.1	359.5	431.9
Imports	298.0	299.8	322.3	454.0	803.3	1040.7	874.3	823.9	1007.9
Balance	-108.2	-98.0	-101.0	-154.6	-482.0	-750.6	-530.2	-463.4	-576.0
Czechoslovakia									
Exports	604.5	694.0	798.0	1077.1	1289.6	1358.8	1410.0	1553.3	1794.1
Imports	724.5	853.9	936.3	1273.1	1631.4	1765.7	1952.9	1949.8	2158.4
Balance	-80.0	-159.9	-138.3	-196.0	-341.8	-406.9	-542.9	-395.5	-364.3
G.D.R.									
Exports	331.0	341.8	420.3	539.8	777.4	809.7	851.0	909.8	1094.1
Imports	420.6	486.6	608.2	750.5	990.9	1133.4	1286.6	1149.8	1495.1
Balance	-89.6	-144.6	-187.9	-210.7	-213.5	-323.7	-429.6	-240.0	-401.0
Hungary									
Exports	451.6	490.1	681.7	968.9	1159.9	1068.3	1228.3	1428.7	1598.5
Imports	631.3	767.6	876.1	1164.0	1970.7	1942.9	1899.6	2420.2	3106.0
Balance	-179.7	-277.5	-194.4	-195.1	-810.8	-874.6	-671.3	-991.5	-1507.5
Poland									
Exports	863.2	989.4	1258.6	1757.5	2297.9	2534.0	2964.4	3193.4	3630.4
Imports	802.8	973.5	1566.9	2999.6	4355.5	5209.2	5190.2	4728.1	5268.1
Balance	60.4	16.1	-308.3	-1242.1	-2057.6	-2675.2	-2225.8	-1534.7	-1637.7
Romania									
Exports	541.7	657.4	813.0	1178.3	1885.8	1641.6	1877.0	1915.5	1853.9
Imports	747.9	801.6	1028.4	1427.2	2423.9	2153.2	2086.9	2413.7	2769.4
Balance	-206.8	-144.2	-215.4	-248.9	-538.1	-511.6	-290.9	-498.2	-915.5
U.S.S.R.									
Exports	2171.0	2320.0	2632.0	4230.0	6255.0	6516.0	8033.0	9577.0	11010.0
Imports	2218.0	2243.0	3334.0	4977.0	6260.0	10731.0	11662.0	11442.0	13391.0
Balance	-47.0	77.0	-702.0	-747.0	-5.0	-4215.0	-3629.0	-1865.0	-2381.0

*United States, Canada, Japan, Austria, Belgium, Denmark, France, West Germany, Italy, Netherlands, Norway, Sweden, Switzerland, United Kingdom, except trade between East and West Germany. Exports f.o.b.; imports f.o.b. for all except G.D.R. and Hungary.

Source: International Monetary Fund, *Direction of Trade 1971-77* and *1972-78.*

state can reduce at least part of imports at will and can reduce domestic consumption in order to make exports available. The fact that the 1976–1980 plans provide for increased imports from the West and the fact that Western banks and governments are eager to advance credits to the East are indicative of the creditworthiness of the CPEs. Moreover, it would be unlikely for the USSR to let the CPEs (with the possible exception of Romania) default. The creditworthiness of the whole bloc would be at stake. Even in the West, the OECD and the United States have not let Turkey or Zaire down, nor have the commercial banks reduced their loans to these countries, although their ability to manage their economies is nonexistent in comparison with the CPEs'.

I do not wish to minimize the importance of the rising debt. The bulk of CPE imports from the West is capital equipment, and reduction of such imports would disrupt the economic plans. Indeed the asymmetry of imports of the CPEs from the West in 1974–1976 may be a compromise between the desire to import and the rising debt. Compared with the period 1971–1974, Western exports to the USSR exploded in 1975 and 1976, while exports to the rest of the CPEs followed the opposite pattern (see Table 14). This is also indicative of the USSR's greater capacity to borrow in the Western markets. But in both cases, the rising debt would not be present if Western firms and governments were not eager to compete for export markets. In the process, Western savings finance the modernization of the CPEs, a far cry from Khruschchev's "We will bury you" slogan.

Table 14 separates the data on CPE imports from, and exports to, the West in order to concentrate on hard currencies. The industrial West is where the CPEs are looking for both capital imports and credits. However, the reader should notice that Table 14, like all other tables here, refers to trade in commodities. Invisible accounts, such as tourism, pensions, and interest, are not reflected in trade statistics. Tourist receipts from the hard currencies area should be positive, but, because of interest payments, the current account for invisibles should be negative and growing for the whole area. The deficit in invisibles increased from $236 million in 1973 to $1.14 billion in 1976.

Trade Structure

The commodity composition of most CPEs has changed dramatically since the prewar period. With the exception of Czechoslovakia and East Germany, the CPEs were exporters of agricultural goods and a few raw materials, and importers of manufactured goods. Moreover, their exports were concentrated in a few products. All the CPEs had the typical profiles of underdeveloped countries, and the Soviet Union still resembles a developing country in its trade with the industrial West. Before the war, Western Europe imported 17 percent of its total cereal imports from Eastern Europe. In the late 1940s, cereals were still imported from the East (mainly the USSR) but at their peak, cereal imports amounted to only 50 percent of the prewar level.

Throughout the postwar period, Eastern economists, administrators, and commentators have taken pride in the achievements of socialism in the transformation of the predominantly agricultural societies of Eastern Europe into industrial economies. For example, E. D. Matrievskaya wrote: The general growth in production in the European members of CMEA has been reflected in the rapid expansion of their engineering: thus, in a mere decade (1950–1960) the volume of engineering production grew 7.8 times in Poland, 7.2 times in Bulgaria, 5.8 times in Rumania, 4.6 times in Czechoslovakia, 3.8 times in the G.D.R., and 3.3 times in Hungary."[53]

Table 15 shows the commodity composition of CMEA trade, according to the broad economic categories, as a percentage of each category of the total value of exports and imports. The share of machinery and equipment increased dramatically in both exports and imports during the first twenty-five years of CMEA. This constitutes a testimony to both the "success" of CMEA in transforming the primarily agricultural economies into industrial economies and to its failure in developing manufacturing industries independent of the West. As Table 10 shows, CMEA has a deficit in the trade of manufactured goods, especially in engineering—the sector that is the pride of the East. But even when one looks into machinery and equipment alone, the East has a deficit (32 percent of exports versus 36 percent of imports). Given that the value of imports exceeded the value of exports in both 1975 and 1976, the deficit is larger than the one indicated by Table 15.

The rising importance of machinery and equipment in the values of total exports and imports is not, of course, equally distributed among the CMEA countries. For example, in 1972 the share of machinery and equipment varied from 19 percent of the USSR's exports to 51 percent of the GDR's exports. Czechoslovakia and the GDR have always had about 50 percent of their exports originating in the machinery and equipment category. Bulgaria, one of the least industrialized countries in the 1940s and 1950s, has made a big jump in this sector, with machinery and equipment accounting for 26 percent of export revenue in 1968 and 43 percent in 1976. The shares in the imports of machinery and equipment were much closer together, varying from 32 percent of the imports to the GDR, Hungary, and Romania to 42 percent of the imports to Bulgaria.

TABLE 15

THE COMPOSITION OF CMEA TRADE IN SELECTED YEARS

(PERCENT OF TOTAL VALUE)

	Machinery & Equipment	Raw Materials & Semifinished Goods	Foodstuffs & Raw Materials for Food	Consumer Goods
Exports				
1950	14	41	22	11
1963	27	49	15	9
1968	29	47	14	10
1975	32	48	9	11
1976	32	50	8	10
1977	32	50	8	10
Imports				
1950	24	54	14	6
1963	34	41	13	10
1968	37	39	12	12
1975	36	42	15	8
1976	36	41	15	8
1977	37	40	14	9

Note: Exclusive of the G.D.R. for the years prior to 1975.

Sources: Based on United Nations, *Yearbook of International Trade Statistics* and ECE, *Economic Bulletin for Europe*, Vols. 21, 28, 29, and 30.

While the above percentages refer to the total trade of the seven countries with the world, Table 16 shows the intra-CMEA trade in machinery and equipment.

In spite of the growth of machinery in CMEA exports, the bloc faces a deficit in this item in its trade with the industrialized West. Indeed, as Table 17 shows, Western imports of machinery from the East accounted for only 21 percent (C.I.F.) of the value of Western exports (F.O.B.) to the East. The modernization programs undertaken in the 1976–1980 plans would require much more imports of machinery from the West than actually imported. It seems that the growing deficit of the East in its trade with the West put the brakes on the growth of the import of machinery. On the other hand, Eastern exports to the West are dominated by energy materials such as gas (from the Soviet Union), petroleum and petroleum products (86 percent from the USSR), and coal and coke (mainly from Poland).

Although in its trade with the West, the East still retains the profile of a developing area, in its trade with the developing countries, the East acts as a highly industrialized region. That is, manufactured goods dominate Eastern exports to the developing countries, and foodstuffs and raw

TABLE 16

SHARE OF MACHINERY AND EQUIPMENT IN INTRA-CMEA TRADE

(PERCENTAGES)

Exporting Country	1955	1960	1965	1967
Bulgaria	3	15	30	32
Czechoslovakia	51	47	56	57
Eastern Germany	--	56	59	58
Hungary	38	46	43	42
Poland	17	38	49	49
Romania	6	16	25	25
U.S.S.R.	17	13	18	23

Source: ECE, *Economic Bulletin for Europe*, Vol. 21, No. 1
          (1970), p. 21.

materials dominate Eastern imports. In 1972 and 1974, 65 percent and 55 percent, respectively, of the value of CMEA exports to the developing countries were in the categories of machinery and other manufactured goods. On the other hand, foodstuffs and raw materials accounted for over 70 percent of CMEA imports from the developing countries. Recent efforts to increase cooperation between CMEA and the developing countries are likely to alter trade composition in the future.

U.S. trade with the CPEs is dominated by agricultural products. Taking all CPEs, not just the European CMEA, as a group, in 1978, 54.5 percent of U.S. exports to those countries were SITC 0-1 categories (food, beverages, and tobacco), while these categories accounted for only 14.9 percent of U.S. exports to the world. "When soybeans, an agricultural product classified as crude material, are added, this share of exports to the NMEs [nonmarket economies] increases to 62.6 percent."[54] On the import side one finds greater diversification. SITC 0-1 categories accounted for about 17 percent of imports from the CPEs, while chemicals, mineral fuels, and manufactured goods accounted for over two-thirds. The USSR has been the main destination of U.S. exports of cereals; the value of these exports amounted to $1,347 million in 1976, $849 million in 1977, and $1,290 million during the first nine months of 1978.[55] Poland has been the second most important destination of U.S. cereals exported to the CPEs. In 1978, China emerged as the third most important market, within the group of CPEs, for U.S. exports of cereals. Moreover, U.S. trade with the CPEs increased substantially in 1978 over 1977.

TABLE 17

COMMODITY COMPOSITION OF EAST-WEST TRADE:
WESTERN EXPORTS TO THE EAST (F.O.B.) AND
WESTERN IMPORTS FROM THE EAST (C.I.F.)

(MILLIONS OF CURRENT DOLLARS)

	Exports			Imports		
	1975	1976	1977*	1975	1976	1977*
Food & live animals	2,974	3,910	2,597	1,732	1,884	1,696
Beverages & tobacco	180	198	153	125	146	135
Crude materials (excluding fuels)	1,126	1,268	1,283	3,005	3,320	3,293
Mineral fuels, etc.	206	220	230	6,850	8,648	7,972
Animal & vegetable oils & fats	106	78	85	290	141	146
Chemicals	3,136	3,067	3,323	1,034	1,174	1,383
Basic manufactures	8,238	8,173	7,281	3,276	3,598	3,528
Machinery & transport equipment	9,854	10,121	10,262	1,841	2,217	1,782
Miscellaneous manufactured articles	1,286	1,467	1,185	1,377	1,592	1,763
Goods not classified by kind	172	213	179	120	164	183
Total	27,278	28,731	26,579	19,650	22,889	21,882

*Yugoslavian trade excluded for 1977.

Source: Economic Commission for Europe, *Economic Bulletin for Europe*, Vols. 28, 29, and 30. (New York: United Nations; 1976, 1977, 1979.)

Prospects for the Future

As Table 1 shows, trade of the European CMEA with the developed MEs made a dramatic turn in 1973. The interdependence between East and West created by the web of trade agreements, agreements on cooperation, joint ventures, financial relations, and the politics of détente has been promoted with vigor, not only because it promotes economic welfare in both the East and the West, but also because it is presumed to have certain by-products that have been judged to be good in themselves.

Presumably, one of the by-products is that the web increases the independence of the European CPEs from the control of the USSR by creating alternative sources for their imports as well as markets for their exports. Moreover, the technology and capital that the CPEs are importing from the West create continuous flows of linkages. The technology imported is complex and thus creates ties that cannot be severed without high penalties. Therefore, return to autarky, or even interdependence within the CMEA only, is likely to be very costly.

It is true that trade shares with the Soviet Union have declined for all countries except Bulgaria. However, there are limits to how far the East European economies can divorce themselves from the Soviet economy.

Moreover, although the record shows a declining relative importance of the USSR in the trade of the East European countries, the agreements of cooperation within the CMEA indicate an increased interdependence in the future.

A second by-product is that the Soviet Union itself is interwoven with the capitalistic world. In the first half of the 1970s, imports from the developed MEs increased by an average rate of 19 percent per year versus 8 percent per year for imports from European CPEs, and this gap accelerated further in 1975–1976 (see Table 14). Exports to the West increased twice as fast as exports to the East. Moreover, the Soviet Union accounts for over one-half of the CMEA imports of machinery from the West, and the technological dependence mentioned above applies to the USSR as well. The share of Soviet imports from the advanced market economies increased from 24 percent in 1967 to 41 percent in 1976, while the share of imports from CMEA declined from 60 percent to 42 percent. However, the share of imports from the advanced market economies declined to 36 percent in 1977 and 35 percent in 1978, while the share of the CPEs increased to 49 and 51 percent in those two years, respectively.

Relations between the Soviet Union and the United States mellowed in the 1970s, but the two countries still remain predominantly rivals on the international scene. East-West trade has created vested interests but it has also helped to sharpen some of the contradictions, such as those created by the imbalance of, and the readiness of the United States to prohibit sales of, high technology. Besides, no matter how many reforms are introduced, Soviet bureaucracy retains its aversion toward risk. But above all, as Marshall I. Goldman has observed, "if Russian history tells us anything, it is that the Russians have been able to tighten their belts and make do without foreign help, both in industry and in agriculture."[56]

Following the Soviet invasion of Afghanistan, President Carter announced on January 4, 1980, the imposition of controls on exports of grain and high-technology items to the USSR. The value of the embargoed items is estimated at about $3 billion for 1980. The Soviet Union is expected to make up part of the embargoed grain purchases through other sources, although it will likely pay higher prices. Total U.S. exports to the USSR amounted to $2.3 billion in 1978, and $2.7 billion during the first nine months of 1979.

The embargo on high-technology items is likely to have a smaller impact on Soviet imports of these items, unless the Coordinating Committee (Cocom), consisting of the NATO allies plus Japan, fully agrees to the tough U.S. controls. West Germany, Japan, and France—not the United States—have been the important sources of Soviet imports of high-technology items. It is doubtful that the United States will be able to pressure these countries into sacrificing economic benefits for the sake of Afghanistan. The new embargo shows, however, that the USSR has not been successful in its attempt to divorce economic matters from foreign affairs.

The increased interdependence between the two camps may be viewed as an erosion of the cohesiveness of the East. Yet, no matter how far trade between the two camps goes, we should not expect the erosion to be very significant. After all, Marxism may have been modified to meet national interests but it has not been abandoned.

Because of the long-term effects of East-West cooperation agreements, trade between the two camps is likely to keep growing in the 1980s. As both East and West learn more about one another, imbalances are likely to decline. However, the West will have to absorb an increasing flow of Eastern goods if imbalances are to be kept within manageable limits.

Futurology is very inexact; when it comes to predictions about Soviet trade it becomes speculation. For example, what kind of leaders will succeed the aged Soviet leadership? Some of us like to think that the time for another Stalin is gone and that economic interdependence is irreversible. Yet Stalin has not been a unique phenomenon in the Russian pantheon.

Within CMEA there are two basic contradictions. The cooperation agreements are concrete steps to further integration. Moreover, the agreements appear to be increasing the dependence of the East European economies on the Soviet Union. Yet Soviet economic policies, especially after the price revisions of 1975, seem to indicate a trend on the part of the Soviet Union toward freeing itself from subsidizing Eastern Europe.

Notes

1. Eastern Europe, CPEs, and CMEA are used interchangeably here and include the seven countries. Albania is excluded because of lack of data; Yugoslavia is classified as a "Western" country.

2. Quoted in Frederic L. Pryor, *The Communist Foreign Trade System* (Cambridge, Mass.: M.I.T. Press, 1963), p. 23.

3. Quoted in U.S., Senate, Committee on Foreign Relations, *A Background Study on East-West Trade* (Washington, D.C.: Government Printing Office, 1965), p. 3.

4. The most exhaustive study on Western economic policies of the strategic embargo is G. Adler-Karlsson, *Western Economic Warfare 1947–67* (Stockholm: Amqvist and Wicksell, 1968).

5. Quoted in Michael Kaser, *Comecon: Integration Problems of the Planned Economies*, 2nd ed. (New York: Oxford University Press, 1967), p. 12.

6. See, for example, Egon Neuberger, "Is the U.S.S.R. Superior to the West for

Primary Products?" *Review of Economics and Statistics* 46 (1964): 287–293; George J. Staller, "Patterns of Stability in Foreign Trade," *American Economic Review* 57 (1967): 879–888; Eleftherios N. Botsas, "Trade Stability of the Balkan Economies, 1956–1970," *Weltwirtschaftliches Archiv,* Band 111 (1975):573–584.

7. Josef Wilczynski, *The Economics and Politics of East-West Trade* (New York: Frederick A. Praeger, 1969), p. 60.

8. Quoted in U.S., Congress, Joint Economic Committee (JEC), *Current Economic Indicators in the U.S.S.R.* (Washington, D.C.: Government Printing Office, 1965), p. 160.

9. For a further discussion of this topic and inconvertibility see Franklyn D. Holzman, "Foreign Trade Behavior of Centrally Planned Economies," in Henry Rosovsky, ed., *Industrialization in Two Systems: Essays in Honor of Alexander Gerschenkron* (New York: John Wiley and Sons, 1966), pp. 237–265; Pryor, *op. cit.;* and Wilczynski, *op. cit.*

10. Wilczynski, *op. cit.,* pp. 108–109.

11. Pryor, *op. cit.,* p. 27.

12. See Alan A. Brown and Paul Marer, "Foreign Trade in the East European Reforms," in Morris Bornstein, ed., *Plan and Market* (New Haven: Yale University Press, 1973), pp. 153–205.

13. Kaser, *op. cit.,* p. 143.

14. Economic Commission for Europe, *Economic Bulletin for Europe,* vol. 21 (New York: United Nations, 1970), p. 48.

15. Economic Commission for Europe, *Economic Survey of Europe in 1976,* Part II (New York: United Nations, 1977), pp. 119–125. (Hereafter cited as *Survey.*)

16. Quoted in Kaser, *op cit.,* p. 31.

17. Quoted in Herthor W. Heiss, "The Council for Mutual Economic Assistance—Developments Since the Mid-1960's," in U.S., Congress, Joint Economic Committee, *Economic Developments in Countries of Eastern Europe: A Compendium of Papers* (Washington: Government Printing Office, 1970), p. 529.

18. For an excellent discussion of the origin of the dispute, see John M. Montias, "Background and Origins of the Rumanian Dispute with Comecon," *Soviet Studies* 16, no. 2 (1964):125–151.

19. *Voprosy Economiski,* June 1965, quoted in U.S., Senate, Committee on Foreign Relations, *Background Study,* p. 30.

20. Economic Commission for Europe, *Survey 1976,* Part II, p. 126.

21. *Ibid.*

22. *Ibid.*

23. *Ibid.,* p. 127.

24. *Ibid.*

25. See H. Hendershausen, "Terms of Trade Between the Soviet Union and Smaller Communist Countries," *Review of Economics and Statistics* 41 (1959): 106–118 and his "Broadened Analysis," *Review of Economics and Statistics* 42 (1960):152–163; Franklyn D. Holzman, "Soviet Foreign Trade Pricing and the Question of Discrimination," *Review of Economics and Statistics* 44 (1962):

134–147, and his "More on Soviet Bloc Trade Discrimination," *Soviet Studies* 17 (1965):44–65.

26. Pryor, *op. cit.*, pp. 172–173.

27. Martin J. Kohn, "Developments in Soviet-Eastern European Terms of Trade, 1971–1975," in U.S., Congress, Joint Economic Committee, *Soviet Economy in a New Perspective* (Washington: Government Printing Office, 1976), (p. 68).

28. Economic Commission for Europe, *Survey 1976*, Part I, p. 125.

29. Martin J. Kohn and Nicholas R. Lang, "The Intra-CEMA Foreign Trade System: Major Price Changes, Little Reform," in U.S., Congress, Joint Economic Committee, *East European Economics Post-Helsinki* (Washington: Government Printing Office, 1977), p. 136. (Hereafter cited as JEC, *Post-Helsinki.*)

30. Economic Commission for Europe, *Survey 1975*, p. 139.

31. Economic Commission for Europe, *Economic Bulletin for Europe*, vol. 29 (New York: United Nations, 1977), p. 66.

32. Wilczynski, *op. cit.*, p. 23.

33. *New York Times*, September 18, 1955, quoted in Wilczynski, *op. cit.*, p. 237.

34. U.S., Senate, Committee on Foreign Relations, *Background Study*, p. 57.

35. *Ibid.*, p. 56.

36. Abram Bergson, "Development Under Two Systems: Productivity Growth Since 1950," *World Politics* 23, no.4 (1971):579–607.

37. Economic Commission for Europe, *Survey 1965*, p. 3.

38. Thad P. Alton, "Economic Structure and Growth in Eastern Europe," in JEC, *Economic Developments: A Compendium*, p. 42.

39. *Ibid.* In the same *Compendium* see the papers by John P. Hardt, "East European Economic Development: Two Decades of Interrelationships and Interactions With the Soviet Union," pp. 5–40; Gregory Lazarcick, "Growth of Output, Expenses, and Gross and Net Product in East European Agriculture," pp. 463–527; and Laszlo Czirjak, "Industrial Structure, Growth, and Productivity in Eastern Europe," pp. 434–462.

40. Economic Commission for Europe, *Survey 1976*, Part I, p. 130.

41. Carl H. McMillan, in his "East-West Industrial Cooperation," in JEC, *Post-Helsinki*, pp. 1175–1224, estimated 2302 interfirm agreements as of 1976. However, McMillan's study includes Yugoslavia, which accounts for as many agreements as the seven CMEA members combined.

42. For a detailed discussion of countertrade agreements, see Jenelle Matheson et al., "Countertrade Practices in Eastern Europe," in JEC, *Post-Helsinki*, pp. 1277–1311.

43. Economic Commission for Europe, *Survey 1976*, Part II, p. 129.

44. U.S., International Trade Commission, *Special Report to the Congress and the East-West Trade Board* (Washington, D.C.: April 1977), p. 12. (Hereafter publications of USITC will be cited as USITC and publication number.)

45. USITC, Publication 876 (March 1978), p. 17.

46. Franklyn D. Holzman and Robert Legvold, "The Economics and Politics of

East-West Relations," *International Organization 29*, no. 1 (1975):293.

47. Thomas A. Wolf, "East-West European Trade Relations," in JEC, *Post-Helsinki*, pp. 1043-1044.

48. Economic Commission for Europe, *Survey 1976*, Part II, p. 129.

49. Economic Commission for Europe, *Survey 1975*, p. 144.

50. Richard Portes, "East Europe's Debt to the West: Interdependence Is a Two-Way Street," *Foreign Affairs*, July 1977, p. 753.

51. *Ibid.*, p. 759.

52. *Ibid.*, p. 769.

53. E.D. Matrievskaya, "The Role of Engineering in the Development of Foreign Trade Between the European Members of CMEA," in M. C. Kaser, ed., *Economic Development for Eastern Europe* (New York: St. Martin's Press, 1968), p. 136.

54. USITC, Publication 934 (December 1978), p. 3.

55. *Ibid.*, p. 13.

56. Marshall I. Goldman, "Autarchy or Integration—the U.S.S.R. and the World Economy," in JEC, *Soviet Economy in a New Perspective*, p. 84.

Trond Gilberg   **5**

The Political Order

Introduction

The political order in Eastern Europe has undergone great changes since the establishment of Communist-dominated regimes in the area thirty years ago. During this life span of a generation, the countries of the area have experienced fundamental changes in all aspects of societal life, and these changes have largely been engineered by the Communist political elites. These changes in society have in turn resulted in altered relationships between policy and society, between the citizen and political authority, and between the individual and the collectivity. At the same time, older values and behavior patterns have reasserted themselves in all of the East European countries, thus demonstrating the extent to which even political elites dedicated to the implementation of a radical program of societal transformation must coexist with the traditional aspects of political behavior and outlooks. In fact, the political elites of the area have grasped the significance of such values and have attempted to utilize them for the purposes of political legitimization.

Under such circumstances, the "synchronization" of the political order, which was imposed upon the East European political systems during the Stalinist era, has given way to considerable diversification. National differences have once again become a striking feature of the political and social order in Eastern Europe, and any meaningful analysis of these countries must take this fundamental fact into consideration. But even such important differences are contained within certain basic parameters of political institutions and behavior, which make it possible to classify the political systems of the area as essentially "Communist." This interaction between unity and diversity in the political order provides the essential dynamic of contemporary Eastern Europe.

Elements of Commonality:
The Imposition of External Parameters

While the considerable political diversification that has taken place in
Eastern Europe during the last decade makes it difficult to speak of the
area as a "zone" of political commonality, it is nevertheless clear that certain fundamental aspects of life remain unchanged. First and foremost,
the countries of Eastern Europe continue to be dominated politically by
their respective Communist parties, and these parties in turn must relate
to the Communist Party of the Soviet Union (CPSU) within the Moscow-
defined parameters of "proletarian internationalism." Since the Communist parties of Eastern Europe control the policymaking process of
their respective countries, and thus in fact are *state* parties, the relations
between these parties and the CPSU set the stage for relations among the
states of Eastern Europe and the Soviet Union. State relations in the area
therefore exist and develop under the auspices of "socialist internationalism."

Albania and Yugoslavia, however, have rejected this set of imposed
parameters and have succeeded in maintaining their autonomy. As for
the other countries, Leonid Brezhnev has made it absolutely clear that
the Soviet Union demands the adherence of all East European Communist leaders to certain basic principles of domestic and foreign policy
and that the Kremlin considers it a right *and* a duty to intervene by
whatever means necessary (including military occupation) whenever
these principles are violated. The judgment as to such violations will be
made in Moscow, not in the capitals of Eastern Europe; an example of
this kind of Soviet predominance was the invasion of Czechoslovakia in
1968, when the leaders of the Kremlin decided that "socialism" was in
dire danger in Prague and Bratislava, despite Alexander Dubcek's
protestations to the contrary.[1]

According to Brezhnev and the CPSU, the following political and
socioeconomic preconditions must be met by the local Communist
regimes in Eastern Europe:

1. The political hegemony of the local Communist parties must be
preserved. Under no circumstances will the CPSU and the Soviet state
permit real political pluralism in its "front yard"; the existence of
political alternatives to the ruling Communist party is outlawed, and
consequently, political opposition cannot be permitted. Furthermore, the
local Communist parties must maintain their monopoly of political *initiative*, in the sense that only such parties can propose, legislate, and exe-
cute the political and socioeconomic programs that in all cases are

termed "the building of socialism and communism." That several of the East European countries have a multiparty system is of no consequence in this context; the non-Communist parties in countries such as Poland and the German Democratic Republic (GDR) are in all cases mere adjuncts of the local Communist party and act as front organizations and mobilization agents for these ruling parties.[2]

2. The right of the local Communist parties to define the socioeconomic development programs in Eastern Europe must not be violated, and the economic program itself must conform to certain specific guidelines that are subsumed under the heading "socialism." Specifically, "public" ownership of the means of production must be maintained, and the private sector should be reduced to a minimum, especially in industry and in services; however, there is considerable administrative leeway in the execution of agricultural policies. Furthermore, in an era of economic reform in Eastern Europe, decentralization, the development of worker participation in economic management, and the expansion of localized incentive mechanisms must never be allowed to jeopardize the final control of economic decision making and the execution, which must rest with the central authorities.[3]

3. The local Communist parties must retain the right to define the relationship between the individual and the collectivity, i.e., between the citizen and the state and party; in other words, the Communist elites remain the final definers and arbiters of political authority and the sole executors of political power. All the parties of the area remain formally dedicated (both by choice and by Moscow-imposed necessity) to the concept of "making the new socialist man and woman" in preparation for the final goals of socialism and Communism. This aspect of fundamental human transformation, including the restructuring and change of human values and behavioral norms, sets the Communist parties of Eastern Europe apart from other authoritarian ruling parties. Moscow watches this role with considerable attention at a time of ideological erosion in the Communist world.[4]

4. In the field of interparty relations, relations among socialist states, and general foreign policy, the Kremlin has made it clear that it will insist upon certain manifestations of solidarity in the East European capitals. First of all, Moscow demands that the East European states conduct their foreign policy to support the foreign policy of the Soviet state in its major manifestations. Conversely, the Kremlin insists that certain kinds of foreign policy behavior be avoided; in this context, it is expected that the East European countries refrain from support of the "forces of imperialism" (especially the United States, West Germany, and other members

of the Western alliance). Any attempt by an East European country to withdraw from the COMECON or the Warsaw Pact would undoubtedly trigger a sharp Soviet reaction, very likely military intervention. Similarly, consistent East European support for "imperialist" states would, undoubtedly, draw Moscow's unmitigated ire and retribution.[5]

While the requirements of "socialist internationalism" (referring to the support of general Soviet foreign policy as well as to relations among socialist states) are rather clear and well articulated, relations among Communist parties and the principles underlying these relationships are much less clearly defined. The concept of the Soviet Union as the model of socioeconomic development and the recognized center of the international Communist movement has been officially challenged by several East European leaders (notably in Romania), and the 1976 conference of Communist parties in East Berlin went as far as redefining the principle of relations among Communist parties.[6] The concept of "national roads" to socialism and Communism has become well entrenched in many East European Communist parties, once again most notably in Romania (and Yugoslavia). The CPSU has been unsuccessful in its efforts to call an international conference of Communist parties that would exclude the Chinese from the Communist movement, and the relatively recent phenomenon of "Eurocommunism" has also been evaluated quite differently in the East European parties. The CPSU seems primarily concerned with preventing any East European party from endorsing the Chinese Communist party (CCP) in the Sino-Soviet dispute, rather than enforcing acceptance of Soviet supremacy in the international Communist movement; furthermore, the prevention of dangerous experiments à la Eurocommunism in the field of internal party management, rather than imposition of the operating principles of Soviet party organization, appears to be the main principle in this decade.[7]

Elements of Commonality: The East European Quest for Political and Socioeconomic Monopoly

The parameters established by the CPSU and the Soviet state in Eastern Europe are by no means entirely alien to the ruling elites in the area. In fact, in several fields, they correspond well with the vital interests and needs of the East European elites themselves. All the East European Communist party leaders are dedicated to the enhancement of their personal power as well as the power of their organizations in society. To further that end, the ruling elites in Eastern Europe have striven mightily to develop the party organizations and related and subordinate structures. Table 1 examines the party strength of the East European Com-

TABLE 1

PARTY MEMBERSHIP IN EASTERN EUROPE
(ALBANIA AND YUGOSLAVIA EXCLUDED), 1967/68-1976/77
(It should be noted that in some cases, the official sources separate full members and candidates; in other cases, the figures are collapsed in the source material available.)

	1967/68		1970/71		1972/73		1974/75		1976		1979/80	
	Membership	% of Tot. Pop.	Membership	% of Tot. Pop.	Membership	% of Tot. Pop.	Membership	% of Tot. Pop.	Membership	% of Tot. Pop.	Membership	% of Tot. Pop.
Bulgaria	613,000('68)	7.5	700,000('71)	8	--	--	--	--	789,796('76)	9	817,000	9.2
Czecho-slovakia	1,700,000('67)	12.0	1,200,000('71)	8.3	1,200,000('73)	8.2	1,100,000('75)	7.4	1,382,860('76)	9.3	1,500,000	9.9
GDR	1,700,000('68)	10.0	1,845,859('71)	11	1,902,809('72)	11	1,900,000('75)	11.1	2,043,697('76)	12.1	2,100,000	12.5
Hungary	600,000('68)	8.5	662,397('70)	6.4	724,000('72)	6.9	754,353('75)	7.2	--	--	797,000	7.5
Poland	2,029,968('68)	6.3	2,296,000('70)	7	2,300,000('72)	6.8	2,453,000('75)	7.2	2,500,000('76)	7.3	3,100,000	8.8
Romania	1,761,000('68)	13.0	1,999,720('70)	9.9	2,336,000('73)	9.9	2,500,000('74)	11.2	2,577,434	12	2,930,000	13.3

Source: Yearbook on International Communist Affairs (Stanford, Calif.: Hoover Institution Press) for the following years: 1969, 1971, 1972, 1973, 1974, 1976, 1977, and 1980, appropriate country profiles.

munist parties. While the proportion of the population enrolled in the Communist party generally constitutes a small percentage of all citizens, these structures are nevertheless mass organizations and they carry considerable organizational weight on the basis of numbers alone. Furthermore, the parties are extremely important in key segments of the population, such as among army officers, police personnel, and the general and technical intelligentsia. Thus, in the 1960s, the Romanian Communist party (PCR) had enrolled fully 85 percent of all military officers and 42 percent of university professors; other key personnel were also well represented in the PCR, and the situation was much the same elsewhere in Eastern Europe.[8]

This kind of organizational coverage of key occupational groups allows the East European parties increased control over the "commanding elites" of their respective societies. With such coverage and control, there is little chance that the political and socioeconomic monopoly of decision making will be lost in the near future.

Structural control is further enhanced by the numerous front organizations established and maintained by the East European Communist parties. In all cases, there are umbrella organizations such as the Socialist Unity Front in Romania or the National Front in the GDR, in which the Communist party is the leading force, with Communist personnel controlling the crucial posts. Furthermore, the youth organizations of each country are under the firm control of the Communist parties, and there are numerous other organizations for special categories of people, such as women's organizations and groups for pensioners, war veterans, and ethnic minorities; in all cases, such organizations are under the firm control of the respective Communist parties, and Communist functionaries hold the top positions.[9] Table 2 summarizes the available evidence on East European mass organizations.

The work force in Communist-dominated countries is thoroughly controlled through an extensive network of professional organizations. The trade unions are still considered "transmission belts" for supervision and control, and these organizations enroll virtually every gainfully employed person in the East European economic systems.[10] In each field of professional activity there is a specialized union that exercises a monopoly on decisions in matters such as the relationship between the individual employee and the plant administration, health, recreation, and, in many cases, housing; in the writers' and artists' unions, the professional survival of the membership is based on the respective union, since this body decides upon scholarships, royalties, and the very question of whether or not an individual's work will be published or his

TABLE 2

The Most Important Mass Organizations and
Their Memberships in the East European
Political Systems in the 1970s

Bulgaria

    Fatherland Front - 3,500,000 (1976); 4,000,000 (1979/80) - includes:
        Bulgarian Komsomol - 1,200,000 (1976); 1,400,000 (1979/80)
        Trade Unions - 2,500,000 (1976); 2,500,000 (1979/80)

Czechoslovakia

    Swazarm (paramilitary) - 350,000 (1975)
    Socialist Union of Youth - 600,000 (1972)*
    Pioneers - 750,000 (1972)*

GDR

    Free German Youth - 2,157,734 (1976); 2,300,000 (1979/80)
    Ernst Thälmann Pioneers - 1,900,000 (1976); 1,700,000 (1978)
    Trade Unions - 8,000,000 (1976); 8,300,000 (1979/80)

Hungary

    Trade Unions - 4,000,000 (1976)
    Communist Youth League - 800,000 (1976); 840,000 (1979/80)
    Pioneers - 1,000,000 (1979/80)

Poland

    Trade Unions - 12,300,000 (1976); 12,500,000 (1979/80)
    Federation of the Socialist Unions of Polish Youth - over 5,000,000 (1976)
    League of Women - 454,000 (1976); 450,000 (1979/80)
    Union of Fighters for Freedom (Zbowid) - 422,000 (1976); 640,000 (1979/80)

Romania

    All mass organizations are in the Front of Socialist Unity, which
    has a monopoly of political activity. Automatic membership by
    occupational or educational category is standard.

Source: Yearbook on International Communist Affairs, 1968-1980.

*Source: Otto Ulc, Politics in Czechoslovakia (San Francisco, Calif.:
       W. H. Freeman and Co., 1974), pp. 65-66.

paintings exhibited. Through the principle of self-criticism and the alert eye and ear of the party apparatus inside each individual's place of employment, political control is ever-present.

Organizational control over the masses of the population is but one of the mechanisms employed to ensure the hegemony of the East European Communist parties in their societies. The principle of overlapping membership at the elite level is still firmly entrenched in political practice, and the result is that the party's presence is felt at all levels of East European life. Figure 1 shows the extent to which "interlocking directorates" dominated political control in Romania in the mid-1970s.

Figure 1: The Romanian Interlocking Directorate, Late 1976

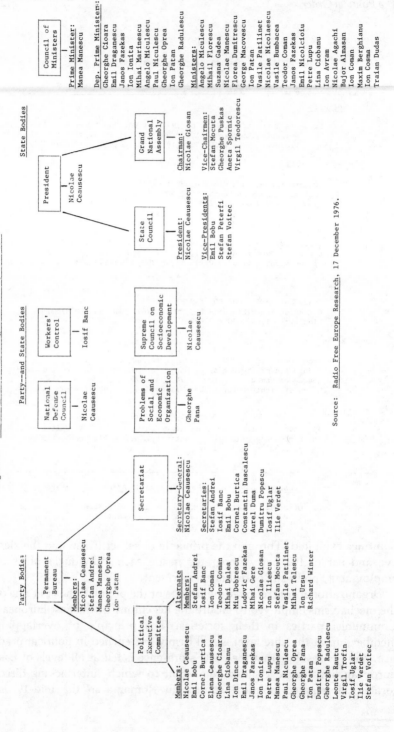

Source: Radio Free Europe Research, 17 December 1976.

Although it is true that Romania is the most centralized (and personalized in the hands of Nicolae Ceauşescu) of all the East European states and political systems, much the same kind of control mechanisms and functions exist throughout the entire region. Patterns similar to the Romanian can be found in other East European countries as well, as shown in Table 3, which examines the interlocking directorates of Poland, the GDR, Czechoslovakia, Hungary, and Bulgaria as of 1974/75.

Impresssive as the control mechanisms of overlapping memberships and interlocking directorates are, they are not considered sufficient by the ruling elites of Eastern Europe. In each of the states, organizational control is backed by large and relatively efficient structures of coercion, such as the security police, the censorship offices, and various vigilante organizations, such as "druzhiniki" and "people's guards," that attempt to assist in the maintenance of law and order and also help ferret out "anti-state" or "anti-socialist" elements and behavior.[11] The power of the coercive structures in Eastern Europe has been demonstrated in graphic fashion in the GDR and Czechoslovakia during the recent spate of dissident activity, and ethnic minorities in Romania have also charged the Ceauşescu regime with methods reminiscent of Stalinist police states.[12]

In addition to administrative/organizational and coercive methods of societal control, the regimes of Eastern Europe maintain their socio-political and economic hegemony by means of their monopoly over economic planning and implementation as well as by their ideological monopoly. Despite varying degrees of reform in the planning agencies and the process of plan establishment and fulfillment, all the economies of Eastern Europe remain essentially centralized rather than market oriented, and political authorities retain their predominance in setting economic priorities for development and deciding on the indicators of success in economic endeavor, be it profit, quantitative output, quality of goods produced, employment, labor productivity, or a combination of these elements.[13] Command over the East European economies is firmly held by the respective political elites, and the differences among the systems of the area are a function of political interests of these ruling cliques.[14]

The political elites of Eastern Europe have also successfully retained their monopoly of ideological pace-setting, insofar as other competing views of political and socioeconomic matters have been removed, destroyed, or at least pushed back to a peripheral position in the political realm. This is not to say that ideological uniformity prevails in Eastern Europe, or that challenges are unimportant; rather, the present regimes have managed to retain their right to decide what *official* ideology is, thereby also establishing the standard against which all other ideological

TABLE 3

The Number of Overlapping Memberships in Top Party and
State Bodies in Eastern Europe, mid-1970's
(Number of positions held by top party officials in party
and state bodies denoted by "P" or "S")

Bulgaria	Czechoslovakia	GDR	Hungary	Poland
Todor Zhivkov 2P,1S	Gustav Husak 2P	Erich Honecker 2P,2S	Janos Kadar 2P	Edward Gierek 2P
Tsola Dragoycheva 1P	Vasil Bilak 2P	Hermann Axen 2P	Gyorgy Aczel 2P,1S	Edward Babiuch 2P,1S
Grisha Filipov 1P	Peter Colotka 1P,1S	Friedrich Ebert 2P,2S	Antal Apro 1P,1S	Henryk Jablonski 1P,1S
Pencho Kubadinski 1P,1S	Karel Hoffmann 1P	Gerhard Grueneberg 2P,1S	Valeria Benke 1P	Mieczyslaw Jagielski 1P,1S
Alexander Lilov 2P	Alois Indra 1P,1S	Kurt Hager 2P	Bela Biszku 3P	Piotr Jaroszewicz 1P,1S
Ivan Mihailov 1P	Antonin Kapek 1P	Heinz Hoffmann 1P,1S	Lajos Feher 1P	Wojciech Jaruzelski 1P
Todor Pavlov 1P	Josef Kempny 2P	Werner Krolikowski 2P	Jeno Fock 1P,1S	Wladyslaw Kruczek 1P,1S
Ivan Popov 1P,1S	Josef Korcak 1P,1S	Werner Lamberz 2P	Sandor Gaspar 1P	Stefan Olszowski 1P
Stanko Todorov 1P,1S	Jozef Lenart 2P	Guenter Mittag 1P,1S	Gyula Kallai 1P	Franciszek Szlachcic 1P,1S
Tano Tsolov 1P,LS	Lubomir Strougal 1P,1S	Erich Mueckenberger 2P	Dezso Nemes 1P	Jan Szydlak 2P
Boris Velchev 2P	Ludvik Svoboda 1P,1S	Alfred Neumann 1P,1S	Karoly Nemeth 4P	Jozef Tejchma 1P,1S
ZhivkoZhivkov 1P,1S	Miloslav Hruskovic 1P	Horst Sindermann 1P,2S	Rezso Nyers 1P	Kazimierz Barcikowski 1P
Dobri Dzhurov 1P	Vaclav Hula 1P,1S	Willi Stoph 1P,2S	Imre Gyori 1P	Zdzislaw Grudzien 1P
Petar Mladenov 1P	Jan Baryl 1P	Paul Verner 2P,2S	Miklos Ovari 2P	Stanislaw Kania 2P
Todor Stoychev 1P	Jan Fojtik 1P	Herbert Warnke 1P,1S	Arpad Pullai 2P	Jozef Kepa 1P
Peko Takov 1P,1S	Frantisek Ondrich 1P	Werner Felfe 1P	Janos Brutyo 1P	Stanislaw Kowalczyk 1P
Krastyu Trichkov 1P,1S	Oldrich Svestka 1P	Joachim Herrmann 1P	Pal Romany 1P	Wincenty Krasko 1P,1S
Drazha Valcheva 1P	Miroslav Moc 1P	Werner Jarowinsky 2P		Jerzy Lukaszewicz 1P
Penyu Kiratsov 1P	Milos Jakes 1P	Guenther Kleiber 1P,1S		Jozef Pinkowski 1P
Ivan Pramov 1P		Ingeborg Lange 2P		Andrzej Werblan 1P,1S
Konstantin Tellalov 1P		Erich Mielke 1P,1S		Ryszard Frelek 1P
Georgi Bokov 1P		Margarete Mueller 1P,1S		Zdzislaw Zandarowski 1P
Vladimir Bonev 1P,1S		Konrad Naumann 1P		Stefan Misiaszek 1P
Sava Dalbokov 1P		Gerhard Schuerer 1P,1S		
Georgi Yordanov 1P		Harry Tisch 1P		
Stoyan Karadzhov 1P		Horst Dohlus 1P		
		Kurt Seibt 1P		

Source: Radio Free Europe Research, 22 July 1974, "Communist Party-Government Line-Up."

manifestations are judged. This situation produces great advantages to the respective regimes, since they can define orthodoxy, establish deviations, and take the appropriate measures of purges and expulsions. Thus, despite the considerable political fervor in Eastern Europe during the last decade, fundamental changes in the ideological sphere have not taken place.[15]

Factors of Diversification

While the essential nature of the East European political systems has not been drastically changed during the 1970s, there have, nevertheless, been many developments of a less substantial nature, which, taken together, add up to considerable change—change that may result in fundamental alterations of political and socioeconomic relationships and foreign relations if the process continues unabated in the 1980s. These changes have been brought about by a confluence of internal and external events and developments.

As pointed out above, the countries of Eastern Europe (with the exception of Yugoslavia and Albania) remain locked in the Soviet sphere of influence, but the nature of that influence has been altered considerably during the last decade. It is in this period that the Soviet Union has moved toward the practical implementation of détente in relations with the West, for the purpose of reducing tension in one arena so that the troublesome conflict (at both the party and state level) with China can be contained. Furthermore, the Soviet Union, grappling with fundamental socioeconomic problems resulting from its forced modernization policies, has attempted to utilize political détente for the purpose of gaining access to Western technology and know-how, ingredients vital to the very survival of the Soviet system. Détente was also a necessary backdrop for the Helsinki Agreement, which finally granted the Kremlin its long-standing wish of formalizing the post–World War II expansion of Soviet power and influence in Europe by legalizing the existing boundaries.[16]

Political détente with the West was designed to reestablish Soviet hegemony in Eastern Europe on the firmer footing of political agreements with the main competitor, the United States, but in the process of producing this kind of agreement, the Kremlin found it also necessary to accept greater interaction between the West and the Eastern European Communist systems. Once the principle had been established that trade and scientific cooperation across the ideological boundary lines of Europe was acceptable, it became impossible to refuse increased political interaction as well. With the new opportunities for East-West relations thus established, the East European elites moved in differing ways and differing degrees to take advantage of the situation.

Among the elites of Eastern Europe, the Romanians were the most anxious to establish new relations with the West or to expand already existing ties. Nicolae Ceaușescu and his close associates perceived the "opening to the West" as a golden opportunity for strengthening the autonomy of Romanian foreign policy, which had been established as official doctrine in the famous "declaration of independence" of 1964.[17] Furthermore, increased economic cooperation with the advanced societies of the West could help the development of the Romanian economy, which had entered a stage where "extensive" policies were no longer sufficient and high-level technology was required; Western credits and know-how could significantly assist the regime in its quest for the "multilaterally developed society," a prerequisite for the achievement of socialism and Communism, which are based upon a high level of socioeconomic achievement. Expanded relations with the West became an integrated part of general Romanian foreign—and domestic—policy. As for the anticipated dangers of ideological imports from the West, the Ceaușescu regime countered by instituting ideological offensives of its own, coupled with rigid internal control, the development of a Ceaușescu personality cult, and the concentration of unparalleled powers in the hands of the PCR general secretary.[18] Such political measures, it was felt, would serve the double purpose of ensuring the continuation of the general secretary's personal power and the power of the PCR in Romanian society, while at the same time showing the Kremlin that "Czechoslovak conditions" would not develop in Romania.

Among the other states of Eastern Europe, expanded relations with the West were effectuated much more slowly and hesitantly. The greatest hesitation was shown by the GDR, where the Ulbricht regime (and subsequently the Honecker leadership) perceived the whole process of détente as potentially dangerous to the very survival of the East German state; Pankow instead followed a policy of sharp *Abgrenzung* ("rigid separation") in regard to the Federal Republic, and relations with the "other Germany" west of the Elbe did not improve until the de facto recognition of the GDR by Bonn later in the 1970s.[19]

Poland at first reacted negatively to those aspects of détente that promised more frequent relations with the West. This hesitancy was undoubtedly caused by fear of West German revanchism and the need to wait for clear Soviet signals, but of perhaps even greater importance was the political outlook of Wladyslaw Gomulka, the Polish party leader. This erstwhile "domesticist" and "nationalist"[20] had become increasingly rigid in his conceptions of ideology and foreign policy, and by the end of the 1960s he had succeeded in reinstituting firm political control in all walks of life and strict centralization in economic matters. This dogmatic revival in Poland also ushered in greater reluctance to deal with the West.

After the demise of Gomulka, the new Polish leadership under Edward Gierek showed a much more conciliatory attitude toward the West European countries and the United States, and throughout the 1970s Warsaw has been in the forefront of East-West détente, especially in the field of economic cooperation. This break with the Gomulka tradition was partly brought about by sheer economic necessity; the Stalinist regime of the 1960s had been toppled by worker unrest, and Edward Gierek found himself forced to rely on Western credits and know-how for the needed imports of consumer goods and technology, necessary ingredients in the regime's quest to maintain a reasonable level of popular satisfaction while at the same time ensuring the modernization of the Polish economy. But despite such economic necessities, Polish-Western détente reflected general political trends as well—trends that at the same time allowed the Polish leadership to engage in foreign policymaking of an autonomist nature and also ensured Western interest in expanded relations. Thus, the 1970s have seen the development of considerable initiative in Warsaw in foreign policymaking.[21]

In Czechoslovakia, 1968 stands as the watershed of foreign affairs and relations with the West. While the pre-invasion leadership was willing to expand its ties with Western Europe and even the United States (albeit cautiously, so that the Kremlin would not be unduly worried), the Husak leadership, presiding over the "normalization" of the political system, chose to realign itself unquestioningly with the Kremlin and consequently instituted a rigid and at times rejectionist attitude toward the West. This approach continues to this day, even though commercial relations have been considerably expanded.[22]

While the Poles cautiously expanded their relations with the West throughout the decade and the Czechs severely restricted theirs, Hungary and Bulgaria followed somewhat divergent patterns, which nevertheless showed that relations with the Soviet Union continued to dominate foreign policymaking in the capitals of Eastern Europe, and that relations with the West remained a "dependent variable" whose extent and intensity would depend upon the extent of national policymaking autonomy allowed by the Kremlin. Hungary, which had gone further than any other East European state in the matter of internal economic reform, cautiously expanded its ties with Western Europe and the United States, especially in economic relations.[23] Bulgaria, which had consistently remained the closest follower of Moscow in domestic and foreign policy during the 1960s, remained the Kremlin's closest associate during the 1970s as well. No foreign policy initiative toward the West emanated from the Bulgarian capital without full clearance from Moscow, and in most cases the Zhivkov leadership merely followed the initiatives of the CPSU and the Soviet foreign ministry. In this case at least, there was no noticeable difference during the decade of the 1970s.[24]

The differing policies pursued by the various East European leaderships as East-West détente developed during the 1970s ushered in considerable variations in domestic policies. While increased East-West relations provided opportunities for expanded economic and scientific credits as well as export markets, it soon became clear that East European economic enterprises were severely hampered in their relationships with capitalist systems in terms of quality of production, marketing, and general ability to respond to fast-changing conditions of a free market. This realization hastened the trend toward economic reform that had already been underway since the early 1960s. In the field of economic reform, the policies produced were markedly different from one country to the next. In Hungary, a thoroughgoing economic reform significantly reduced the influence of the central political authorities on day-to-day planning and management, and important elements of the market economy were introduced.[25] In Romania, early attempts to decentralize (albeit in a cautious manner) were opposed by the central planning authorities and their counterparts within the party apparatus, and the decade of the 1970s experienced a slow but steady recentralization of decision making, culminating in the establishment of a set of central bodies—composed of party and government cadres and technical and academic experts—that were designed to coordinate political and economic decision making for the greater efficiency of both. In almost all these bodies, Nicolae Ceauşescu was member ex officio, and his political style soon asserted itself in matters large and small, thus producing the highest kind of centralized leadership in the form of personalized decision making, even in this sphere.[26] In Bulgaria, early efforts to decentralize were also soon superseded by a trend toward increased centralization, a process that was to be based upon an unprecedented expansion of technical and scientific inputs into political and socioeconomic decision making. The Bulgarian leaders envisioned a system of computerized forecasting and planning that would enable the central authorities to make economic decisions with unprecedented accuracy, based upon a much more thorough knowledge base than had hitherto been possible. As of this writing, this Bulgarian "initiative" has been rather unsuccessful in producing a new era of centralized economic efficiency.[27]

In the remaining East European states, economic decentralization and reform were undertaken cautiously, and the trend has been toward greater reform during the 1970s, producing somewhat altered relationships between the political decision makers and the planners and experts charged with the execution of the regimes' programs. In the GDR some decentralization and considerable autonomy for the technical and administrative experts have produced a highly efficient economic machinery by socialist standards.[28] The Polish reforms of the economic system in the 1970s have resulted in considerable improvement in the standard of living of the population, but chronic problems of low labor productivity and a wage system that stands in a tenuous relationship to the supply of goods and services continue to plague Poland. Periodic regime efforts intended to raise efficiency and reduce surplus purchasing power by means of increased political control have brought the workers out in the streets on several occasions, with subsequent partial withdrawal of the regime's goals.[29] Thus, the Polish regime has rather tenuous control over the economic system and over the primary socioeconomic class, the industrial workers. Such a relationship is conducive to considerable political instability. In Czechoslovakia, on the other hand, cautious decentralization of the economy was a conscious strategy of the postinvasion political elite and was utilized as an important element in the process of "normalization"; the reestablishment of firm political rule, replete with massive party purges, the re-introduction of full-scale censorship, and heightened emphasis on ideological orthodoxy, was perceived as more palatable in a climate of relative economic affluence. Throughout the 1970s, the Czechoslovak political elite has largely escaped the Polish dilemma, which essentially equates political stability with economic consumerism—a highly dangerous combination in Communist-dominated systems.[30]

The different approaches to the problems of economic performance and regime control of economic activity were but one of the manifestations of political variations within the East European socialist states and people's democracies. Throughout the last decade, every regime in the area was forced to face several crucial questions pertaining to political power, authority, legitimacy, and the means and methods of maintaining or enhancing these basic aspects of political rule in *any* system. Some of these problems were the fruit of circumstances and others of the regime's own making; first and foremost, however, these fundamental questions arose in new and more urgent form as a result of the dynamics of political and socioeconomic development launched under Communist auspices a generation earlier. This modernization process has succeeded in drastically transforming East European society during the thirty years of Communist rule, and it was therefore to be expected that the socioeconomic and political "feedback" of such achievements would sooner or later confront the initiators. This point of rendezvous with history and the legacy of the Communist political order occurred during the 1970s in all of the East European states.

As the East European leaders faced this legacy, they were forced to confront several vexing questions, the solutions of which were crucial to their own survival and the continuation of the regimes and the sociopolitical systems that they erected. First, a modern society, with considerable socioeconomic stratification, must presumably be ruled differently than the relatively underdeveloped rural societies that were taken over by the local Communist parties of Eastern Europe in the 1940s. How does a centralized regime maintain its close control over the increasingly diversified population that has developed in such modernizing societies? The East European regimes have responded differently to the challenge of political power emanating from the societies that they themselves fashioned.

Second, the modernization process has created a need for highly skilled technical and managerial personnel as well as experts in other fields. How does a political leadership staffed primarily by professional party apparatchiks deal with the problem of political control, based on power and supervision, in relationships with experts whose main base of strength is indispensable knowledge? This problem also poses the questions of how the political elite deals with the need for political recruitment and provides access to the decision-making structures for new, centrally located societal elites.

Third, the main thrust of Marxism-Leninism (and the local variations thereof in Eastern Europe) is toward the achievement of material affluence as a necessary prerequisite for the establishment of socialism and Communism. In the beginning stages of the modernization process it is perhaps possible to convince elements of the population that the end result of this Communist-supervised process is justified, and that material sacrifices today will redound to the advantage of the next generation. But now, after thirty years of forced socioeconomic development, in which the emphasis has always been on heavy industry and fuels, the question is posed with increasing frequency and intensity: How long must we continue to sacrifice for a distant tomorrow, the image of which seems to recede like the end of the rainbow? In short, the economic policies of the East European regimes deal not only with economics, but with the entire issue of regime authority and legitimacy, which revolves around the fundamental question of popular perceptions of regime performance.

Fourth, Marxist-Leninist doctrine is also being challenged in the modernizing systems of Eastern Europe for its effect on individual freedom and societal responsibility. Marxism as a presumed doctrine of human liberation from control and manipulation has produced a system of authoritarian and often exploitative relationships between ruler and ruled, between employer and employee. This kind of political and socioeconomic system rests upon the use or the threat of coercion as a mechanism for maintaining power and authority. Furthermore, it severely restricts the element of human freedom and choice in all areas of activity, and, in an essential sense, redefines the concept of "freedom" to mean that the individual is free to do the best he or she can *within* the parameters established by the regime. By the same token, the individual cannot choose to set himself outside of the community as defined by the political leadership; this would indeed be "parasitism" and "antisocial behavior," which is liable to be severely punished.

Fifth, increasingly, citizens of East European societies are beginning to question these fundamental premises of the regimes concerning socialist society and the relationships of human beings within it. Questions have arisen regarding human freedom, in which "Western" definitions of the concept are juxtaposed to "Eastern" practice. There are charges that the East European regimes are violating their own constitutions as well as international agreements signed by the respective leaders. There are demands for a reevaluation of the whole question of political and societal authority and power in the context of human, i.e., individual, freedom. All of these questions go to the very heart of politics everywhere. When the East European regimes attempt to face these questions, they are in a very real sense confronting the problem of the nature of politics in this decade and in the foreseeable future. No wonder that responses to these essential questions vary from country to country.

This development of greater citizen concern about the nature of East European politics was predictable. As a society modernizes, it educates its citizenry, and with education comes the ability to question and to wonder about alternatives. Since the Eastern European regimes have been concerned with the rapid diffusion of knowledge, political and otherwise, it may be said that they in fact invited this kind of problem. Throughout the last generation of societal development in Eastern Europe, the political regimes relied on the twin mechanisms of control and political indoctrination to forestall just this kind of fundamental reassessment of the entire political system and the processes within it. It is a monument to the failure of these two mechanisms that increasing numbers of citizens now raise their voices with important questions. Of greatest concern (and the sixth major problem confronting the East European political elites in the 1970s) is the attitude of youth in the area.

The generation under thirty has lived its entire life under Communist political and socioeconomic domination, and it was always assumed in leadership circles that such individuals, properly socialized and educated, would be fervent supporters of the regimes and the systems, since they did not carry the heavy burden of "bourgeois-landowner mentality" and "retrograde views" so prevalent among the older generation. Yet in the 1970s it is precisely this generation of socialist youth that is confronting the respective regimes with fundamental questions about the nature of the political and social order. In this field, too, regime responses vary considerably from one system to the next.

Finally, each political elite in Eastern Europe is increasingly faced with the need to define its own system in relation to the other East European regimes, to the international Communist movement, and thus ultimately to the Soviet Union. There is considerable pride concerning socioeconomic achievements in the East European populations, and this pride often manifests itself as nationalism, occasionally chauvinism. Furthermore, the political "decompression" that has taken place since the death of Stalin has made it possible for older forms of nationalism (and also the resurrection of old animosities) to be resurrected. While it is a commonplace that political nationalism has been in drastic upswing in Eastern Europe during the 1960s and 1970s, it should be noted that the forms and intensity vary considerably from country to country.

Nationalism is not only of great importance as a response to altered socioeconomic and political conditions; it is also an important source of popular legitimacy for the regimes of the area. Regimes that have fundamentally altered the societal conditions of life for every citizen and have instituted political structures and processes that are repressive and often economically exploitative cannot expect massive public support on instrumental grounds, and alternate sources of legitimacy and authority must be found. The historical tradition of nationalism (and on occasion, chauvinism) in Eastern Europe has proved to be of considerable value in this respect, even to political elites who are officially dedicated to the making of a new society and new relations between nations and states.

The regimes of Eastern Europe have responded to the multifaceted social, economic, and political challenges discussed above in a variety of ways. The problem of political power is everywhere answered by a firm reiteration of the principle that the Communist party is the leading, indeed dominant, force in society and must so remain, even after the establishment of socialism and Communism. This firm programmatic response, seemingly imposing uniform policies throughout the area, in fact masks a great deal of difference in practical political response to the challenges of the 1970s.

Essentially, the regimes of Eastern Europe can be classified in three major categories in terms of their approach to the maintenance of political power under rapidly changing societal conditions. First of all there are the "orthodox" regimes, which have answered the challenge to the party's monopoly by expansion of organizational and administrative control and an intensified use of political propaganda and indoctrination, coupled with renewed emphasis on ideological orthodoxy in all areas of human endeavor. Both Romania and Czechoslovakia, and, to some extent, Bulgaria, fall in this category. In Romania, social stratification and pluralization have been met by expanded party authority in all areas and an unprecedented tendency toward personalized leadership under General Secretary Nicolae Ceauşescu. Furthermore, since the summer of 1971, the Romanian party leadership has been carrying out a massive ideological campaign designed to enhance the political commitment of the rank and file and the apparatchiki, while at the same time expanding the PCR's control over other apparats in society. The ideological campaign has been coupled with a constant process of organizational change that has been designed to reduce the size of the centralized bureaucracy by removing personnel to the provinces and into actual "productive" (rather than administrative) work. Such rapid administrative change has further reduced the possibility that alternative centers of power can develop and has considerably enhanced the power of the party and of Nicolae Ceauşescu personally. All of these ideological and organizational programs have been undertaken at considerable expense in terms of ordered processes of policy execution, and disruption of the economic functions of planning and management has been considerable. Despite such economic and social considerations, the PCR under Ceauşescu has persisted in these policies. It is clear that in Romania, the regime, and in particular its leader, is unwilling to compromise in the question of maintaining centralized and absolute power in both the polity and the economy, regardless of cost.[31]

The process of postinvasion "normalization" in Czechoslovakia was a development that gradually but inexorably reestablished political and societal hegemony for the party after a period of relative pluralism in all areas of life, including the political realm. This process has not led to personalized political rule, as in Romania, nor has the mobilization program of the elite been carried out in such a thoroughgoing fashion as in Romania. Nevertheless, normalization meant the reestablishment of the party as the leading force in society, through the re-imposition of ideological orthodoxy and political purges of those who fell outside the category of orthodoxy; furthermore, the position of the political authorities in fields such as education, the arts, and literature was considerably strengthened. The "profile" of the party in Czechoslovak society was thus considerably enhanced during the decade, and, in a fashion similar to that of Nicolae Ceauşescu, the Husak leadership firmly emphasized the principle that societal change will not reduce political control from the center, but may in actuality demand increases in political control and expansion of the party's political power.[32]

The relationship between the individual and political authority has always been a very restrictive one in Bulgaria, and no essential changes emerged during the 1970s. The Zhivkov regime, like its counterparts in Romania and Czechoslovakia, emphasized ideological orthodoxy, strict centralization of political power, and a correspondingly authoritarian relationship between the political and the technical-managerial elites of the country. Censorship remained tight in the arts, literature, and education, and the Bulgarian leadership closely followed the Soviet line in any question dealing with political authority and the application of Marxism-Leninism. General Secretary Zhivkov did not acquire the personalized power of Ceauşescu, but, by the same token, the bureaucratized leadership of the Bulgarian Communist party (BKP) was firmly maintained in a fashion that left little doubt as to the location of political power. Bulgaria therefore remained firmly in the category of political orthodoxy.[33]

In considerable contrast to the centralized political power exercised by the "orthodox" regimes in Romania, Czechoslovakia, and Bulgaria, the leaders of Hungary and Poland have shown willingness to accept some decentralization of power and authority in their societies. It should be emphasized that neither Janos Kadar nor Edward Gierek have abandoned the concept of party supremacy in their respective societies, but it is also a fact that both of these men have supervised the output of practical policies that represent a good deal of innovation in the East European context. Kadar's famous slogan that "those who are not against us are for us" neatly summarizes this approach. The regime is not primarily concerned with the need for making "new socialist men and women," but would rather concentrate on power maintenance and the monopoly of formal decision making. In such a system, regime "profile" is relatively low, there is a considerable amount of autonomy for the individual citizen in socioeconomic terms, and in the political realm, the regime will allow measured autonomy as long as individuals or groups do not engage in activities designed to weaken or replace the political system or the socioeconomic development program devised and executed by the political elite. Such a system may perhaps be characterized as a modernizing authoritarian system, in which considerable social pluralism exists along with political monopoly as exercised by the dominant party.[34]

The post-Gomulka leadership in Poland has not officially accepted the "low profile" concept espoused by Kadar, yet many of the policies produced by Edward Gierek's regime in fact bear close resemblance to the Kadar principle. The very ascension to power of Gierek bore the marks of some political pluralism; Gomulka was toppled by worker unrest, and Gierek's first act as head of the Polish Workers' party (PZPR) was to make significant concessions to the demands voiced by the organized working class in the Baltic Sea ports.[35] Since the events of early 1971, the Gierek leadership has significantly strengthened its position, first by considerable personnel change in the party leadership and in the governmental apparatus, and also by means of some expansion of political controls in working-class organizations and in many other fields of socioeconomic activity; but it is clear that the party's control still rests on an uneasy coalition between Gierek and the organized working class, a coalition based on the regime's ability to provide consumer goods and a steadily rising standard of living. Under such circumstances, the party leadership has been forced to grant some autonomy to other elements of society, notably the technical intelligentsia and the academic elite of the country. The need for increased (and more economical and efficient) production has produced a situation in which the traditional relationships between political power and technical expertise no longer hold in the same measure as before. By the same token, the increasing complexity of Polish society demands greater expertise in many other fields, especially in the social sciences, and the party must reckon with this in its relationship with these groups. Thus, the Polish political elite finds itself in a situation of increased social pluralism and decreased overt political power as exercised by the PZPR, whether such was its intention or not.[36]

The GDR represents an interim category between the "orthodox," represented by Romania, Czechoslovakia, and Bulgaria, and the "liberal," represented by Hungary and Poland. The East German regime has met the problems of the 1970s by means of increased control by the Socialist Unity party (SED) over the cultural and artistic elite and the general population. The Honecker leadership is certainly as centralist in these matters as was its predecessor. At the same time, the SED has been willing to accord considerable autonomy to the country's economic planners and managers (while retaining essential control over "the commanding elites" of the economic mechanism) in return for the highest per capita production figures and the greatest efficiency of any East European economy. This interplay between political centralization and relative economic decentralization is designed to ensure unquestioned party control over the nation-building process, while the relatively high level of economic performance is considered an important source of legitimacy and popular support for the regime.[37] Popular response, however, has not been as favorable as might be expected; the numerous requests for exit visas to the Federal Republic, initiated under the auspices of the Helsinki Agreement's "Basket Three," eloquently testify to this.

As discussed above, the East European regimes have had to face the problem of maintaining political monopoly in a societal context of rapid change. One of the most important aspects of this relationship is the extent to which the political elites can meaningfully relate to the new societal elites that have arisen, especially the technical and managerial elite, whose services are indispensable for the continued economic performance of the systems. In all of Eastern Europe, there has been a concerted attempt by the political elite to maintain this indispensable control by means of a mixture of co-optation, overlapping memberships and "interlocking directorates," and outright coercion. The process of co-optation, whereby the party attempts to recruit individuals with valuable skills of a technical or managerial nature into important positions in the party apparat, has been extensively used in all of the East European countries during the 1970s, particularly in the GDR, Poland, and to some extent Hungary; in Czechoslovakia and Romania, the importance of the professional party apparatchiki has been enhanced at the expense of all other categories, due to the processes of normalization in Czechoslovakia and the trend toward personalized political leadership under the auspices of Ceaușescu in Romania.[38] In Bulgaria the significant increase in the representation of technical experts in political leadership positions, ushered in by the trend toward "scientific management" of the economy, has slackened off considerably, and the hegemony of the party apparat is once again unquestioned.[39]

Despite the success of the East European political elites in maintaining control over the emerging and expanding societal elites of the 1970s, the trend toward increasing interdependence of the political and expert elites is likely to produce problems of control in the future. As the societies move toward higher levels of educational and scientific sophistication, the party leaders have attempted to absorb the new elites by means of recruitment into the party structure. Table 4 illustrates this development.

As shown by Table 4, no ruling party in Eastern Europe can classify itself as a workers' party in the 1970s; in these party structures, significant numbers of individuals can be found whose educational level and occupational skills are considerably above the average. Furthermore, the discrepancy between party members and the rest of the population in terms of socioeconomic status and educational achievement widens even further as one moves up the ladder of the political hierarchy.[40] This

TABLE 4

Social Categories in East European Party Memberships, 1960's and 1970's

Country	Year	Percent of Total Membership			
		Workers	Peasants	White Collar Intellectuals, Functionaries	Women
Albania	1970	35.2	29.0	35.8	
	1971	36.4	29.7	33.9	22.05
	1972				24.0
	1974	37.9			
	1975	37.7	29.2	33.9	26.0
	1976	37.5	29.0	33.5	27
	1979				27
Bulgaria	1969	39.0	27.0	27.0	
	1971	40.1	26.1	28.1	
	1976	41.4	23.1	35.6	27.5
Czechoslovakia	1971	26.1			
	1976	62 ("of working class origin")			
	1978	62 ("of working class origin")			
GDR	1968				25.0
	1969				25.0
	1971 (candidates to 8th SED Congress)	60.0	10.5	26.6	
	1973	56.6			
	1974	58.0			29.4
	1976	56.1	5.2 (coop. farmers)	31.5	31.3
	(1976: university and higher school graduates. - 27.4%)				
	1979/80	56.7	4.8	33.0	32.5
Hungary	1966	42.4	6.0 (collective farms)		22.9
	(1966: university degree holders - 34.7%)				
	1968	42.7		38.1	
	1969			41.2	
	1970	41.7	18.9		
	1973	58.3	14.2		
	1975 "original occupation"	59.2	13.0	25.2	
	1975 "current occupation"	45.5		40.0	
	(1975: 6.1% "immediate supervisors of production")				
Poland	1970	40.2	11.6	42.5	
	1971	40.1	11.0	43.2	
	1979/80	45.6	10.0	33.5	26.0
Romania	1967	42.0	30.0		
	1968	70		17	
	1969	43.0	28.0	23.0	
	1970	43.4	26.6	24.0	
	1971	44.3	25.5	23.0	
	1973				30.0
	1974	50.0	20.0	22.0	25.0
	1975	50.0	20.0	22.0	
	1979/80	54.0	18.0	29.0	28.0
Yugolsavia	1969	30.0			
	1973	28.0			
	1975	31.3	6.0	33.6	
	1976	28.1	5.1 ("private peasants")	41.8	
	(1976: students and pupils - 7.5%, "others" - 17.5%)				
	1977	29.0	5.0	40.0	

Source: *Yearbook on International Communist Affairs, 1968-1980*

trend, which is well known both in Communist and in non-Communist systems,[41] has established the ruling parties of Eastern Europe as significant elites in their own right. Increasingly, therefore, the parties have responded to the question of control over societal elites by means of co-optation at higher levels *and* direct recruitment of skilled personnel at the grass-roots level of the apparat. As the decade of the 1980s begins, this steady influx of "special category" individuals threatens to fundamentally change the nature of the ruling parties of the area, with broad policy ramifications.

One of the most significant ramifications has already manifested itself, i.e., the widespread perception among the East European populations that the ruling elites represent a new caste of chieftains, a set of "bosses" as far removed from the general population as the boyars and absentee landlords of the past.[42] As this perception takes hold, the entire question of regime-citizen relations moves to center stage of the political scene in Eastern Europe. During the 1970s, significant mass dissent as well as considerable discussion of the nature of the political system developed. This reassessment of political reality, discussed above, has manifested itself differently in the states under examination, and, once again, regime response has varied. In the GDR, thousands of people (one source estimated up to two hundred thousand) responded to the Honecker signature of the Helsinki Agreement by demanding exit visas for resettlement in the Federal Republic. There was a significant level of political dissent among the writers, artists, and other elements in East German cultural life, and several of the most important of these individuals found themselves barred from re-entry after visits to the West, or, in some cases, behind bars. The Honecker leadership reacted strongly to the dissent and firmly resisted any attempts at reassessment of the relationship between the individual and the regime. The principles of party supremacy, democratic centralism, and personal freedom within the narrow confines of societal needs (as defined by the political leadership) were reconfirmed, defended, and even expanded.[43] The East German press and the SED theoretical journal *Einheit* carried out several campaigns designed to defuse popular resentment and bolster party authority. As of this writing, there is no sign that the regime intends to yield any of its control over defining the nature of the political system and the relationship between the elite and the individual.

Czechoslovak dissent had even greater effects, both on the domestic political scene and in terms of ramifications abroad. Dissent was important during the early years of normalization when the residual effects of the Prague Spring were felt in a major way, both in the party and elsewhere in society. As the Husak regime consolidated its position in the political system, severe purges spread throughout the party apparat and spilled over into the governmental and administrative structures, the mass organizations, and organizations of the artistic and cultural elite.[44] Such developments dampened the voices of dissent during the mid-1970s, but after the Helsinki Agreement, the question of the nature of Czechoslovak society and its political system reappeared in various forms. During 1977, a movement called Charter '77 became a rallying point for this dissent, which reached a high point in March 1977 when eleven former members of the Central Committee of the Czechoslovak Communist party (KSC) openly appealed to other European Communist parties for help in ensuring that the Czech and Slovak authorities would act in accordance with the Helsinki Agreement on matters pertaining to human rights under socialism.[45]

Once again, the regime's response was swift and harsh. Many of the leading members of this and other movements were jailed or exiled, pamphlets were confiscated, and many lost their positions. The purges continue at this time, and there is little likelihood that any reconciliation with the dissenters is possible. But it is also unlikely that the other side will be bludgeoned into silence. The battle has been joined, and it will produce considerable political controversy and societal instability in the years to come.

In Poland, too, significant challenges were launched against the entire concept of directed society under Communist auspices. During the 1970s, challenges to the party's hegemonistic rule were launched from elements within the Roman Catholic church, part of the student body at some universities, important groups and individuals within the artistic and literary intelligentsia, and even parts of the general population, especially the industrial working class. These multifaceted voices of criticism and even outright dissent were raised at a time when the Gierek regime struggled with problems of political consolidation after the traumatic experience of the forced resignation of Wladyslaw Gomulka. Due partly to the relative weakness of the new regime, and partly to an increased willingness on the part of Gierek the pragmatist to consider some of the problems raised by the critics rather than dismissing them outright, regime response to the challenge in Poland was considerably more moderate than had been the case in the GDR and Czechoslovakia. Some of the most stridently aggressive dissidents, who questioned the very nature of Polish society under socialism, were brought to trial, but the punishment meted out was rather moderate;[46] many others were ignored. Since 1978 the Polish government has sought further reconciliation with the Catholic Church, and this has produced a more moderate political climate as well. Literary and artistic "freedom," although still curtailed in contemporary Poland, has been considerably expanded during the last few years, and Polish literature and theater now openly discuss some of the most fundamental problems of human existence in a socialist system.[47] The overall result of these trends and the regime's response to them is a Polish system in which the political elite has deliberately chosen a relatively "low profile" in society, and where a certain amount of dissent is tolerated.

Dissent developed in other East European countries as well during the 1970s, although the extent and intensity were not as significant as in the GDR, Poland, and Czechoslovakia. Both the number of incidents and the intensity of protest were significantly less in Bulgaria and Hungary. In Romania, on the other hand, a small but vocal group of dissidents, centered around Paul Goma, one of the most controversial novelists in the country, succeeded in launching their complaints in such a context that they received a great deal of attention, both at home and abroad.

The arguments of the Romanian dissidents emphasized familiar themes. Firstly, there were complaints about regime violations of basic civil rights as guaranteed in the Romanian constitution and the existing code of law. Secondly, it was maintained that the Helsinki Agreement was systematically violated by Romanian authorities. Thirdly, elements of the German and Hungarian minorities charged the Ceauşescu leadership with blatant and substantial discrimination against ethnic minorities.[48] All of these arguments gathered momentum in the aftermath of widespread destruction caused by the earthquake of March 1977; this crisis situation tapped already widespread dissatisfaction over the economic conditions in the country. Since the volatile issue of minority rights and the regime's nationality policies had entered the discussion, the dissidents in Romania were ensured of a major audience, especially in the West, where President Carter's stand on human rights had become a major focal point.

The Romanian regime at first approached this problem with considerable flexibility. Goma was invited to discuss the problems that most concerned the dissidents, and no immediate repressive action was undertaken against those who had signed the manifestos of the group. Subsequently, several of the most prominent spokesmen for the dissidents were encouraged to leave Romania, and quite a few did so. Later on in the year, however, the regime chose to engage in considerable harrassment of the dissenters, and spokesmen of the PCR began to issue threatening statements about "anti-state activity" among the protesters. One of the most active participants in this campaign was Ceauşescu himself, who repeatedly castigated the behavior of the dissenters and at

times came close to equating their actions with treason.[49] Of particular
concern to Ceaușescu was the issue of emigration of ethnic minorities,
especially Germans; the general secretary made plain his view that the
individual citizen does not have the right to set himself or herself outside
of society or the political and socioeconomic programs launched and
supervised by the party, and he especially attacked the idea of severing
ties with the "socialist fatherland" through emigration. The PCR leader
also emphasized his determination to ensure compliance with the party's
directives by whatever means necessary, and he vowed to continue the
ideological-educational campaign to eliminate "retrograde views" and
the "bourgeois-landowner mentality" from the minds of citizens, thereby
removing also the quest for permission to leave the country.[50] This de-
fiant stand on political socialization and indoctrination as well as the
question of emigration once again served to illustrate the orthodox and
centralist nature of the contemporary Romanian regime. This attitude
was further underscored by the continuing ideological campaign, designed to raise the level of political consciousness in party members and
general citizens alike. Frequent governmental and administrative reor-
ganizations put teeth into the PCR's claim of supreme authority in Romanian society.[51] There is little prospect for a reduced regime "profile" in
the treatment of political and social dissent as long as Nicolae Ceaușescu
remains the supreme party leader.

The rising concern in Eastern Europe with human rights, "socialist
legality," and the nature of the citizen-regime relationship has called into
question the very legitimacy of Communist rule. To meet this challenge,
the East European regimes have produced policies that emphasize instrumental, ideological, and other symbolic forms of legitimacy, in an
attempt to offset the manifest problems of dissent, now apparent in virtually every socialist system.

The instrumental approach to political legitimacy emphasizes economic performance as measured in the increased provision of goods and
services (as well as the continued development of heavy and extractive
industry, transportation, and fuels). For some time, the political leaders
of most of the East European states have operated on the assumption that
"a fat citizen is a happy citizen," and thus, a continued increase in the
standard of living has become a mainstay of economic policy and an important element in the regimes' overall policy output.

The results of this policy have been mixed. As discussed in some detail
in Chapters 3 and 4 of this volume, there has been a steady increase in the
standard of living of all the East European countries. There is more
food than previously; the production of consumer goods (and increasingly also of consumer durables) has been considerably expanded, and

social and health services, pensions, and free education have become standard features of the East European systems. Despite such advances, the states of Eastern Europe lag far behind Western Europe (not to mention the United States) in all measures of the standard of living. There are frequent bottlenecks in the supply of goods and services, and the quality of consumer goods leaves much to be desired—so much so, in fact, that East European finished goods are by and large noncompetitive on the world market. With increased interaction between East and West in an era of détente, these differences between "capitalism" and "socialism" are readily apparent to many citizens of the socialist states and people's democracies, and there is some evidence that such perceptions have given rise to dissatisfaction and certainly to the adoption of Western life-styles by many (insofar as this is materially possible), especially the younger generation.[52] Instrumental legitimacy in the form of good economic performance, therefore, seems to be eluding the regimes of Eastern Europe in the 1970s. To be sure, there are significant differences among the Eastern European countries in terms of economic performance; the GDR is ahead of all of the others, with Czechoslovakia a close second, and Hungary and Poland following at some distance. Bulgaria and Romania remain at the bottom of the scale as measured by the standard of living. But even those systems with relatively high performance records in the standard of living do not compare favorably with the West, and it appears that it is the *comparative* perspective (rather than the year-to-year improvements internally) that reduces or eliminates the regimes' quest for instrumental legitimacy.

Ideological legitimacy, as discussed above, has also proved an elusive goal, and in many cases, the continued emphasis on this aspect of political life has contributed to the deterioration of public support. In a similar vein, it can be said that the attempts to produce acceptance by means of medals, honorary titles, or other awards conferred upon meritorious citizens have yielded minimal results.[53] Clearly, such standard methods of attaining legitimacy—Communist style—have been of little benefit to the East European regimes in the 1970s, and it was therefore clear that other elements must be employed in order to ensure the kind of popular support necessary for the fulfillment of the regimes' political and socioeconomic programs. One of the most important of these methods in the 1970s was the expansion of political and cultural nationalism after its initial resurgence in the late 1950s and early 1960s.

Political nationalism may be defined as a state of mind (coupled with actual policies) that emphasizes the importance of national sovereignty over any form of internationalism and, furthermore, often expresses reservations about the political and socioeconomic systems of others; in addition, political nationalism tends to take a longitudinal view of historical development and attempts to find continuities between the present system and the heritage of the past. In multiethnic societies, the emphasis on the national past and heritage may produce significant stress and strain in relations among ethnic groups, insofar as the historical legacy and the "collective past" will vary from group to group. Thus, political nationalism may be a major source of integration for those who belong to the same ethnic group as that of the nationalistic political and socioeconomic elites; by the same token, this element may be a considerable destabilizing force, insofar as it may produce overt ethnic conflict or at least some covert hostility.[54]

Political nationalism is often based upon (and in turn helps strengthen) cultural nationalism and even chauvinism. The symbols of the historical past, as expressed in the language, arts, literature, and general social and behavioral mores constitute a massive integrative force for those who are "in," partly because they help keep others "out." Each nation (and its leaders) develops a cultural "hierarchy," in which it takes pride of place as a matter of course, while other nations and cultures are ranked in terms of compatibility and perceived quality.[55] Such perceptions, while conducive to internal integration, are likely to produce friction in relations among nations and their political machinery, the states.

Eastern Europe has had a tradition of considerable political instability resulting from political and cultural nationalism and chauvinism.[56] During the Stalin era, however, the overwhelming influence of the Soviet Union and of Stalin personally prevented the continuation of the traditional national struggles of the area and instead instigated full-scale "synchronization" of foreign policy behavior, presumably based on the principles of "socialist" and "proletarian" internationalism. Nationalism as a force for increased regime legitimacy internally in each of the East European Communist systems was considered unnecessary by the USSR because the local regimes maintained themselves in power by means of coercion, terror, and the presence of the Red Army; indeed, nationalism was seen as highly detrimental to the development of internationalism, which in practical terms meant the complete hegemony of Moscow in all of the East European countries.

As discussed above, one of the most important developments in Eastern Europe in the post-Stalin era has been the relative decline of firm Soviet control over the detailed policies of the local regimes. As this "decompression" developed, political and sociocultural nationalism once again became a major factor of political life in Eastern Europe. As the societies of the area modernized, with resulting social stratification and the corresponding problems of maintaining political control, the

emergence of dissent was a natural development. Under these circumstances, the East European regimes resorted to political, and in some
cases, cultural nationalism as a vehicle for their legitimatization. Since
nationalism as a doctrine is inclusive ("our nation") and also exclusive
("all the others"), the East European regimes who want to rely on nationalism in its various forms as a source of legitimacy must also perforce
accept an increased level of interstate and interparty controversy. Thus,
Eastern Europe has experienced a marked upswing in nationalism (as
defined above) and, consequently, a more critical and at times hostile
atmosphere in the foreign and cultural sphere.

The regimes of Eastern Europe have varied greatly in their use of political and cultural nationalism as a source of legitimacy, although all of
them have utilized this element to some extent. In the GDR, nationalism
has long been a dangerous subject, since the East Germans are members
of a much larger cultural tradition that includes the chief political rival of
Pankow on the other side of the Iron Curtain. Furthermore, the Soviet
experience with the German nationalism of the past contributed greatly
to the SED's determination to hew close to the CPSU and to make few
nationalistic moves.[57]

All of this changed with the erection of the Berlin Wall. For the first
time in GDR history, the state borders were "secure," and the Ulbricht
regime could proceed with the process of internal political and socioeconomic consolidation. The principle of *Abgrenzung* became the primary
guiding light for Ulbricht and his successor Erich Honecker; *Abgrenzung*
connotes division from something else, in this case the Federal Republic
and its polity and culture, but it also indicates the existence of internal
forces for cohesion, so that one knows what it is that the regime wants to
protect *against*, as well as what must be preserved internally. For the East
Germans, then, *Abgrenzung* also connoted the development of a
separate nationality in the GDR. Such a nationality, however, must have
a history and a heritage, and the regime's realization of this need had a
great deal of impact upon the SED's treatment of German history and national traditions. From the early 1960s, then, nationalism became an important part of the regime's quest for domestic legitimacy and also
diplomatic recognition as a separate entity in the concert of nations.[58]

The use of political and cultural nationalism as a vehicle for increased
regime legitimacy has taken on quite diversified forms in the GDR.
Among the most important of these forms are the following assertions
and policies:

1. The GDR and the SED *alone* represent the German leftist tradition. During the 1970s, the Honecker regime increasingly laid claim to Karl Marx,
Friedrich Engels, Karl Liebknecht, and Rosa Luxemburg as the precur-

sors of the present-day regime, and, therefore, "the first workers' and peasant state on German soil" is billed as a natural, indeed inevitable, outgrowth of German national traditions. In the spirit of *Abgrenzung* the Federal Republic is also considered part of the German tradition, but in this case the present regime in Bonn is seen as the personification of the dangerous and reactionary elements of German history, while the GDR represents the "progressive" forces in German history.[59]

2. In a similar vein, East German culture traces its roots in the "progressive" cultural traditions of German history. Hence, Pankow has laid claim to Beethoven and other cultural giants of the German past, while Bonn is once again consigned to the scrap heap of history, the depository of traditional reactionism and militarism.[60]

3. The achievements of the GDR in political and especially socioeconomic matters have been increasingly considered with pride, and during the 1970s, the East Germans frequently discussed the economic performance of their COMECON partners in a somewhat overbearing way, emphasizing the "traditionally strong" economic performance in German history. There is certainly a great deal of nationalism, perhaps even chauvinism, in this kind of discourse, and it is so perceived by the GDR's partners in Eastern Europe.[61]

Thus, nationalism has become an important legitimizing agent in the GDR. It should be emphasized, however, that Honecker and his colleagues are anxious to avoid any implication of anti-Sovietism (although such feelings appear to be widespread in the general population). In fact, Pankow goes out of its way to emphasize the "organic unity" of the progressive traditions of German nationalism with Communist internationalism under unquestioned Soviet leadership. In this manner, contemporary East German nationalism represents no threat to the Kremlin and its position in Eastern Europe.

Political and cultural nationalism have always been major factors in Poland as well. It was the popular (and elite) perception of Wladyslaw Gomulka as an ardent nationalist that helped to propel him to power in 1956, and the subsequent disillusionment with his seeming departure from this principle, indeed his full return to orthodox Marxism, had a great deal to do with his demise fourteen years later. Since then, the Gierek regime has maintained an uneasy coexistence with traditional Polish nationalism. On the one hand, the regime has frequently referred to the glorious past of the Polish nation, and national symbols abound; on the other hand, the general secretary is always quick to emphasize that the expansionist and anti-Russian elements of Polish nationalism have been buried forever. In a manner similar to the East German example, Gierek seeks to identify himself with the selected elements of the national tradition that are classified as progressive. But in contradistinction to the situation in the GDR, the Polish regime must contend with a formidable competitor, which represents the *real* tradition in the eyes of most Poles. This competitor is the Roman Catholic church, which has retained the devotion of the overwhelming majority of the Poles even in the 1970s. The church hierarchy, under the leadership of aggressive and principled men, has actively competed with the party for the historical legacy, and the result has been an uneasy relationship between the two structures—a situation that prevailed during the 1970s.[62]

In Czechoslovakia, on the other hand, nationalism is a distinctly two-edged sword. Throughout the existence of Czechoslovakia as a separate political entity in the twentieth century, nationalism has been traditionally associated with Czech nationalism, whereas Slovak nationalism, which developed in a major way in the 1920s and 1930s, always took a back seat to its Czech neighbor. During the first twenty years of the existence of the Communist regime in Czechoslovakia, this traditional dominance of the Czechs continued under the auspices of Gottwald, Zapotocky, and Novotny. After the invasion of 1968, this situation was partially reversed, and several prominent leaders of the Slovak national tradition came to the very top of the political pyramid of the federal power structure. Under these circumstances, Gustav Husak has been careful in his utilization of nationalism as a legitimizing force, even though he stands as one of the staunchest spokesmen for the Slovak tradition. Instead, the present Czechoslovak leadership has emphasized the achievements of the Communist regime, and since 1968 there has been considerable stress on the full agreement between Prague and Moscow on all questions pertaining to nationalism and socialist and proletarian internationalism. In fact, reference to the past in the Czechoslovak context is likely to conjure up images of the interwar republic or the Prague Spring, both of which are very bothersome for the present regime. Thus, nationalism seems to play less of a role in the regime's quest for legitimacy in Czechoslovakia than is the case in the GDR and Poland.[63]

Among the remaining states of Eastern Europe, the resurgence of political and cultural nationalism in the 1960s has been followed by the incorporation of these elements into the daily political decision-making processes of each system. Nationalism is clearly of the greatest importance in Romania, but plays a considerable role in Hungary as well. In Bulgaria, nationalism is primarily utilized in the ongoing conflict with Yugoslavia over Macedonia, while in other fields, the Zhivkov regime has been careful not to alienate Moscow and its quest for hegemony in international Communism.

The development of political and cultural nationalism in Romania has been one of the most remarkable events in Eastern Europe in the 1960s and 1970s. A political regime that had been imposed upon a reluctant, even hostile, population with a minimal amount of support in 1944 emerged as the self-styled protector of the national heritage twenty years later, with the famous "declaration of independence" of early 1964.[64] During the 1970s, nationalism became even more of a factor in Romanian politics. Nicolae Ceauşescu, who ascended to the position of first secretary of the PCR in 1965, soon began to expand the nationalistic elements of both foreign and domestic policy that had been introduced by Ghorghe Gheorghiu-Dej in the 1950s. Ceauşescu increasingly associated the Communist regime with the era of Romanian greatness in the Middle Ages, and his speeches were filled with references to Stephen the Great, Michael the Brave, and the "organic ties" between the present regime and those famous leaders of the Romanian nation. In foreign policy, the quest for Romanian autonomy within the bloc was advocated as a measure of national sovereignty, and Ceauşescu repeatedly emphasized the supremacy of national Communism over "proletarian" and "socialist" internationalism. In the arts, literature, and education, the themes of Romanian greatness and the links between the past and the present were forcefully emphasized, and the Ceauşescu era has witnessed a remarkable renaissance of Romanian historical research, especially on the establishment of national independence in the nineteenth century, but also on the Latin and Roman heritage of the Romanian people. Archaeology has delved into the cultural past with a vengeance, and anthropological research has been expanded to help support the present argument that the Geto-Dacians preceded all others in the Danubian basin in terms of settlement and cultural development. In education, the traditional Communist emphasis on Marxism-Leninism has been coupled with "Ceauşescuism," which includes a very generous dose of old-fashioned nationalism. The PCR cadre organizations are enjoined to help, indeed to supervise, the national revival, and thus the apparatchiki must be good nationalists as well as good Marxists, Romanian style.[65]

This emphasis on political and cultural nationalism culminated in the celebration of the centennial of Romanian independence in 1976, with the ideological conference of the PCR that summer and the festival "Hymn to Romania," which continued throughout the entire year. The festival was a vehicle for mass mobilization around the ideals of Romanian nationalism and a major part of the campaign to increase the legitimacy of the Ceauşescu regime. Although the results in this respect seem to have been mixed, there is little doubt that the festival succeeded in bringing the nationalist message to even larger segments of the population.[66]

It is a commonplace that systematic measure of popular attitudes is impossible in Communist systems, due to the restrictions placed on surveys and interviews. This handicap is perhaps more severe in Romania than elsewhere in Eastern Europe, but it is still possible to draw general conclusions about the effects of the nationalistic policy of Ceauşescu and the PCR. Many observers have agreed[67] that the emphasis on traditional nationalism and the association of the present regime with the Romanian past have been the major sources of political legitimacy for the PCR in Romania during the 1970s. Since Romanian nationalism emphasizes a tradition and a collective memory that are different from the legacy of the ethnic minorities of Romania, the effects among the latter groups have been largely negative, insofar as it is possible to judge from the unsystematic evidence available. Popular support for the contemporary nationalists in Romania therefore comes primarily from the ethnic Romanian population. Since the Romanians constitute the overwhelming majority of the total population, nationalism has contributed significantly to the strengthening of the regime. By the same token, the minorities do constitute an important segment of the population, and the plight of the Hungarians and the Germans has received a great deal of attention abroad. Thus the disaffection of many in these groups is an important element in the contemporary political scene. Nationalism in Romania therefore acted as both a stabilizing and a destabilizing factor in the 1970s.[68]

The unprecedented emphasis on national traditions in Romania has helped the renaissance of Hungarian nationalism as well. It is clear that Budapest was determined to expand *its* legitimacy in the general population by emphasizing the "Hungarian road" to socialism as soon as it was clear that this path could be undertaken without severe reprisals from Moscow. During the 1960s, the New Economic Mechanism (NEM) in Hungary set the country apart from most of the others in Eastern Europe because of its emphasis on decentralization and, to some extent, on market forces. A cautious revival of political nationalism was also evident in referrals to the "Hungarian road," and, in practical policies, the Kadar regime's liberalization policy in fact did set Hungary apart from the other states, even though Budapest continued to emphasize the similarities of the Hungarian experience to those of the other fraternal states, especially the Soviet Union.[69]

All of these developments in Hungary in the direction of a cautious expansion of political and cultural nationalism were spurred by the widespread perception of Romanian discrimination against its Hungarian minority. During the 1970s, there were several clashes between Hungarian party officials and their Romanian counterparts over this question. The most serious clash erupted in the summer of 1971, when Zoltan Komocsin, a member of the Hungarian Politburo, castigated Romanian policy toward the Hungarians of Romanian Transylvania, and Paul Niculescu-Mizil, a member of the PCR Politburo, responded with a major statement on national sovereignty and noninterference in internal affairs.[70] Since that time, the debate has continued in academic circles with research designed to "prove" that the Hungarians were the first organized settlers in the disputed Transylvanian area, or that the Romanians there were incapable of national consciousness and political organization at an earlier stage (the Hungarian position), or, conversely, that the Geto-Dacians, forefathers to the Romanians, preceded the other ethnic groups in the area, both in settlement and in culture (the Romanian position).[71]

There is little doubt, then, that nationalism has been an important element in the legitimacy of the Hungarian regime in the 1970s, primarily because of Kadar's determination to protect Hungarian rights and traditions even when they are being violated (or perceived as being violated) in a neighboring socialist state. The dispute between the two parties and governments has tapered off somewhat since the middle of the 1970s, but it is still simmering, and it serves as a source of internal legitimacy, both in Budapest and in Bucharest.

In a fashion similar to that of the Kadar regime, the Bulgarian party leadership has utilized the existence of traditional nationalistic controversies among Balkan states as a vehicle for internal legitimization. Unlike the Hungarians, however, whose tradition is distinctly anti-Russian and has been for centuries, the Bulgarians can point to the existence of a strong pro-Russian element in Bulgarian history and in the population in general. Bulgarian historians are therefore much more active than their Hungarian counterparts in tying the present system to the policies of Bulgarian "progressivism" and agrarianism in the nineteenth century. As for the legitimizing role of foreign policy disputes, the controversy with Belgrade over the status and tradition of Macedonia has served the Zhivkov regime as a source of popular support.

The Macedonian dispute is reminiscent of the Romanian-Hungarian dispute over Transylvania. As in the latter case, the Yugoslavs and the Bulgarians disagree over the heritage of the peoples living in Macedonia and their contemporary ethnic status. The Bulgarian argument essentially postulates that the Macedonians are ethnic Bulgarians, that the language is also essentially Bulgarian, and that the historical experiences of the Macedonian people closely align them with Bulgaria, at least in Pirin Macedonia.[72] The Yugoslavs, by contrast, have argued that the Macedonians constitute a separate nationality, that the language has features that clearly distinguish it from Bulgarian, and that the

Macedonians historically had very close ties with the Serbs and other ethnic groups incorporated in the Yugoslav federation.[73]

For the Bulgarian leadership of the 1970s, the utilization of the Macedonian question as a source of internal legitimacy has been forceful at times, hesitant in other periods—vacillations that reflect Sofia's need to coordinate its policy with that of Moscow on this and other sensitive questions. It is nevertheless fair to state that the Zhivkov leadership gained some measure of public support because of its position on this issue during the 1970s.

The Mavericks: Albania and Yugoslavia

The comparative analysis of the East European political systems in the 1970s does not hold for two of the states of the area. Neither Albania nor Yugoslavia can be classified as belonging to the same group of states as the GDR, Poland, Czechoslovakia, Hungary, Romania, and Bulgaria. Both the domestic and the foreign policies of these two systems differ drastically, even fundamentally, from those of the other states and Communist parties of the area. One of the most important of these differences is the simple fact that both Albania and Yugoslavia are outside of the Soviet sphere of direct influence. The concepts of "proletarian" and "socialist internationalism," which hold at least partly for the other East European parties and states, therefore have little direct influence on policymaking in the two maverick systems, although both Tirana and Belgrade ostensibly subscribe to their own versions of these two "isms." In fact, Enver Hoxha and Josip Broz Tito and his successors, each in their own way, have argued that these two principles of international relations among Communist parties and socialist states have been seriously violated by the CPSU and the Soviet state and by the "loyalist" parties and states that have supported the Kremlin in these matters.

These leaders, therefore, reject the idea that Moscow can intervene in the affairs of another party or state and claim instead that each Communist leadership has the right to choose its road to socialism and Communism. In the case of Albania, this road has been similar to that of the Chinese Communist party (CCP) up until very recently; during the last two years, significant conflicts have developed between Tirana and Peking, and the leaders in the former capital increasingly argue that they alone have the correct policies of political and socioeconomic development.

In addition to claiming the right of independent foreign policies, Hoxha and Tito severely criticized Soviet interventionist doctrines and actual practices as examples of big power chauvinism and imperialism.

In both cases, the outrage expressed reflected both the doctrines of separate or alternative development (the Yugoslav and Albanian positions, respectively) as well as fear of possible Soviet moves to enforce its own principles of international relations. Under such circumstances, the criticisms launched in the two maverick capitals have been predictably vehement.[74]

Even though the Brezhnev Doctrine as a definition of Soviet foreign policy goals has been rejected by Tirana and Belgrade, some of the basic aspects of the doctrine have largely been accepted in the two capitals as guidelines for the respective regime's policy (although there is no willingness in either leadership to attribute this correspondence of views to good relations with Moscow). First of all, the leaders agree with the principle that the political hegemony of the Communist party in society must be preserved, albeit in different degrees. Hoxha has consolidated his political position by means of a series of violent purges, the most recent of which is still underway. The purges have been backed up by massive ideological campaigns and the partial militarization of labor and the educational system to ensure compliance. Rigid ideology and constant cultural revolution have shaken Albanian society for years, leaving little doubt as to the superiority of the Communist party over all other organizations and groups in the country.[75]

In Yugoslavia, the relative weakness of the central party leadership (apart from Tito himself) in relation to the republic parties has occasionally resulted in "national" deviations, which in fact focus on the political autonomy of the republics rather than on the strength of the federation. Such deviations resulted in forceful intervention by Tito for the purpose of reestablishing the principle that the League of Communists (LCY) still maintained political control in Yugoslavia. One of the most important of these involvements by the center was the forceful reaction to the 1971/72 Croatian affair, in which important elements in the Croatian party leadership openly associated themselves with the demands of Zagreb university students and emigré groups in the West for greater Croatian autonomy, both political and economic. During the last few years, Tito forcefully moved to strengthen the authority of the central party bodies, in anticipation of his own physical demise.[76]

Hoxha and Tito also agreed with the maxims of the Brezhnev Doctrine that state that the Communist parties of Eastern Europe have the right to decide on the socioeconomic development programs of their respective systems, but here the extent of the agreement varies widely. Hoxha's Albania has gone further than any other country in Eastern Europe in implementation of this principle by centrally directing all planning and policy-execution of economic decision making and by completely mobilizing, indeed militarizing, the work force.[77] In Yugoslavia, on the other hand, the decentralized nature of the economic system that developed in earlier decades continued in the 1970s—a system in which much of the decision making is decentralized, where the profit motive and market forces continue to have important influence, and where central planning is primarily "parameter planning" rather than directly binding in detail. The Yugoslav system operates on the premise that non-Communist forces must not be allowed to gain control over the economic system, but short of this preventative function, the regime will provide only moderate control and guidance of the economy.[78]

Considerable differences also exist between the two maverick leaderships in defining the relationship between the individual and political authority. Here, Hoxha has instituted an Albanian version of "the permanent purge" and also continuous ideological campaigns, which leave the individual citizen little opportunity for personal autonomy and privacy. These policies have created an extremely high regime "profile" in Albanian society, surely the most dominant regime position vis-à-vis the individual in all of Eastern Europe.[79] The Yugoslav system, on the other hand, has produced a relatively low regime "profile," in which considerable individual autonomy exists, including the possibility of withdrawal from society and the political and socioeconomic development programs. Politically, the Yugoslav federal party shares center stage with the republican parties, and voices have been raised in favor of a political system of collective elites, in which the LCY is but one of the structures. In this field, then, the two maverick systems differ significantly from each other, and each in its own way is also quite different from the other systems in Eastern Europe in the 1970s.

The quest for political control is pursued through the Albanian and Yugoslav versions of party organization, overlapping membership, and interlocking directorates. Table 5 illustrates this aspect of political life in Albania and Yugoslavia. As shown by Table 5, the organizational power of the Albanian Workers party (PPS) and the LCY is considerable. Once again, major differences do exist, in that the PPS exercises control in a centralized system, while the Yugoslav counterpart must contend with several semiautonomous parties in the republics of the federation. This major difference became even more marked during the 1970s, when the Albanian party continued its persistent pursuit of political and organizational hegemony even more forcefully than before.

While the two maverick systems differ considerably from each other in organizational control and in the doctrines and practices pertaining to the party's position in society and the relationships between the individual and political authority, they share a similar problem in the

TABLE 5

Party Membership in Albania and Yugoslavia, 1967/68-1976/77
(It should be noted that in some cases, the official figures separate full members
and candidates; in other cases the two sets of figures are collapsed)

	1967/68		1970/71		1972/73		1974/75		1976	
	Membership	% of Tot. Pop.	Membership	% of Tot. Pop.	Membership	% of Tot. Pop.	Membership	% of Tot. Pop.	Membership	% of Tot. Pop.
Albania	63,000('68)	3.2	75,673('70)	3.6	86,987('71)	3.7	100,000('75)	4.2	101,500	4.2
Yugoslavia	1,146,084('66)	5.7	1,046,084('70)	5.1	1,025,476('72)	4.9	1,192,446('75)	5.6	1,400,000	6.5

Source: Yearbook on International Communist Affairs (Stanford, Calif.: Hoover Institution Press),
for the following years: 1969, 1971, 1974, 1976, 1977.

struggle against "retrograde views" and "deviationist political behavior." This problem is clearly more severe in Yugoslavia, which, as a semipluralist system, must contend with the expectations of societal elites, the general citizenry, and the various ethnic groups, all at the same time. For Tito, the biggest problem was always to prevent these centrifugal forces from pulling Yugoslavia apart politically, socioeconomically, and culturally. Under such circumstances, some of the forces of integration and legitimization utilized in other countries of Eastern Europe, notably political and cultural nationalism, have been reduced to relative insignificance in Yugoslavia; in fact, nationalism is in itself a disintegrative force in this diverse federation, and Tito, after an initial attempt to develop a sense of "Yugoslavism," ceased to rely upon this element. For Yugoslavia, the primary source of legitimacy is increasingly instrumental, i.e., the performance of the system, especially in the socioeconomic field, but also in terms of maintaining foreign policy autonomy. Nationalism, on the other hand, is frequently classified as a "retrograde" view, designed to pull Yugoslavia apart, rather than help cement it. Ideology is increasingly utilized to provide a unity that nationalism cannot deliver. In this respect, Yugoslavia differs substantially from the other countries of Eastern Europe.

Albania represents yet another configuration of ideological and nationalistic interaction. The Albanian regime has struggled against "retrograde attitudes and values" in a determined fashion, and many of the views that have been attacked are in fact remnants of a not so distant past, when Albania was a tribal society operating in an almost medieval cultural setting and pastoral economy. At the same time, the heavy infusion of Marxist-Leninist orthodoxy in Albanian society has increased the likelihood that "incorrect" views will be found, both in the political elite and in the general citizenry; hence the frequent purges and the ongoing cultural revolution. The Albanian regime will continue to find many enemies domestically as long as it persists in maintaining its high "profile" and pursuing rigid ideological orthodoxy.[80]

While traditional Albanian nationalism, based upon the semifeudal values and mores that existed prior to the Communist takeover of political power, is castigated as "retrograde," the very emphasis on ideological orthodoxy in Tirana has generated its own form of nationalism. Albania dramatically broke with the Soviet Union and the CPSU in 1960—certainly a very courageous act for a small country without nearby allies. The break came over ideology, and the Albanians claimed that *they* were the real Marxists, while the Soviets were perpetrating unpardonable deviations from the correct doctrine. For over fifteen years, Albania accepted the Chinese claim that Peking had the correct interpretation of the

Marxist classics, and Albania became China's outpost in Europe. Since the middle of the 1970s, relations with China have cooled considerably, amid dark hints from Tirana that Peking was also committing deviations, especially in its cautious détente with Washington. Recent statements and actions in Tirana have in fact established that the Hoxha leadership has determined to "go it alone," as it were, in ideological matters.[81] According to this view, ideological deviations are found in all of the Communist systems, including the Soviet Union and China; only Albania has the right view of the ideological classics and the only correct implementation of the principles. This is indeed a form of ideological nationalism, indeed chauvinism; a small country with a minuscule party in comparison to the "deviationist" structures elsewhere has decided to set itself up as the center of world Communism and ideological orthodoxy. There may be a sense of pride in elements of the Albanian population over this ideological nationalism, but by and large it is too far removed from any pre-Communist value base to have the kind of staying power and emotional attraction that traditional nationalism has in many other socialist states, notably Romania. In the field of nationalism, too, Albania has been a maverick of considerable proportions in Eastern Europe in the 1970s.

Conclusion: Whither Eastern Europe in the 1980s?

The problems that confronted the East European political elites in the 1970s are not temporary nuisances that can be expected to disappear in the 1980s; rather, they are fundamental and intractable problems that are likely to remain, indeed become exacerbated, as the new decade unfolds. The multifaceted challenges of foreign policy, domestic legitimacy, party control, societal development, and increasing dissent (and occasionally organized opposition) will continue to demand the full attention of the Communist elites in this rapidly changing area. Their successes or failures in handling these challenges will increasingly depend upon their ability (or lack of such) to innovate, improvise, and compromise between demands of one sector of society and the requirements of another, between the needs of the domestic economy and polity and the external requirements of "socialist" and "proletarian" internationalism. Thus, the political elites of Eastern Europe must, in all likelihood, face increased social and political pluralism in the 1980s.

Specifically, the following areas of major concern can be identified. Firstly, increased political and cultural nationalism will be utilized as a major mechanism for the achievement of legitimacy by the local Communist leaderships. In multiethnic societies, this process will tend to increase the apprehension of ethnic minorities, and a certain amount of political instability can be expected. Nationalism will also lead to more troublesome relations between the states of Eastern Europe, and it will confront the Soviet Union and the CPSU with an increased challenge to political and military control.

Secondly, the public emphasis on improved economic performance will continue, and the masses of the population are likely to become increasingly vocal in their demands for an improved standard of living, based on better performances in agriculture and in the production of consumer goods and services. At the same time, the massive industrialization programs under way in Eastern Europe will continue to draw heavily upon scarce resources and manpower. A further complication in the economic field is the existence of energy shortages, which will probably become worse in the 1980s. The regimes of the area are therefore confronted with classical problems of allocation of scarce resources in a citizenry with rising expectations.

Political dissent is also likely to continue, even to increase, in the 1980s. The concern over human rights became "internationalized" in the 1970s, and this trend is likely to continue in the foreseeable future. The regimes of Eastern Europe cannot expect to be able to maintain separate standards of human rights without increasing problems of control over the citizenry. The old nemesis of coercion and mobilization versus individual political autonomy will become a major problem in the 1980s.

As discussed above, the Communist-supervised modernization process is creating new socioeconomic classes and societal elites, and the political regimes of the area are constantly confronted with the twin needs of political integration of these new elites and control over them. This problem is likely to be exacerbated in the 1980s, especially since the aging apparatchiki of Eastern Europe will leave the political pinnacle in large numbers. The political party leaders will be faced with increasingly difficult questions of recruitment, co-optation, and personnel policy in the 1980s.

These major problems will be met by political elites whose members are increasingly sophisticated in terms of education, knowledge, and political outlook. The old emphasis on "frontal attacks" and coercion will fade to a considerable degree in the new decade. All the same, there are certain fundamentals, political "givens," that will not be tampered with by the regimes in response to the many difficult challenges of the new decade. Firstly, the dominant political position of the respective Communist parties of the area will not be compromised. New societal elites will be co-opted, but the co-optation process will be slow and measured, designed to properly train and socialize the new elite entrants in the values and behavioral norms of the apparat. Dissent of the masses and elements of the intelligentsia will be allowed only insofar as it does not jeopardize the political and socioeconomic hegemony of the party. The utilization of nationalism as a vehicle for increasing popular support will not be carried so far as to establish tradition as a counterpoint to the existing, future-oriented regimes and their programs. In foreign policy, overt challenges to Soviet hegemony and control are unlikely in the new decade, but the regimes will attempt to expand their autonomy in various ways, chief of which will be increased participation in international organizations such as the United Nations; attempts will also be made to relate to Eurocommunism in such a way that the internal political order of Eastern Europe is not challenged, but at the same time foreign relations at the party and state levels are enhanced; furthermore, the ongoing dispute between Moscow and Peking will be utilized for increased political and ideological autonomy, and there will be utilization of East-West détente (insofar as the process of détente survives the current rift between the global powers) for expanded relations with the West, once again in such a manner that the East European political order will not be upset.

The predictions discussed above add up to "more of the same" in terms of regime response to the challenges of the 1980s—that is, the tried and tested policy formulas of the 1970s seem likely to be repeated in the 1980s, without drastic innovation. The fundamental question that faces analyst and policymaker alike in 1981 is this: In view of the increasing complexity and magnitude of the social, economic, and political problems that will confront the political elites of Eastern Europe in the 1980s, will the policies of the 1970s be sufficient? Herein lies the key, not only to the future of Eastern Europe, but to the future of "maturing" (and "mature") Communist systems everywhere.

APPENDIX:
List of Party Names and Abbreviations

Albania: Albanian Workers' party—Partija e Punës të Shqiperisë—PPS

Bulgaria: Bulgarian Communist party—Bulgarska Kommunisticheská Partiia—BKP

Czechoslovakia: Communist party of Czechoslovakia—Komunistická Strana Československa—KSČ

German Democratic Republic (GDR): Socialist Unity party—Sozialistische Einheitspartei Deutschlands—SED

Hungary: Hungarian Socialist Workers' party—Magyar Szocialista Munkás-párt—MSM

Poland: Polish United Workers' party—Polska Zjednoczana   Partia Robot-nicza—PZPR

Romania: Romanian Communist party—Partidul Comunist Român—PCR

Yugoslavia: League of Communists of Yugoslavia—Savez Komunista Jugoslav-ije—SKJ or LCY

Notes

1. A great deal has been written on the Brezhnev Doctrine; see, for example, Vernon V. Aspaturian, "East European Relations with the USSR," in Peter A. Toma (ed.), *The Changing Face of Communism in Eastern Europe* (Tucson: University of Arizona Press, 1970), pp. 281–311.

2. This aspect of East European politics has been discussed in many volumes, e.g., Charles Gati (ed.), *The Politics of Modernization in Eastern Europe: Testing the Soviet Model* (New York: Praeger Publishers, 1974), esp. Part II.

3. *Ibid.*

4. The Soviet version of ideological orthodoxy in the era of "Eurocommunism" was forcefully stated at the ideological conference in Moscow, November 10-12, 1977, in honor of the October Revolution, see *Pravda,* November 11, 12, and 13, 1977.

5. For a very thorough analysis of Soviet foreign policy, see Vernon V. Aspaturian, *Process and Power in Soviet Foreign Policy* (Boston: Little, Brown and Co., 1971).

6. Heinz Timmermann, "Moskan und der europäische Kommunismus nach der Gipfelkonferunz von Ost-Berlin," *Osteuropa,* April 1977, pp. 282–303.

7. See *Pravda,* November 11, 12, and 13, 1977.

8. For a thorough discussion of Romania, see Nicolae Ceausescu's speech to the Eleventh PCR Congress, in *Congresul al XI-lea al Partidului Comunist Român,* (Bucharest: Editura Politica, 1975), pp. 68–69; the figures for military officers and professors were taken from speeches by Virgil Trofin and General Ion Ionita at the December 1967 PCR conference (see *Scinteia,* December 6 and 8, 1967).

9. In many parties, notably the East German SED, a whole section of the party's Central Committee is devoted primarily to control over such organiza-tions.

10. The exception is the countryside, where the East European parties have had considerable problems of organizational control.

11. For an in-depth examination of this system in one East European country, see Otto Ulc, *Politics in Czechoslovakia* (San Francisco: W. H. Freeman and Company, 1974), esp. Chapter 7.

12. The debate over this issue has flared in Romania for over a year. For the

regime's version, see the campaign against dissent and minority emigration in the Romanian press, e.g., Friedrich Böhmches in *Scinteia*, April 13, 1977; Simion Roth in *Scinteia*, April 20, 1977; and Dan Zamfirescu in *Romania Libera*, April 11, 1977.

13. This is basically true even in Hungary, where the economic reforms went quite far in decentralization. See, for example William F. Robinson, *The Pattern of Reform in Hungary: Economic and Cultural Analysis* (New York: Praeger Publishers, 1973).

14. In this respect, there have been some restrictive moves even in Hungary during the 1970s; see *ibid.*

15. The differences among the countries of the area are nevertheless visible; see, for example, Ferenc Varnai in *Nepszabadsag*, January 29, 1977, where he discusses Eurocommunism but also the Hungarian view of official ideology and the socialist state; Robert R. King, "Ideological Mobilization in Romania," *RAD Background Report* (Romania) no. 40, February 21, 1977; Zdenek Haba in *Hospodarske Noviny*, September 9, 1977, on Czechoslovakia's road toward socialism and Communism; Thomas E. Heneghan, "The Loyal Opposition: Party Programs and Church Response in Poland," *RAD Background Report* (Poland), no. 45, February 28, 1977.

16. See Vernon V. Aspaturian, "Has Eastern Europe Become a Liability to the Soviet Union? The Political-Ideological Aspects," in Charles Gati (ed.), *The International Politics of Eastern Europe* (New York: Praeger Publishers, 1976), pp. 17–35.

17. For a discussion of this development, see Stephen Fischer-Galati, *Twentieth Century Rumania* (New York: Columbia University Press, 1970), Chapter 8.

18. E.g., my "Ceauşescu's Romania," *Problems of Communism* 23 (July-August 1974):29–44.

19. Andrew Gyorgy, "Ostpolitik and Eastern Europe," in Gati, *International Politics*, Chapter 8.

20. These characterizations were used against Gomulka in the Stalinist era; see Zbigniew K. Brzezinski, *The Soviet Bloc* (Cambridge, Mass.: Harvard University Press, 1969), esp. Chapter 5.

21. E.g., Adam Bromke, "A New Juncture in Poland," *Problems of Communism* 25 (September-October 1976):1–18.

22. For a thorough analysis of the process of "normalization" see Robin Alison Remington (ed.), *Winter in Prague* (Cambridge, Mass.: M.I.T. Press, 1969) and Tad Szulc, *Czechoslovakia Since World War II* (New York: Viking Press, 1971).

23. Robinson, *Pattern of Reform in Hungary.*

24. For a discussion of the extent of Bulgarian coordination with the Kremlin in domestic policies as well, see F. Stephen Larrabee, "Neue Tendenzen in der bulgarischen Innenpolitik," *Osteuropa*, March 1973, pp. 174–185.

25. Robinson, *Pattern of Reform in Hungary.*

26. Gilberg, "Ceauşescu's Romania."

27. See Larrabee, "Neue Tendenzen," for a discussion of these plans.

28. An interesting discussion of the relationship between the political leadership and the technical intelligentsia can be found in Thomas A. Baylis, *The*

Technical Intelligentsia and the East German Elite: Legitimacy and Social Change in Mature Communism (Berkeley: University of California Press, 1974).

29. Bromke, "New Juncture in Poland."

30. A good overview is Jan F. Triska's "Messages from Czechoslovakia," *Problems of Communism* 24 (November-December 1975):26-43.

31. See my *Modernization in Romania since World War II* (New York: Praeger Publishers, 1975).

32. A recent discussion of this puts the question in the context of socialist law and its application; see Jan Nemic, minister of justice, in an interview in *Tvorba*, December 15, 1976.

33. The Bulgarian performance has been well discussed in Nissan Oren, *Revolution Administered: Agrarianism and Communism in Bulgaria* (Baltimore, Md.: Johns Hopkins University Press, 1973), esp. Chapters 5, 6, and 7.

34. Even so, ideological orthodoxy was reintroduced to some extent at the Eleventh Congress of the Hungarian party; see Kurt Kwasny, "Pragmatismus weicht der Ideologie. Zun XI Parteikongress der ungarischen Kommunisten," *Osteuropa*, October 1975, pp. 868-879.

35. Adam Bromke, "Poland under Gierek: A New Political Style," *Problems of Communism* 21 (September-October 1972):1-20.

36. Bromke, "New Juncture in Poland."

37. See Baylis, *Technical Intelligentsia*, esp. Chapter 1.

38. Gilberg, "Ceaușescu's Romania," and Robert R. King, "Romania," *Yearbook on International Communist Affairs* (1976), pp. 58-68.

39. *Rabotnichesko Delo*, October 14, 1977, on the "new approach" to planning, which emphasizes trade union participation as well as party control in the planning mechanism.

40. Thus, most of the high level apparatchiki can only claim "working-class origin," since they have in fact been functionaries for many years.

41. See Carl Beck et al., *Comparative Communist Political Leadership* (New York: David McKay Company, 1973).

42. This problem is at the heart of contemporary dissent in Eastern Europe. An example of the views of some writers on political "bossism" can be found in Augustin Buzura's novel on Romanian "worker heroes," published in *Viata Romaneasca*, no. 2 (1977), and translated in *RAD Background Report* (Romania), no. 80, April 21, 1977.

43. The reaction of the SED leadership was described and criticized by Bernard Umbrecht in *L'Humanite*, December 13, 1977.

44. Triska, "Messages from Czechoslovakia."

45. *Radio Free Europe Research* (Czechoslovakia), no. 11, March 23, 1977.

46. A thorough discussion of Polish dissent can be found in Harald Laeuen, "Opposition in Polen," *Osteuropa*, June 1975, pp. 389-407.

47. *Ibid.*

48. A series of articles on dissent in Romania appeared in *Süddeutsche Zeitung*, February 8, 14, and 16, 1977.

49. E.g., Ceaușescu in *Scinteia*, April 19 and 21, 1977, and in an interview in *Agerpres*, May 2, 1977.

50. *Ibid.*

51. The most recent comprehensive reshuffle in Romania took place in late January 1977; see *Scinteia*, January 26 and 27, 1977.

52. Social scientists have examined the phenomenon of spare-time use in Czechoslovakia and have found much "Western" influence; see Jan Sirbek in *Tribuna*, March 23, 1977.

53. Even in Romania, material incentives have increasingly become important. In this vein, Nicolae Ceauşescu severely criticized the performance of the light and consumer goods industries and promised improvements in the 1977 plan; see *Scinteia*, November 6, 1977.

54. See my *Modernization in Romania*, esp. Chapter 8.

55. *Ibid.*

56. See, for example, Peter Sugar and Ivo J. Lederer, *Nationalism in Eastern Europe* (Seattle: University of Washington Press, 1969).

57. For a good overall discussion of East German policy under Ulbricht, see Donald D. Dalgleish, "Walter Ulbricht's German Democratic Republic," in Toma, *The Changing Face of Communism*, Chapter 5.

58. Gyorgy, "Ostpolitik and Eastern Europe."

59. Honecker discussed this in a speech to the SED Central Committee, printed in *Neues Deutschland*, October 29, 1976.

60. See, for example, *GDR: 100 Questions, 100 Answers* (Berlin, 1974), esp. Chapter 6.

61. Despite such impressive economic performance, the GDR also has problems; see *Der Spiegel*, August 1977.

62. Bromke, "New Juncture in Poland."

63. See the discussion of Czechoslovak achievements in *Hospodarske Noviny*, September 9, 1977, by Zdenek Jaba.

64. Fischer-Galati, *Twentieth Century Rumania*, Chapter 8.

65. Gilberg, "Ceauşescu's Romania."

66. The ideological foundations of the campaign were discussed in detail in *Scinteia*, March 6, 1976.

67. See, for example, Anneli Ute Gabanyi, "Der Rumänische Kulturkongress Permanente Revolution und neuer Nationalismus," *Osteuropa*, February 1977, pp. 131–138.

68. I have argued this in a book on the East European ruling parties edited by Stephen Fischer-Galati, *The Communist Parties of Eastern Europe* (New York: Columbia University Press, 1978).

69. See Kwasny, "Pragmatismus weicht der Ideologie."

70. The Hungarian view was published in *Nepszabadsag*, June 25, 1971; the Romanian reply can be found in *Scinteia*, July 9, 1971.

71. Recently the Romanians have in fact argued that cultural developments among the Romanians *preceded* developments in all other countries—an argument relevant in the polemics between Budapest and Bucharest on cultural "firsts." See, for example, Serafina Duicu in *Tribuna*, September 15, 1977.

72. For a thorough study of this controversy, see Stephen E. Palmer, Jr. and Robert R. King, *Yugoslav Communism and the Macedonian Question* (Hamden,

Conn.: Shoe String Press, 1971).

73. *Ibid.*

74. A good overview of Albanian politics is Nicholas A. Pano, "The Albanian Cultural Revolution," *Problems of Communism* 23 (July-August 1974):44–58; on Yugoslavia, William Zimmerman has written well in "The Tito Legacy and Yugoslavia's Future," *Problems of Communism* 26 (May-June 1977):33–49.

75. *Ibid.*

76. *Ibid.*

77. Editorial in the Albanian daily *Zeri i Popullit*, November 20, 1977, discussing the proceedings of the Central committee plenum of the Albanian party.

78. Zimmerman, "The Tito Legacy."

79. Pano, "The Albanian Cultural Revolution."

80. There is considerable evidence that this policy is also causing problems internally in the Albanian party; see, e.g., Jorgji Sota in *Rruga e Partise*, September 1977, also discussed in *RAD Background Report* (Albania), no. 214, November 4, 1977.

81. Evidence of this can be found in Enver Hoxha's speech to the congress of the Albanian party in 1976; see *Zeri i Popullit*, November 2, 1976.

Robin Alison Remington   **6**

Eastern Europe
and World Communism

Contemporary Eastern Europe belongs to what among Communist states is often referred to as the "family of socialist nations." It is part of an international ideological/political movement dedicated to radically changing the international status quo, united on the goal if widely split on issues of strategy, tactics, and timing. The world Communist movement includes both ruling and nonruling parties all influenced in varying degrees by

> that ensemble of norms, standards, and values which is current in the Communist system, common to party members and separating them from nonmembers: "reactionaries," "capitalists," "imperialists" and the like. This culture is embodied in its own prolific literature, has its own distinct language and symbols, its own history and its own heroes, villains, and martyrs, and its own special ritual behavior.[1]

Communist states perceive themselves as existing separate from the non-Communist international system in a political world where rules apply that do not maintain on the outside. Relations among Communist states are expected to have attributes different from those among non-Communist states or between a Communist and a non-Communist state. That there is deep, sometimes violent disagreement on just what those rules and attributes are does not negate the feeling among Communists in and out of power that there is a "right" course at any given time that can and must be found. Analytically, the Communist world can usefully be understood as a subsystem within which substantial political energy is devoted to battles over conflicting interpretations of appropriate in-group behavior.

This process is complicated by the fact that the subsystem involved is characterized by expanding membership, in which the status of more recent members is ambiguous and the impacts upon the power configuration are complex. The Communist world has a 133-year history, dating back to the League of Communists of 1847, an essentially egalitarian organization of nonruling parties that commissioned Karl Marx to write the *Communist Manifesto*. From the Russian Revolution of 1917 until the end of World War II in the 1940s, the Communist party of the Soviet Union (CPSU) occupied a unique position as the ruling party of the only state in the international system dedicated to the construction of Communism. The CPSU towered above nonruling parties. The Third International (the Comintern) operated as an instrument of Soviet foreign policy via which nonruling parties subordinated their domestic goals to the perceived exigencies of Soviet survival. The Soviet Union was the superpower of the Communist subsystem. Russian national Communism dominated the transnational Communist movement. Moscow became the Mecca of the Communist world.

After World War II, a new category of political actor appeared within the Communist subsystem, i.e., ruling parties in Eastern Europe and Asia; thus the position of the Soviet Union was changed to that of first among what in reality were substantially less than equals. In 1962, Khrushchev's somewhat reluctant acceptance of Cuban socialism expanded the Communist world to Latin America at the expense of ideological rigor, military risk, and economic costs undoubtedly far greater than the Soviet leaders' original calculations. With the end of the Vietnam War, the Communist world spread still further to include a united and regionally powerful Vietnam, as well as Laos and Cambodia. The Communist subsystem is still convulsed by its attempt to integrate these new Asian acquisitions. At the same time, the 1970s saw Soviet efforts to expand into Africa and the Middle East. In short, the number of political actors that East European policymakers must relate to in the Communist world of the 1980s has grown precipitously and involves numerous complex distinctions.

First, in the 1980s the power configuration of the Communist world includes not just one but two superpowers whose continued hostility despite intermittent conciliatory gestures[2] continues to influence East European policy options. Second, that world includes an increasing number of ruling parties that operate as powerful political actors in their own right even if substantially less powerful than decisionmakers in Moscow and Peking. East European relationships with each other, perhaps most particularly with Yugoslavia, are for the most part closer than their relations with non-European Communist states. Yet like it or not, that Cuba joined the Council for Mutual Economic Assistance (CMEA) in 1972 and Vietnam joined in 1978 are major considerations for

East European interactions within the Communist world. For one must not forget that East Europeans also relate to two organizations that function simultaneously as instruments of Soviet policy and as arenas of intra-Communist political maneuver, i.e., the Warsaw Pact and CMEA.

Moreover in the Communist world of the 1980s, the importance of nonruling parties has grown dramatically. This is most visible in the behavior of the autonomist parties, somewhat inappropriately labeled "Eurocommunist." Indeed, as an additional complication, East European leaders must decide upon their responses to the "people's democracies" of the 1970s, parties that have been accepted as somewhere, but no one seems quite sure exactly where, on the road to socialism with varying degrees of obligation on the part of more established members of the "family." Leaving aside Afghanistan, it is helpful to view the situation of Angola, Ethiopia, and South Yemen as similar to that of a probation period before adoption becomes legal.

Beyond these considerations, there remains the historical, realpolitik factor. Eastern Europe has a vital military importance to any policy-maker sitting in Moscow. Long before there was a Soviet Union, geography, reinforced by religious and cultural pan-Slavism, made Eastern Europe central to tsarist foreign policy. The revolution added an ideological concern that fed into an already well-developed tendency to consider the area as Russia's backyard, a natural sphere-of-influence to be consolidated. This makes Soviet–East European relations multidimensional. The Soviet Union is not only the first and most powerful socialist state, it is the closest superpower, and the intensity of Moscow's anxiety over the outcomes of East European domestic and foreign policy far outstrips its concern over the Chinese, or for that matter Italian, Communists.

In contrast, there is no natural Chinese–East European connection apart from Sino-Soviet relations. The Chinese role in Eastern Europe is one aspect of Peking's challenge to Moscow. Hence, the nature of bilateral Chinese–East European relations can be expected either to reflect or anticipate Sino-Soviet dialogue.

Lastly, the Communist regimes in Eastern Europe have moved beyond the periods of revolutionary takeover and consolidation. They are maintaining political systems increasingly tied to national political cultures. Not only do they govern peoples with pre-Communist memories, but it is fair to say that "throughout the European Communist world the societal base is tending to reassert its sovereignty over the political super-structure."[3] Thus, to a significant degree regime legitimacy in these circumstances has come to depend on performance in defense of indigenous national interests within, as well as outside, the "family of socialist nations." Thereby the line between socialist patriotism (national interests) and proletarian internationalism as operating principles has become ever more blurred.

To write of Eastern Europe in relation to world Communism is an analytical fiction. Eastern Europe is an artificial grouping of eight nations with very different circumstances, policies, and options for political maneuver. Even then one is faced with both the dilemma of data far too broad for a country-by-country discussion and the pitfalls inherent in presuming a collective treatment.

Therefore this chapter focuses on three developments that in my judgment will substantially determine East European relations with the Communist world as we enter the 1980s: the future of Eurocommunism as a political force, the nature of East European dependence on Soviet energy resources, and the uncertainty introduced by the transition to post-Tito Yugoslavia.

Eurocommunism and Eastern Europe

Names and labels are essential for conversation and political analysis. By nature they define the problem and identify the political phenomena. Wrong labels create confusion and misunderstanding and hamper the ability to think clearly about events. Unfortunately, perhaps because political labels tend to be the product of journalists with an eye to headlines, they stick far better than Elmer's glue. Eurocommunism is an extremely misleading label. There is no way to get rid of it, so one must examine the component parts to fit Eastern Europe into the scheme.

It is an hypothesis of this chapter that what is called Eurocommunism is not primarily domestic in origin, nor is it primarily confined to Western Europe although that is where much of the action has been at present.[4] Rather Eurocommunism is an international phenomenon that has existed since the late 1940s variously identified as domesticism, national Communism, reform Communism, polycentrism, and autonomist tendencies. The process of Eurocommunism is one of ongoing change in the balance of forces within the international Communist movement resulting from the end of the Soviet Union's unique position as the first and only socialist state. Eurocommunism began in Eastern Europe. It spread to Western Europe, has an active East European component, and is returning to Eastern Europe in admittedly new forms and with new implications.

On the most fundamental level, Eurocommunism is a demand to change the rules of the game within the Communist world. After 1917, as before, the international Communist movement was dedicated to proletarian internationalism. This meant that Communists in any given country owed their loyalty not to their country but to their class; that in principle, for example, French workers should not fight German workers during World War I no matter what their capitalist government's decisions were regarding war. Yet after 1917, in practice proletarian internationalism came to mean love of Comrade Stalin, uncritical loyalty to Soviet policy priorities, and an assumption on the part of the Soviets that what was good for the Soviet Union was good for world Communism.

From the beginning, Eurocommunism has been a challenge to this dominate-subordinate relationship, a challenge on two fronts. First, there is an insistence that within the Communist world the concept of "nation" be rehabilitated and reunited with the concept of "class" to form national roads to socialism. Second, the Soviet definition of proletarian internationalism has been rejected in favor of emphasis on equality, sovereignty, noninterference in internal affairs, and mutual advantage. In short, this is a move toward "democratization" of decisionmaking within world Communism with an emphasis on Soviet responsibility to other members of the movement. Much confusion has resulted from the fact that these demands for domestic autonomy were combined with an attempt to redefine Communist political relationships and organizational principles at the international level.

At first the "democratic" tendency appeared harmless and it almost seemed as if Moscow would go along. At the end of World War II, East European Communist leaders played coalition politics. In 1944, the Hungarians insisted that these were not tactical maneuvers but long-term alliances. Even Rakosi, the head of the Hungarian Communist party until 1956, stressed the Hungarian road to socialism.[5] Then Polish party leader Gomulka insisted on the possibility of a peaceful road to socialism that eliminated the need for a dictatorship of any kind, proletariat or otherwise. In retrospect such statements are often interpreted as dishonest maneuvers designed to lull suspicions and facilitate Communist consolidation, an opinion held by some with respect to current Italian Communist pronouncements as well. In fairness, there is no evidence that East European leaders preferred the subsequent forced turn to dictatorship of the proletariat, internal class struggle, and show trials.

Whatever tolerance existed in Moscow for domestic diversity within Eastern Europe vanished with Tito's defiance in 1948. Yugoslavia was the first of the Eurocommunists to split with Moscow. Moreover, Tito became a "national communist" only after the split, not before. Previously, Yugoslavia had been the most enthusiastic follower of the Soviet model within the bloc, Kardelj, the Yugoslav Communist leader and ideologist, even going so far as to suggest that eventually the country become a Soviet republic. The issue of Tito's revolutionary expansionism in the Balkans, symbolized by his attempts to mobilize a Balkan federation and to aid the Greek Communists over Soviet opposition, was far more serious than the Yugoslav leadership's domestic deviations. The Yugoslav alternative with its emphasis on socialist self-management at home and emancipation from Soviet ideological hegemony within Communist subsystems grew out of the break with Moscow, as did Stalin's determination that there would be no more East European deviations from the Soviet norm.

Stalinist uniformity could not survive the Soviet dictator's death. Sparked by de-Stalinization, the 1956 Polish October and the Hungarian Revolution of 1956 were more national than international manifestations of what we now call Eurocommunism. With the Sino-Soviet dispute, however, the process again shifted to an international challenge to Soviet dominance of world Communism. The Chinese attack on Moscow's hegemony not only led to Soviet pressure on ruling and nonruling parties alike to take sides, but gave rise to neutrals who remained legitimate political actors. Soviet indecisiveness, the oscillation between attempting to pressure and to woo such parties, increased both the importance and attractiveness of neutralism. Paradoxically, the result amounted to sanctioning virtual nonalignment in interparty relations.[6]

Throughout the early 1960s, the arena of maneuver was largely organizational and centered on the issue of Moscow's drive for a world Communist conference to expel the Chinese. The Italians, still working for a "unity in diversity" formula, opposed such a conference as did the Yugoslavs. With the visit of Togliatti, the head of the Italian Communist party (PCI), to Belgrade in January 1964, Italian-Yugoslav united opposition to isolating Peking at such a conference went public and was soon joined by the Romanians.[7] This was the nucleus of what has come to be known as the "southern axis," the backbone of an East and West Eurocommunism alliance in the 1970s. The euphoria of the Prague Spring in 1968 was a factor in these developments as it spread from Czechoslovakia to the Communist parties of Western Europe. Socialism with a human face was in line with Italian Communist party positions and also answered the needs of British and Scandinavian electoral pressures. Eurocommunist nonruling parties maneuvered desperately to head off the resort to a military solution in Czechoslovakia during the long, hot summer of 1968. (Indeed, from my conversations in Prague in June 1969, it is clear that many otherwise well-informed Czechs and Slovaks considerably overestimated the degree to which, particularly Italian, Communist concern would function as a restraining force in Moscow. Then general secretary of the PCI Luigi Longo was in Moscow desperately maneuvering for a last minute compromise when Soviet troops invaded in August 1968.)

Their failure was anything but the end of the matter. The invasion of Czechoslovakia led to formerly virtually unthinkable public criticism of the Soviet Union by parties that had no intention of joining the Chinese or splitting with Moscow. Even the French Communist party joined in the chorus of dismay. For the first time a major Soviet foreign policy move came under concerted attack from numerically significant sections of the world Communist movement. The West European parties faced the dilemma of whether they could be uncritically pro-Soviet and, at the same time, viable political alternatives in their own countries. The majority resolved the issue by opting for criticism of the Soviet Union and, therefore, electoral credibility. The Romanians and Yugoslavs buttressed public condemnation of the USSR by building peoples' militias, territorial defense units to join the professional military in defending national borders.

Moreover, the issue of Czechoslovakia became inextricably tangled with Moscow's plans for a world Communist conference. When finally held in June of 1969, this meeting must have been a bitter, pyrrhic victory for the Soviets. The conditions existing at the time gutted the desired content. Delegates made their views public. The hoped-for collective condemnation of Peking proved impossible to mobilize. The tactic of having willing pro-Soviet parties attack China publicly at the meeting only led Eurocommunist parties to openly condemn the invasion of Czechoslovakia to the chagrin of both Brezhnev and Czechoslovak leader Gustav Husak. The concluding declaration was not signed by some parties, signed only in part by others, and with public reservations by still others. To use Kevin Devlin's expression, this lack of agreement was the "institutionalization of diversity" within world Communism.[8] Such diversity could not help but affect Eastern Europe.

Thus, whatever advantages Moscow had gained by aborting the Eurocommunist domestic alternative in Eastern Europe by invading Czechoslovakia must be weighed against the impact upon Soviet goals in the international Communist arena, much more substantial than supposed from the first wave of criticism. The substance of the Prague Spring— socialist pluralism and demands for intellectual freedom, inner party democracy, and an end to censorship and repression of dissidents— survives as the core of Eurocommunism in Western Europe where it is much harder to stamp out or denounce as illegitimate. This survival of Eurocommunism is the victory of the proponents of the Prague Spring; of Czech playwright Vaclav Havel, who maintains his opposition despite his subsequent persecution as a result of the Charter of '77;

of Zdenek Mlynar, a member of the 1968 Czechoslovak Party Presidium, who continues to advocate socialist pluralism whether or not he too suffers economic and political harassment. Nor has the fate of these ideas and individuals in Husak's Czechoslovakia improved Moscow's negotiating position in multiparty forums.

By the early 1970s, winds of change swept the European political scene. Once again the Soviets were caught in a vise of conflicting priorities. There were political and economic crises convulsing Portugal, Spain, and Greece. Potentially, the domestic balance of power was shifting in Italy and France. In Latin America, President Salvadore Allende appeared to be moving down a peaceful road to socialism. Power was not lying in the streets, but anticipation that it soon might be made it crucial for both Moscow and the West European parties to evaluate the situation.

Hence, the impetus toward the pan-European Communist conference, which finally took place in 1976. Moscow saw the conference as setting the tone for a collective response in which the Soviets would have a decisive voice. The autonomist parties started from the assumption that the only viable response to Moscow's aims for calling the conference was on an individual basis. However, they too wanted the conference in order to legitimize their electoral strategies and thus avoid "consensus" decisions. On one level, the conference route can be seen as an organizational struggle over the issue of peaceful versus violent roads to socialism. The fall of Allende in Chile in September 1973 was a blow to supporters of socialist pluralism. Nonetheless, the evident collapse of Moscow's protégé Cunhal in Portugal by the summer of 1975 recouped that loss, leaving the Soviets with little choice but to temporarily settle for influence short of control over the reformist West Europeans.[9] The drawn out preparations for a European Communist conference, much like those prior to the 1975 Helsinki conference on European Security and Cooperation, became an increasingly important arena of interparty maneuvering for both Yugoslavia and Romania.

Yugoslav participation was the key to holding such a meeting. From the West European parties' perspective, Belgrade's presence was an index of Moscow's good faith. Without the Yugoslavs there would be no conference, and the Yugoslavs had a price. At the 1974 preparatory meeting in Warsaw, the Soviets reluctantly agreed to Yugoslav procedural conditions that the meeting be public, not devoted to attacking parties that stayed home (i.e., the Chinese), and limited to decisions upon which everyone agreed.[10]

Decisionmaking by consensus was the heart of these procedural demands. Once Moscow conceded consensus, those parties pushing for the lowest common denominator of agreement had virtual veto power. During the next two years, the Soviets tried unsuccessfully to renege. But subsquent preparatory meetings simply crystallized East and West Euro-communist resistance. The Yugoslavs and Romanians allied with the Italian and Spanish parties. By 1975 the French Communist party had also swung into the "southern axis," which effectively blocked support for Soviet policy objectives.

The success of this united opposition rested to a significant degree on the tactical skill of its East European members. This in turn increased both the power base and the stature of Yugoslavia and Romania within the European Communist world. For Yugoslavia such organizational maneuvering was the continuation of a policy shift evident during the preparation for the Helsinki meeting as well—redirection of nonaligned principles and tactics toward the small and medium-sized states of Europe, both Communist and non-Communist.[11]

Narrowly speaking, nonalignment is an alliance-building, issue-oriented strategy based on lowest common denominators of agreement. Broadly, it is the demand for democratization of international relations, and the institutionalization of the right to disagree in all arenas. Not only was nonalignment recognized in the final document of the 1975 East Berlin meeting; the process of preparing for that meeting epitomized what the Yugoslavs have consistently held to be nonaligned principles for achieving agreement.

Further, as long as these negotiations went on, it was more difficult for Moscow to pressure Belgrade and Bucharest in other respects. The 1975 Yugoslav polemics, followed by trials of Cominformists (the euphemism for pro-Soviet forces within Yugoslavia), may have been a message to Moscow, signaling Yugoslav adamance on the conference issue as well as general flouting of Soviet pressures.

It is not suprising that Moscow decided to abandon its hope for a pan-European conference prior to the February 1976 CPSU Twenty-Fifth Congress. At the conference a sudden push for a document referring to "some obligations for all parties" might have succeeded. Certainly it was not the first time Moscow had changed the ground rules—by giving up the pan-European conference—at an interparty meeting at the last minute.

Unlike the 1957 Moscow meeting, this time the ploy did not work. Brezhnev might well have considered that a weakly worded document presented to the congress would be more damaging than none at all.[12] He was faced with unintended repercussions. Although the Soviet leaders may have expected Tito and the leader of the French Communist party (PCF), George Marchais, to stay home, it is less likely that Brezhnev anticipated the behavior of the head of the Italian Communist party (PCI), Enrico Berlinguer, who did attend.

For the first time, a Soviet party congress became a platform for an alternative to Soviet socialism. The PCI leader put forward the Eurocommunism package of independence, autonomy, and equality of all parties. He went further to inform the congress of the Italian party's support for religious, cultural, and intellectual freedom in the context of a pluralistic, democratic socialist society. The ghost of the Prague Spring echoed in Berlinguer's message to the Soviet congress delegates.

Thus, rather than repudiate either the Italian party or its leader, the Soviets returned to the pan-European conference route with a sudden urgency in the summer of 1976. This signaled what appears to have been another shift in a submerged policy struggle between those in the Kremlin who agreed with the Soviet ideologist Mikhail Suslov that West European Communist regionalism amounted to "right opportunism"[13] and the somewhat more flexible view identified with the CPSU secretary in charge of relations with nonruling Communist parties, Boris Ponomarev.[14] The result was hardly encouraging from a Soviet perspective.

Soviet leaders may have taken some consolation from the fact that the conference, attended by twenty-nine European Communist parties (only the Albanian and Icelandic parties stayed home), endorsed the main lines of Soviet foreign policy. Nevertheless, on balance the gathering was a procedural victory for the Eurocommunists. The preferred Soviet ideological basis for interparty relations—proletarian internationalism, the general party line, the dictatorship of the proletariat—received no mention. It was replaced by emphasis on "voluntary cooperation" rooted in the principles of equality, sovereignty, noninterference in internal affairs, and respect for different roads to socialism.[15] In short, the Romanian-Yugoslav formula became the public platform of European Communism, East and West. Collaboration between Communist and socialist or social democratic parties was welcomed. To Yugoslav delight, the movement of nonaligned countries was characterized as "one of the most important factors in world politics."

The meeting made no mention of Soviet moral or political leadership. It encouraged dialogue with non-Communist progressives and praised nonalignment as a significant force in world politics. Soviet attempts to get even minimal acceptance of common strategy or commitment to common ideology failed. Organizationally, Tito had insisted that this be a meeting with "no past and no future." The Italian and Spanish party leaders took the occasion to reaffirm their Eurocommunist stance and announced that they would not come to such a meeting again.

The 1976 conference of European parties became a watershed in European Communist politics. Although by agreement the East Germans had to publish complete texts of all speeches, the Soviet Union and the more orthodox East European countries omitted whatever they disagreed with in their accounts of the meeting. All references to ideological differences disappeared. Indeed, if one relied on Soviet sources there would be an impression that proletarian internationalism and the dictatorship of the proletariat had survived the conference intact. The Yugoslavs polemicized against these distortions, while the West European parties largely ignored them.

By the end of the summer of 1976, charges and countercharges centered first on the anniversary of the invasion of Czechoslovakia and subsequently on the nature and meaning of Eurocommunism. Within this context Soviet-Yugoslav relations again deteriorated. Whether or not Brezhnev pressed for a Soviet naval base in Yugoslavia and Yugoslav participation in the Warsaw Pact as rumored, his visit to Belgrade did not improve matters. Nor did the December article by Bulgarian leader Todor Zhivkov in *Problems of Peace and Socialism*, which denounced Eurocommunism as "subversion aimed against proletarian internationalism" and as "anti-Sovietism."[16]

The Zhivkov article set off a new round of polemics in which the Hungarians, who had treated the issue of Eurocommunism gingerly, were drawn into the discussion. Kadar, the Hungarian leader, happened to be in Vienna at the time. When asked by an Italian journalist if he considered Eurocommunism "anti-Sovietism," he indicated that he did not. Then in January, Kadar wrote a carefully worded article dealing with Hungarian socialism that combined support for the "leading role of the party" with the view that socialism can be built in a multiparty system as well as a one-party system.[17] One-party systems had a particular responsibility, according to the Hungarian leader, to recognize and reconcile "the existence of various group and individual interests," and to ensure such interests are given "proper consideration." With this cautious endorsement of socialist pluralism, a tentative Eurocommunist line-up in Eastern Europe put the Yugoslavs[18] and Romanians in a leading role, the Hungarians as supporters of substance intent on staying out of the limelight, and the Czechoslovak, Bulgarian, and East German parties flatly opposed to a situation they feared could potentially undermine East European domestic stability.

The Poles, due to their complex domestic scene, waffled. Yet with the rise of the workers' opposition, which led to the fall of Gomulka in December 1970 and severely shook the Gierek regime in June 1976,[19] Poland provides a potentially destabilizing alternative to the Soviet model in Eastern Europe.

At a minimum, Polish domestic developments have made the Soviets more sensitive to workers' complaints within the USSR. (Worker protest in the Soviet Union in the form of complaints centering on working conditions, injury rates, exploitive production norms, and trade union indifference have become increasingly insistent. In December 1977, some seventy workers from all over the country addressed an open letter to the Supreme Soviet asserting that they were "a vast army of Soviet unemployed, thrown out of the gates of Soviet enterprises" for attempting to improve their situation. Copies of the letter were sent to foreign correspondents. Official awareness of the need for reform is evident in Central Committee member Alexei I. Shibayev's address to the December session of the Supreme Soviet stressing that the economic plan for 1978 must cover industrial safety.)[20] Polish domestic instability has also led the USSR to maintain a preventive policy by supplying continued high-level economic aid to prop up the Polish regime. How Soviet leaders view the cost of further destabilization and working-class demands in Poland also acts to limit Soviet options in the rest of Eastern Europe.

In addition, the workers' opposition in Poland is symbiotically tied to Eurocommunism. Poland epitomizes the national, autonomist component of the Eurocommunist phenomenon. Polish internal solutions are carefully watched by West European Communists, who offer more than moral support to Polish intellectuals rallying to the cause of the workers. West European Communists are allies, a potential source of funds, and a point of access to world media for drawing attention to regime repression and thus making such repression more costly.

At the same time, Poland underscores the dilemma of East Europeans engaging in Eurocommunist coalition politics. Publication of the June 1976 Berlin conference speeches gave Marxist legitimization to Soviet and East European dissidents. The reinforcing nature of Eurocommunism and such dissident activity reemerged in 1977 in the context of preparations for the Belgrade Conference to discuss Basket Three of the 1975 Helsinki Agreement and President Carter's declaration on human rights. Dissidents are further encouraged by West European parties who publicly deplore the repressive nature of USSR response to Bukovsky; Bierman's forced exile from East Germany; the sentences given Polish workers; and Czechoslovak harassment of the signers of "Charter '77," a manifesto calling for the civil rights guaranteed by the Helsinki Agreement.

The issue of human rights is the dividing line between East and West

Eurocommunist proponents. Alliance with domestic dissidents in another country is a delicate business for any ruling Communist party. The Gierek regime did shrink from ordering Polish soldiers to shoot Polish workers, did favor a Polish cultural renaissance, accepted the necessity of hosting the Polish pope, and tolerated a deeply religious component in the Polish road to socialism. Nonetheless, Gierek's survival depended on containing the workers' opposition. Given its track record in dealing with rising nationalism in the 1970s, the Yugoslav government is not particularly interested in seeking out human rights violations on the part of its neighbors, whereas the Romanians conceive of autonomy as justification for their own hard-line policies at home.

So far the explosiveness of the human rights issue has been subordinated to a united front against Soviet pressure tactics on the international ideological level.[21] However, the options of East and West European Communist parties are tied to very different domestic imperatives, a reality perhaps best understood by examining the impact of the politics of energy on Eastern Europe's place in the Communist world.

Energy Politics in Eastern Europe

Economic relations between the Soviet Union and Eastern Europe are institutionalized in CMEA, established in 1949 as Moscow's answer to the Marshall Plan. Throughout Stalin's lifetime the dynamics of those relationships operated much like a one-way street. Raw materials, machinery, and entire plants went from Eastern Europe to the Soviet Union. The uncompensated flow of resources from Eastern Europe to the USSR before Stalin's death in 1953 was about 14 billion dollars, roughly equal to U.S. aid to Western Europe under the Marshall Plan.[22]

By the 1960s, economic traffic between Eastern Europe and the Soviet Union had become a two-way affair. The Soviet Union supplied raw materials, energy, machinery, equipment, and turnkey plants. In return, CMEA partners sent machinery, equipment, and industrial consumer goods; the quality of these consumer goods has led to Soviet complaints and observations by Westerners that the Soviet Union has become a dumping ground for substandard consumer goods exports from Eastern Europe. Western economists dispute the issue of gains and losses in CMEA trade for the 1960s. Nonetheless, two major studies independently concluded that it was costing the Soviets more labor, capital, and natural resources to import CMEA goods than it would have cost for them to produce those goods at home.[23]

Thus, there is reason to believe that the Cold War relationship of reparation-type deliveries from Eastern Europe to the service of Soviet reconstruction was replaced by mutual exchange increasingly to Soviet disadvantage. This situation took on new and complicated dimensions with the Soviet declining rate of growth and domestic economic pressures, factors that were exacerbated by the bad harvests of 1972 and 1975 that required huge unplanned grain purchases abroad. Moreover, economic normalization, hoped for as a component of détente, raised the tempting possibility of Western hard-currency markets for Soviet raw materials and of prospects for better-quality consumer merchandise. In short, in terms of opportunity cost, Eastern Europe was becoming a perceived economic liability to Moscow.

The energy crunch that sent world prices of oil skyrocketing after the Yom Kippur War in 1973 further complicated matters. In 1970 CMEA agreements specified that the Soviets would provide Eastern Europe with increasing quantities of raw materials and energy at fixed world-market prices (the average prices of 1966–1970). To do so meant the Soviets were visibly losing money; not to do so or to demand sudden compensating adjustments would jeopardize East European standards of living, potentially destabilizing East European regimes.

Even before 1975, the Soviets had tried to cut their losses by pressuring East European countries to invest in developing new energy and raw material sources within the Soviet Union. There was considerable foot-dragging, but by 1974, when the seriousness of the energy predicament could not be ignored, a significant number of such investment agreements were signed, even some with Romanian participation. Then in 1975, the Soviets reneged on the 1970 flat-rate agreements and insisted on changing the rules of the game.

The Hungarians were the first to be hit, with an oil price hike 2.3 times 1974 CMEA prices. Based on an average of 1972–1974 prices, the new cost per metric ton was about one-half the world market price at the end of 1974, which, given the slight decline in world prices in 1975, meant that Budapest had to pay roughly two-thirds what it would have cost to import oil from the Middle East. The resulting Hungarian deficit was to be financed by applying the 1974 trade surplus to the debt and by a series of ten-year Soviet loans at low interest rates.[24]

Nor was this an idiosyncratic move. Agreements on 1975 oil prices with other CMEA countries were also based on the 1972–1974 average. Furthermore, the method of CMEA price determination was restructured. The standard fixed-price system was replaced by a moving average price base in which each year's price was to be calculated on the average world-market price for the preceding five years.

To what extent the Soviets were as cooperative on the matter of deficit financing in terms of other CMEA partners as they were with Hungary is unknown. Obviously, the impact of the new prices varied depending on the degree to which an East European country was locked into using large amounts of Soviet oil.

Eastern Europe is not blessed with large energy resources. Romania does have significant oil reserves, although not enough to be self-sufficient in the foreseeable future. Poland has coal. All the other CMEA states are energy deficient, with the Soviet Union providing 95 percent of their oil needs. To aggravate the matter, energy consumption in Eastern Europe has grown even faster than in Western Europe. Even with the best of will, it is questionable whether the Soviets could supply an East European yearly estimated demand of 170 tons by 1980.[25] In such circumstances, it is not surprising that Moscow is pushing its East European allies to start looking elsewhere for energy sources. Problems in transporting Middle Eastern oil to Eastern Europe have been a major stumbling block. Yet, if the planned Adriatica pipeline materializes, large supplies of Middle Eastern oil will be available to Hungary and Czechoslovakia via Yugoslavia. There is a possibility of Libya and Kuwait helping with the financing, and Hungary is already making plans to buy more oil from Iraq and Libya when the pipeline opens. All of which makes the "after Tito" question even more vital to policymakers sitting in Budapest, Prague, or, for that matter, in Moscow.

The political significance of these economic facts of life is anything but a matter of straightforward correlations. Turning economic dependence into political advantage on other fronts is a delicate business. At each step along the way political and economic trade-offs must be weighed in an environment of shifting priorities.

It is undoubtedly true that the Soviet Union has been able to gain some support for its socialist integration schemes from CMEA due either to the economic plight of various East European regimes after the 1975 price increase or perhaps to East European calculations concerning the potential costs of noncompliance. Whether Moscow's increased economic power can be translated into political clout in other areas remains to be seen. The dilemma of being a superpower in the modern world is that of turning power into desired policy outcomes, of actually implementing influence in such a way as to make things happen in a world where client states in both the East and West have become increasingly sophisticated, evasive, and skilled at sliding out from under. This is the crux of Eastern Europe's relations with world Communism in the 1980s. And now we come to one of the most compelling questions, a crucial variable for determining political options in the Communist world: After Tito—what?

The Yugoslav Experiment

Yugoslavia presents a peculiar conceptual problem: In analyzing the impact of post-Tito Yugoslavia on Eastern Europe, one is dealing with a problem that to some extent defies Western-style categorization. For Yugoslavia both is and is not a part of Eastern Europe. (For example, the State Department has separate East European and Yugoslav desks, and at a conference on East European stability and change at Airlie House in 1975, I was told it was relevant to discuss the consequences of Brezhnev's succession but not Tito's.)

For our purposes, we will accept that thirty years of experimenting with self-managing socialism has produced a distinct Yugoslav alternative within the Communist subsystem. Yugoslavia is separated ideologically as well as politically from other East European Communist states. The League of Communists of Yugoslavia (LCY) is unique among ruling Communist parties in that it has given up its monopoly on political life, if not party organization, to permit political conflict in the form of self-managing institutions with varying degrees of autonomy. The survival of Tito despite Stalin's mini–cold war against him and the gradual, if grudging, Soviet acceptance of a nonaligned Yugoslavia have influenced both domestic politics and foreign policy options of other East European Communist decisionmakers.

The impact of the transition to post-Tito Yugoslavia produces a cluster of questions: Can Titoism survive without Tito? Or more academically, is the Yugoslav experiment sufficiently institutionalized to function without Tito's personal charismatic authority? On the one hand, this is a question of the viability of the complex succession mechanism; on the other, a question of popular political will. Did the multiethnic peoples of Yugoslavia actually support the concept of nonaligned, self-managing socialism or were they swept forward by the personality cult of the godfather of Yugoslav Communism? Can these peoples submerge historic national and ethnic hatreds to work together or will they be torn apart by political separatism?[26] In short, what are the chances that domestic dysfunction and Soviet pressure will sweep Yugoslavia back onto a more orthodox road to socialism? Or, to put it differently, can post-Tito Yugoslavia remain a member in good standing of both the Communist and the nonaligned worlds?

Ever since Brezhnev denounced the Brezhnev Doctrine as a "Western fabrication" in Belgrade in 1971,[27] the public Soviet line has been a formal commitment to noninterference in Yugoslav internal affairs. This was reaffirmed during the Soviet leader's 1976[28] trip to Yugoslavia, again when Tito visited Moscow in 1979,[29] and when Brezhnev went to Tito's funeral in May 1980.

Moscow tolerates the current version of Yugoslav nonaligned self-management. Time and historical acceptance have won accommodation. Should it appear that the wheel of history was about to tear Yugoslavia from even this deviant path of socialism, that would be another matter. However, even then, to send Soviet troops into Yugoslavia would be a high-risk venture. This brings us to some basic cost calculations that face the Soviets in attempting to exploit options in post-Tito Yugoslavia. Even if there are doubts among Soviet leaders as to the extent of commitment involved in the concern expressed by President Carter for Yugoslavia's territorial integrity during his June 1980 visit to Belgrade, the possibility that a military move against Yugoslavia might rapidly escalate into an East-West confrontation cannot be dismissed. The 270,000-man Yugoslav army, supplemented by territorial defense units totaling one million Yugoslavs, is an even more persuasive deterrent.[30] The Yugoslav record during World War II is unambiguous. To invade Yugoslavia would be costly, to conquer and occupy the country even more expensive and difficult. Afghanistan may not be the Soviet Union's Vietnam; there is every reason to think that Yugoslavia would be.

Consequently, Soviet military intervention in post-Tito Yugoslavia is unlikely, short of a crisis in which Yugoslavia is thrown into civil war and a Yugoslav splinter group asks Soviet assistance in the name of preserving Yugoslav socialism. Such a scenario has an air of unreality. Civil war would explode, if at all, over the issue of Croatian separatism and independence, but the LCY and the Yugoslav army have both socialist credentials and vastly superior military forces over the Croats. The winning side does not usually ask for outside help. Also, the possibility of Soviet troops aiding "socialist" Croatia against the Yugoslav federal government would have potentially inflammable domestic implications for the multinational Soviet Union.

It is much more plausible that Moscow would scrupulously observe its official hands-off policy during the transition period and attempt to develop a more viable pro-Soviet faction within Yugoslavia's new collective leadership than the out-dated, often persecuted Cominformists. The success of such a policy would depend on persuasion rather than force, a lack of cohesion within the post-Tito leadership, and what the Soviets were willing to offer.

All of which brings us back to the question of the viability of Yugoslavia's current collective leadership. Soviet options or restraints are much more a function of Yugoslav domestic development than of Soviet goals or Western commitments to maintaining a united, nonaligned Yugoslavia. The new system is complex, poorly understood, and dismissed as unworkable by those who considered Tito the linchpin holding together an inherently unstable grouping of hostile nationalities.

Yet, political outcomes depend on institutions as well as personalities. And perhaps the least understood aspect of Yugoslav politics has been the constant organizational experimentation with the role of the Communist party itself. Ever since the historic Sixth Party Congress in 1952, the LCY has struggled to sort out the party's relationships, first to the new political forces known as the self-managing institutions, and second, to its own regional branches, the republic and provincial party organizations.

The result of what is frequently referred to as the "republicanization" of the LCY has been a lopsided pattern of political institutionalization in which the regional party organizations were stronger than the central organization. The temporary reversal, which is probably better called a flirtation than a return to Leninism,[31] of the early 1970s did not survive the reorganization of party bodies that took place at the June 1978 Eleventh Party Congress. This congress put in place the current collective leadership and a complex power-sharing arrangement among nine organizational political actors—the six republic party organizations, the two party organizations representing the autonomous provinces, and the party organization in the Yugoslav People's Army (JNA).

At the highest level, the twelve-member former Executive Committee was dropped. The Party Presidium was cut back to twenty-four members—three from each republic, two from each autonomous province, and one representing the party organization in the army, plus Tito. A secretariat was created with executive secretaries representing each republic, province, and army party organization. The Central Committee was also tied to proportional representation: twenty from each republic, fifteen from each autonomous province, and fifteen from the army.

In this fashion, the center of the party has been firmly tied to its regional bases, with the possibility of playing a positive role as a mediating and integrating institution. Such a method of party organization is one in which there can be a realistic expectation that the multinational peoples of Yugoslavia will feel that they can get a fair deal when it comes to resolving their differences. It is an attempt to channel and contain national and ethnic conflict and potential regional bureaucratic power struggles by allowing the LCY itself to operate as a legitimate arena of conflict resolution.

Moreover, the Eleventh Party Congress further institutionalized the political mission of the Yugoslav military implied in Tito's blunt statement in 1971 that it was the duty of the army to defend the Yugoslav revolution not only at its borders but internally as well.[32] Although at the time this was taken as a warning that the JNA would move militarily against any nationalist uprising, subsequent emphasis has been on the political dimension. In 1974 the number of high-ranking officers in top party posts increased significantly. Active army General Franjo Herljevic became head of the civilian security apparatus, the UDBA. The new public prosecutor was an army general. Military men made up 10 percent of the Central Committee, and the new constitution formalized the role of military delegations in the legislative process. This trend was reaffirmed and expanded at the 1978 party congress.

Currently, Defense Minister Nikola Ljubicic sits on the new LCY Presidium. There are twenty-three generals (14 percent) in the Central Committee, fifteen generals as delegates of the party organization in the JNA, and others, including General Herljevic, who were elected to the Yugoslav National Assembly to represent their republic or province party organizations. Nor is this the full measure of military influence. In June 1979, Tito appointed General Ivan Dolnicar as secretary-general of the collective State Presidency. One of the nine party executive secretaries is an army general. Six generals sit on the National Defense Council that advises the State Presidency. Internal security head Herljevic and Defense Minister Ljubicic are members of the Federal Council for Protection of Constitutional Order. A general serves as president of the Council for Civil Defense; another, not himself a member of the Presidium, is chairman of the Party Presidium's Commission for Nationwide Defense. In the spring of 1979, army Colonel Veljko Mladinovic became editor-in-chief of the party theoretical journal, *Komunist.*

In sum, Western speculation that the army might take over in post-Tito Yugoslavia in the sense of replacing the Communist party is a misunderstanding of Yugoslav party-army relations. Throughout the 1970s, penetration of the top party-army-security apparatus took place to the extent, as I have argued elsewhere,[33] that there is a strong possibility that the army will operate as the vanguard of the party, at least during the transitional period. There is precedent for such a situation.[34] Nor does it imply that the army would operate against the wishes of civilian party leaders. For the most part, both the civilian and military men at the top of the party during the transition period belong to the "club of 1941," those who joined the party during the partisan struggle against German occupation and who have provided an enduring infrastructure ever since. At the same time, the explicit power-sharing arrangement guaranteeing the republics and provinces access to top party bodies operates as an assurance that, by dealing the military in, other political actors are not being squeezed out. Indeed, one might tentatively say that the present arrangement increased the actual political influence of the military, while limiting its potential influence, by establishing a formula of regional proportional representation.

Undoubtedly the solution of 1978 could change at the next LCY party congress scheduled for 1982. Nonetheless, it is Yugoslav reality for the moment—the reality that Soviet and East European foreign policy alike must respond to.

Tentative Conclusions

Reports that Eurocommunism as a political force collapsed with the defection of the PCF in support of the Soviet invasion of Afghanistan are premature. Rather the impact of Moscow's resort to force to prop up an unpopular Soviet puppet in Kabul added momentum to a process already evident in Eurocommunism in the 1970s, i.e., boundary disintegration of the Communist world in which socialist, nonaligned, and other non-Communist allies became increasingly important to autonomist parties in Western and Eastern Europe alike. Note that the PCI condemnation of Soviet "imperialism" was combined with a move to initiate a "Euroleft" dialogue with French socialist and German social democratic parties, and that Romania and Yugoslavia both boycotted the Soviet-sponsored April 1980 meeting of European Communist parties in Paris.[35]

The last years of the 1970s saw the Soviets moderating their insistence that Eurocommunism represented imperialist maneuvers to undermine the Communist movement in both Western and Eastern Europe. The shift was in the direction of gradual conciliation, which culminated with Berlinguer's visits to Paris, Moscow, and Belgrade in October 1978. The Afghanistan adventure has severely strained this emerging, if limited, rapprochement. Italian, Spanish, British, Swedish, and Japanese parties have all criticized the Soviet occupation. The simultaneous hard line toward domestic dissent shown by the January 1980 exile of Soviet dissident Andrei Sakharov from Moscow can be expected to create still further tensions.

As for Eastern Europe, the Romanians abstained in the United Nations vote condemning the Soviet invasion of Afghanistan and have cautiously demonstrated their dismay. Hungary and Poland came forward with reluctant, highly qualified support while reportedly letting the Soviets know privately that they see the invasion as "a serious and damaging mistake."[36] For our purposes, the importance of this discrete East European distancing from Moscow is the extent to which such behavior demonstrates the increasing concern of the East European leaders with protecting their economic and political relations with the West, i.e., protecting indigenous national interests even when Soviet policy priorities are involved. In this sense, despite formal East European support, the invasion of Afghanistan has expanded autonomist (i.e., Eurocommunist) tendencies in Eastern Europe.

Moreover, whatever Soviet intentions are toward post-Tito Yugoslavia, they will be more difficult to carry out in the current climate. Yugoslavia voted to condemn the Afghanistan invasion in the United Nations and has kept up steady polemics against what it considers a violation of the territorial integrity and interference in the internal affairs of nonaligned Afghanistan. These verbal attacks have been combined with intensified security precautions that make effective exploitation of the post-Tito transition even less likely.

The role of the Yugoslav military as a stabilizing factor is undoubtedly a mixed blessing from the Soviet viewpoint. On the one hand, there are certain ideological advantages. Despite pledges of dedication to Yugoslavia's self-managing socialist system, the military itself is the one all-Yugoslav institution with little experience in self-management. Yugoslavia does not have a self-managing army, nor have army officers had to operate within enterprise workers' councils, as have so many party members. In addition, we may assume that military leaders in Communist and non-Communist countries alike give high priority to domestic tranquility, dislike opposition and criticism, may even be suspicious of in-system dissent, and prefer administrative decisionmaking to uninhibited discussion. Whether or not they are correct, the Soviets have some reason to suppose that military influence at the highest level of the LCY will tilt the party toward centralism and away from Kardelj's theme of the pluralism of self-managing interests, which dominated the 1978 congress. Undoubtedly, an increasing centralized party dedicated to reestablishing its "leading role" would narrow the ideological distance between Moscow and Belgrade.

From the strategic perspective, however, the army as the vanguard of the party can only intensify Yugoslav commitment to national independence, of which nonalignment is a crucial component, thus making even more unlikely the Soviet goal of bringing Yugoslavia into the Warsaw Pact.[37]

An ambiguous "affiliate" status similar to the Yugoslav relationship with the CMEA might become a negotiating point. Yet to move seriously in that direction risks not only unpredictable Western reaction, but demands that the Soviets abandon their consistent support of the Bulgarians in the long-standing Yugoslav-Bulgarian conflict over Macedonia. Nor could the Soviets be certain what such a move would mean vis-à-vis Romanian maneuvering within the Warsaw Treaty Organization. At a minimum it could be expected to legitimize Bucharest's claim that the Warsaw Pact does not prevent a nonaligned foreign policy,[38] which could hardly add up to a policy benefit for Moscow.

But to return to the impact of Soviet troops in Afghanistan on East European relations with the Communist world, the invasion intensified the need of both Yugoslavia and Romania to cultivate Chinese contacts in order to counter Soviet pressure. Chinese interest in Yugoslav self-management, evident since Hua's visit in August 1978, can be expected to flourish and Chinese, Yugoslav, and Romanian foreign policy lines to dovetail.

Let us consider the following:

1. The rules of the game in inter-Communist relations are substantially those of the autonomist parties East and West, despite Soviet objections. After the Berlin conference of 1976, there was some evidence that Moscow might be abandoning its faith in the advantages of multilateral conferences to reestablish Soviet influence. Now even the cautious bilateral gains may have been jeopardized.

2. Despite the ability to get grudging East European support for the Afghanistan occupation, Soviet ability to control political developments in Eastern Europe has become ever more expensive. Soviet energy resources are expected to peak in 1980. Moscow is already telling the East Europeans to look elsewhere for oil and insisting that they contribute to developing internal Soviet energy industries with hard currency. Throughout the 1980s this will result in declining control, in which the Soviet–East European relationship will be further complicated by Soviet pressure on these regimes to pay a Moscow-defined percentage of the bill for Vietnamese economic development via CMEA.

During the inevitable Soviet succession crisis of the 1980s, the temptation on the part of would-be successors to Brezhnev to seek allies in Eastern Europe will become a factor. How the power struggle in Moscow affects Eastern Europe's relationship to world Communism depends on a complex of unknowns—including the outcome of U.S. elections in November 1980. But that the power struggle will be a determining variable is certain.

In short, in my view, in the 1980s the Soviets confront a potentially deteriorating situation in Eastern Europe as well as in other sections of the Communist subsystem, in which their attempt to precipitously expand the membership of the Communist world will in the long run increase Eastern Europe's political options and weaken Moscow's ability to contain, never mind control, the situation.

Notes

1. George Modelski, *The Communist International System*, Princeton University, Center for International Studies Monograph (Princeton, 1960), p. 45.

2. For a useful recent analysis see Harry Gelman, "Outlook for Sino-Soviet Relations," *Problems of Communism* 28 (September-December 1979):50-66

3. Alfred G. Meyer, "The Comparative Study of Communist Political Systems," in Frederic J. Fleron, Jr., ed., *Communist States and the Social Sciences* (Chicago: Rand McNally, 1969), p. 194.

4. This is not to take issue with William Griffith's hypothesis that Eurocommunist diplomacy is best studied on a nation-state basis for a detailed understanding of the process. It is certainly true that the international impetus of Eurocommunism cannot be separate from its domestic manifestations. For our purposes, however, the world Communist dimension, i.e., interparty alliances challenging Soviet hegemony, is more salient. See William E. Griffith, "The Diplomacy of Eurocommunism," in Rudolf Tökés, ed., *Eurocommunism and Détente* (New York: New York University Press for the Council on Foreign Relations, 1978).

5. Zbigniew K. Brzezinski, *The Soviet Bloc: Unity and Conflict*, 4th ed. rev. (Cambridge, Mass.: Harvard University Press, 1971), p. 21.

6. The Yugoslavs have pointedly called attention to the applicability of nonaligned concepts to current interparty relations. See, for example, the commentary of Zeljko Brihta, foreign policy editor of the Zagreb paper, *Vjesnik*, December 17, 1977. For an analysis, see Slobodan Stankovic, "Yugoslavs Suggest 'Eurocommunism' Should be Called 'Nonaligned Communism'," *Radio Free Europe Background Report*, December 21, 1977.

7. "Statement on the Stand of the Rumanian Workers' Party Concerning the Problems of the International Communist and Working-Class Movement," adopted April 1964; complete text in William E. Griffith, ed., *Sino-Soviet Relations, 1964-1965* (Cambridge, Mass.: MIT Press, 1967), pp. 269-296.

8. Kevin Devlin, "The Interparty Drama," *Problems of Communism* 24 (July-August 1975):18-35.

9. See Joan Barth Urban, "Contemporary Soviet Perspectives on Revolution in the West," *Orbis* (Winter 1976):1359-1402.

10. For a more detailed analysis, see Kevin Devlin, "The Challenge of Eurocommunism," *Problems of Communism* 26 (January-February 1977):1-20.

11. Radovan Vukadinovic, "Small States and the Policy of Nonalignment," in August Schou and Arne Olv Brundtland, eds., *Small States in International Relations* (New York: John Wiley and Sons, 1971), pp. 99-114. Also Vlado Benko, "Deconcentration of Power in the International Community and the Position of Small and Medium Sized States," in Ljubivoje Acimovic, ed., *Nonalignment in the World Today*, International Symposium, January 16-18, 1969 (Belgrade: Institute of International Politics and Economics, 1969), pp. 131-152.

12. The Soviet leader's passing reference to the role of regional party meetings

in his report to the CPSU Central Committee put such gatherings firmly in the context of the long-delayed Soviet goal of a world Communist conference; *Pravda*, February 25, 1976.

13. *Washington Post*, March 18, 1976.

14. For a provocative analysis, see Joan Barth Urban, "The Impact of Eurocommunism on the Socialist Community," in Andrew Gyorgy and James Kuhlman, eds., *Innovation in Communist Systems* (Boulder, Co.: Westview Press, 1978), pp. 115–140.

15. *New Times* 28 (July 1976):17–32.

16. Todor Zhivkov, "A Year of Peace, A Year of Struggle," *Problems of Peace and Socialism*, December 1976.

17. Janos Kadar, "On Several Hungarian Experiences in Building Socialism," *Problems of Peace and Socialism*, January 1977. Analysis C.A. "The Hungarian Party's Cautious Interest in Eurocommunism," *Radio Free Europe Background Report*, January 26, 1977.

18. Aleksandar Grlickov, head of the LCY International Department, came out with the most authoritative statement to date distinguishing between national and international interests; See *Borba*, February 22–28, 1977.

19. For an excellent, detailed analysis of these events and their implications see Thomas E. Heneghan, "One Year After the Polish Price Protests," *Radio Free Europe Background Report*, no. 132, June 1977.

20. For a good journalistic analysis see Paul Wohl in the *Christian Science Monitor*, February 2, 1978.

21. Reported to include threats of splits and promises of additional orders for Italian export firms; see Viktor Meier in *Frankfurter Allgemeine*, March 19, 1977.

22. See Paul Marer, "Has Eastern Europe Become a Liability to the Soviet Union? (III) The Economic Aspect," in Charles Gati, ed., *The International Politics of Eastern Europe* (New York: Praeger, 1976), pp. 56–80.

23. *Ibid*, pp. 68–69.

24. *Nepszabadsag*, February 23, 1975.

25. Arthur Jay Klinghoffer, *The Soviet Union and International Oil Politics* (New York: Columbia University Press, 1977), p. 186. For a recent analysis see *Christian Science Monitor*, February 21, 1980.

26. As illustrated by the one-half page ad of the Croatian National Congress dedicated to the proposition that Yugoslavia will not survive Tito's death; *New York Times*, March 14, 1980. For an analysis, see *ibid.*, March 23, 1980.

27. *Borba*, September 22, 1971.

28. *Pravda*, November 16, 1976. At the time Brezhnev explicitly scoffed at "fairytales" depicting Yugoslavia as "Little Red Ridinghood" and the Soviet Union as a "rapacious wolf."

29. *Pravda*, May 19, 1979. The language is considerably more ambiguous than during the earlier Brezhnev visit to Yugoslavia, however.

30. A good collection of Yugoslav explanations of this concept can be found in Olga Mladenovic, ed., *Opstenarodna Odbrana Jugoslavije*, translated into English under the title, *The Yugoslav Concept of General Peoples' Defense*

(Belgrade: Medjunarodna Politika, 1970). For a Western analysis, see A. Ross Johnson, "Yugoslav Total National Defense," *Survival* 15 (March-April 1973):54–58.

31. Note the dialogue between A. Ross Johnson and William Zimmerman, "Is Yugoslavia Leninist?" *Studies in Comparative Communism* (Winter 1977):403–411.

32. *Borba*, December 23, 1971.

33. Robin Alison Remington, "Armed Forces and Society in Yugoslavia," in Catherine McArdle Kelleher, ed., *Political-Military Systems: Comparative Perspectives* (Beverly Hills: Sage Publications, 1974), pp. 163–190.

34. By the spring of 1956, for example, Communists in the armed forces were ordered to take a more active part in local government, the Socialist Alliance, and other sociopolitical organizations to help combat "stagnation" in the party. *Borba*, March 14–15, 1956; for an analysis, see George W. Haffman and Fred W. Neal, *Yugoslavia and the New Communism* (New York: Twentieth Century Fund, 1962), p. 200.

35. Elizabeth Pond, in the *Christian Science Monitor*, April 30, 1980.

36. Eric Bourne, in the *Christian Science Monitor*, June 4, 1980.

37. This interpretation is supported by George Klein's persuasive institutional argument. To bring the Yugoslav army into the Warsaw Pact would most likely lead to major purges of the officer corps and might well appear undesirable to even pro-Soviet sympathizers in the Yugoslav armed forces. See George Klein, "Soviet Foreign Policy Options in the Contemporary Balkans," in Phillip A. Petersen, ed., *Soviet Foreign Policy in the Post-Tito Balkans*, Studies in Communist Affairs, vol. 4 (U.S. Government Printing Office, 1979), p. 146. Klein also correctly makes the point that, centralizing preferences of the internal security apparatus notwithstanding, the UDBA (the Yugoslav secret police) would be inhibited in moving closer to the Soviets by that organization's diligence in arresting Cominformists throughout the 1970s.

38. Ever since April 1975 when the Romanians sought Yugoslav support for their request for observer status at the nonaligned summit scheduled for 1976 in Sri Lanka, Bucharest has attempted to establish institutional links with the nonaligned movement—what Ceauşescu called "de jure recognition of existing reality . . . of Romania's relations with nonaligned countries." See the Romanian leader's press conference in *Le Monde*, July 25, 1975.

Selected Bibliography

Aspaturian, V. V., Valenta, Jiri, and Burke, David, eds. *Eurocommunism Between East and West*. Bloomington: Indiana University Press, 1980.

Bromke, Adam, and Strong, John W., eds. *Gierek's Poland*. New York: Praeger, 1973.

Brzezinski, Zbigniew K. *The Soviet Bloc: Unity and Conflict*. 4th ed. rev. Cambridge, Mass.: Harvard University Press, 1971.

Devlin, Kevin. "The Challenge of Eurocommunism." *Problems of Communism* 26 (January-February 1977):1-20.

————. "The Interparty Drama." *Problems of Communism* 24 (July-August 1975):18-35.

Gati, Charles. "The 'Europeanization' of Communism." *Foreign Affairs* (April 1977).

Gati, Charles, ed. *The International Politics of Eastern Europe*. New York: Praeger, 1976.

Gitelman, Zvi Y. *The Diffusion of Political Innovation: From Eastern Europe to the Soviet Union*. A Sage Professional Paper. London and Beverly Hills: Sage Publications, 1972.

Griffith, William E., ed. *Albania and the Sino-Soviet Rift*. Cambridge, Mass.: MIT Press, 1973.

————. "The Diplomacy of Eurocommunism." In Rudolf Tökés, ed., *Eurocommunism and Détente*. New York: New York University Press, for the Council on Foreign Relations, 1978.

Johnson, A. Ross. "Eastern Europe Looks West." Rand Paper Series, P-6032, November 1972.

Klinghoffer, Arthur Jay. *The Soviet Union and International Oil Politics*. New York: Columbia University Press, 1977.

Prifti, Peter R. *Socialist Albania Since 1944: Domestic and Foreign Developments*. Cambridge, Mass.: MIT Press, 1978.

Rakowska-Harmstone, Teresa, and Gyorgy, Andrew. *Communism in Eastern Europe*. Bloomington and London: Indiana University Press, 1979.

Daniel N. Nelson   **7**

Eastern Europe and
the Non-Communist World

Introduction

"The Communist camp," wrote Zbigniew Brzezinski in 1966, "is neither homogeneous, monolithic nor unchanging." Both evolutionary processes and "antagonistic contradictions" were seen by Brzezinski to be engendering a transformation in the Soviet bloc. During the late 1960s and 1970s, disparities between worldwide interests of a dominant power such as the USSR and dependent regimes of Eastern Europe have, as Brzezinski postulated, led occasionally to "open antagonisms and contradictory objectives."

Such blatant divisions between Soviet and East European foreign policies have, however, been rare. Particularly with respect to interactions between Communist states and the non-Communist world, East European regimes continue to behave more like, than different from, their large neighbor. Continued economic and energy dependencies, ideological ties, institutional links such as the Warsaw Pact (WTO) and the Council on Mutual Economic Assistance (CMEA), and the Soviet military presence in most of Eastern Europe are among many factors which restrict in obvious ways the foreign policy latitude of these states.

Arising from such observations, this brief overview of East European relations with the non-Communist world will begin with a broad characterization of East European foreign policies in a section that contrasts the "revolutionary rhetoric" with the "conservative realities" facing these nation-states. Second, relations with NATO countries, nonruling Communist parties, and the Third World (primarily Latin America, Black Africa, the Islamic nations of North Africa and the Middle East, and non-Communist Asia) will be summarized. Finally, I intend to conclude with a segment assessing trends in Eastern Europe's relations with non-Communist states, an effort meant to focus on dynamic elements in those systems' foreign policies likely to be evident through the 1980s.

Revolutionary Rhetoric and Conservative Realities
of East European Foreign Policies

Revolutionary slogans calling for working-class solidarity, anti-imperialist wars of national liberation, and other forms of political change are frequent components of East European rhetoric concerning the non-Communist world. Likewise, it is not uncommon for such words to accompany visits by the leaders of guerilla armies, nationalist front organizations, or newly installed revolutionary governments to the capitals of Eastern Europe. In terms quite typical of East European governments, the highest Communist party organ (the Politburo) in East Germany recently described its foreign policy toward the Third World as follows:

> The national and social liberation revolutions in Africa, Asia and Latin America make a major contribution to further changes in the international balance of forces. The principles of our foreign policy include support for the political and economic independence of the states that have emerged from such revolutions, their struggle against colonial and neo-colonial exploitation, imperialist oppression and attempts at hegemony. We attach special importance to the countries with a socialist orientation and to the formation and growth of revolutionary-democratic and vanguard parties in Africa and Asia, since they are the embodiment of social progress and represent another great victory for scientific socialism.[1]

These ostensibly radical words and ceremonies are, however, ironic symbols—ironic because few governments are more desperate in their efforts to *avoid* any form of political change than the regimes of Eastern Europe. Stated succinctly, the foreign relations of Eastern Europe exhibit the characteristics of small ruling elites trying to protect the political status quo.

An important point of departure in the analysis of East European foreign relations is the "elite" nature of policymaking. The making of foreign policy is, of course, an artifact of a narrow stratum in any political system. But in Communist Europe, it seems fair to say that the nature of national security sought through foreign policies is that which *only* the elites identify, i.e., what the highest echelon of the party views as security, having little to do with public sentiments or group interests. While the latter are parts of the foreign policy environment of Eastern Europe, public opinion or group needs ought not be confused with the immediate behavior of East European governments. That architects of

East European foreign policy exist in an elitist environment is then integral to the policies they produce. Without institutional rivals to the party leadership (e.g., no congress to limit a president's prerogatives), no competitive parties with alternative foreign policies, and no interaction between government and associational groups openly trying to influence relations with other nation-states, one does not exaggerate by saying that Romania's foreign policies are those of Ceauşescu and a few close associates, that Warsaw's interactions with the non-Communist world reflect the perceptions of Polish security as seen by the troubled leadership of Gierek, etc.

As with the Soviet system, the elite character of policymaking does not mean that conflict over policy is excluded. Indeed, when the political future of a regime is in question (perhaps as in the case of Gierek in Poland), conflict may be intensified. Certainly, Ceauşescu's actions in foreign relations are not uniformly supported among members of the Political Executive Committee, given differing perspectives on Romania's domestic needs and how to best use foreign relations in the pursuit of industrial development. Nevertheless, one can assume with confidence that the spectrum of decision makers' views are narrow and the number of people involved very few.

All of this does not suggest that East European leaders are ignorant of, or purposefully overlook, the advantages of public support for governmental policies or the need to assure that foreign policies serve interests of important groups (e.g., that sources for needed foreign technology are secured via diplomacy, or that the military budget satisfies the high command). But authority for the making of decisions regarding relations with non-Communist states is not diffused in Eastern Europe. Although the degree to which decision-making authority is centralized may differ slightly, the kind of process is uniform; a presidium or politburo of the party is the locus for decisions that are then implemented through automatic appropriations by the national assembly when needed and administered by the relevant ministry of state. When expert advice or data are needed for the making of foreign policy decisions, the party's own department of external relations (an equivalent existing in all East European systems) within the secretariat will produce required documents, occasionally via contract research with scholars at the party's academy or other specialized institutes.

For Western observers, recognition of the elitist context in which East European foreign policies are made and the controls placed on inputs into that process should preface any summary of relations with non-Communist states. Simultaneously, however, one must be aware of domestic factors beyond the immediate control of East European leaders that can be very influential on policymaking and the outcomes of such policies. Although other portions of this volume have detailed the domestic political conditions of Eastern Europe, some additional emphasis is germane here.

The link between political currents inside East European states and the foreign policies of those regimes is crucial. No single event made that linkage more clear than the Soviet-led invasion of Czechoslovakia in August 1968. As articulated by the so-called Brezhnev Doctrine, no decision regarding a country's development by its ruling Communist party can be allowed to damage socialism in that country or the "fundamental interests of the other socialist countries nor the worldwide workers' movement. . . . The sovereignty of individual socialist countries cannot be counterposed to the interests of world socialism. . . . "[2] In such blunt language, the Soviets reasserted forcefully their erstwhile de facto position that the USSR's interests would prevail over any socioeconomic or political trends within East European systems. By 1980, it was apparent that Soviet interests in non-WTO states bordering the USSR were included in such a doctrine, as was evident in Afghanistan. Domestic conditions of East European Communist states—at least those within the Warsaw Pact—necessarily are viewed by leaders of those countries as integral to the relations of their regimes with a dominant "ally," the Soviet Union. To the extent that relations with the non-Communist world might exacerbate the potential for domestic conditions viewed negatively by Moscow, foreign policymakers in Eastern Europe must be attuned to socioeconomic and political currents within their own country.

At the core of East European relations with the non-Communist world are the efforts by party elites to avoid ideological nuances or threats of domestic deviation that might provoke Soviet intervention. Not only must policymakers in Eastern Europe live within the bounds of Soviet interests worldwide, but they also must take care that their country's domestic political life fulfills Soviet expectations. Within such an environment, it is unlikely that men will rise to leadership posts for whom "risk taking" comes casually. Neither the elitist character of foreign policy processes nor watchful Soviet eyes is conducive to experimentation. Indeed, we find the foreign policies of East European systems to be defined within implicit norms and, sometimes (e.g., 1956 and 1968), explicit limits imposed by the Soviet military. Careful and cautious, East European party leaders have no choice but to gauge their range of actions on the basis of volatile domestic politics plus an ever-watchful dominant neighbor.

Put in perspective, Western observers must differentiate revolutionary posturing from conservative realities. Most of the East European party leaders not only confront difficult political environments at home, but face clear dependencies on both East and West as well. In short, most regimes of Eastern Europe cannot afford to be in a precarious international position vis-à-vis *anyone*. Remaining outside the Warsaw Pact, Yugoslavia has been able to adopt distinct domestic and international positions because of Tito's indigenous legitimacy as a resistance leader, because the break with Stalin took place before the USSR had recovered from World War II and at a time when U.S. nuclear monopoly still existed, and because Yugoslavia's commitment to fight back was evident. Albania's independent posture during the 1960s and 1970s can be attributed to that country's relative insignificance as an international actor, its now-terminated association with China, and its geographical isolation. Only Romania within the WTO has adopted significantly different policies regarding the non-Communist world, the content of which seem to reflect a cost-benefit analysis which concluded that Romania could ill afford more cautious and conservative behavior. (I will return to the details of such policies below.) But a Ceauşescu "gambit," such as in November 1978 when he left the WTO's Political Consulative Committee meeting in Moscow to announce what had transpired while refusing to cooperate with the alliance's decisions about defense expenditures, could *not* have been undertaken by Gierek, Kadar, Husak, or others. Ceauşescu ought not be credited with "innovative" or "original" foreign policies, but with the recognition that low-risk confrontations with the USSR on matters of foreign relations are mandatory if Romania is to devote its limited resources to socioeconomic development.

What appear as exceptions to the cautious and conservative norm of East European foreign relations, then, can be explained by specific circumstances and requirements. In no way do the three cases mentioned above alter the fundamental foreign policy issue for East European systems, i.e., how to maintain political security, a concern directed not West but East. Although all the revolutionary rhetoric of Eastern Europe would deny this thesis, the absence of any plausible Western military threat (evident not only in the military imbalance of the 1970s but also in the West's commitment to détente notwithstanding Soviet military buildup, human rights violations, or overt invasion of Czechoslovakia) has focused the attention of East Europeans on their role in a Russian view of security.

Being part of the Soviet security system *does* give East European regimes some influence with the USSR, insofar as the cooperation of Eastern Europe is required to implement any Soviet policies regarding NATO. There is some evidence, for example, that Eastern Europe has been able to minimize economic integration under Soviet auspices implicitly in return for unflinching diplomatic and military support. While that trade-off has never been articulated in Moscow or Eastern Europe, events of the past decade and a half suggest such collective and individual capacity to "advance or protect . . . national interests against those of Soviet Union and other bloc countries."[3]

Nevertheless, whenever an East European state interacts with non-Communist systems there will be a nervous glance "over the shoulder" to assess the USSR's reaction. Relations with the non-Communist world are, then, conducted by cautious party elites, aware that their regime's political security continues to rest on the balance between domestic needs and Soviet perceptions.

NATO and Eastern Europe

A Restructuring of Relations

The era when the North Atlantic Treaty Organization could have been a military threat to the security of Communist Eastern Europe has passed. Precisely when such a potential began to recede or when it ceased to be a significant factor in East European relations with NATO members cannot be assessed with precision. Before 1956, European Communist leaders had reason to be suspicious of U.S. intentions for the Atlantic Alliance; John Foster Dulles spoke of containment and liberating Eastern Europe, U.S. arms opposed Communist forces in Korea and Greece while the French fought the first Vietnam War and Britain dealt with Malay guerillas, West Germany was re-armed and included in NATO, and CIA-engineered coups ended governments sympathetic to socialism in places as diverse as Tehran and Guatemala City. While it may not have been the intention of Western policymakers to convey such an aggressive posture, one can see that regimes with little public support would have viewed U.S./NATO actions and statements as threatening.

During the 1980s, however, no East European leader can view NATO as such a malevolent adversary. The WTO is clearly superior in almost every quantitative measure of military equipment and personnel (see Table 1). NATO aggressive action in the 1980s is certainly a scenario as absurd to East Europeans as it has been, for some time, to Western political and military leaders. At a time when aggressors require perhaps a 3:1 advantage in equipment and personnel to counter the edge possessed by the defense—because massing for attack can be detected by satellite and then impaired by nuclear weapons—the Western alliance is almost at that disadvantage vis-à-vis the WTO. Leaders and the informed public of Eastern Europe are well aware of such conditions. The com-

TABLE 1

NATO–WTO FORCE COMPARISONS: NUMBER OF DIVISIONS OR
EQUIVALENT UNITS AND NUMBER OF MAIN BATTLE TANKS

		1970	1972	1974	1976	1978
Number of Divisions	WTO	103	94	100	100	103
	NATO	58	61	63	70	66
Number of Main Battle Tanks	WTO	19,000	21,200	26,500	26,500	27,900
	NATO	7,600	8,100	10,000	11,000	11,300

Source: The Military Balance (London: International Institute of Strategic Studies, various years).

bined experiences of 1956 and 1968 have, moreover, taught Eastern Europe that the NATO states would not jeopardize peace to alter the status quo (i.e., Soviet control) in Eastern Europe.

The mere absence of a NATO-focused threat, however, does not *yield* the "breakup" of the Soviet bloc, the disintegration of the Soviet empire, or other metaphorical processes. While empirical research has suggested that WTO alliance cohesion is related to perceived threat,[4] the negligible military threat of NATO through the late 1960s and 1970s and into the 1980s would not, itself, have sufficed to alter the post–World War II status quo. If WTO cohesion has decreased to any degree over the 1960–1980 period coincident with a decline in perceived NATO threat, any assumption that the latter "caused" the former would be dangerously oversimplistic. Instead, détente required diplomatic initiatives from both NATO and WTO members. These initiatives were not taken on either side by principal alliance partners; moreover, the motivations had as much to do with the political security of nations involved as with any idea of immediate military threat. In addition, the combination of several other domestic and international factors encouraged changes in East-West relations.

For NATO, initiatives came from Willy Brandt as West German foreign minister during the Grand Coalition from 1966–1969 and as Social Democratic party chancellor with a Bundestag majority beginning in 1969. Eastern Europe was led toward rapprochement by Romania when Ceauşescu reestablished diplomatic ties with Bonn in 1967. SPD

Ostpolitik and Romanian ties to Western Europe, it must be remembered, came at a time when the United States was militant in its anti-Communism—in Vietnam and in the Dominican Republic occupation of 1965, to name but two obvious examples. The USSR, likewise, was engaged in a forceful reassertion of its hegemony in Eastern Europe via the Czech invasion and the Brezhnev Doctrine.

In such an international environment, it might have seemed ill-advised for a small state such as Romania to take any kind of initiative that differed from Soviet foreign policy norms. Both the Romanian action of 1967 and similar events in which other East European states participated in the 1960s or early 1970s, however, can be interpreted as "conservative" policy. Accepting rapprochement with Bonn, for example, broke less new ground than one might suspect. Given the Romanian party's April 1964 statement rejecting Soviet plans for East European socioeconomic development that would have minimized Romanian industry, the new (1965) leadership of Nicolae Ceaușescu had no choice but to seek links that would enable his regime to survive. His alternative was not a true alternative, i.e., to witness the gradual application of Soviet economic and diplomatic pressure to force Romania into conformity and dependence on the USSR. Thus the political security of the Romanian regime, and its ability to authoritatively allocate resources within that country, were at stake.

A general reduction in the threatening nature of NATO simultaneous with diplomatic initiatives from West Germany and Romania were two important components of a "restructuring" of NATO–East European relations over the past decade and a half. Other factors played a role in promoting the growth of East European–U.S. or East European–West European contact. The lure of Western consumer goods and technology certainly had some impact on East European elites and masses, albeit an effect we cannot measure. Likewise, the Sino-Soviet conflict cannot be ignored as an impetus for careful divergence from Russian interests. To remain neutral in that struggle was, perhaps, the most noteworthy action that a Soviet bloc state could take as an initial step toward national identity and/or political diversity in the 1960s. The Chinese, for their part, made concerted efforts in the late 1960s through 1970 to gain influence in Eastern Europe, no doubt seeking to dissipate Soviet hegemony in that area. The Chinese differentiated among East European regimes quite studiously, devoting far more diplomatic and propaganda attention to Romania and Poland. For the most part, none of the East European states could welcome Chinese overtures with enthusiasm, although Romania clearly went farthest in that regard. Although there is no clear way to measure the weight of the Sino-Soviet rift in East European relations with the West, it seems entirely accurate to agree with Zbigniew Brzezinski when he notes: "The restoration of the primacy of the interstate relations, and the consequent decline in the relative importance of the formerly paramount party channels were prompted by the disruptive impact of the Sino-Soviet rift on Communist ideology and unity."[5] Had the Sino-Soviet dispute not occurred, it seems unlikely that the East Europeans would have had the opportunity for great contact with the West in the 1960s notwithstanding any desire or rationale to do so.

By the time the USSR, itself, had shifted its policies toward NATO—most notably in mid-1969 as signaled by Gromyko's speech on July 19 of that year to the Supreme Soviet indicating Russian willingness to negotiate on a renunciation-of-force treaty prior to a de jure settlement of Central European boundaries—East European states had moved toward de facto relations with major Western powers such as France and West Germany. Enterprise-level agreements, trade delegations, and permanent commercial missions were all in evidence several years before the Soviet Union's policy decision was announced. Indeed, if one examines East European trade from the mid-1950s through 1967 (when the first embassy-level relations were resumed between an East European state and Bonn), several of the Soviet bloc governments had a quarter of their total foreign trade (or more) with NATO members. Over half of Yugoslavia's trade, of course, was with Western allies during the period 1956–1967.[6]

Once the USSR had sanctioned negotiations with NATO states, however, a second stage of East European–NATO relations began in which formal accords marked an acceleration in East European contacts with the West. Treaties in Moscow and Warsaw during 1970 resolved outstanding disputes such as the Oder-Neisse boundary in Central Europe, while the September 1971 Berlin Accord ended some of the most difficult problems regarding access to the divided city. With these and other legal issues set aside, a broad development in bilateral and multilateral relations commenced involving both economic and diplomatic contacts.

East-West Economic Relations

As suggested above, several of the East European states already were involved in East-West trade to a significant degree prior to diplomatic breakthroughs in the early 1970s, and Yugoslavia was trading principally with the West. Although East Germany (the GDR) did not rank highly in trade with the West, fully 10 percent of the GDR's foreign trade was with West Germany (the German Federal Republic—GFR) alone by the late

1960s, making the GFR a trading partner second only to the USSR. Czechoslovakia, likewise, had a mean of only a sixth of its foreign trade with NATO states before the late 1960s, but again almost 10 percent was devoted to trade with Bonn. Poland and Romania had been, through the 1950s and 1960s, the most active among East European states in concluding trade and commercial agreements with the West, but Bulgaria was not far behind—suggesting, at least, that while trade volume was not high, the Bulgarians sought to expand that trade with non-Communist Europe.[7]

Much of the 1970s witnessed a strenuous effort by Eastern Europe to import technologies and finished products from Western Europe and the United States while acquiring credit for such purchases from the same countries. Diplomatic leverage has often been applied in order to gain economic concessions. The East Germans, for example, used Berlin's vulnerability even after the Four Power Accord of 1971. Offers to deliver electric power to Berlin, improve railroad and auto links, open up new stations for border crossings, and other gestures were the lure for Bonn to extend long-term credits approaching 700 million deutsche marks a year through the 1970s, to enter into cooperative economic ventures such as chemical plants, etc., and to sell equipment and goods ranging from railroad cars and meat-packing machinery to women's clothing. Occasionally, East Europeans have gone to the West not only for consumer and high-technology items, but for foodstuffs as well. Severe droughts in 1976 in the GDR, for example, necessitated a second straight year of major grain imports from the United States and Canada (over three million tons).

The expansion of trade with NATO states was less dramatic for its quantitative increases (which were actually quite modest during the 1970s) than for qualitative changes (see Table 2). Romania, for example, became the first Communist country to establish a joint bank with Western commercial banks in 1973 and to allow on its soil jointly owned and operated industrial corporations with 51 percent Western participation. A major Control Data computer-component assembly line was to be established following that accord, with Italian and German companies joining in Romanian ventures shortly after. Hungary and Poland, by 1973, had begun joint ventures of a similar nature. The Poles, for instance, negotiated cooperative production arrangements with Berliet of France, Fiat of Italy, and U.S. corporations such as Clark Equipment and International Harvester, all to manufacture equipment (such as buses, cars, and factory or farm utility vehicles) under license in Poland. Both Romania and Poland began to permit, by mid-1973, U.S. Department of

TABLE 2

EASTERN EUROPE'S (CMEA STATES) FOREIGN TRADE

	GDR	Poland	Czech.	Hungary	Romania	Bulg.
Foreign trade in billions of $ (year)	22.2 (1975)	25 (1976)	20.9 (1977)	13.3 (1976)	14 (1977)	11 (1976)
Percent with Communist states[a]	70	66	66	62	49	73
Percent with non-Communist states	30	34	34	38	51	27

Sources: Background Notes, Department of State; Countries of the World and Their
          Leaders, 4th Edition (Detroit, Michigan: Gale Research Co., 1978).
          Adapted from 1980 Great Decision (Washington: Foreign Policy Association,
          1980).

[a]A more recent estimate suggests that intra-CMEA trade, which of course excludes
a few communist states, accounts for about 75% of Bulgarian trade, two-thirds
for Czechoslovakia and the GDR, half for Hungary and Poland, and a third for
Romania. See Morris Bornstein, "East-West Economic Relations and Soviet-East
European Economic Relations" in U.S. Congress Joint Economic Committee, Soviet
Economy in a Time of Change (Washington: GPO, 1979).

Agriculture inspectors to observe the packing of meat destined for export to American markets. By contrast, the Soviet Union was unwilling to allow any inspection visits of production facilities or natural resource extraction processes.

Into the mid-1970s, East European efforts to expand exports to the West in exchange for consumer goods and technology continued unabated, and the contrasts with Moscow grew. While the Soviets cancelled a U.S. trade agreement in January 1975 due to the Jackson-Vanik Amendment—an amendment to the 1973 Trade Reform Act, which, the USSR asserted, intruded in the domestic politics of another state by insisting on the lifting of emigration curbs prior to any U.S. trade concessions—the East Europeans sought to convince the United States that they were in compliance with the amendment. When Polish chief Edward Gierek visited Washington in October 1974, for instance, part of his argument for expanding U.S.-Polish trade beyond one billion dollars by 1976 was the relatively liberal domestic political environment, which included few political prisoners, a 1974 amnesty for almost 150,000 common criminals, and the conspicuous absence of any political purges.[8]

The extent to which trade development was a priority among East Europeans in the 1970s was suggested by Bulgaria's obvious efforts in 1973–1974 to court U.S. favor by such measures as issuing exit visas for five dozen individuals with close relatives in the United States who had fled Bulgaria illegally, agreeing to end jamming of Voice of America radio broadcasts, signing a consular convention that accorded greater protection for Americans in Bulgaria, and by generally improving the environment for American diplomats stationed in Bulgaria (e.g., by allowing multiple entry visas so that short trips could be made to Greece and Yugoslavia and by granting increased access to Bulgarian officials). When Bulgarian Deputy Premier Ivan Popov came to the United States in November 1974, the expectation was clear; concessions during that year were seen as preliminary to an expansion of trade, particularly the purchase of heavy machinery. To some extent, Bulgarian efforts were successful insofar as annual trade, which had been only $11 million a year in 1973, rose to $30.4 million in 1974 and continued to grow in the next few years. That U.S.-Bulgarian ties did not expand geometrically, however, was due to Sofia's inability to adopt a policy to any degree at odds with the USSR; when the Soviets abrogated a trade accord in early 1975, the Bulgarians had to abandon their efforts to expand trade with the United States, despite their compliance with the letter of the Jackson-Vanik Amendment (most Bulgarian Jews and other minorities had left at the regime's urging immediately following World War II). Nevertheless, Bulgarian officials continued to indicate in press interviews their eagerness for good relations with the United States and an expansion of trade.[9]

Romanian leader Ceauşescu, meanwhile, became nothing less than a traveling salesman during the 1970s, promoting his brand of détente and internationalism hand-in-hand with the economic interests of his regime—the latter being increasing levels of foreign trade with the West for its technology and investments, with the Third World for inexpensive raw materials, and within COMECON for finished products and some crucial raw materials (e.g., oil and gas). In the two-year span of 1972–1973, for example, Ceauşescu personally went in 1972 to the USSR, Africa, Western Europe, and South Asia, and then to Italy and West Germany in early 1973, followed by a major trip to the United States and through much of Latin America. Throughout the decade these journeys continued, the fanfare being particularly notable when Ceauşescu visited Western Europe and the United States. Such events as Ceauşescu's discussions with President Carter and Prime Minister Callaghan in 1978–1979 were lavishly covered by the Romanian media for domestic consumption, as was President Gerald Ford's brief stop in Bucharest in 1975 when "most favored nation" (MFN) status was granted to Romania. Coupled with such vists were several large credit arrangements, first through the World Bank and then, in 1975, via the Import Bank of the United States, amounting to more than three-quarters of a billioı dollars. International Monetary Fund membership also made Romania unique in Eastern Europe during the 1970s.

The surge of East European desire for trade with the West, and specifically NATO states, began before inflationary pressures led to spiraling prices for Western products. But most of the East European states—perhaps the most developed states such as the GDR and Czechoslovakia are exceptions—have had little choice but to continue their purchases. Having squeezed all they could out of labor-intensive growth, which meant the massive influx of peasants and women into industrial employment, Eastern Europe increasingly began to depend in the 1960s on import-fed development. The kind of sophisticated technology required to propel Poland, Romania, Hungary, Bulgaria, and Yugoslavia into mass-industrialized economies was, and is, available in the United States, West Germany, France, Italy, the United Kingdom, and other West European states. By the mid-1970s, however, prices for such machinery and equipment had skyrocketed, and Eastern Europe had no way to recoup the growing trade imbalance with the West. Simultaneously, in January 1975, the Russians announced that their de facto subsidization of East European economies through oil shipments of 1.25 million barrels a day in 1973-1974 at about a third of the world price would change dramatically because Soviet oil would double in price (up to thirty-six rubles a metric ton from sixteen in 1974, or six dollars per barrel up from three dollars). Other Soviet pressures on East European economies were also related to energy supplies. Although the Soviets were willing to tap natural gas reserves and sell the gas to the East Europeans, for example, the purchasing states within COMECON had to supply labor battalions for the construction of pipelines during 1975-1977, involving, for example, up to 6,000 East Germans—a not insignificant loss of skilled manpower in the GDR in areas such as welding.

With Eastern Europe thus caught between rising prices in the industrial states of NATO and a not altogether sympathetic ally in the East, which controls supplies of most natural resources required for industrial output, Communist regimes from Sofia to Warsaw have seen their trade deficits mount through the 1970s. In 1974, Poland's exports to NATO members fell behind imports by over $1.4 billion, and the total trade deficit of COMECON members with the West in the first four years of 1970 rose to more than $8 billion.[10] Hungary, relatively prosperous by East European standards, felt the impact of worldwide inflation a bit later, but severely nonetheless. Huge deficits of $700 million in 1974 and close to $1 billion in 1975 plus related difficulties brought an end to the political careers of Jeno Fock, who resigned as premier in May of 1975, and Rezso Nyers, author of the New Economic Mechanism (NEM), who

TABLE 3

THE HARD CURRENCY DEBT OF EASTERN EUROPE (IN BILLIONS OF $)

	1970	1974	1975	1976	1977
Bulgaria	0.7	1.2	1.8	2.3	2.7
Czechoslovakia	.3	1.1	1.5	2.1	2.7
G.D.R.	1.0	2.8	3.8	6.0	5.9
Hungary	.6	1.5	2.1	2.8	3.4
Poland	.8	3.9	6.9	10.2	13.0
Romania	1.2	2.6	3.0	.3	4.0
Total, Eastern Europe	4.6	13.1	19.1	25.7	31.7

Source: Adapted from Paul Marer, "Statement in U.S. Policy Toward Eastern
          Europe" (Washington: GPO, 1979), p. 100.

was ousted as a party secretary in 1974 and lost his Politburo post in early 1975.

When inflation mushroomed in 1974–1976, European Communist states (the USSR included) began to live on credit, borrowing at a furious rate. In 1975, the USSR and its COMECON partners borrowed more from the West than they had throughout the earlier part of the decade, i.e., some $9 billion, bringing the total loans since 1970 to about $30 billion (see Table 3). Poland, alone, had received $13 billion in Western credits through 1977—a much higher proportion of its GNP than the $16 billion received by the Soviets through the end of the same year. By 1979, Polish debt had risen to $15 billion as well. Borrowing such huge amounts of capital from Western banks or governments was necessary, of course, because of a growing annual trade deficit of the USSR and Eastern Europe that passed the $12 billion mark in 1975 alone, up from about $5 billion in 1974.

Coupled with their mounting payments to the Soviet Union for oil and other raw materials, at a time when sales to the NATO states were declining due to a worldwide recession, East European nations found their economic relations with Western Europe and the United States complicated by a variety of other concerns. Even Romania, beneficiary of MFN status in 1975, was unable to reach its trade goals with the United States. Although trade topped $450 million in 1976, and a November 1976 agreement suggested that close cooperation would follow, the opposition of organized labor in the United States to alleged "dumping" of textiles, shoes, sheet glass, and other products by Romania in the U.S. market, and American worries that high-technology U.S. exports to Bucharest would be transferred to the Soviet Union, limited the flow of trade in both directions.

For Yugoslavia, another complication arose when the flow of Yugoslav laborers to West German and other Common Market nations was slowed in the late 1970s by public pressure and government action in Western Europe. The *Gastarbeiter* (guest worker) phenomenon in the German Federal Republic had been of enormous benefit to Yugoslavia in the 1960s and early 1970s, siphoning off excess labor and thereby reducing the potential for serious unemployment, while Organization of Economic Cooperation and Development (OECD) economic surveys in 1974 and 1975 suggested that hard currency sent back to families in Yugoslavia (over $1 billion a year by 1974) was a very significant factor in providing development capital. By 1972, 500,000 Yugoslavs worked in the GFR alone, a fifth of all foreign workers employed in the West German economy. In 1975, over one million Yugoslavs worked in Western Europe. One can gain dramatic indication of Yugoslav labor migration to the West during the 1960s and early 1970s by recalling that in 1960 there were fewer than 9,000 Yugoslav workers in the GFR.[11] Confronted with new visa restrictions in most Western European states and the return of laborers put out of work by a recessionary environment, the rapid rise in labor migration leveled off by the mid-1970s. Such conditions, coupled with Western price increases and general stagnation, sent Yugoslav unemployment to over 10 percent (of 5 million workers), with inflation reaching a rate of 32 percent in 1975.

As the 1970s ended, Eastern Europe had witnessed—and fostered—an intriguing change in its economic relationship with the West. Prior to 1970, i.e., before the rudimentary economic and diplomatic links of the 1960s had led to legal resolutions of outstanding problems in 1969-1971, there was negligible debt to the West. By 1979, however, servicing the debt to NATO governments and private banks in those nations was an onerous burden for more than one East European state, with Poland clearly in the greatest economic peril. Moreover, the dependence on the West as both a source of machinery, equipment, high technology, and consumer items and as a market for meats, textiles, produce, and some raw materials meant that East European economics were very much intertwined with the West. The decade had, indeed, wrought considerable changes in the economic fortunes of Eastern Europe.

Diplomatic Relations Between Eastern Europe and the West

Any effort to separate "economic" from "diplomatic" relations is an analytic device, and world events of the late 1960s through 1980 forcefully exhibited such a connection. Nevertheless, it seems useful to focus on several occurrences over the past decade and a half that set the tone for East European diplomatic interactions with the West during the 1980s.

The 1970s began, as was mentioned earlier, with the legal resolution of several issues—Central European borders, the emigration of Germans from Eastern Europe, and the status of Berlin—by means of the Four Power Berlin Accord of 1971 and a series of accords at Moscow and Warsaw involving the USSR, Poland, and the GFR. After several years of Soviet and WTO urging, a thirty-four nation (all of Europe plus the United States and Canada) session was held at Helsinki in late 1972 ostensibly to prepare for a European security conference. From the Soviet perspective, the security conference and the 1972 preliminary meeting were to formalize the status quo in Europe, i.e., to achieve a Western recognition of Soviet hegemony in Eastern Europe. But, as had been the case during the 1960s, the USSR was unable to insist that all of its allies maintain an obedient silence. Romania was at the forefront of those participants insisting that a European security conference must subsume Central European force reduction negotiations (later called the Mutual and Balanced Force Reduction, or MBFR, talks), negotiations that major NATO and WTO states were soon to undertake. Joining Romania in opposing the separation of the two processes were Yugoslavia, Finland, and Austria. That two sets of diplomatic efforts were nevertheless carried out may suggest, of course, the impotence of small powers in a forum of European states. On the other hand, twenty or even ten years before Helsinki, the thought of diversity within the Soviet bloc was unthinkable.

On an individual basis, East European states took important diplomatic initiatives during the 1970s disassociated from immediate Soviet concerns. Faced by a very large Roman Catholic population, for example, Poland's Communist leaders have been forced to compromise with the Vatican, both before and after Cracow Cardinal Woytila's election as Pope John Paul II. John Paul II's triumphant tour of Poland in mid-1979 was preceded by several conciliatory gestures from the Gierek regime toward the Catholic church, including the return of rights to property owned by German churches before 1945 in the Oder-Neisse region. For its part, the Vatican gave tacit acknowledgement to the Oder-Neisse border in 1972 by establishing Polish bishoprics in what had been

German land before 1945 and formally recognizing Polish sovereignty over those territories in 1973. Stefan Cardinal Wyszynski visited the Vatican in November–December 1972, laying the foundation for the resumption of diplomatic relations.[12] These compromises, however, must be seen amid a general background of continued church-party acrimony, with no permanent resolution in sight.

Vatican diplomats such as Archbishop Casaroli and Jan Cardinal Willebrands were sent to Eastern Europe as early as 1969 to test reactions to some degree of rapprochement. Positive indications were received from all East European states with sizeable Catholic populations. The first break in over two decades of icy relations took place, for instance, when the Hungarian party agreed to Vatican appointments of permanent bishops. Czechoslovak authorities likewise agreed to normalize relations in the early 1970s, while 1973 saw successful negotiations between Warsaw and papal emissaries about the resumption of formal ties (once the Vatican had acknowledged the Oder-Neisse line, as mentioned above).

Some of the steps taken by East European states represented initiatives no doubt approved by the USSR. Nevertheless, as departures from past practice, such events are significant. The East Germans, noted during the Ulbricht regime for their hostility to détente in any form (especially to Brandt's Ostpolitik), made numerous concessions during the early to mid-1970s, surely designed to gain more trade and diplomatic recognition. In the first three years after the Four Power Berlin Accord, for example, access to the divided city was made much easier, with the East Germans even cooperating to allow additional lanes at border checkpoints to accommodate the much higher volume of auto traffic. West Germans were allowed to visit with comparative ease after 1971 and were far less subject to searches of luggage or person. This and other evidence of "good behavior," within a general environment of East-West rapprochement during the early and mid-1970s, paid off for the GDR. Strengthened by increasing trade, the East German economy grew at a healthy pace, and diplomatic recognition occurred rapidly. In September 1974, the United States signed a document with the East Germans to exchange ambassadors, thus ending two and a half decades of Western (U.S. inspired) refusal to recognize the GDR as anything more than a Soviet-occupied territory. The GDR's entry into the United Nations also occurred in September 1974.

The GDR followed its diplomatic advances with an offer of wide-ranging concessions to the GFR in December of 1974, a move directly related to Bonn's agreement to provide the East Germans with credits of $340 million per year through 1981. Such credits, announced in early December, were certainly the sine qua non for a number of measures announced the following week by East Berlin including an exemption of pensioners from currency-exchange fees when visiting East Germany, an East German invitation to Krupp and Hoechst (giant West German corporations) to build plants in the GDR (Krupp to construct a nuclear power plant and Hoechst to build a chemical plant), an offer to build a new autobahn from Berlin to Hamburg and to improve rail links, and a suggestion that the Teltow Canal around Berlin be enlarged (for better electricity supply, sewage disposal, etc.).

Most provocative among East European diplomatic actions vis-à-vis the West since the 1960s have been those of Romania and its President Nicolae Ceauşescu. An extended account of Romanian "deviance" since, at least, 1964 is beyond the scope of this essay. Nevertheless, it is important that one recognize the carefully balanced nature of Romanian foreign policy differences with the USSR's positions—a balance that, when combined with Romanian political vulnerability and veiled intentions to resist, has probably kept Russian forces from reentering Romania. As suggested in the introduction to this essay, it may be erroneous to regard Ceauşescu as an innovative or risk-taking actor in foreign policy. Instead, the fundamental decision to break with early 1960s CMEA plans for Romania's economy—to concentrate investments on agriculture, leaving industry underdeveloped—necessitated cultivating ties with the non-Communist world. The regime's political survival, then, became dependent on a carefully executed strategy of bridge building to the West for technology, credits, and a market for products such as textiles, meat, shoes, and other low-technology items, while articulating their commitment to socialism and their continuing alliance (WTO) status notwithstanding limited participation.

Romanian deviations from Soviet-led positions usually have been quiet and/or limited. Romania supported Arab claims in 1973, but did not condemn Israel or break relations. Romania votes with the Soviets at the U.N. and objected to its exclusion in 1975 from the East European representatives to a U.N. committee designed to review the charter. Ceauşescu's failure to join Soviet bloc leaders in the summer of 1974 at the almost-annual Crimean retreat was another clear, but limited, signal of independence. When the Chinese invaded Vietnam in early 1979, Romanian criticism of China was veiled by references to ending all aggression, withdrawing all troops from other states (by which was meant the Vietnamese occupation of Cambodia), etc. Perhaps the boldest ploy of the Romanian leadership was Ceauşescu's public statements in November 1978 upon returning from a Political Consultative Committee meeting of the WTO in Moscow. Contrary to any precedent in the Communist world, Ceaușescu refused to agree to the increased defense expenditures sought by Soviet leaders and publicly announced that refusal once he returned to Bucharest.

To view such events as rash or ill-conceived actions, however, would misinterpret Romania's calculated interests. To encourage relations with the West—gaining low-interest West European credit arrangements, MFN trading status with the United States, and sizeable Western investments, all necessary in order to make the 1964 break with CMEA economic integration plans appear rational and beneficial—an independent stance on some foreign policy issues was very helpful. Moreover, there can be little question that anti-Soviet sentiment provided a reservoir of support from which the Romanian government could draw. Even Ceaușescu's November 1978 action, which startled some observers, can be viewed from the perspective of Romanian economic need; throughout the 1960s and 1970s, Romanian expenditures for defense have been lowest among WTO members measured either as a proportion of national income or the national product,[13] while the rates of industrial investment have been among the highest. The trade-off is direct, and Ceaușescu knows that his party's vision of an industrialized Romania cannot currently coincide with an expansion of regular military forces. East European states gave tacit support to the Romanian position in November 1978 as well; only East Germany raised defense expenditures relative to inflation.

One of the most intriguing diplomatic processes that began in the late 1970s was the emergence of Albania from self-imposed exile. Although no one could say as the 1980s began that Tirana was accessible for diplomatic or economic initiatives, party leader Enver Hoxha had little choice other than to seek economic links to Western Europe. For seventeen years (1961–1978), China had supported the Albanian regime with huge amounts of economic assistance and, to a lesser degree, military supplies. The death of Mao in 1976 and the pragmatic regime of Deng and Hua rapidly soured the ties between Peking and Tirana until the Chinese stopped their assistance in 1978 after the Albanians failed to halt criticism of new Peking policies.

During 1979, the economic crises created by the aid cutoff apparently led Albania to renew requests that West Germany and Britain settle outstanding disputes with Tirana as a first step toward reestablishing diplomatic relations. Both disputes involve small amounts of money. Bonn is being asked to pay several million dollars for Nazi wartime destruction in Albania and the British are asked to return $25–30 million in gold confiscated by London in 1946 as compensation for the sinking of two

British warships that year due to Albanian mines in the Straits of Corfu (the gold now worth far more than in 1946, of course). These issues remain, however, unresolved in 1980.

Nevertheless, Albanian students were sent to West European universities for the first time since World War II in the fall of 1979, and Albanian trade missions appeared in Bonn, Rome, Brussels, Vienna, Paris, and other capitals. A major exporter of chrome (ranking third in the world), Albania is also able to export some oil to the Italians and Greeks. These natural resources plus a variety of fruits are being marketed in return for industrial assistance.

The record of East European diplomatic relations with the West during the era of détente did not exhibit uniformly positive trends. Many complications arose to dampen the otherwise heady atmosphere of Ostpolitik, détente, and peaceful coexistence. Even in the case of U.S.-Yugoslav relations, the latter having been a beneficiary of huge Western economic credits and military aid from 1948 through the mid-1960s, disputes widened during 1973-1975 that threatened to disrupt long-standing Washington-Belgrade understandings. U.S. foreign policy, specifically its support of Israel in the October 1973 war, was viewed as alarming by the Tito leadership. Despite a December 1973 speech by Yugoslav Foreign Minister Milos Minic indicating a desire for improved ties with Washington, in the same month *Kommunist* (a party journal) harshly criticized unspecified U.S. agencies for subverting Yugoslavia. In what was apparently Tito's own decision, Yugoslav media and government statements fueled the acrimony for over a year. While precise motives are uncertain, Tito certainly viewed the criticism of the United States as a means to raise Yugoslavia's slipping international prestige and to constrain the domestic turmoil that had plagued the country since 1971.

Such domestic turmoil came in the form of nationalist terrorism, principally from the Republic of Croatia. Arson, bombing, and assassination were among the techniques that began to plague Yugoslavia seriously in the 1970s, and such difficulties affected that state's relations with the West. Croatian separatists (a movement called Ustashi) established ties with emigré guerilla cells in Western Europe and North America, receiving money and weapons as well as occasional terrorist "support," e.g., airline hijackings. Clandestine Yugoslav pursuit of separatists abroad and Belgrade's assertions that the West was not cooperating adequately—and was even harboring anti-Tito organizations—did nothing to help relations with the West.

Other difficulties appeared in Eastern Europe's diplomatic ties to the West, most notably in the realm of human rights. Long before the human rights theme was sounded by President Carter in 1977, East European treatment of dissidents had been criticized in the West, while Communist leaders had denounced any criticism as interference in domestic affairs. Thus, Yugoslavia's Tito alleged in February 1975 in a televised speech that a campaign had been going on in the Western press to raise a "hue and cry" against Belgrade over treatment of regime critics such as Mahajlo Mihajlov. The trial of dissident writer Mihajlov in early 1975, of course, was not the only action being taken by Tito to silence criticism. The intellectual journal *Praxis*, known for its open views of Yugoslav socialism, was shut down by government order in February 1975, and eight philosophy professors were fired from Belgrade University at the same time. Crackdowns continued into 1976 with the arrest of journalist Viktor Blazic and Judge Franz Miklavic, both allegedly having written articles for foreign magazines regarding limits to free expression in Slovenia.

We can see in the Yugoslav case further issues that hamper normal diplomatic relations. Claiming that Nazi elements in Austria and territorially ambitious Fascists in Italy had found allies in Washington, Belgrade created a stormy campaign in 1975 against Austria over Slovenian and Croatian national issues and against Italy regarding the Adriatic port of Trieste. In the former dispute, Belgrade claimed Austria was tolerating right-wing terrorist organizations (i.e., Croatian or Slovenian nationalists) and moreover was not protecting the rights of those minorities in Austria, particularly of Slovenes in the province of Carinthia. Austrian Chancellor Kreisky rejected such accusations and recalled the Austrian ambassador. Meanwhile, 1974 witnessed the inflammation of an old diplomatic problem in the Trieste issue. Supposedly resolved at the end of World War II when provisions were signed to make Trieste a "free port," the city in fact became divided between Italian and Yugoslav zones of occupation. When Italians objected in 1974 to road signs that implied Yugoslav sovereignty over both zones, Belgrade protested and brought the issue to the Geneva Conference on European Security. Little of substance came of the flare-up and a legal resolution is not yet at hand.

The Yugoslav case is notable because Belgrade's ties with NATO states had been very close for more than a decade and a half after Tito's break with the USSR in 1948. U.S. and NATO commitments to Yugoslav independence and nonalignment were central to the West's relations with the USSR and WTO. That policy disagreements (regarding the Arab-Israeli conflict, for example), economic disruptions, border disputes, and the human rights issue could disturb bilateral and multilateral relations even in the years of détente suggest the fragility of East European links to the West. Many conflictual elements remain in such relationships that preclude any presumption that economic or diplomatic ties are permanent or destined to improve.

Human rights constituted a recurring theme of tension in Eastern Europe's diplomatic relations with NATO states; the details of internal repression are cited elsewhere in this volume. Notwithstanding the 1975 Helsinki Agreement, Romanian artistic and intellectual expression became more constrained in the late 1970s; scores of Czech historians and other intellectuals were purged in 1975–1976, resulting in the Charter '77 dissident movement (inaugurated with a 3,000-word petition signed by over 300 Czechoslovaks calling for the Husak regime to implement the Helsinki Agreement); and East German writers, poets, and other artists have been sent into exile (such as balladeer Wolf Biermann), arrested (as in the case of author Rudolf Bahro), or harassed during 1977–1979. Although such violations of fundamental liberties continued, the momentum of détente was sufficient during the October 1977 Belgrade Review Conference on Security and Cooperation in Europe to dim the volatile nature of the human rights issue. Nevertheless, although the August 1975 Helsinki Agreement remained at the forefront of East-West diplomacy throughout the 1970s, there existed a clear recognition among Western states that Basket Three of the Helsinki Agreement, which was meant to promote freer circulation of peoples and ideas, had not been implemented by Communist regimes. For East European leaders there is the certain knowledge that a complete implementation of such an agreement is ill-advised for their own domestic control, not to mention political security vis-à-vis the USSR.

On several occasions, revelations of espionage have served to weaken East-West relations as they affect Eastern Europe. Defections from Romania's spy network, including Ion Pacepa, who ranked among the leaders of Ceauşescu's security apparatus, and Virgil Tipanut, an agent assigned to the Romanian Embassy in Oslo, were of immense aid to Western intelligence agencies but damaged bilateral and multilateral relations. The inverse could also be said of Colonel Jerzy Pawlowski's arrest in Poland. Pawlowski, an Olympic fencing gold medalist, was tried for spying on behalf of MI-6 and the CIA in 1975.

Most dramatically, Willy Brandt was forced to resign as West German chancellor in May 1974 because of the discovery that the GDR had placed a spy in Brandt's personal office. Guenter Guillaume, who had been a close Brandt aide for years, confessed to his role as an East German spy in April of 1974, after which a storm of protest arose from the opposition party in Bonn, the CDU. For the remainder of 1974 and into 1975, serious disruptions in the process of normalizing inter-German relations resulted, including the delay of talks to establish de facto diplomatic relations between the two governments.

Eastern Europe and the Third World

Close ties between East European states and African or Asian governments are not new and, in some cases, have not paralleled Soviet relations with the same Third World nations. In the broadest respect, of course, Soviet and East European interests differ regarding Southern Hemisphere nations; put quite simply, the Third World means more economically to Poland, Romania, Hungary, and the other CMEA states than to the USSR. (Yugoslavia, one must remember, has been closely linked to Asian and African nations via the nonaligned movement for several decades.) Deficient in raw materials, unlike the USSR, and lacking a large hard-currency market for their industrial products, East European states have necessarily regarded good relations with Black Africa, the Moslem world, South Asia, and other regions as integral to their well-being.

In general, East European trade, cultural exchanges, and military assistance have been received favorably or enthusiastically in the Third World, often without the restraints Soviet aid would have faced. Eastern Europe poses much less of a threat to Third World governments, as those Communist regimes lack colonial pasts or records of imperialistic conquest.

As long ago as the 1950s, commercial and military accords were signed between the smaller Communist states of Europe and new governments in Asia and Africa. These were, and remain, primarily bilateral agreements, rather than tacit alliances with all CMEA or WTO states. In many cases, East European countries preceded the USSR by several years in solidifying commercial and military arrangements, the foci of Communist attention being nations such as Guinea, Somalia, and Mali in Africa; Iraq, Egypt, Syria, and Yemen in the Middle East; and Afghanistan in South Asia. There was little overt effort to penetrate the U.S. "sphere of influence" in Latin America until the success of Castro's revolution in Cuba. Cases such as the Guzman regime in Guatemala, which the CIA overthrew in 1954, do not represent formal commercial or military links of Communist Europe to Central or South America. The East European regimes most active in extending aid to the East African countries cited above were Czechoslovakia, East Germany, and Poland, i.e., the more advanced states of Communist Europe in socioeconomic terms. Hungary, Romania, and Bulgaria participated much less in pursuing ties with Third World nations through the first two decades of Communist rule in Eastern Europe. As will be discussed below, however,

Romania's activism during the past decade and a half, and the nature of Ceauşescu's policies vis-à-vis the Third World, distinguish that Balkan state from other WTO members.

While the economic aspect of Eastern Europe's interests in Southern Hemisphere states may be primary, the political benefits must be considered as well. The degree to which a Kadar, Gierek, or Ceauşescu receives international recognition cannot be disassociated from either a leader's domestic prestige or his ability to press for his nation's interests in CMEA discussions with the Soviet Union. Without any specific information about face-to-face bilateral talks involving the USSR and other CMEA members, it is nonetheless plausible that the number of trade accords with Third World nations and the monetary value of such agreements will widen the latitude of an East European state's action within CMEA. For small states such as those in Eastern Europe, the political benefits of economic aid packages, cultural exchanges, and related links to Third World nations can be enormous—much more so than if the United States or the USSR offered aid in the same proportion. In simple terms, it costs relatively little to offer genuine and important assistance to states of Africa and Asia, thereby fostering an image of helpfulness and comradeship. Building a hospital for several million dollars in Ethiopia, for example, is not a major undertaking for Czechoslovakia, but provides a dramatic increase in health services for such a poor nation. The positive sentiment generated by such assistance, and a lesser-developed country's perception that imperialistic motives do not underlie aid from other small states (even if that is a *mis*-perception), offer the possibility of spectacular diplomatic success at "cut-rate prices."[14]

Political intentions considerably overlap, of course, economic aid and cultural exchanges. Tens of thousands of Africans and Asians have studied in Eastern Europe or competed in sports contests, both ostensibly nonpolitical experiences. But the GDR's effort to inculcate ideology in higher education has been quite evident in the curriculum of Wilhelm Pieck Youth College at Bogensee, as has the intention of Poland's Lumumba Scholarships for university study and Czechoslovakia's "University of November 17." Also quite transparent are Communist efforts to utilize international student organizations such as the World Federation of Democratic Youth to attract adolescents and young adults to Marxism-Leninism and, if possible, to encourage positive attitudes toward Soviet-led states. Similarly, the World Federation of Trade Unions has been employed to organize Third World working-class opinion against the West, a task often made easier by the specter of economic imperialism seen by former colonies.

It is by no means clear that Communist Europe has been successful in relations with the Third World. In cases as diverse as Syria, Egypt, and Uganda, the Soviets have been thrown out and relations with Eastern Europe curtailed. Although the late 1970s witnessed some successes for the USSR—and subsequent expansion of East European involvement—in Angola, South Yemen, Mozambique, and Ethiopia, the combat role of Cuban troops played the major role in securing such ostensibly pro-Soviet regimes. But Afro-Marxism is not a political genre with which the ruling European Communist parties can easily mix, and Middle East socialism (e.g., the Arab Socialist Union in Egypt or the Iraqi Baathists) has never been identified with the Russian model. Indeed, as one observer has noted, Islam has not only prevented solid inroads by Communists in the Arab world, but "Arab socialism," where it does exist, "has turned out to be a pragmatic version of state capitalism, i.e., industrialization carried out under various mixes of private and government ownership."[15] In the Far East, East European and Soviet aid, which reached a combined total of $1.5 billion, was for naught in Indonesia, and the 1965 military coup resulted in the deaths of thousands of Communists (and innumerable innocent citizens as well). Fifteen years later, only a small contingent of Soviet technicians has been readmitted to Indonesia, with the East European role very minor.

At the beginning of the 1980s, the GDR, Czechoslovakia, and Romania were the most active East European states regarding Third World contacts, the former two countries clearly acting as adjuncts to Soviet policy, and the Ceauşescu regime striking out on its own in several important directions. Czechoslovak foreign aid, including technical assistance for industry, construction projects, training programs, and financial credits, exceeded that of other East European states. Some military equipment of Czech origin was also provided to African, Middle East, and South Asian socialist states, often as part of general assistance from the WTO arranged by the USSR. East Germany occasionally played a more active role, supplying military advisers in Ethiopia, and weapons to SWAPO forces in Namibia (Southwest Africa) for their guerilla war against the Union of South Africa.

Romania's activities vis-à-vis the Third World differed from other WTO members. Throughout the late 1960s and 1970s, Ceauşescu was a frequent visitor to Southern Hemisphere nations striving for an identity as a "developing state." To be sure, there is considerable reason to call Romania a developing state, insofar as its economic indicators continue to place it among the two or three poorest nations of Europe. Nevertheless, the Romanian campaign to achieve "observer status" in the Group of 77 was an important departure from established norms within the Soviet-led alliance.

Eastern Europe and Eurocommunism

Communist parties of Western Europe, together referred to as "Eurocommunism" because of both their nonruling status and ideological distinctions from Soviet-inspired doctrine, have had difficult relations with their comrades in Eastern Europe. The French and Italian Communist parties (PCF and PCI, respectively) are very large and have long had considerable electoral support. In the Italian case, the PCI had the potential to enter the government during the 1970s on several occasions by achieving a third or more of the popular vote in parliamentary elections. Such electoral successes, and the emergence of a legal Communist party in Spain (PCE) led by Santiago Carillo, are not without implications for Eastern Europe's foreign relations.

Expectations that Eurocommunism will foster an "infection" in Eastern Europe more severe than Titoism have little immediate support. We cannot ignore, however, the potential long-term effect of Communist party participation in West European governments. Although PCI or PCF governmental participation is likely to have minimal short-run effects on governmental policies in Eastern Europe, except for additional repressive measures imposed on political expression, workers' rights, or artistic liberty, the extent to which East European elites view Eurocommunism as a threat to their political security vis-à-vis the USSR will strain relations with the nonruling parties in Western Europe.

The principal issue between Eurocommunism and most WTO states (the Romanians are an exception) is that of national autonomy. The Italian, French, and Spanish Communists, usually in concert with the Yugoslav and Romanian parties, have stressed on many occasions their belief in separate roads to Communism dictated by national conditions. These voices of Eurocommunism became louder in the 1970s and were particularly evident at the European Communist party conference held at Berlin, at the French Twenty-Second Party Congress, and at the CPSU Twenty-Fifth Party Congress, all held in 1976. An implicit rejection of the Soviet position on CPSU leadership was in evidence at all three meetings, with PCF General Secretary Marchais boycotting the Twenty-Fifth Party Congress in Moscow and dropping the term "dictatorship of the proletariat" from the stated goals of the PCF when the French party convened. The latter step was in accordance with a joint statement made by the PCI and PCF in November of 1975 asserting that political power would be sought through the democratic systems of their countries. Such blatant renunciation of revolutionary means was coupled with French, Italian and Spanish Communist criticism of Soviet actions against dissidents, published openly in the press (e.g., *L'Humanite* in Paris and

L'Unita in Rome). In 1977–1978, these anti-Soviet actions continued; Marchais refused to meet with Brezhnev when the Soviet leader visited France in the spring of 1977 and Berlinguer, the Italian party leader, wrote a letter in November 1977 to Bishop Bettazzi in Rome guaranteeing full respect for religion if the PCI were to enter the government.

Eurocommunism has not retained a unified front vis-à-vis Soviet policies, however, as the Afghanistan invasion demonstrated. While Berlinguer and Carillo, the Spanish Communist leader, castigated the USSR, Marchais supported uncritically the Soviet excuse that the coup and occupation were entirely justified by "capitalist" interference. Ironically, the PCF undertook a more vocal defense of the Soviet aggression than did several WTO members. Romania, as usual, said nothing to defend the Soviet position, while studiously avoiding outright condemnation. Yugoslavia's overt criticism came as no surprise, but the careful reporting in Poland and Hungary was significant—local commentary was absent and Tass (the USSR's wire service) stories were simply carried without further elaboration.

Quite apart from issues of foreign policy, West European Communists pose a dilemma for East European regimes. As proponents of national independence and separate paths to Communism, Eurocommunists suggest models for reformers in WTO states. "Socialism with a human face" was tried once in Eastern Europe and crushed, when Soviet forces occupied Prague in 1968. But precisely the same view of Communist party rule is advocated by the PCI, PCF, and PCE and emerged clearly after August 1968. With consistency, those three parties, joined by smaller Communist political organizations elsewhere, supported the Czechoslovak exiles and continued dissent while censuring the invasion.

For Eastern Europe's leaders, the nonruling parties of Western Europe often constituted unwelcome intervention in politics ostensibly "domestic" in nature. Polish dissident Jacek Kuron's 1976 appeal to the PCI for support against crackdowns on workers or the 1977 Eurocommunist condemnation of Czechoslovak handling of Charter '77 signers exemplify the thorny side of Eurocommunism for East European elites. We cannot be certain that Eurocommunism "causes" social turmoil in Eastern Europe since data crucial for testing such a proposition are not generally available. These data would include statistics on strikes, demonstrations, and crime plus national samples of public opinion. Lacking such indicators, we can nevertheless see a suggestive coincidence between dissident activity in Communist Europe and Eurocommunist support. The monitoring efforts by Eurocommunist parties and the appeals of Eastern Europe's dissenters to Western Europe's Communist parties together produce an environment of mutual identity of which East

European political elites cannot be sanguine. If the PCE labels as "particularly scandalous" the performance of Communist states regarding "freedom of expression," and dissident Czechs "praise the PCI's 'authentic democracy,'" then Eurocommunism must be perceived as a not altogether welcome phenomenon by Gierek, Husak, or other WTO regimes.

In the 1980s: A Summary

Eastern Europe possesses few of the attributes that would encourage autonomous foreign policy. With the exception of Yugoslavia and Albania, all states of the region are linked institutionally to the Soviet Union. Within the institutional ties of CMEA and WTO, only Romania has no Soviet troops garrisoned on its soil and only Romania retains a degree of energy independence by virtue of importing no Soviet oil. All regimes of Eastern Europe must consider political security vis-à-vis the USSR, not military security vis-à-vis NATO, as their principal goal of foreign policy. In such circumstances, conservative policies, limited innovation, and cautious statements predominate.

Almost fifteen years of momentum toward East-West rapprochement has had decided effects on Eastern Europe, fostering a significant degree of economic interdependence with NATO states and, in some cases, mammoth debt to Western banks and governments. Many legal impediments to better relations were resolved, and commitments were made at Helsinki to create an atmosphere of reconciliation. Impediments to détente persisted through the 1970s, but the important setback in the USSR's image fostered by the Afghanistan invasion in 1980 will affect Eastern Europe as well. Clearly, because of their greater dependency on foreign trade and concern about economic performance, East European leaders will seek to avoid anything more than rhetorical endorsement of the Soviet actions in central Asia. If a "new Cold War" was to become an accepted model of international relations during the 1980s and Western sanctions were applied to non-Soviet WTO members, Eastern Europe would suffer economic dislocation far greater than the USSR. For their own economic welfare, East Europeans will strive to avoid "guilt by association," while for their political welfare, there will be no overt criticism of Soviet aggression among WTO members in Eastern Europe. This suggests, therefore, another decade of very limited maneuvering for East European relations with the West, now further complicated by Soviet actions that alienate non-Communist states from the USSR and its allies.

Selectively targeted economic aid, technical advice, and military assistance will continue to be Eastern Europe's principal role in the Third World, primarily in Africa and Asia. In return, aside from political support at the international level that might accrue to Communist states, Eastern Europe will seek natural resources in exchange for manufactured items that are less suited for advanced markets. Relations with Eurocommunism, and specifically the largest parties in Italy, France, and Spain, will not improve as long as the domestic conditions of East European systems are the subject of criticism from PCI, PCE, or PCF leaders. Although Georges Marchais defended the Soviet invasion of Afghanistan, he and the PCF are not likely to become close comrades of Gierek, Husak, or other party elites in Eastern Europe.

Conclusions from this overview of relations between Eastern Europe and the non-Communist world can be portrayed in deceptively simple terms: conservative rulers of WTO states will, in the coming decade, have to make and implement foreign policies within the bounds of Soviet security interests. But, as this summary of such foreign relations has suggested, much more complex issues pervade the interaction of East European states with the non-Communist world—issues of economic interdependence, legal and diplomatic negotiations, the relationship between domestic dissent and Eurocommunism, and political aims of economic assistance and cultural exchanges with the Third World. Because of these complexities, we would be ill-advised to subsume Eastern Europe's relations with the non-Communist world in the 1980s under Soviet interests alone.

Notes

1. GDR Press Department, Ministry of Foreign Affairs, *Foreign Affairs Bulletin* (Berlin), no. 34 (December 27, 1979):293.

2. *Pravda*, September 25, 1968.

3. William Kintner and Wolfgang Klaiber, *Eastern Europe and European Security* (New York: Dunellen, 1971), p. 207.

4. Terrence Hopmann, "International Conflict and Cohesion in the Communist System," *International Studies Quarterly* 11 (1967):212–236.

5. Zbigniew Brzezinski, *The Soviet Bloc* (Cambridge, Mass.: Harvard University Press, 1967), p. 433.

6. Kintner and Klaiber, *Eastern Europe*, pp. 242–243.

7. *Ibid.*, pp. 248–249.

8. "As Gierek Visits U.S., Poland Basks in Stability and Economic Prosperity," *New York Times*, October 11, 1974.

9. "Bulgaria is Striving to Improve U.S. Ties," *New York Times*, May 1, 1975.

10. "How Eastern Europe Ran Into the Red," *Manchester Guardian*, May 3, 1975.

11. "Tito Preparing for the Succession," *New York Times*, March 4, 1975.

12. "Poland, Vatican Said to Strive for Better Ties," *Baltimore Sun*, November 19, 1972.

13. *The Military Balance* (London: International Institute of Strategic Studies, various years).

14. Herbert Dinerstein, "Soviet Doctrines on Developing Countries," in Kurt London, ed., *New Nations in a Divided World* (New York: Praeger, 1963), p. 87.

15. John K. Cooley, "Arab Communists," *Problems of Communism* 24 (March-April 1975):42.

Roy E. Heath   **8**

Education

Education in Eastern Europe has always been the product of a variety of factors and influences. It has also frequently reflected local conditions and needs as well as outside developments. The situation is no different today in either the realm of educational theory or in actual educational practice, although the specific factors may vary. This chapter will deal with the current situation of education in Eastern Europe, in terms of general trends and developments and in reference to the specific educational structures.

Much of the educational situation in Eastern Europe today is the product of significant post–World War II developments. Immediately after the war and the subsequent coming to power of the Communist regimes, the respective educational systems of Eastern Europe underwent drastic alterations, with the Soviet Union serving as the model. The aim of these changes was to help solidify the new political order in each country and to ensure its survival. Older textbooks were replaced by new ones reflecting socialist values and worldviews. Pedagogical cadres were subjected to intense scrutiny in order to weed out those who might be hostile to or incompatible with the new governments. Education was regarded no longer as a privilege of the few but as the duty of every citizen of the socialist state. Education was to serve as the chief vehicle for creating the new socialist man. In order to accommodate such a goal, however, a mere reshuffling of texts and faculty was not enough. Educational facilities were vastly expanded, especially if compulsory primary education was instituted where it had not previously existed. In countries where such compulsory education laws already existed, they were now strictly enforced. The goal was to educate, at least on the primary level, every segment of the population. This process, called "democratization" by Eastern Europeans, is still an ongoing process. In the more advanced countries, however, such as Hungary, Czechoslovakia and the German Democratic Republic, the emphasis now is on making secondary education and higher education available to all.

The next important phase in East European educational development came during the late 1950s and early 1960s, when Khrushchev held power in the Soviet Union. An overwhelming concern that education be closely linked with real-life situations characterized this period of development, a period in which Eastern Europe was still very much under the sway of Soviet influence in every aspect of life and politics. The demand by Khrushchev that education be closely tied to real life had two motivations. First, the events of 1956 in Hungary and Poland called attention to the fact that a tremendous gap existed between the masses and the educated elite, especially party officials. Second, Soviet and East European officials wished education to reflect the increasing tempo of industrial development in Eastern Europe. Thus, the calls for more ties between school and life were translated into an increased emphasis on polytechnical instruction. Soviet as well as East European systems were altered to include more courses in mathematics and natural and physical sciences. New class schedules included several hours of factory or field work during regular school hours, and special courses were implemented that aimed at cultivating love and respect for labor in the students of the basic (primary) schools. The German Democratic Republic and Bulgaria launched ambitious programs to make the entire primary-school system polytechnical in content and format. However, the other East European countries carried out Soviet recommendations to a lesser extent. This trend lasted well into the 1960s, when a reevaluation of the emphasis on polytechnical instruction raised questions about the value or success of such instruction. Countries such as Poland and Yugoslavia, which had always been lukewarm toward such instruction, quietly began to deemphasize or at least to curb the extent of polytechnical instruction. The German Democratic Republic and Bulgaria, however, still remain firmly committed to maximizing polytechnical instruction.

Without any doubt, the hallmarks of the 1960s in East European education were a trend toward what Western observers have labelled "polycentrism," as well as a tendency toward a great deal of introspection, in regard to education, by educators and government officials. Polycentrism, a phenomenon not confined to educational affairs, involves a willingness to look outside of the socialist system for new ideas and developments in the field of education, rather than exclusively following the Soviet lead. Thus, when East European educators consider changes in teaching methods, for example, they are just as apt to look to Sweden or Japan as they are to the Soviet Union for possible improvements. The other chief trend of the 1960s was a tendency in almost all the countries of the area to make detailed studies of their entire educational systems.

The results of such studies were both encouraging and disheartening and gave rise to many of the reform movements that characterized the 1970s. The self-examinations conducted by such countries as Poland and Romania revealed many significant achievements in terms of democratizing educational opportunities. The majority of the population in every country of Eastern Europe has received at least some elementary education, and new educational facilities were constructed in order to make this feasible and permanent. On the other hand, East European educators were also reminded by conclusions of such studies that many chronic problems still defy resolution while new ones also beg attention. In brief, the chronic problems, which are especially evident in the rural areas, include such things as continuing shortages of equipment, classroom space, and teachers. This, in turn, continues to frustrate attempts to eliminate inequalities in the education of rural as opposed to urban students. Rural children often suffer in competition with children educated in the better urban schools, especially when the time comes for them to find jobs or to apply to higher educational institutions. Another disturbing holdover from previous decades is the tendency throughout Eastern Europe for the children of the educated elite to enter secondary schools that emphasize preparation for college, while children of the less privileged train for technical careers or enter the labor market immediately after the completion of primary school.

Some of the newer worries involve demographic and economic pressures, which ironically are due to the successes of the democratization process. In other words, as a larger segment of the population than ever before passed through and finished the primary cycle of education, a correspondingly larger number demanded and expected to receive at least a secondary, if not an even higher education. Bulgarian authorities, for example, have discovered that many of the less costly primary education facilities will soon become redundant as the postwar demographic surge levels off. At the same time, the much more expensive secondary facilities will have to be expanded at a rate that may well tax the country's resources to the limits. These are only a few of the important questions that must be discussed in any examination of contemporary East European education.

Goals and Functions of Education

The basic foundation of the educational systems of Eastern Europe, as indeed in any country, is comprised of the goals and the tasks assigned to educators and education. The general goals of education in Eastern Europe in the 1970s may be roughly divided into philosophical and

228 *Roy E. Heath*

pragmatic ones. The philosophical goals included: promoting the intellectual, physical, moral, and aesthetic growth and development of citizens in a socialist society and advancing the dialectical materialist concept of society and nature. Put more simply: encouraging the development of all aspects of the socialist personality in a society of progress and economic prosperity.

More pragmatic goals, which are in a sense implicit in the philosophical statements, include inculcation of a love for labor, preparation of the student for useful employment, creation of a ruling elite for the socialist state, cultivation of the love of the state and its ideals, and provision of free, public, and universal education. All of these goals and functions can be found in the preambles of laws, five-year plans, and constitutions.

In order to achieve the goals established for its educational system, each of the East European countries has a complicated system for the administration of school affairs. These administrative systems have remained fairly stable, with few significant developments.

Management and Administration of Education

The pattern of educational administration typical of all Eastern Europe, except Yugoslavia, which will receive special attention, revolves around a ministry of education and supportive organs in a highly centralized and tightly controlled system, some with mechanisms provided for public participation. The Ministry of Education has the responsibility for the general organization, guidance, and supervision of the educational system in all aspects of theory and practice. This would also include such specific duties as formulating and coordinating curricula, managing scholarships and grants, encouraging or initiating research, supervising and inspecting various networks of education, collecting data, and establishing central records. However, many of these specific duties are delegated to support groups, and the actions of the educational ministries always reflect a whole network of stimuli and influences from government, industrial, agricultural, and party agencies or organizations.

Also, the direct management of schools is carried out by agencies not part of the nuclear structure of the ministry. For example, in Bulgaria, secondary schools are managed by departmental peoples' councils with the Ministry of Education supervising. This points out another feature of educational administration in Eastern Europe, which is that different levels of education are sometimes managed by different levels of government. For example, in Czechoslovakia, pre-primary institutions are run by the most immediate local authorities, while secondary schools are managed by larger regional committees, and universities are run directly by the Ministry of Education. Czechoslovakia has two ministries of education, one for the Czech Republic and one for Slovakia. An educational council led by a deputy prime minister of the federal government coordinates the educational affairs affecting the entire country.

Two areas usually remain outside of, or in special relation with, the regular administrative system; these are higher educational affairs and the political management of education. The party in all countries maintains a separate apparatus for implementing and supervising political education in the regular school system (as opposed to special indoctrination or party cadre education). This is in addition to the tasks performed by party officials and committees within the Ministry of Education.

Higher education is also in a separate category because it is, in all East European countries, directly administered by the Ministry of Education. However, much more leeway and participation is given to academic personnel in higher educational institutions. The government keeps close ties to the universities because the university functions as a major source of research and plays a crucial role in the country's development. Yet, a certain amount of independence is mandatory for such research to be effective. Also, various branches of the university must work with ministries other than the Ministry of Education: agricultural colleges with the corresponding ministry, etc. In some cases, a higher educational institution, such as an engineering institute, can and will conclude contracts with an industrial enterprise for particular research and receive money for that purpose.[1]

In contrast to higher education, the lower levels of the educational structure are marked by much more control and input from local sources and private citizens. Various youth groups, industrial committees, party organizations, parents' groups, clubs, trade unions, and cultural committees take some part in formulating the educational process, be it curricula, policy, textbooks, or work-study programs.

In Bulgaria, for example, the immediate organization of education is vested in the district councils' public education departments, which in turn are organs of both the Ministry of Public Instruction and the district people's councils. The important point is that the schools are directly managed by individuals close to the particular schools. East Germany and Romania have very elaborate systems designed to ensure participation of local groups, especially parents, in school affairs in their vicinity. These local school councils have sometimes been compared to the U.S.'s local school boards, but they have less autonomy. Such a comparison is specious, considering that autonomy is the essential feature of the U.S. school system.

Another system often compared to the U.S. one is the Yugoslav system of school committees. Unlike the rest of Eastern Europe, Yugoslavia's educational structure is extremely decentralized as a result of deliberate measures to ensure that end. Geographic, ethnic, and political reasons account for this. The country is somewhat of an artificial creation of six independent republics and two autonomous regions, organized largely around major ethnic groups. The republics and various ethnic groups have significant differences in language, religion, and historical experience, as well as differences in standards of living. Thus, it is difficult, if not impossible, to impose a uniform centralized system on the federation. The Yugoslav situation is also colored by an insistence on "the withering away of the state," to be achieved by encouraging popular participation in all affairs of the country, including education. The result of these conditions is that educational responsibilities are diffused throughout the republics and self-management councils. There is an educational council at the national level, but its influence is marginal.

Yugoslavia has taken the principle of decentralization to such an extreme that every single school is managed directly by its own teachers' council, principal, and school committee. Each unit has its own duties as defined by law. The school committee itself is composed of representatives of three groups: the Municipal People's Committee, the Council of Teachers, and the voters of the municipality where the school is located. Principals are members ex officio, and, in secondary schools, students are also voting members. Sometimes schools are set up by economic, social, or professional organizations. In such cases, representatives of the founding group are included on the school committees. The only government interference comes in defining the duties of various units. Higher levels of this administrative system are also designed to ensure participation in every aspect of school affairs from budget to curricula.[2]

Attempts by other East European countries to encourage public participation or less emphasis on centralized control still pale in comparison to the Yugoslavian example of school administration.

Pre-Primary Education

The actual school network, administered by whatever means, in Eastern Europe begins with a first cycle of pre-primary education, although it is not considered part of the formal educational system.

All countries make a distinction between nurseries (for the very young) and kindergartens (for those closer to regular school entrance age). But the goals of pre-primary education are the same for nurseries and kindergartens. Generally, these include: development of motor skills; development of perception and sense of balance between excitation and inhibition; development of concentration, memorization, and speech; and training in play, rest, habits, hygiene, and attitudes. More concrete functions include preparation of children for elementary schools, and child-care for working or handicapped parents. The age levels for such institutions vary from country to country; but most nurseries accommodate children up to three years of age, while kindergartens train children from three or four to whatever the school entrance age may be, usually six or seven. Attendance is not mandatory anywhere, although increased attendance is a universal goal of all the countries. Czechoslovakia wished to have all five-year-olds enrolled in kindergarten by 1975, but did not achieve that goal.

If pre-primary education in Eastern Europe is not compulsory, neither is it entirely free. However, a number of methods are used to finance the operation of the establishments; usually it is a combination of government funding and tuition fees. Sometimes an industrial or agricultural concern will pay for either all or part of the nursery or kindergarten fees, especially if such a school was established by the firm.

In Czechoslovakia, the government gives special consideration to working mothers or those in poor health and unable to take care of their children. In Bulgaria, a priority system for entry is set up when availability of spaces exceeds demand. In such cases, preference is given to low-income or large families and to the children of widows, single mothers, students, soldiers, war veterans, and Heroes of Socialist Labor. Bulgaria has a very wide variety of pre-primary establishments, ranging from half-day and seasonal schools in rural areas to full-day ones in the cities. These institutions throughout Eastern Europe are staffed almost completely by women and often function in a manner similar to day-care or child-care centers.

The percentage of preschool-age children in attendance varies from approximately 10 percent in Yugoslavia, to 25 percent in Poland, to a high of 65 percent in Czechoslovakia. Pre-primary education is vastly underemphasized in Yugoslavia, where participation in such education ranges from only 0.9 percent of pre-primary age children in Montenegro to the still low figure of 9.1 percent in Slovenia.[3] These discrepancies are due, no doubt, to varying levels of industrialization, as well as to the goals of each country for achievements at each level. Official UNESCO statistics on pre-primary education (Table 1) show the comparative figures for each country in Eastern Europe in the early 1970s.

TABLE 1

PRE-PRIMARY EDUCATION

Country	No. of Institutions	No. of Teachers	No. of Students
Albania (1971)	NA	2,713	52,727
Bulgaria (1973)	7,692	20,847	360,582
Czechoslovakia (1973)	8,642	31,077	414,433
East Germany (1973)	11,442	49,114	675,104
Hungary (1973)	3,785	16,452	296,101
Poland (1973)	30,095	NA	1,021,271
Romania (1973)	12,438	27,640	704,950
Yugoslavia (1972)	1,860	12,610	147,626

Source: United Nations Educational, Social, and Cultural Organization, Statistical Yearbook 1975, New York: 1976, pp. 122-133.

Such is the complex ethnic composition of East European countries that even on this very basic level provision is made for minority groups to have their own schools. In Czechoslovakia, for example, the Hungarian, Polish, and Ukrainian minorities may establish and run their own schools, but the children are taught Czech or Slovak in addition to their native language.

Primary Education

The next cycle of education in Eastern Europe, primary education, or general education, is the first formal stage and is compulsory in every country. However, the length of primary education varies widely from country to country, as shown in Table 2.

Although East European nations have lengthened the compulsory education process, they have also tried to avoid delaying eventual entry of the young into the labor market. To accomplish this, state officials have lowered the school entry age and offered more polytechnical education in the primary school. (The latter step curbs the need for further training on the job or at the secondary level.) The actual numbers involved in primary education, country by country, are shown in Table 3.

The duration of compulsory education is not the only aspect that differs from country to country. The content and format of the education

TABLE 2

COMPULSORY EDUCATION

Country	Age Limits	Duration In Years
Albania	7 - 15	8
Bulgaria	7 - 16	8
Czechoslovakia	6 - 15	9
East Germany	7 - 16	10
Hungary	6 - 16	10
Poland	7 - 15	8
Romania	6 - 16	10
Yugoslavia	7 - 15	8

Source: United Nations Educational, Social, and Cultural Organization, Statistical Yearbook 1975, New York: 1976, pp. 72-84.

also vary. In general, primary education throughout the area is a stage of preparation for future careers and jobs. Since relatively few of the students who enter the school systems of Eastern Europe will ever see the inside of a college classroom, most of the emphasis is on preparation for a nonacademic future. Thus, there is much heavier emphasis on math and science than in U.S. schools. For example, East Germans have taken this to the extreme by converting their primary school into a ten-year polytechnical school. The East German experiment has generated a lot of discussion and criticism and is unique in Eastern Europe, if not the whole world. East German motivations are twofold. First, as socialism progresses, the future state will necessarily become more and more technically oriented, and education must keep pace with this evolving society. Second, since most students even now are channeled into technological employment, it is only natural that their education should occur in a basic school that heavily emphasizes math, physics, chemistry, biology, and geography, but also offers nonscientific subjects.

Critics in East Germany and abroad have pointed out that under such a system, the humanities and liberal arts suffer and the product of such a heavy scientific and technical education will be mere machine-like

TABLE 3

PRIMARY EDUCATION

Country	Year	No. of Institutions	No. of Teachers	No. of Students	Student: Teacher Ratio
Albania	1971	1,429	20,555	518,002	25:1
Bulgaria	1973	3,435	47,667	992,835	21:1
Czechoslovakia	1973	10,247	96,781	1,890,081	20:1
East Germany	1973	5,042	151,989	2,608,074	17:1
Hungary	1973	4,978	64,605	1,032,786	16:1
Poland	1973	18,889	213,017	4,634,316	22:1
Romania	1973	14,761	135,454	2,658,916	20:1
Yugoslavia	1972	13,761	123,860	2,856,491	18:1

Source: United Nations Educational, Social, and Cultural Organization, Statistical Yearbook 1975, New York: 1976, pp. 147-151.

workers. East German educational leaders have no plans for abandoning the experiment, however, and have answered their critics by maintaining that such schools simply reflect the reality of the dominance of technology in modern socialist states. The East Germans also argue that *all* citizens must be acquainted with such things, just as they are with music, history, and so on.[4]

East Germany, however, is not alone in its attempt to incorporate more polytechnical instruction into the basic schooling process. Every country in Eastern Europe has taken measures to this end. Bulgaria comes closest to East Germany in its willingness to make such a transformation, although not quite so radically. It has planned an increase in polytechnical instruction and, a component of such education, more first-hand opportunities for the students in factories and agricultural complexes in the first four years of school. Yugoslavia, despite recent signs of wariness, has also included polytechnical education in the fourth year of school on an intensive level. In Poland, as well as in East Germany, a subject entitled "Education by Labor" is taught as early as the first grade.[5] Ironically, most of the East European countries cannot adequately provide the modern equipment and instructional aids needed for such education. All of them cite this as a major weakness in their educational systems.

One less obvious reason for the heavy emphasis on polytechnical education is to curb the demands on general secondary schools and on universities and to help overcome negative attitudes toward labor on the part of the young, but progress in these areas has been slow.

The East European primary schools remain much more formal and demanding than their U.S. counterparts, especially in terms of curricula. There have been changes, however. Bulgaria, for example, achieved significant results in its efforts to reduce the problem of repeated classes, which Bulgarian educators believed had unacceptable psychological consequences for many students. Romania and Hungary initiated significant reductions in the work-load of students at the primary as well as at higher levels. On the other hand, another noteworthy development of the 1970s was the appearance of all-day primary schools to accommodate working mothers and to provide a structured school environment for the preparation of homework assignments. Czechoslovakia and East Germany have developed these facilities most, and East Germany plans for a vast increase of such schools in the future.

Hungary has already implemented some of the general reforms that were planned in the early 1970s. Some of the Hungarian reforms were prompted by parental complaints that the schools had longer days than did industrial establishments. A complete overhaul, with a deadline in 1978, was sanctioned in 1972 by the Central Committee. The reforms were to be carried out in three stages: 1) curing immediate problems, 2) revamping curricula in time for 1978 implementation, and 3) preparing long-range improvements for the 1980s. An immediate change was to cut the teaching load 20 percent across the board by eliminating chapters in textbooks. Since then, new texts and curricula have been issued. Private tutoring over four hours a week was forbidden. Recent experiments have even toyed with the idea of decentralizing educational planning and giving teachers more leeway in choosing texts to suit their own style of teaching. These changes, if implemented, would radically alter the face of Hungarian education.

Romania's educational system has also undergone a radical series of transformations that deserve much more discussion than can possibly be given in this chapter. Romanian education continued to reflect Soviet patterns in education for only a short time after the country decided to pursue a more independent foreign policy. In the late 1960s, intense discussion and debate centered around the "Directions of the Central Committee of the Communist Party Concerning the Development of Education in Romania, April 1968." The result was a series of new laws, beginning in May 1968. Both political and academic motives were evident in the new laws. The political goals stressed a denigration of Soviet educational influence, rehabilitation of the progressive heritage of Romanian education before World War II, and an effort to bring Romanian education closer to the more advanced systems and features of its counterparts in the West.

Major academic goals, in general, included an extension of compulsory education to ten years, improvement of evening and correspondence courses, modernization of curricula, texts, and teaching methods, improvement of civic and patriotic education, revamping and updating of teacher-training and retraining, diversification of secondary education, establishment of postuniversity refresher courses for specialists, and establishment of new intermediate schools for training junior engineers and architectural foremen. Also, the new curricula tend to deemphasize Marxism by submerging it in the study of philosophy in grades eleven and twelve. At the same time, there has been a corresponding emphasis on Romanian aspects of Communism and the role of Romania in the development of world Communism. Romanian authorities carefully point out that social patriotism does not conflict with proletarian internationalism.[6]

Insofar as chronic problems of education in Eastern Europe are concerned, Yugoslavia continues to have its unique ones, along with those problems common to all of the countries. The challenges that still have not been met include a continued lag by East European standards (and world standards) in pre-primary educational facilities. The multifarious ethnic scene has also led to problems that continue to defy resolution, such as the disparity of educational achievement among and between the federal republics and autonomous regions. Seriously high rates of illiteracy and dropping-out are still common in the southern regions of Kosovo-Metohija (Kosmet) and Montenegro. There also exists the problem of providing equal opportunities for education to the numerous minorities within each autonomous republic. These minorities often comprise significant percentages of the population and complicate efforts to develop uniform texts, standards, etc.

An important element in the curricula of all East European primary schools is language instruction. Only one foreign language is ever required, additional foreign languages are optional. The required language is Russian, except in Romania and Yugoslavia, and is introduced at various grade levels depending on the country. In Hungary and East Germany, for example, it is required in grades five through eight. Other languages are offered as an optional second language, the most popular being English, French, German, Spanish, and Italian. All countries have difficulty coping with the demand for English language instruction (at every level of the school system). Bulgaria operates several schools in which all instruction is in Russian. Russian is not mandatory in Yugoslavia and Romania for political reasons. Romania only recently dropped Russian as a requirement, as part of its de-Sovietization program. (It also replaced the traditional Russian five-point grading system with a new ten-point one.)

Upon reaching the end of the compulsory general education, the student is then faced with a choice of continuing into secondary education or directly entering the work force. The overwhelming majority of students decide to continue their schooling in some form of secondary education.

Secondary Education

The hallmarks of secondary education in Eastern Europe in the 1970s, as in preceding years, were diversity and narrow specialization. With the exception of the general secondary school, which prepares students for the university, all other secondary schools—especially vocational ones—offer very specialized training for hundreds of different jobs. There are three basic types of secondary schools in Eastern Europe: a general secondary school of four to five years oriented toward the university, technological secondary schools of four to five years that train technicians and industrial managers, and vocational training schools of two to three years aimed at producing skilled workers. The last category garners the majority of primary school graduates throughout Eastern Europe.

All three types of schools have seen profound changes due to the trend throughout Eastern Europe to lengthen the period of compulsory education. The compulsory education period at the primary level now includes two to three years of what was previously secondary education. Thus, those who do not enter general secondary schools or vocational secondary schools after eighth grade must still, for example in Romania, continue some form of education.

The old pattern was a short period of primary education, a longer period of secondary education (six to ten years), and another short term of higher education. This pattern has increasingly evolved into one of a long period of primary education, a shortened period of secondary education (two to five years), and a short term of higher education. The result has been some confusion as to the role of secondary education. The traditional role of secondary education was to provide an average level of vocational education or prepare for admission into higher studies. Increasingly, these roles are delegated to very specialized types of schools (either vocational or general in nature), and both can lead to

TABLE 4

HUNGARIAN PUPILS CONTINUING EDUCATION
AFTER THE EIGHTH GRADE

	1962	1969/70
General secondary schools	44.1%	34.4%
Vocational schools	27.8%	46.9%
Secretarial schools	2.6%	2.0%
Final two years of primary school	13.4%	5.2%
Total	87.8%	89.5%

higher education. Romania, Bulgaria, and Poland all plan for some amount of compulsory secondary education for the 1980s. The biggest developments of the 1970s, however, were the push toward more vocational education and increasing the percentage of students going on to secondary education.[7] In East Germany, for example, 16 percent of primary-school graduates went on to ninth and tenth grade in 1952; the figure rose to 73 percent in 1965 and to 88.6 percent in 1972. This trend is common to all of Eastern Europe. Figures for Hungary illustrate how quickly enrollments shifted from general secondary to vocational technical schools (see Table 4). In only seven years a significant shift occurred. Again, this pattern held true for all of Eastern Europe and was the result of intense pressure by governments to increase polytechnical enrollments.

These campaigns were spurred by two serious problems common to all of Eastern Europe, but not exclusive to the region by any means. The lingering prestige associated with general secondary schools (as opposed to technical or vocational) is one of these problems. From Yugoslavia to Poland, government officials have tackled this issue with only minimal success. Influenced by, or aware of, the traditional status of such schools, the political and social elite sends its children to the lyceum or gymnasium, while the average worker sends his or her children to some form of technical or vocational school. Since only the general secondary-school graduate has the right to apply to the university, all the benefits and positions accruing to people with a college degree tend to remain in the same societal circles. This, in turn, breeds a host of political problems emanating from feelings of resentment in the working class. Ironically, however, Hungarian officials have discovered that many workers do not wish to enroll their children in general secondary schools, no matter how prestigious. The parents feel that if the children obtain a general school degree but fail to be admitted to college, they will have no marketable skills, skills they would have obtained if they attended a vocationally oriented school. Such attitudes no doubt will continue to hamper public officials who must face the long-term social consequences from a fossilized system.

The other major problem stems from a demand from youth for more and more postprimary education, no matter what type. This flies in the face of the urgent economic need for skilled laborers with specialized training in every country in Eastern Europe. In states with chronic labor shortages, extended time for education is a luxury that cannot be easily afforded. This problem of state needs versus popular demand plagued educators and government officials in the 1970s, and the likelihood that it will be effectively eliminated is not great for the 1980s.

However, serious measures have been taken to overcome both problems. The most popular and effective measure, by far, to deal with the problem of gymnasium prestige has been curriculum reform, since the only real difference between gymnasium and polytechnical education is in the manner in which curricula are constructed. Polytechnical schools give little attention to general subjects, and gymnasiums to technical subjects. Thus, in almost every country in Eastern Europe, curricula are being juggled around so as to allow students to transfer from one type of school to another. More technical subjects are injected into the general school curriculum, and more general subjects appear on the list of courses offered in polytechnical schools. This arrangement, of course, allows more of the graduates of vocational and technical secondary schools to go on to higher education. Although it does tend to keep these students out of the work force for a longer time, at least they have, at the end of their coursework, skills that the country urgently needs.

Another very important and perhaps overdue step was to eliminate the barriers to higher education. All too often, vocational schooling meant a dead end, but this situation was radically altered in the 1970s. Czechoslovakia in 1968 and Poland in 1970 set up a new type of polytechnical school with a course lasting as long as that of the gymnasium, and most importantly, giving graduates the right to apply to institutions of higher education. Since then, such measures have spread to all of Eastern Europe, although only recently to Yugoslavia. East Germany, of course, has completely transformed most of its secondary educational institutions into polytechnical ones, so that only a few general schools still exist. The latest complete figures on secondary education

TABLE 5

TEACHER-STUDENT POPULATION IN SECONDARY SCHOOLS

Country	Data Year		Total Secondary Schools	General Education Schools	Teacher Training Schools	Vocational Technical Schools
Albania	1971	Teachers	3,030	1,318	N.A.	N.A.
		Pupils	85,441	23,229	N.A.	N.A.
Bulgaria	1973	Teachers	26,102	7,245	N.A.	18,857
		Pupils	391,509	94,723	N.A.	296,786
Czechoslovakia	1973	Teachers	24,103	7,829	457	15,817
		Pupils	397,492	119,547	10,240	267,705
East Germany	1973	Teachers	N.A.	N.A.	N.A.	N.A.
		Pupils	483,572	51,609	N.A.	431,963
Hungary	1973	Teachers	23,511	7,196	N.A.	N.A.
		Pupils	400,758	105,449	N.A.	293,242
Poland	1970	Teachers	164,353	22,358	3,742	138,253
		Pupils	1,361,343	401,306	26,585	933,452
Romania	1973	Teachers	38,648	13,115	1,377	24,156
		Pupils	719,167	214,057	21,724	483,386
Yugoslavia	1972	Teachers	25,144	10,230	850	14,064
		Pupils	770,665	193,275	10,174	567,216

Source: United Nations Educational, Social, and Cultural Organization, Statistical Yearbook 1975, New York: 1976, pp. 200-211.

enrollments in Eastern Europe (Table 5) show the distribution of students and teachers according to the various categories of schools.

While many countries are striving to make polytechnical secondary education more attractive, others such as Yugoslavia are worried about too much emphasis on this kind of education. This concern is one of the distinguishing characteristics of Yugoslav educational reform. Yugoslav educators of the 1970s believed that there had been, in the previous decade, too much emphasis on technological education aimed at greater productivity and efficiency, all at the expense of general education. In other words, broad education was replaced by mere training, which also stressed quantity rather than quality or understanding of what was learned. Education had become simply a valuable thing to possess in the marketplace. Reformers believed that even the actions taken to remedy the situation, such as adult education, were too utilitarian. Thus current plans for future educational reform in Yugoslavia stress the need for more attention to the content, not just the quantity, of education.

There is much discussion in some countries of Eastern Europe of the possibility of making all or part of the secondary educational process compulsory. Bulgarian reform guidelines stress the need for compulsory secondary education, although the focus is only on polytechnical schools. Hopes in Bulgaria are for the secondary polytechnical school to add two years (to make a total of ten years). At the same time, colleges will be reduced to four years instead of five, the number of postgraduate courses will be increased, and the age of entry into primary schools will be lowered to six years. The Bulgarians began to implement these reforms in 1975. There is also much discussion in Bulgaria about proposed measures to stimulate more creativity and participation in the school system. Thus, experimental curricula are being devised to allow more independent and individual study and to encourage more active participation by students (through youth groups) in all functions of the school, including the controlling organs. However, measures will be taken to ensure that there is no weakening of central control, by working to strengthen the schools as important ideological institutions.[8]

The problem of creativity in general also figured in Czechoslovakia's reform plans for education in the 1970s. The country has engaged in a program for revamping its entire educational system over an extended period of time. Goals of the reform plan are to bring the educational process closer to the interests and the requirements of the individual, and the development of a socialist society more in step with the progress in all the various fields of human endeavor. Reforms also aim at furthering the process of raising the educational level of all members of society. Much emphasis is placed on the choice and the structure of teaching materials and on Soviet studies of the learning process, in the interest of reducing the time required for learning simple ideas and skills, as well as complex ones, without risking the health of the students.[9]

The third element or category of secondary education in most East European countries stresses apprenticeship and practical training. Where they exist (Bulgaria, Czechoslovakia, Poland, and Yugoslavia), apprenticeship schools are akin to work-study arrangements in the United States. Another type of school similarly stresses practical training, but shifts the emphasis to more general education and less on-the-job training. These managerial schools are all part of the secondary school system as opposed to schools that are less formal. (These will be discussed in a section on special schools.)

Upon completion of secondary education, of whatever sort, graduates may proceed to higher education or enter the job market. The overwhelming majority choose the latter option. For those who wish to enter a higher educational institution, an arduous series of examinations, interviews, and more examinations must first be endured.

Higher Education

Despite increased numbers of secondary school graduates and growing demand for more opportunities, little has been done to make higher education more accessible in Eastern Europe. The primary reason is the chronic shortage of manpower and especially of skilled workers, a situation that does not encourage prolonging the educational process. And, in the face of outright attempts to discourage students from going on, the race for admission to higher education in Eastern Europe is as intense as ever.

A number of factors determine who will go on, including scholastic achievement, the ambition of parents for their child, student aspiration, location of schools, and financial position of the parents. While East Germany adamantly claims that no special privileges are accorded to any class, other countries reluctantly admit that "elitism" infects even the universities. But the most important factor by far in determining who or how many will enroll is the central government. Since entry into higher education in Eastern Europe is a virtual guarantee of a job, governments must try to balance supply with demand. This is a very risky and imprecise task at best. Each year the government (usually the Ministry of Education) consults with all potential employers and determines the number of job openings that will be available. The number of students with diplomas, however, outstrips the number of positions available each year. To further complicate the situation, many graduates demand or expect white-collar jobs in large urban centers, a trend not in keeping with the needs of East European countries. There is often a shortage of jobs for graduates simply because they have the kind of nontechnical preparation that the country needs in only limited quantities, while technical and agricultural jobs go begging. The result is that East European universities do not admit all who wish to study or even all who are eligible to enter. Admissions procedures are thus correspondingly strict and complicated.

The most immediate and drastic selection comes as the result of an initial entrance exam, which, if failed, can be repeated several times. (The particular exam taken is determined by the specific subjects that the student indicates he or she wishes to study.) Exemptions from these exams are rare and usually involve only those who have competed successfully in so-called Olympiads, a type of competition in mathematics and science. Poland offers a fairly typical example of the next steps in the selection process. Officials take the exam results and try to assess the candidates' chances of success at the university, for about 20 percent of all first-year students drop out. (This is a vexing problem for all of Eastern Europe.) In some faculties there are only a fixed number of places, and another exam is almost always necessary to eliminate surplus applicants. One must achieve a certain number of points on this exam (between fifteen and twenty-five), with the cutoff point varying. Children of peasants and workers automatically get a number of preference points (three) to help them compete with the children of families enjoying a higher standard of living or more cultural experiences—a practice criticized by those who claim that such inequalities have been eliminated. This typical process used by Poland shows how the selection procedure weeds out surplus candidates.[10]

The successful candidate has a wide variety of higher educational facilities from which to choose. The variety in part reflects some of the goals of higher education in Eastern Europe in the 1970s. All of the countries of Eastern Europe look upon higher educational institutions as one of the most important factors in the country's economic development. Thus, a primary goal of education is to provide graduates who are equipped with the means to help advance such development. Other important goals include the formation of a socialist personality and the preparation of students for active participation as leaders of social and cultural life in their respective countries. Also highly stressed is the need to preserve the cultural identity of the nation. Surely, the most difficult goal is to meet the enormous demand for well-trained specialists, while preserving the highest standards of scientific training.[11]

In every country of Eastern Europe, a whole network of universities, technical colleges, academies, and conservatories awaits the prospective student. In some countries, notably Bulgaria and Yugoslavia, there are also two-year schools that are postsecondary but not really full-fledged institutions of higher education. Bulgaria has what translates as "semi-higher" institutes of two years' duration, offering library training, winter agriculture, and telecommunications. Mostly these two-year schools are teacher-training facilities for kindergarten and primary school teachers.

Yugoslavia has "higher schools" that enroll about 31 percent of secondary school graduates and are often compared to U.S. community colleges. These schools are similar to their Bulgarian counterparts, offering mostly vocational and technical programs in agriculture, social work, engineering, and so on. Some graduates of these schools can and do go on to enter the university at upper levels.

Most degree work at higher educational institutions in Eastern Europe lasts considerably longer than two years. Universities are few in number, but some, such as Charles University in Prague, founded in 1348, are centuries old and have enjoyed great fame. Technical colleges, however, exist in greater numbers. Czechoslovakia, for example, has six universities, ten technical colleges, eight colleges of arts (music and fine arts),

TABLE 6

STUDENT ENROLLMENT IN HIGHER EDUCATION

Country	All Institutions	Universities & Equivalent Institutions	Nonuniversity Teacher Training Institutions	Other Non-university Institutions
Albania	28,668	18,449	5,243	4,976
Bulgaria	121,798	105,722	12,134	3,942
Czechoslovakia	135,874	135,874	N.A.	N.A.
East Germany	325,113	161,459	28,548	135,106
Hungary	98,122	62,225	8,613	27,284
Poland	N.A.	42,415	N.A.	N.A.
Romania	143,656	143,656	N.A.	N.A.
Yugoslavia	328,536	234,639	22,820	71,077

Source: United Nations Educational, Social, and Cultural Organization, Statistical Yearbook 1975, New York: 1976, pp. 256-262.

two colleges of economics, five colleges for agriculture, forestry, and veterinary medicine, and seven theological colleges. Bulgaria, to use another example, has only one university, seven technical or engineering institutes, three chemical-engineering institutes, three institutes of rural economy, three colleges of economics, three schools of fine arts, and one school of physical culture. The numbers involved in higher education throughout Eastern Europe are shown in Table 6. The figures for Albania are from 1971, all others are from 1973.

In every country, students in higher education receive some form of financial support, ranging from free tuition, book subsidies, low-cost housing and meals, to monthly stipends. There are also, of course, special scholarships that combine all of the above or simply make large cash payments per month to the student. Nevertheless, higher education is by no means absolutely free, and many students cannot attend simply because the combined costs are prohibitive. (This is especially the case for students who are not natives of the city or town where the school is located.)

Not all students receive outright and direct aid. For example, in 1968/69, 53.3 percent of all students in higher education in Hungary were given some form of financial aid: 48.5 percent lived in student hostels, and if inexpensive meal plans are taken into account, 91.3 percent of all students received some type of state subsidy. In 1970, Hungary revised its grant system and established a new one with three categories: 1) study grant, 2) social benefits, and 3) workshop-training allowances. The study grant allots 100–500 forints per month according to the applicant's scholastic record and evidence of activity in the student community. This category also includes scholarships for students with extremely high grades and scholarships established by firms. The social assistance category is based on a mathematical calculation of the student's share of his or her family income. Very low amounts result in free room and board, plus 300 forints per month. The third category consists of scholarships for workshop-training, which range from 700 to 1,000 forints per month.[12]

This system exists, with variations, throughout Eastern Europe. More costly forms of education, however, carry special responsibilities with them. For example, a newly graduated doctor in Bulgaria is obliged to spend two or three years working in remote rural areas chosen by the government before he or she is free to go where he or she pleases. The only way to avoid this duty is to go on for yet another advanced degree.

Postgraduate work in Eastern Europe can be done either at the university or at the Academy of Sciences. The Academy of Sciences holds a unique place in East European cultural life and has no exact equivalent in the United States. It is a state institution for research in almost every field and discipline. Although it is not, strictly speaking, a part of the formal educational system, it has enormous impact on it. Members of the academy are held in as high, if not higher, regard as university professors, who have always been deeply respected in Eastern Europe. There is close cooperation between the academy and higher educational establishments. Indeed, much of the research leading to reforms in school practice or revisions of textbooks occurs at the academies, usually at the pedagogical institute. The field of educational research has been the scene of very interesting new developments in East European education.

One significant new development is the growing integration of research with higher education and production processes. This often takes the form of a state-coordinated enterprise that unites and combines three of the most crucial factors in development: scientific research, education, and the economy. East European countries increasingly perceive this arrangement as a way to guarantee the maximum participation of their citizens in the process of world development. Bulgaria is an example of this process in its extreme form. The country has established huge complexes that combine scientific research institutes and industrial production units, such as the industrial complex at Titon in Plovdiv.

Romania has attempted similar complexes in Cluj and Timişoara. Bulgaria, it is estimated, has about 68 percent of its scientific potential invested in such complexes.[13]

Increasingly, many of the new developments in East European education are the result of specialized research, and Romania offers good examples of some typical new developments in educational research. During the watershed years of 1968 and 1969, many Romanian educators called for more emphasis on, and control of, educational research. A teachers' conference in 1969 demanded more research to buttress changes in curriculum, better organization of research, and better definition of the relationship of research to school practice and administration. The goal was, and is, to make the development of education not just a matter of school practice and policy, but a result of educational research as well—thus making research a more important factor in school progress.[14] Some of the tasks and goals of educational research not only in Romania but in all of Eastern Europe include: assessing future needs of school practice, devising ways to accelerate change by encouraging receptivity to change, preventing superficial or simplistic solutions to complex educational problems, and analyzing curricula and pedagogical practice, all with the cooperation of educators.

Current educational research in Eastern Europe is also heavily involved with such topics as adult education, development of new instructional materials to reflect the most recent advances, cybernetics, and efficiency of education. Most East European countries are aware that they lag behind the West in the application of advanced audio-visual methods, but this is due more to lack of financial resources than to any lack of desire to make use of such technology.

Except, perhaps, for East Germany and Bulgaria, most East European countries were more apt in the 1970s than previously to be part of the world educational scene. Articles by East European educators, especially Yugoslavs, Poles, and Romanians, are increasingly found in all the important international journals dealing with education. Also, there was more of a tendency in the 1970s for Western sources to play a role in educational reform. Czechoslovakian researchers, for example, in current work on educational reform use outstanding authorities in each sector of educational theory, whether it be B. F. Skinner (United States) and I. V. Zankov (USSR) for programmed instruction, or H. Heimpel (West Germany) for instruction by example. However, much more emphasis is given to Soviet authorities on learning processes and development of the learner.[15]

Czech researchers are currently excited about their development of what they call the "parallel-progressive" system of learning, which stresses teaching basic units of a subject first and interrelationships only later. It proceeds from general to complex considerations to specific and partial concepts.

Bulgarians have attracted attention (along with the Soviets) for their research on shortening the learning process without harming the health of students. Bulgarian researchers, however, are also interested in better application of research to education and studies on efficiency of education.

Not all of this research occurs only at the pedagogical institutes, however. The university also plays a part, for the university in Eastern Europe has always had an important role as a vehicle of research, and the decades of the 1950s and 1960s saw a tremendous emphasis on polytechnical education at the university level. The distinctions between universities and technical colleges became increasingly confused, to the extent that the issue was one of the most controversial in East European higher education in the 1970s.

The crux of the continuing debate over specialization really concerns the definition of the role of university education. Should it be purely professional and specialized, or should it impart broad general knowledge? Should it be more closely tied to practical polytechnical and industrial work or continue to foster theoretical research? Should the university train people for specific professions or provide an education applicable to many professions?

These were the controversial questions of the 1970s and so far none has been adequately resolved. On the one hand, employers and graduates pressure universities to prepare students in such a way that there will be few problems when students take jobs in their specific professions. This demand has been buttressed by increased government control over curricula to satisfy such concerns. On the other side are those who maintain that a university is a repository of general knowledge and also a generator of original research. They have criticized the "school-like" nature of university education. The university, they claim, is also a public institution, which, in the words of the sixteenth-century Czech educator Johan Amos Komensky (1592–1671), must let "everybody know all about everything." The universities, they argue, must be intellectual centers that promote the exchange of thought and learned discussions. But the days when professors were free to arrange and structure their courses and when students were free to choose from such courses without any state interference are long since gone.[16]

There have been some efforts to seek a compromise solution by allowing more autonomy to university administrators. Such cautious attempts are underway, for example, in Romania and Hungary. In both countries, the tendency is away from government control. Reforms in Hungary in the early 1970s aimed at aiding the development of democracy and limiting government regulations to only the most important problems. Also, the reforms attempted to revitalize university and faculty councils, while also experimenting with more student control over university life. Seminar forms of instruction were introduced, and experiments allowed students to have an opportunity to choose more electives. Universities will have more power to implement plans of their own. Romania has introduced similar reform plans.

While discussion and debate on these issues continue, other problems also receive serious consideration. Throughout Eastern Europe, the equipment and materials needed to meet impossibly high goals are rarely available in sufficient quantities. Another problem involves the same conflict found in higher education but on the secondary level: state goals and needs versus the personal goals of individual students. Such conflicts are not uncommon, yet much needs to be accomplished in this area throughout Eastern Europe. The most serious situation of all, however, is that despite careful attempts in each country to match job openings and needs with university admissions, an unacceptably large percentage of graduates eventually take jobs unrelated to their professional training—approximately 35 percent according to some estimates.

Special and Specialized Education

There are some educational facilities that do not fit into the normal school system because they are highly specialized and thus deserve separate treatment. Into this category fall special schools for workers, schools for the handicapped, teacher-training schools, party schools, ideological education, adult education, minority schools, and audio-visual instruction. In some cases, what is specialized or special education in one country is a regular feature of the educational system of another. For example, vocational education is a special category in Romania, Poland, and Yugoslavia, but more closely tied to regular school systems in East Germany and Bulgaria. All countries, however, have schools for vocational technical education that are difficult to classify. Usually these take the form of one- or two-year courses, consisting of instruction in a specific skill, such as carpentry, automotive maintenance, or culinary skills. These schools are usually at the secondary level, but Hungary has over 500 extremely specialized schools on the primary level (specializing in gymnastics, music, Russian, or even Esperanto). Recently, however, a director of educational planning, Lazlo Toth, criticized such schools for their narrowness of concentration and for their failure to give students a well-rounded background.[17]

This problem is less crucial, however, when such schools exist on the secondary level. Every country has its equivalent of the People's Arts and Language Schools in Czechoslovakia, which offer intensive programs in arts, music, dance, or foreign languages to young people who have proven talent. Bulgaria has several high schools in which all instruction is in Russian, French, German, or English—with intense competition for entry, particularly into those schools conducted in Western languages.

For those already working, special provisions are usually made to help them complete education or to acquire special skills. A variety of workers' schools exist throughout the area, and some are part of more formal adult education programs. The status of adult education varies considerably from country to country, but is developing rapidly everywhere. East Germany launched an ambitious program in 1970 to develop an already complicated structure of adult education facilities. Yugoslavia gave considerable attention to adult education in the 1970s. All East European countries recognize that the future will bring increasing need for continuing education in the face of rapidly and constantly changing technology. But not all of these adult education programs have been or will be geared toward only the practical needs of the country or its citizens.

Another special type of education in Eastern Europe is that provided for training teachers, and as with adult education, this type of education varies greatly from country to country. Up until the 1970s, most countries had both secondary and higher educational institutions to serve this purpose. The trend of the 1970s, however, was toward a more simplified structure. Bulgaria, Poland, Czechoslovakia, and Yugoslavia abolished secondary pedagogical schools in favor of either higher pedagogical institutes (postsecondary) (as in Poland or Yugoslavia) or regular enrollment in existing faculties at colleges and universities, with pedagogical courses as part of the curriculum (such as in Czechoslovakia and Bulgaria). This, of course, has resulted in a higher level and longer duration of training for all teachers. (Kindergarten teachers are often exempt from such high requirements.) Romania is an exception to the trend. Up until the 1970s, there was a distinct division of training for lower and upper secondary school teachers, but this is also on the way out in favor of unified training systems.[18]

Czechoslovakia is an example of the newer system in operation. Teachers for kindergarten are still trained in a four-year course at special vocational secondary schools, where they receive instruction in child-care and academic subjects. An experimental program, set up in 1971, offered some of these students education courses at the university level. Students training to be teachers in the primary schools attend four-year programs in education at the university level, while those planning to teach secondary school follow a five-year program at a specific faculty on the university level. The diplomas of these graduates indicate their respective areas of specialization and the level at which they are qualified to teach.

Ministries of education in Eastern Europe have also begun to formulate plans for mandatory graduate courses for all teachers. Czechoslovakia already requires that teachers undertake a four-semester graduate pedagogical program sometime during the first ten years of their teaching experience.[19]

There is one special and extremely important form of education in Eastern Europe yet to be discussed, and that is ideological education. This form of education has many varieties and takes place in a number of ways. Much ideological instruction occurs in the regular classroom, always an important vehicle for education. There are also special youth organizations that are designed to impart ideological training and that work closely with educators inside and outside of the regular school system. Finally, there are special schools for the training of future party cadres.

The goals of ideological training, as defined by various governments, all begin with acquainting the students with the fundamentals of Marxist-Leninist ideology. This is hardly the only task of ideological education, although it is without question the most important. Other goals include helping the students share socialist convictions and consciousness as well as shaping the socialist personality. More pragmatic functions stress inculcation of love for labor, active patriotism, and appreciation of the goals of the state in the construction of socialism.

There has been a growing trend toward injecting more and more of these ideas into the regular classrooms via courses on civic education. Such courses often begin in the earliest grades. East German schools, for example, now teach this subject in the first grade with two classes weekly until the fourth grade, when three more classes are added that stress civic education, field work, and premilitary activity.[20]

Outright political indoctrination classes usually begin in Eastern Europe only in the upper levels of the educational system. The combination of politics and the classroom has provoked criticism from Western educators. But East Europeans earnestly defend such instruction by claiming that capitalist countries do much the same thing—only the politics of the latter are deplorable. Also, they contend, if children disregard politics, they will simply become the pawns of politics made by others.

Another popular system of political education used throughout Eastern Europe involves Communist-run youth organizations. These are always divided into two distinct age groups. All countries have an organization called "Young Pioneers" for the age group of six- or seven-year-olds to that of fourteen- or fifteen-year-olds. The organizations for older children are modelled more closely after the actual party structure. These groups carry a variety of names, such as Communist Youth Union in Romania, Free German Youth in the German Democratic Republic, and the Young Communist League in Bulgaria. All of the youth organizations, however, perform the same kinds of duties and provide a wide range of activities for their school-age members.

The Young Pioneer groups are usually organized according to grades in local schools, in order to build on already existing peer groups. Activities for this junior branch are usually physical in nature and include participating in summer camps, picnics, and field trips to historical sites and museums, as well as a minor amount of actual discussion of politics.

The older youths' activities are much more serious, although physical exercise and sports activities are still important. Cultural events play a larger role, and the children spend more time in study circles and political education. Also, more of their activities tend to be socially and economically useful. Members will often help with particular agricultural chores at sowing and harvest times. Sometimes, they will raise money for needed equipment such as a train locomotive, which will then be named for the group. Members of these organizations are often encouraged to involve themselves in technically oriented hobbies, such as building transistors and robots.

The authority and importance of such youth groups are immense. There are few extracurricular activities or clubs in Eastern Europe that are not supervised, in some way or another, by Communist youth groups. Every school has a representative of such groups, and in secondary and higher educational levels there is usually a member of the youth groups on policymaking or control boards.

Recently, however, there has been growing criticism of the effectiveness not only of the youth groups but of ideological education programs in general. Romania's Communist Youth Union was heavily criticized by the Central Committee of the Romanian Communist party for its general failure in the guidance of youth. The Central Committee accused the youth groups of encouraging negative attitudes toward labor—something they were supposed to be correcting. Also, according to high party leaders, the youth groups offered fossilized, outdated, and unappealing programs to their members. To remedy the situation, the Romanian Communist party stripped the youth union of some important duties and responsibilities, investing them instead in educational and cultural organs. While such drastic measures occurred only in Romania, problems with ideological education were not limited to that nation. Bulgaria, for example, cited its own ideological education program for failure to achieve designated goals. Party leaders especially noted signs of nationalism, as well as a lack of discipline and enthusiasm in many chapters of the youth groups. The groups also failed to promote any rapport between authorities and young people, especially those of college age.[21] Other typical complaints of failures of ideological instruction programs involve the persistent interest of East European youth in the West and in the United States, outright resistance to youth organization work, and worst of all, apathy toward the goals of the state in the promotion of socialism.

Conclusion

Whatever the changes and reforms that took place in Eastern Europe in the 1970s, they were all the result of much thought, discussion, and, in many cases, research. Change has always proceeded on a continuum, and a slow-moving one at that. In the past, East European nations have been able to leisurely pick and choose among the advances in educational practices or technology developed by other countries, unless of course the Soviet Union mandated a new approach or practice. However, this luxury is rapidly becoming a thing of the past since East European countries are all painfully aware of serious lags in the application of more advanced teaching methods and technological improvements. Yet overcoming such shortages and lags may prove easier than overcoming the chronic problems of morale and attitude that still exist from earlier periods. The recent cries of concern over the apathy of the young have led to very tentative moves toward encouraging more participation and creativity on the part of the young. Such moves could have interesting and important consequences and merit close attention.

The problems and challenges facing Eastern Europe are not unique to that area, and without any doubt, the area's increasing participation and involvement in world educational affairs will lead to more experimentation with, or at least attention to, foreign methods of solving universal problems of education. The tendency to polycentrism in educational affairs will no doubt continue—a trend not without certain risks in terms of possible reaction from the Soviet Union.

It will be interesting to watch the denouement of other important trends and developments. What effect, if any, will Romania's radical anti-Soviet measures have on the educational programs of other countries in the area? What will be the outcome of the debate on the nature and role of the university in the future educational systems of Eastern Europe? How well will the area meet the demands for more higher educational opportunities? These are but a few of the questions facing the future of education in Eastern Europe. Perhaps, the growing emphasis on educational research will make it easier to cope with these issues.

No matter what the future may hold for East European education, the area will certainly remain a fascinating one for international observers in all fields of education.

Notes

1. Jan Szczepanski, *Higher Education in Eastern Europe* (New York, 1974), p. 19.
2. S. A. Farmerie, "Educational Organization in Yugoslavia," *Educational Forum* (November 1974):71–76.
3. S. A. Farmerie, "Education in Yugoslavia," *Clearing House* 44 (November 1972):146.
4. Wolfgang Reischock, *Education for Today and Tomorrow* (Dresden, 1973), pp. 26–27.
5. J. Nica and C. Birzea, "Educational Innovation in European Socialist Countries," *International Review of Education* 19, no. 4 (October 1973):454
6. Randolph L. Braham, *Education in Romania: A Decade of Change* (Washington, D.C., 1972), p. 59.
7. Nica and Birzea, "Educational Innovation," pp. 451ff.
8. N. Grant, "Educational Reforms in Bulgaria," *Comparative Education* (November 1970):180–188.
9. Bogumir Kujal, "Research into New Educational Methods in Czechoslovakia," *Prospects* 5, no. 1 (Spring 1975):105.
10. Szczepanski, *Higher Education*, pp. 13–14.
11. *Ibid.*, pp. 10–11; B. Suchodolski, "The East European University," in Brian Holmes and David Scanlon, eds., *The World Yearbook of Education 1971/72: Higher Education in a Changing World* (London, 1971), p. 125.
12. Hungary, Ministry of Education, *Education and Cultural Activities in Hungary, 1945–1970* (Budapest, 1970), pp. 13–14.
13. Nica and Birzea, "Educational Innovation," p. 455.
14. Dumitru Muster and G. Văideanu, "Contemporary Romanian Education," *Journal of Education* 152, no. 3 (February 1970):66.
15. Kujal, "Research," p. 106.
16. Suchodolski, "East European University," pp. 123–133.
17. F. Lipsius, "Five Year Plan Lays Stress on Flexibility," *London Times Edu-*

cational Supplement, December 6, 1974, p. 14.
18. N. Grant, "Teacher Training in the USSR and Eastern Europe," *Comparative Education* 8 (April 1972):11–12.
19. Peter A. Toma, *The Educational System of Czechoslovakia* (Washington, D.C., 1976), p. 9.
20. Nica and Birzea, "Educational Innovation," p. 456.
21. N. Grant, "Educational Reforms," p. 187.

Selected Bibliography

Anweiler, Oskar. "Towards a Comparative Study of the Educational Systems in the Socialist Countries of Europe." *Comparative Education 11* (March 1975):3–11.

Avramova, Bistra. *Education in Bulgaria.* Sofia, 1969.

Berger, Guy P. "The Planned Establishment of a National Educational Technology Center in Hungary." *Educational Media International* 1 (March 1974):19–22.

Braham, Randolph L. *Education in the Hungarian People's Republic.* Washington, D.C., 1970.

_____.*Education in Romania: A Decade of Change.* Washington, D.C., 1972.

Chabe, A. M. "Soviet Education Faces the 70's." *Educational Leadership* 27 (April 1970): 678–682.

Cohen, G. "What's Happening in Eastern European Schools." *National Association of Secondary School Principals Bulletin,* 55 (November 1971):40–52.

Commins, E. "Kindergarten: Yugoslavian Style." *Young Children* 28 (October 1972):20–25.

Farmerie, S. A. "Education in Yugoslavia." *Clearing House* 47 (November 1972): 145–149.

_____."Educational Organization in Yugoslavia." *Educational Forum* 39 (November 1974):71–76.

Georgeoff, John. "Innovations in Balkan Education." *National Association of Secondary School Principals Bulletin* 55 (November 1971):10–17

Grant, N. "Educational Reform in Bulgaria." *Comparative Education* 6 (November 1970):179–191.

_____."Teacher Training in the USSR and Eastern Europe." *Comparative Education* 8 (April 1972):7–29.

Hahn, W. "Teachers under Communism: The Case of East Germany." *Educational Leadership* 30 (January 1973):331–335.

Hearndon, A. "Individual Freedom and State Intervention in East and West German Education." *Comparative Education* 10 (June 1974):131–135.

Holowinsky, I.Z. "Special Education in Eastern Europe." *Journal of Special Education* 9 (Winter 1975):435–437; and 10 (Spring 1976):107–110.

Hungary. Ministry of Education. *Education and Cultural Activities in Hungary,*

1945-1970. Budapest, 1970.

Kuberski, Jerzy, and Wolczyk, Jerzy. "The Bases of the Reform of the Educational System in Poland." *Prospects* 5 (1975):301-311.

Kujal, Bogumir. "Research into New Educational Methods in Czechoslovakia." *Prospects* 5 (1975):105-110.

Lipsius, F. "Five Year Plan Lays Stress on Flexibility." *London Times Educational Supplement.* December 6, 1974.

Muster, Dumitru, and Văideanu, G. "Contemporary Romanian Education." *Journal of Education* 152 (February 1970):64-71.

Nast, Manfred. "The Planning of Higher Education in the German Democratic Republic." *Higher Education* 3 (1974):201-212.

Nica, I., and Birzea, C. "Educational Innovation in European Socialist Countries." *International Review of Education* 19 (October 1973):447-459.

Parker, Franklin. "Observations on Education in Hungary, Romania, the USSR, and Poland." *National Association of Secondary School Principals Bulletin* 56 (December 1972):65-71.

Pecherski, Mieczyslaw. "Changes in the Polish System of Teacher Education Since 1972." *International Review of Education* 21 (1975):407-421.

Reischock, Wolfgang. *Education for Today and Tomorrow.* Dresden, 1973.

Schmitt, K. "Education and Politics in the German Democratic Republic." *Comparative Education Review* 19 (February 1975):31-50.

Schneider, Gottfried. "Adult Education in the German Democratic Republic." *Prospects* 11 (1977):263-271.

Snow, Carl B. "Educational Technology in Three Iron Curtain Countries." *Audiovisual Instruction* 16 (October 1971):71-74.

Šoljan, Nikša Nikola. "Some Problems of Educational Theory and Policy in Yugoslavia." *Prospects* 7 (1977):184-194.

Sosnovskii, T. "Secondary Vocational-Technical Schools in the Polish People's Republic." *Soviet Education* 14 (May 1972):41-46.

Suchodolski, B. "The East European University." In Brian Holmes and David Scanlon, eds., *The World Yearbook of Education 1971/72: Higher Education in a Changing World.* London, 1971.

Sufin, Zbigniew. "Planning and Implementation of Educational Reform in Poland." *Educational Planning* 2 (March 1976):45-52.

Szczepanski, Jan. *Higher Education in Eastern Europe.* New York, 1974.

Toma, Peter A. *The Educational System of Czechoslovakia. Education Around the World.* Washington, D.C., 1976.

United Nations Educational, Scientific, and Cultural Organization. *Statistical Yearbook, 1975.* Louvain, 1976.

Zelenskii, G. "Vocational-Technical Training in the GDR." *Soviet Education* 14 (May 1972):34-40.

Joseph Held

9

Cultural Development

From the very beginning of their activities, the aims of all East European Communist leaders included the creation of a "new socialist man." This man was to make the triumph of Marxism-Leninism in their societies come to pass. Leninist theory maintained that culture was "the aggregate of material and spiritual values, and the means of . . . passing them on, created by society in the course of history"[1] and was, therefore, open to manipulation by the new social engineers. In fact, the cultural patterns that were about to be imposed upon the peoples of the region were so alien to their historical experiences that they could not be expected to embrace them wholeheartedly. Consequently, the Communist leaders mistrusted their own peoples, considering that even the proletariat was infected by "bourgeois ideals"; hence, the need for the creation of the "new man."

One of the means—besides outright coercion—by which the new culture was to be established was "socialist realism." This vague notion was based on the assertion that creative people in bourgeois society could view the struggles of the proletariat only "from outside." This condition allegedly led intellectuals to misunderstand or even deliberately distort workers' culture.[2] Once these intellectuals accepted "socialist realism," however, as their guiding principle, they could no longer remain disinterested observers of socialist construction. Instead, they would become committed cultural workers. As such, they were to be required to labor enthusiastically, together with the local Communist party, for the common goal, the creation of "new socialist men," and the speedy construction of socialist society. This made detached observation not only impossible, but an outright antisocialist activity.[3]

Since socialist construction required a very high level of political consciousness, creative activity in a country building socialism was to reflect mainly the "positive" values of a future socialist society. The writers, artists, and poets of the East European Communist regimes labored to create "positive heroes" in the image of the future new man. Such heroes had no vices or weaknesses and they constantly and heroically struggled against the scoundrel-bourgeois opponents of socialist construction. These superheroes were one-dimensional; the literature and art that produced them was drab, boring, and phony. In the best Orwellian sense, the "new man" was the most unrealistic produced in any age. "Socialist realism" was but a blatant version of neo-romanticism with all the trappings of the real thing without its redeeming virtues. "Truth" was simply a function of the constantly changing party line, and the works of "socialist realism" projected a never-never land flowing with milk and honey. This situation pertained during most of the late 1940s and 1950s in all East European countries.

The consequences, as Francois Fejtö observed, were devastating. There was a drab uniformity, a nihilistic rejection of national traditions, slavish imitation of the Soviet model—whatever that happened to be—and cultural isolation from general European civilization.[4] In short, the East European Communists tried to impose their version of culture on their respective peoples, intent on destroying whatever was left of traditions.

In the early 1960s under Khrushchev's leadership, it seemed that the Soviet Russian leaders had learned from their mistakes and had taken the utter failure of their East European cultural policies to heart. They had largely replaced the rigid, uncompromising Stalinists who ruled the East European empire, which had been shaken by the revolts in East Germany, Poland, and Hungary in the 1950s, with more flexible men. Kadar in Hungary, Gomulka in Poland, Ceauşescu in Romania, and the Svoboda-Dubcek team in Czechoslovakia proceeded to relax censorship. They all tried to live by the slogan, voiced first by Janos Kadar, that "who is not against us is with us." Thus, intellectuals almost everywhere in Eastern Europe were given greater freedom for creative work and there was, as a consequence, a revitalized cultural life in the region. But the Communist leaders did not reckon with the consequences; the "new" cultural life that emerged from the shadow of Stalinist terror and coercion was not necessarily "socialist" in content. In fact, most creative people in the region began to reestablish the European roots of their culture, which were neither socialist nor capitalist, but simply national. The Communist parties of the region were, in fact, simply ignored in the new creative efforts, and the results were often embarrassing for the party leaders. Moreover, there was a revival of the national classics; the works of Ionescu, Kafka, Laszlo Nemeth, and Kolakowski reappeared on the bookshelves, and their books sold rapidly. Thus, the relaxation that threatened the monopoly of the Communist parties over cultural life had to be partially abandoned.

Czechoslovakia's attempt in 1968 to introduce a non-Soviet type of socialism illustrated vividly the possible consequences of the relaxation of controls for the cohesion of the Soviet empire. When some of the controls were reinstated in Eastern Europe in the early 1970s, intellectuals were frequently reminded that the limits—although not as strict as before—were still there, and that the parties were intent on maintaining as much control over creative activity as was prudently possible. But this was a much more difficult matter in the 1970s than before. Thanks to the advancing process of modernization, the East European nations have developed more complex social organisms and Stalinist mass terror could no longer be revived without dangerous consequences. Thus, the cultural policies pursued by the various Communist parties in the region showed greater flexibility and a grudging toleration of some of the nonsocialist manifestations of cultural activities. As Ivan Volgyes remarked, the regimes in the region distinguished between highly desirable, tolerable, and prohibited acts of creativity, and acted in accordance with these distinctions.[5] Almost all of the leaders realized by now the futility of Russification of the East European national cultures. In turn, there emerged tendencies among some of the Communist leaders to encourage identification of their party with at least some of their respective national traditions and aspirations. But they all had to tread carefully in these matters since a revival of nationalism carried potentially dangerous consequences for the entire Soviet empire.

Thus, there emerged a wider variation in cultural policies among the East European Communist regimes than ever before. The most rigid policies are still carried out in Czechoslovakia and Romania. In Hungary and Poland, the atmosphere is more relaxed. In Yugoslavia, fear of the impending death of Tito led to a tightening of control over all spheres of life, including cultural affairs, from 1975 on. In East Germany and Bulgaria, there has never been a relaxation, and cultural policies continue under tight control. One can hardly speak of cultural life in Albania, where the population is just emerging from a premodern age.

Thus, there was less talk of "socialist realism" in the 1970s, in the way it was understood in the 1950s, even in countries where cultural policies remained strict. The adulation of mediocre Soviet writers stopped. The new literature everywhere began focusing on the problems and conflicts, the inner confusion, of the individual human being when confronted by a variety of experiences produced by modernization. A prominent theme of this literature is alienation from society, regardless of its political character. The new heroes often appear as helpless pawns in facing the soul-less bureaucrats of the state, reflecting a general human condition. That this literature is still largely provincial—and that few of the authors have become known in the West—is not surprising. It is the consequence of almost two decades of complete isolation from the currents of European culture.

During the 1970s, the various Communist parties continued to insist that Marxist-Leninist ideology be the basis of cultural life. But these parties have practically given up on the older generation of creative people. What they are currently interested in is the education of the young, their resocialization in the values deemed appropriate for the socialist society. The aim has not changed that much, after all. It is still the creation of a new man, even if the methods applied are somewhat more flexible. And the rewards for compliant intellectuals and artists are a great deal more tangible. It includes the publication of their works, free exhibition places for their paintings, state prizes, and recognition of their sometimes mediocre talents. For adherence to official lines, there are now ample financial rewards, passports to visit the "decadent" West, and opportunities for their children to be admitted to the universities. There are also automobiles, good apartments, and other opportunities for a good life. It seems that these policies have worked to a great extent. By the end of the 1970s, the Communist parties in all East European societies could count on the support of a substantial segment of the intelligentsia. Even if the degree of support varied among the individuals and societies, a modus vivendi had finally been found.

*   *   *

In many ways Czechoslovakia represents an exception to the rule. This is obviously the result of the relatively recent Warsaw Pact invasion of Czechoslovakia and the repression of the intellectuals that followed. The cultural policies of Gustav Husak and his followers were dictated by the needs of "normalization " and the needs of the Communist party to consolidate its hold on the population once again. On the twenty-fifth anniversary of the Communist coup d'etat in Czechoslovakia, Husak declared that his party was determined to retain its leading role in national life in complete loyalty to the Soviet Union, "struggling to the death against the revisionists of 1968."[6]

Miloslav Bruzek, minister of culture between 1968 and 1972, symbolized the policies of the Husak government. He introduced a purge of writers from the Writers' Union, ordered their works to be taken off the bookshelves, and prevented the publication of their newer works. Actors, painters, and other creative artists who participated in the reform era shared the same fate. At the International Historical Congress in San Francisco in August 1975, a list was submitted of 140 Czech historians who were dismissed from their jobs. The list was headed by Josef Macek, former director of the Czechoslovak Historical Institute of the Academy of Sciences.[7] New artists' unions were also organized that excluded all those who had been active during the 1960s, thus depriving them of their livelihood. Prague remained throughout the 1970s the most loyal and consistent supporter of Moscow's foreign policies and ideological line. Husak came out strongly in support of all Russian positions at the 1976 meeting of the European Communist parties, declaring that the socialist countries had common, well-defined interests that required the close coordination of their activities.[8]

Loyalty to the Soviet Union is, therefore, the hallmark of the cultural policies of the Husak regime. This loyalty is expressed in every possible way. For instance, in an interview with Russian Professor Michail S. Dzhunusov in *Mlada Fronta* (the daily paper of the Czechoslovak League of Young Communists) in 1976, the sensitive issues of "socialist patriotism" and the characteristics of the "new" Soviet man were discussed. Dzhunusov asserted that the Soviet Union had succeeded in overcoming ethnic antagonisms and creating a "new socialist man." He further stated that "perspectives for creating socialist men have also appeared in the countries of the socialist community." This meant that conditions were once again ripe for following the Soviet example and coordinating the cultural policies of the East European countries with those of Soviet Russia. That the implication of this published interview was not lost on other members of the socialist bloc was shown by the vehement arguments between Czechoslovakia and Yugoslavia that followed.[9]

But the repression of the reformists in Czechoslovakia constituted only the first phase of "consolidation." Husak himself is a moderate-conservative Communist who suffered during the rule of the Stalinists. Furthermore, the Helsinki Agreement, signed by the Czechoslovak government, had to be considered, if for no other reason than as a sop to Western opinions.

To be sure, the interpretations of the provisions of the agreement were undertaken in the spirit of Marxism-Leninism, and they certainly did not mean the abandonment of the so-called anti-imperialist struggle at home and abroad. Thus, they could easily be circumvented by arguments that, for instance, easy access to literature did not mean to "poisonous works disguised as culture," such as those of Solzhenytsin and Pasternak.[10] But Husak is basically a reformer within the context of his own conservatism; he soon realized that repression had to be eased, as it had been in Hungary and Poland after 1956. Some of the reformers were released from jail; lesser participants in the experiment with "socialism with a human face" were gradually given jobs in areas of their expertise as the 1970s progressed.[11] A sign of this gradual relaxation was that, in

1975, Pavel Kohut was granted a passport to visit Austria and Switzerland, where his plays were being performed, and Milan Kundera was permitted to teach in France.

Although Minister of Culture Bruzek was dismissed in 1972, his replacement, Milan Klusak, did not change the essential characteristics of his predecessor's policies. Klusak, anxious to enlist the cooperation of intellectuals, demanded that they denounce the reformists. Many intellectuals were unwilling to do this, but there were some who because of government pressure could not hold out any longer. Three major literary figures thus condemned their own deviation: Miroslav Holub, Jiri Sotola, and Bohumir Hrabal, the author of *Closely Watched Trains*, proclaimed that they had been in error in 1968. The Marxist philosopher Jiri Cvetl also joined them and openly denounced Dubcek and the reformists.[12]

Shortly after his appointment, Klusak turned his attention to the educational system. Under his personal direction the curricula of elementary and secondary schools were reorganized. They now clearly reflect the Communist party's view that schools are the primary means for the transmission of Marxist-Leninist ideology to the next generation, and thus the major means for the creation of the "new men." A new law on higher education followed shortly in April 1980, which strengthened the control of the Ministry of Education over colleges and universities. Admission policies continued to be based on class criteria; the appointment of university officials and the contents of the various curricula were placed in the hands of the bureaucrats of the ministry.

In order to curtail the influence of various churches in the Czechoslovak state, the party continued to emphasize the antireligious nature of socialism. Although agreements were finally reached with the Vatican over the appointment of four bishops to long-vacant sees, and a new cardinal was created by the pope in the Bishop of Litomerice, Stepan Trochta, this simply represented a change of tactics, not of strategy. The regime continued its militantly antireligious policies and campaigns. Books were published on antireligious themes, and conferences held on practical atheism in the countryside. An exhibit of atheistic traditions in Czechoslovakia was opened in the Slovak National Museum in Bratislava in May 1980, underscoring this theme.[13]

Despite all the efforts of the regime, dissident cultural activities continued. Even in death, prominent dissidents seemed to haunt the present leadership. A long posthumous interview, published in the Western press by Josef Smrkovsky in 1975, greatly embarrassed Husak. Even Dubcek felt compelled to defend himself; in a long letter, also published in the West, he defended his policies of the 1960s. Ludwig Vaculik, the famous writer, complained of political and cultural repression to United Nations Secretary Waldheim during Waldheim's visit to Prague. Vaclav Havel, the writer; Karel Kosik, a Marxist philosopher; and Ivan Malek, a microbiologist and former president of the Czechoslovak Academy of Sciences, all expressed their open disapproval of the "normalization" policies of the Husak regime. Dr. Julius Tomin, a former professor at Charles University, began lecturing at his own home, calling his presentations the Jan Patocka Free University. Tomin's course focused on Aristotelian ethics, the implications of which for the conduct of Czechoslovak internal affairs were obvious. In May 1980, Tomin was arrested together with twelve of his students for unlawful assembly, despite the fact that the Czechoslovak constitution does not prohibit the type of work that he had undertaken. Earlier in the year, two visiting scholars from Oxford were arrested at his home and expelled from Czechoslovakia, creating some stir in the West.[14] Tomin's son was denied admission to high school, and the former professor's activities are constantly monitored by the secret police.

In sum, Czechoslovak cultural life, reflecting political conditions in the country, are going through an ambivalent phase. The Communist leaders are anxious to present the picture of a stable, busy society engaged in the building of socialism. To a certain extent they have succeeded in eliminating the most glaring opposition to their policies. Perhaps one should not exaggerate the dissidents' impact in present-day Czechoslovakia; it is certainly true that for every Tomin there are two or three others who have made their peace with the current leadership. It is also true that the vitality and exuberance that characterized Czechoslovak cultural life in the 1960s was nowhere in evidence in the 1970s, which may be a small price to pay for stability from the point of view of the Communist leaders.

* * *

Cultural life in Romania is as closely controlled by the Communist party as it is in Czechoslovakia. But the situation is more complicated in the Romanian case by the attempts of the party to combine an old-fashioned Stalinist "personality cult" with the requirements of the modernization of society. The modernizing of society is called "multilateral development"; this means the simultaneous development of the economy and all other areas of national life, including culture, in the spirit of a Romanian version of Marxism-Leninism. All cultural endeavors are subordinated to this aim, and Romanian nationalism is a strong component of these efforts. The Communist party of Romania is portrayed as the direct successor to the great patriotic movements of the past. The National Conference of the Union of Artists, held in 1971, represented the opening gambit of these efforts, to identify with the "glorious" past, and it also signalled the consolidation of the power of the Ceauşescu family.

Romania, thus, represents a special case among the East European nations. This is evident in the special role that the Ceauşescu family plays in the affairs of state. The entire family shares in the adulation accorded to the head of the family, Nicolae. The latter is usually described as "the founder of Romania and a wise thinker"; his wife, Elena, is referrred to as "the first lady of Romania" and "the most just woman in the world."[15] Family members occupy important governmental positions. For instance, Elena Ceauşescu was appointed chairperson of the National Council on Science and Technology. Simultaneously with her appointment, the various academies (of agriculture, natural sciences, the arts, etc.) were placed under the direct supervision of the council, that is, under Mrs. Ceauşescu. She has become, therefore, the most important authority, besides her husband, in scientific and cultural affairs. Ilie Ceauşescu, Nicolae's younger brother, has been promoted to the rank of general in the Romanian army. He also usually leads cultural delegations visiting Western countries, an important function in Romania's efforts to strengthen ties with the West.

During the 1970s, the primary concern of the leadership was the indoctrination of young people in Marxism-Leninism of a Romanian type. Consequently, party doctrine was stressed at all levels of schooling and was considered to be the most important subject of study. Besides the schools, the party's youth organizations were entrusted with the task of developing the "new socialist man" in Romania. The ideal type of such a man would be well-versed in his special area of expertise in the economy and fully devoted to the party, its leader, and to Marxism-Leninism. (One has to wonder, if after thirty-five years of Communist rule such a man has not yet emerged, when, and under what conditions, would he make his august appearance?) The failure to create such ideal types was often vividly illustrated in the treatment of youth leaders. For instance, in 1973, twenty-four of the forty county first secretaries of the Union of Communist Youth were dismissed, and within one year, five newcomers to the ranks were also sent home.[16] It seems that it is hard to arouse the enthusiasm of young people by appeals to their sense of the heroic in multilateral development.

There have been tremendous efforts exerted by the Ceauşescu leadership to link the history of the Romanian Communist party with progressive Romanian national traditions. No opportunity was missed to help this trend. For instance, there was a vitriolic argument between

Romanian and Russian historians in 1976 about the history of
Bessarabia, and the true ethnicity of the people living in that region. The
debate stopped short of a confrontation, but the implications were
driven home, however, when Nicolae Ceauşescu proclaimed that
Romania had no territorial or other problems with the Soviet Union or
the neighboring socialist states.[17] But Romanian historians continued to
maintain that Bessarabia rightfully belonged to their country in the
presocialist past.[18]

The Congress on Political Education, called to session in June 1976,
signalled once again that there would be no relaxation of controls over
cultural affairs. The congress confirmed the "correctness" of the cultural
and educational policies of the party as instituted in 1971. Once again,
special emphasis was placed on historical continuity allegedly
represented by the Communist party. Nicolae Ceauşescu declared that
Russian and Hungarian historians were contentiously trying to falsify the
past by treating Bessarabia and Transylvania as having been non-
Romanian political entities in the past. The congress then proceeded to
create a series of guidelines for future cultural activities, emphasizing
their Marxist-Leninist, but also Romanian, character.[19]

In spite of all restrictions, literary life in the 1970s was more vibrant in
Romania than before. It was true that the guidelines of the party were
strictly observed, but this did not prevent the emergence of some lively
controversies. The works of Marin Preda seem especially noteworthy,
since they signal the direction that Romanian literature was moving in
in the 1970s. In his book, entitled *Delirium*,[20] the author reviewed the
policies of former Prime Minister Antonescu. Preda provided a balanced
treatment of his subject. He praised Antonescu for destroying the Romanian fascists—the Iron Guard—and protecting the Jews during World
War II. Even Antonescu's alliance with Nazi Germany received an
understanding treatment. In another book entitled *The Most Beloved
Earthling*, Preda treated the first years of Communist rule in a balanced
manner.[21] Another author, Ion Lancranjan, wrote *The Son of Drought*, a
novel dealing with the socialist revolution in Romania in terms that are
not always flattering to the former Romanian Communist leaders.[22]

It is obvious that these works were written with the approval of the
party leaders. They were intended to provide a trend in Romanian
cultural life. This was evident in the arguments that followed an attack
on *Delirium* in *Literaturnaja Gazeta* by Soviet critic Konstantin Savin.
Preda was defended by Ion Ianosi, professor of aesthetics at Bucharest
University. His argument was that regardless of the merit of the work in
question, Savin's attack was reminiscent of Soviet Russian interference in
Romanian cultural life during the 1950s.[23]

The ideal framework for the promotion of national consciousness and its identification with the Communist party was considered to be the Hymn to Romania Festival. This project originated in 1978. The festival was to emphasize "a thoroughly organized, guided, amateur art form" (a rather strange contradiction of terms), and to commemorate the 2050th(!) anniversary of an allegedly "centralized" Dacian state and the 60th anniversary of the establishment of the Communist party of Romania.[24] Cultural life in general was to be stimulated through the festival, mobilizing people for greater efforts on behalf of multilateral development.

The aim of stimulating national consciousness is also evident in the great emphasis placed on the promotion of the so-called Workers' Theater. Such theaters operated in Romania during the early stages of the cultural revolution after 1947. They were geared to the production of "socialist realist" drama, aimed at educating the people in socialist values.[25] In parallel with the reappearance of these theaters in the 1970s, sharp criticisms were levelled at professional actors and dramatists. Valentin Silvestru, a senior critic at *Era Socialistă*, the party's biweekly journal, charged that Romanian theaters lacked a "unified, correctly based" concept. As a consequence of this pressure, political plays that do not stress socialist realism and cultural values have completely disappeared from the stages of professional theaters.[26] But the outside world seemed to have valued professional drama in Romania more than the local party apparat. For instance, Andras Suto, a Transylvanian dramatist of Hungarian descent, was awarded the Herder Prize in drama in 1979 for his activities as a writer.

An anecdote circulating in Romanian intellectual circles in the late 1970s serves to illustrate the attitude of the party leaders toward creative artists. According to this story, Nicolae Ceauşescu delivered a short speech to selected intellectual leaders upon the anniversary of Romania's liberation in 1945. He instructed them that their first and most important task was to go to the people and learn from them. "Because," he allegedly said, "a simple swine herder has more wisdom than many intellectuals spending a lifetime at their desks." Even if this story is apocryphal, it certainly reflects the cultural policies of the Romanian Communist party as they developed during the 1970s.

*   *   *

Poland had a typically cyclic history during the 1970s, and this was reflected in the cultural life. As the initial promise of Gomulka as a reformist leader failed during the 1960s, Poland went through a series of economic and political crises that resulted in a change of leadership, but not in a change of the general aims of the Communist party leaders.

There was already trouble in 1968, when Poland participated in the invasion of Czechoslovakia. There were demonstrations against the invasion and the Brezhnev Doctrine, especially by the university students. This was followed by an officially inspired wave of anti-Semitism during which many intellectuals of Jewish descent were expelled from positions of authority. But the climax of Gomulka's career seemed to have come in December 1970, when Poland finally signed an agreement with West Germany ending the long drawn-out issues emanating from World War II. But this diplomatic success was nullified by an abrupt change in economic policies that was ill-prepared and aroused great opposition.

In December 1970, just prior to Christmas, the Gomulka government suddenly announced substantial increases in food prices and the prices of other consumer goods. The government also altered the salary scale of workers, which adversely affected their purchasing power. The government was correct in seeking economic reform, since the country was living way beyond its means. Foreign debts were increasing alarmingly, and production indices were decreasing. But there was an immediate response from the workers, who resented the fact that the government did not deem it necessary to consult with the population before making the changes. In four Baltic cities there were riots and protests. These were suppressed by force. But the protests forced the cancellation of the price increases and forced Gomulka out of office. He was replaced by Edward Gierek, a Silesian party leader. Gierek promised more consumer goods and promised closer consultation with the workers before any major alterations of the economic system were undertaken. But he also failed to deliver on his promises. In 1976, and again in early 1980, his government had to face the economic problems that bedeviled his predecesssor. By then, Poland's foreign obligations had reached $6 billion, and consumer goods were, once again, in short supply. In June and July 1980, workers struck in several cities, demanding pay increases, and the government was compelled to oblige.

The cultural policies of the Gierek government reflected these conditions. The aim of the Communist party continued to be the creation of the "new socialist man," who would be willing to make sacrifices in the interest of socialist construction. The major vehicle for the task—as in the other socialist states in Eastern Europe—was to be the Polish educational system. The school curricula were, therefore, geared toward spreading Marxist-Leninist ideals and a rationalist-materialist view of the world. Atheism was a strong component of instruction in every level of education. In the view of the Polish Communist leadership, great strides were being made in this direction. As Jan Szczepanski, a party sociologist, asserted, the party has already succeeded in transforming the intelligentsia's orientation "from amateur dilettantism to scientific-minded professionalism," and from a humanistic to a technological point of view.[27] But this assertion seems a bit premature; if reports coming from Poland are true, even party bureaucrats seem to share in many of the old "amateurish" traits of the old Polish intelligentsia.[28]

There are simply too many counteracting forces in Poland undermining the party's efforts at indoctrinating the people in the tenets of Marxism-Leninism. The most important of these forces is the Roman Catholic church. The election of Cardinal Woytila as Pope John Paul II has strengthened the position of Catholics not only in Poland but in the entire East European region. His visit to his native country in 1978 was greeted with delirious joy by great masses of people to the great embarrassment of the Communist party. Consequently, relations between the Roman Catholic church and the Communist party and the government remained strained. The state continued to stress a vigorous atheistic program in the schools and offices, emphasizing the antireligious nature of its ideology. At the same time, it made some minor concessions to the church, such as the inclusion of priests in the social security system.[29]

But the most important issue for the Polish Communists in the 1970s was the problem of ideological purity. It is this issue that prevents an accommodation with the church, and which threatens the party with continuing social isolation. The danger of "ideological convergence" became especially acute with the onset of détente and the conclusion of the Helsinki Agreement. The party apparently considered the danger so serious that it proceeded to conclude bilateral agreements with the other East European Communist parties and with the party of the Soviet Union to prevent ideological softening.[30] At the same time, Gierek tightened control over the universities and instituted closer oversight by the state authorities over the entire educational system.

It seems, however, that despite all these efforts, there emerged in Poland probably the strongest, most articulate dissident movement in all of Eastern Europe. The underground has a whole series of publications, including periodicals and books. It seems that the Communist leaders, although obviously having the coercive power to stop the movement, decided to tolerate it within certain limits. There are periodic reminders that the limits have been reached, at which point the government delivers a harsh reminder to the culprits. But there is none of the vituperation that exists in Czechoslovakia or the merciless oppression that characterizes the Romanian leaders' response to dissidence. The Poles act with more prudence and circumspection. For instance, the head of the NOWA underground publishing house, Miroslav Chojecki, was arrested in May

1980 and charged with stealing a printing press. What he actually did was to rebuild a printing press that had been discarded by one of the government's printing establishments. But after a few weeks of imprisonment, Chojecki was released. His arrest did arouse protests, and petitions were circulated on his behalf, but it seems that all the government intended all along was to serve notice that Chojecki's activities had reached permissible limits.

What is important is that Poland can no longer be isolated from the rest of the world as it was during Stalin's time. There are now between 8 and 10 million Poles living outside of the Polish state, and they continuously keep in touch with their relatives and friends. Western journals and broadcasts reach Poland with regularity, and books published abroad by Polish writers frequently find their way back to the mother country. Thus, the cultural policies of the regime simply could not be as strict as in Czechoslovakia or Romania. The result is that cultural life in Poland differs greatly from that of other East European states; it is freer and more varied, producing non-Marxist publications, drama, and even films. This augurs well for the future of Polish national culture.

* * *

Hungarian cultural policies were the most relaxed of all the East European states' during the 1970s. The Hungarian Communist leadership seems to have matured and achieved a true compromise with the intellectuals. Janos Kadar pointed out in a speech in May 1980 that the time had passed for trying to provide foolproof answers and unrealistic promises for society, and that all the Hungarian Communist party wanted now was to provide the best possible living conditions for the people, under the given economic and political circumstances.[31]

This does not mean that the Hungarian Communists had given up their aim of creating a Marxist-Leninist oriented society. When they are confronted by open defiance, they are quite able and willing to use harsh methods of repression. But while such methods were quite evident in the early 1970s, there was less need for the party to use them by the end of the decade. A typical example of the harsh methods used was the treatment of the Sociological Group of Andras Hegedus, Mihaly Vajda, and Janis Kis in 1973. They were expelled from the party for discussing Marxism in pluralistic terms. The implication of their argument was that the Communist party had no monopoly over the interpretation of Marxist ideology. Hegedus and his group went further and rejected the notion of historical inevitability as this idea related to the development of socialism. Four other scholars belonging to this group who were not members of the Communist party were also disciplined. They all lost their jobs and were forbidden to travel abroad. Three other sociologists who researched conditions of the workers fared similarly. Laszlo Szelenyi, Istvan Kemeny, and Gyorgy Konrad publicized their findings of inequalities and contradictions in the regime's treatment of the working class. They were arrested, their manuscripts were confiscated, and they were eventually advised to leave Hungary. Since then, Konrad, whose book *The City Builder* had received wide publicity in the West, returned; he is still being ostracized by the regime and prevented from working in his profession. The other two sociologists remain in exile.

However, by the end of the decade, the Hungarian party leaders no longer attempted to prescribe precise ways for the creation of a "socialist man." Nor were they sure any longer as to what was the most valid model to follow on the road to socialism.[32] They had accepted the notion (quietly, without much publicity) that the socialist way of life—as all life in general—was constantly changing, and it could not be based on a rigid, prefabricated model.[33]

There seemed to be a corresponding maturity among Hungarian intellectuals in their approach to creative endeavors. Only a handful of writers continued to consider themselves the "conscience of the nation," the traditional stance of creative people in Hungary. The grand old man of Hungarian poetry and drama, Gyula Illyes, continued to issue ringing declarations and calls for heightened national consciousness, but his calls usually found greater echoes among Hungarians abroad than at home.

Correspondingly, dissidents have less impact on Hungarian cultural life than they do in Czechoslovakia or Poland. By the end of the 1970s, there was hardly need for the Communist party to resort to earlier methods of repression. For instance, when, in 1979, several hundred intellectuals signed a petition addressed to Janos Kadar on behalf of the persecuted Czech reformists, there was hardly any official response. They were not persecuted at all. By ignoring the protest, the party leaders provided no opportunity for the Western press to create a sensational story of the incident, and it was soon forgotten. A similar approach was used to deal with the Free University, organized in Budapest without govermental approval during the last years of the 1970s. Although the participants, sometimes numbering more than a hundred, were obviously observed, there was no official reprisal against them or the lecturers.

Tolerance of deviant behavior—within limits, to be sure—made Hungarian cultural life interesting in the 1970s. One example of this was provided by the activities of Gyula Hernadi and Miklos Jancso, two filmmakers turned drama producers, who produced several controversial plays. One of these, *Mata Hari*, was an avant-garde production, showing the first striptease act in any socialist country. Another one of their plays, *Jack the Ripper*, used nude actors who denigrated historical figures with often vulgar speech. When they were taken to task by the party critics, Jancso replied that "as far as I am concerned, everybody's culture is what he cares for, what he lives with. The statement, 'I give culture to the people,' is simply impertinent. People create culture. The most one can do is to provide them with alternatives."[34] No one could go further in proclaiming the end of "socialist realism."

If the Communist party no longer claims infallibility in Hungary, it certainly did not give up its "right" to set standards of cultural life. But the controls are now more subtle, and they are intended more as a means of socialization than of coercion. The image of the party as a rational, reasonable force in national life is being reinforced by a cautious effort at associating it with moderate Hungarian nationalism. One means to this effect is the Mother Tongue Conference. It has been organized, since 1973, as a forum for the preservation of the Hungarian language among Hungarian exiles and their children. The conference meets periodically in Budapest, attracting large numbers of Hungarians from abroad, and lately some from neighboring socialist countries except Romania. It sponsors textbooks and other publications for use abroad and maintains summer camps for children of Hungarian emigrants.

Another effort in the same direction was the organization of the annual Hungarian language week, dedicated to the cleansing of the language of "incomprehensible and meaningless expressions."[35] The movement is officially sponsored by Minister of Culture Gyorgy Aczel and was first aimed against surrealistic novels and plays that increasingly appeared in Hungary. But it was also intended to help party activists rid themselves of the jargon that made party language a caricature of correct Hungarian usage and that helped to isolate the party from the people during the 1950s. Interestingly enough, the language week was also to remind Hungarians that language plays a crucial role in promoting social equality, and that learning correct usage could help "disadvantaged" Hungarians attain higher status in society. All in all, cultural life in socialist Hungary has been lively during the 1970s.

* * *

Cultural policies in the four Communist East European states discussed above represent the opposite ends of the spectrum, ranging from extreme rigidity to great flexibility. In the case of the other four states, one does not find greater consistency, but rather more complexity in the approaches of the respective parties to cultural life. In East Germany, Yugoslavia, Albania, and Bulgaria, strictness of control varied with periods of relaxation. In most cases the causes in policy changes were extraneous—i.e., not related to prevailing political conditions within the countries and not rigorously planned—but they also had something to do with different styles of leadership as one set of party leaders was exchanged for another.

In East Germany, the Communist leaders were preoccupied throughout the 1970s with the related issues of West German influence, the problems created by the very existence of the two German states, and the changing relations between East Germany and the Soviet Union. During the last years of the 1960s, Walter Ulbricht developed some specifically East German elements of Marxism-Leninism, envisaging the evolution of a special relationship between his state and the Soviet Union. Such a relationship was based on the military power of the USSR on the one hand, and the rapidly developing economy of East Germany on the other. One major element of his thinking was that the Soviet Union and the other East European states would have to abide by the interests of East Germany before making any moves in which these interests were involved. This was specifically the case in dealing with West Germany with whom the Soviet Union, Czechoslovakia, and Poland were conducting negotiations for the normalization of relations. Ulbricht dreamed of the eventual establishment of one socialist Germany, and this was clearly not in the interest of the Soviet Union or the other East European states.[36]

Thus, in 1971, Ulbricht was eased out of power by his former protégé, Honecker, although he retained his ceremonial functions until his death in 1973. Since then, Honecker has quietly dismantled the Ulbrichtian machine and has begun tearing down the ideological framework built by his predecessor.

By the mid-1970s, Honecker had developed his policies. The cornerstones of these policies are complete loyalty to the Soviet Union, a new interpretation of German nationhood, and a strict adherence to Marxism-Leninism. For Honecker, there are actually two German nations, eternally separate and divisible, since his definition of nationhood is functional. On the one hand, there is the capitalist, imperialist German nation, i.e., the Federal Republic of Germany. On the other, there is the socialist nation of the German Democratic Republic (GDR). There is nothing in common between these two nations, since language, historical traditions, and other elements of nationhood do not enter Honecker's equation.[37] To aid the development of this interpretation of nationhood, party historians began the difficult task of reinterpreting German history, largely by disregarding historical facts. But even Honecker and the other party ideologues found it difficult to negate the notion of one German nation. Thus, they developed the idea of two separate concepts, namely, nationhood and nationality. According to this idea, German nationality existed since the early Middle Ages, but nationhood must be intepreted according to the functions of the state. Whether this interpretation will be more acceptable to Germans in the GDR than the one before will have to be decided in the future.

The cultural policies of the Honecker regime fully reflected the tensions that the reinterpretation of German nationhood created. The party certainly wanted to maintain cultural life on a Marxist-Leninist basis. But once the regime received international recognition in 1973 and became a member, together with West Germany, of the United Nations, it felt secure enough to relax controls. After the signing of the Helsinki Agreement in 1975, the East German Communists seemed to be able to relax even more. One evidence of this was the appearance of some remarkable films such as *The Third One* and *The Legend of Paul and Paula*, films that deal with the problems of individual human beings with remarkably little ideological content. On the whole, however, cultural life, education, and ideological questions remain within the realm of party control, and there is no dissident movement to speak of in the East German state. The government simply does not permit the emergence of a dissident movement, and it readily permits the emigration to the West of people who are dissatisfied with its policies.

Yugoslavia has been usually regarded as the relatively freest of East European Communist states. Titoism meant, in cultural life, the abandonment of "socialist realism," and the toleration of a variety of views as long as the written or spoken words did not question socialism or were not "pro-Soviet."[38] In the 1970s all this changed. The aging of Tito brought forth the possibility of internal strife among the nationalities of the state and the threat of Soviet intervention. Correspondingly, there was a tightening of controls in every sphere of national life, and a stricter supervision of all cultural endeavors.

Troubles were brewing in the late 1960s among the country's young people. In 1968, students took over Belgrade University. In 1971, the law faculty of Belgrade University openly called for more intellectual freedom. Students demonstrated at Zagreb University in the same year for greater Croatian autonomy and even independence.

Tito was obviously concerned for the future of the Yugoslav Communist state. Thus, a new constitution was introduced in 1974 that strengthened the controls exercised by the central authorities over the autonomous regions. A collective presidency of eight persons was introduced, headed by Tito as long as he was alive, providing governing experience for his designated successors. But the constitution also increased the power of the Communist party apparat. It declared that the party must assume its rightful role as the moving force in the dictatorship of the proletariat, the latter term being increasingly used in party declarations.[39]

Parallel with these policies, a crackdown on dissidents began. Thus, alternative interpretations of Marxism were banned; individuals such as seventy-four year-old Djuro Djurovic (a former associate of the Croatian *chetnik* leader, Draza Mihailovic) and Mihailo Mihailov, the noted Marxist writer, were charged with antistate propaganda and jailed. In 1975, eight Marxist professors were ousted from the philosophy faculty of Belgrade University, mainly because they argued for the elimination of the vestiges of Stalinism in Yugoslavia and for greater intellectual freedom. They were also charged with attempting to limit the influence of the Communist party and with being tainted by bourgeois ideas through their frequent contacts with Western intellectuals.[40] Their writings were banned, and their journal, *Praxis*, was closed.

In the late 1970s, orthodoxy was increasingly demanded from all creative people, especially teachers and professors. Theaters came in for their share of criticism for not being Marxist enough in their presentations, and all other forms of artistic expression were closely monitored by the party. There were attempts to prevent the dissemination of Western art and literature in Yugoslavia, and there was a renewed stress on the study of Marxism in schools. After the death of Tito in 1980, the ruling group further tightened its control over all aspects of life. Dissidents were warned that they would be tried if they did not cease their activities. Milovan Djilas, the most prominent dissident, received further criticism in the party press. It seems that such strict policies are reflex actions against perceived internal and external threats to the survival of the Yugoslav Communist state, and they are likely to remain in effect for the foreseeable future.

In the late 1960s, the Albanian Communist party inaugurated an ideological and cultural revolution, intended to reflect a similar Chinese development. By then, the break with the Soviet Union had been finalized and Albania depended more and more on Chinese support for its survival as a Communist state. The intended victims of the cultural revolution were the bureaucrats who, according to party leader Enver Hoxha, had deviated from Marxism-Leninism and become the Trojan horse of the Soviet "revisionists." The revolution was expected to complete the reorientation of Albanian society according to the party's tenets. In line with these policies, the educational system was reorganized to reflect the triad of Albanian socialism, academic study, menial work, and military training. All churches were closed, priests unfrocked, and the charters of religious denominations revoked. Women were brought into the workplace in large numbers in order to break the conservative structure of Albanian families. Albania, thus, embarked on a strict Stalinist road to socialism. But it did not work. By 1970, there was unrest among young people, economic problems emerged because of Albania's lack of resources, and divisions appeared within the ruling Politburo as to the remedies necessary to correct the situation.[41]

Fadil Pacrami, one of the members of the ruling elite, became the leading advocate of a relaxation of controls. He argued that it was the conservative attitude of older, badly educated cadres that threatened Albanian socialism, not the decadence of the younger generation or foreign influences. Pacrami himself was a writer by profession; he received support from two other members of the Politburo and the experiment in relaxation was tried between 1970 and 1973.

The new policies, however, were never really given a chance to succeed. By 1973, it became obvious that they did not work. There was increased absenteeism at shops and factories, young people began to assume the manners and dress of Western tourists who came to Albania in increasing numbers, and the indifference of young people to Marxism-Leninism became quite apparent. In 1973, therefore, the Albanian Communist party decided to resume its earlier course of close control over every sphere of life in the country.

While Pacrami had his way, he encouraged intellectuals to abandon "socialist realism" for genuine art forms and literature, permitted the increasing importation of Western films and books, and tolerated socially deviant behavior among young people. Now all this suddenly changed. Pacrami and his two supporters were ousted from the Politburo. A massive purge of the nation's intellectual elite and the leaders of the youth organizations took place. Intellectuals were sent to do menial labor in factories and on collective farms. The educational system was reorganized once again to reflect the party's ideology, and the study of Marxism-Leninism assumed a new, heightened significance. These policies remained in effect throughout the decade of the 1970s, and there seems to be little prospect for change in Albania.

Bulgarian cultural policies in the 1970s were hardly distinguishable from those of Soviet Russia. There was a reliance on the time-worn clichés of "socialist realism" for the publication of books and stories and the exhibition of fine art. Theaters catered almost exclusively to "socialist realist" dramas, in many instances brought directly from the Russian stage. Undeniably, there was a slight relaxation of controls, but certainly no liberalization has taken place. As the Bulgarian Communist party continued to rely on the Russians for both external and internal support, their cultural policies faithfully reflected this situation. The regime, headed by Todor Zhivkov, continued to insist on Marxist-Leninist principles in judging cultural endeavors.

Perhaps the influence of Ludmilla, the daughter of Zhivkov, was felt a little more than many realized. She has been known to advocate a close interrelationship between science, education, and the fine arts, and as a member of the Politburo of the Bulgarian Communist party she had a chance to implement her theories. At the Bulgarian Congress on Education, held on May 12–13, 1980, she declared that "the development of men and society [must proceed] according to the laws of beauty."[42] This statement is certainly far from a customary interpretation of "socialist realism." One must wait to see whether her influence will be beneficial in the liberation of Bulgarian cultural life from the conservatives.

The Bulgarian Communist party, following closely that of the Soviet Union, placed a great emphasis on education as the means of spreading Marxist-Leninist ideas. Here, again, Ludmilla Zhivkov seems important. As a Politburo member, she has been entrusted with the supervision of education and she has taken advantage of her position to fill important posts in the Ministry of Education with her supporters.

As the 1970s drew to a close, however, there was hardly any movement in Bulgarian cultural life to indicate any change in well-established practices. The Communist party is so closely dependent upon and allied with the Soviet Union that there seems very little chance for a more liberal policy and a more exciting cultural life in Bulgaria in the foreseeable future.

In summing up this short survey, one is struck by the variety of approaches to cultural life and policies employed by the respective Communist parties in Eastern Europe. At the same time, one must also note that the aims of the regimes in question have not really changed. They still want to create, through education, indoctrination, and cultural policies, a "new socialist man," who would be more trustworthy to work for socialism than the present population. They continue to insist that Marxist ideology (sometimes Marxism-Leninism) be the basis of most, if not all, cultural endeavors. Although in the more advanced states where the Communist parties feel secure, "socialist realism" has been abandoned (or the leaders pay only lip service to this vague notion, but do not enforce its tenets), in others, it continues to be the yardstick by which the authorities measure cultural creativity. Relaxed or strict, conservative or liberal, the Communist regimes have not given up the idea that somehow they have a superior knowledge of what cultural life ought to be in their respective societies. Even in states where a relaxed approach is evident, there is never any insurance that, if the party so decides, there would not or could not be a return to the harsh policies of the Stalinist era.

Notes

1. M. Rosenthal and P. Yudin, "Filosofskii Slovar" in *A Dictionary of Philosophy*, English edition (Moscow: Progress, 1967), p. 10.

2. Istvan Hermann, *A szocialista kultúra problémái* [Problems of socialist culture] (Budapest: Kossuth, 1970), p. 460.

3. *Ibid.*, p. 461.

4. Francois Fejtö, *Die Geschichte der Volksdemokratien* (Graz, Wien, Köln: Vlg. Styria, 1972), vol. 2, p. 459.

5. See Ivan Volgyes, "Politics, Ideology and Culture. The STP's of Life in Communist Eastern Europe," unpublished MS. I want to thank the author for permitting me to use this work.

6. Radio Free Europe (hereafter: RFE), *Situation Report*, April 5, 1973.

7. Edward Taborsky, "Czechoslovakia under Husak," *Current History* 70 (March 1976):117.

8. RFE, *Situation Report*, August 5, 1976.

9. *Ibid.*

10. Taborsky, "Czechoslovakia," p. 117.

11. *Ibid.*

12. *Tribuna*, September 17, 1975, p. 3.

13. See, for instance, the antireligious work by Ondrej Danyi, *Politici v Sutanach* [Politicians in cassocks] (Bratislava: Obzor, 1979), and Jiri Loukotka, *Vedecky Ateismus a Svetonazarova Vychova* [Scientific atheism and world outlook education] (Prague: Horizon, 1980), and the report in *Rolnicke Noviny*, March 24, 1980.

14. See Anthony Kenny, "Take No Illegal Orders," *New Statesman* (London), April 18, 1980, and by the same author, "Question Czech Secret Police Refuse to Answer," *Sunday Telegraph* (London), April 27, 1980.

15. Radio Bucharest, March 22, 1980, as reported by RFE, *Situation Report*, May 13, 1980.

16. RFE, *Situation Report*, April 5, 1973.

17. *Ibid.*, August 5, 1976.

18. *Ibid.*

19. *Ibid.*

20. *Deliriul* (Bucharest: Cartea Romaneasca, 1975).

21. *Cel Mai Iubit Dintre Paminteni* (Bucharest: Cartea Romaneasca, 1980).

22. *Fiul Secetei* (Bucharest: Albatros, 1980).

23. RFE, *Situation Report*, May 22, 1980.

24. *Romania Libera*, April 8, 1980.

25. *Scinteia*, March 16, 1980.

26. RFE, *Situation Report*, April 22, 1980.

27. M. K. Dziewanowski, "The Communist Party of Poland," in Stephen Fischer-Galati, ed. *The Communist Parties of Eastern Europe* (New York: Columbia University Press, 1979), p. 272.

28. *Ibid.*

29. RFE, *Situation Report*, May 27, 1980.

30. *Tribuna Ludu*, July 18, 1975.

31. Kadar's election speech in *Népszabadság* (Budapest), May 30, 1980.

32. László Cseh-Szombathelyi and Kálmán Kulcscár, "A szocialista életforma kutatásának eredményei,"[Results of the researches into the socialist way of life] *Társadalomtudományi Közlemények* 1(1980):1–3.

33. *Ibid*.

34. *Szinház*, March 1980, p. 4.

35. RFE, *Situation Report*, May 7, 1980.

36. Henry Krisch, "The German Democratic Republic in the Mid-1970s," *Current History* 70 (March 1976):119.

37. *Ibid.*, p. 120.

38. Alex N. Dragonich, "Yugoslavia: Titoism without Tito?" *Current History* 70 (March 1976):111.

39. *Ibid.*, pp. 111–112.

40. *Ibid.*, p. 112.

41. Nicholas C. Pano, "Albania in the Era of Kosygin and Brezhnev," in George W. Simmonds, ed., *Nationalism in the USSR and Eastern Europe in the Era of Brezhnev and Kosygin* (Detroit, Mich.: University of Detroit Press, 1977), pp. 484–485.

42. *Narodna Kultura* (Sofia), no. 22, May 30, 1980.

Stephen Fischer-Galati   **10**

Conclusion: A Balance Sheet

It has long been assumed that as the Communist order consolidates itself in Eastern Europe—at least to the extent of being immutable short of the collapse of the present political order in the Kremlin—its rigidity would diminish. It has also been assumed that the industrialization and corollary modernization of Communist societies would proceed according to plan and thus, by the end of the 1980s, convergence between the Western capitalist and the Eastern socialist systems would be closer than at any time since the death of Stalin. Supporters of these positions have used a plethora of statistical data to give credence and validity to the theory of convergence, within the framework of détente and peaceful coexistence. Occasional deviations from this script, such as the Soviet invasions of Czechoslovakia and Afghanistan, nonobservance by the Soviet bloc of the provisions of the Helsinki Agreement, overt or covert subversion of U.S. interests in the Middle East, Africa, Asia, Latin America, and even Western Europe, have been dismissed as ultimately irrelevant to the achievement of convergence on the assumption that nuclear war cannot be contemplated any more seriously than a return to the Cold War days of the Stalinist period. Yet, the theory of convergence is as questionable as that of inevitable confrontation enunciated by contemporary exponents of the policies of containment, instant retaliation, and constant muscle-flexing, who can discern no essential changes between Eastern Europe of the 1980s and that of the early 1950s.

The fact is that the data and arguments used in support of a theory are used selectively and for a preconceived purpose and, as such, they must be suspect at all times. There are two basic difficulties in seeking an objective assessment of the present status and the foreseeable future of Eastern Europe. The first is the tendency to use all data indiscriminately, at face value, and to extrapolate from it generalizations for the bloc as a whole. The second is to assume either that the Soviet Union has altered its essential relationship with the countries of Eastern Europe in a manner that would obviate the utilization of such terms as "bloc" or "satellite"—since, ostensibly, the Kremlin recognizes the right of individual Communist countries to pursue individual programs of development as long as they do not place socialist security in jeopardy—or, alternately, that nothing has changed since the days of Stalin.

The present volume attempts to present and analyze statistical data and other information within what we have perceived to be a valid pattern for assessing the present and future development of Eastern Europe. That pattern is evaluation of both common and diverse factors affecting the individual Communist states of Eastern Europe, albeit within the general framework of the unquestionable entity that the socialist community of Eastern Europe actually represents. Moreover, it was deemed essential to relate developments in Eastern Europe directly and intimately to the present and future aims of the Soviet Union, the ultimate protector of the security of the states of Eastern Europe and guarantor of their continuing existence as socialist states. Therefore, any balance sheet of achievements, failures, and prognoses cannot concern itself with developments in any one given East European state because case studies are unrepresentative for Eastern Europe and also because the sum of individual parts does not provide a correct understanding of the whole. And this is so because "democratic centralism" has always been an erroneous concept and because the deductive method is far more valid than the inductive one in the study of Soviet and East European affairs.

This is not to say, however, that there are no significant differences among the development and policies of the various countries of Eastern Europe, for indeed there are many. Rather, it is to say that the differences are essentially inconsequential for assessing the general character of Eastern Europe in the 1980s.

The domestic and foreign policies of the Communist states of Eastern Europe show variations determined ostensibly by the prevailing "objective conditions" in each country. Thus, decentralization and the corollary increase in the political activities of regional and local units are clearly more manifest in Yugoslavia and Hungary than in Czechoslovakia, Bulgaria, or Romania. Nevertheless, with the exception of Yugoslavia, decentralization is as cosmetic as the ostensibly prevailing democratic centralism, given the constant increase in the powers of ruling groups in the capital cities, which, in the case of at least Bulgaria and Romania, has led to the virtual deification of Zhivkov and particularly of Ceaușescu. And the ruling elite in Tirana, headed by the venerable Enver Hoxha, is not far behind the Romanian leadership in that respect. More intriguing perhaps is the question of the relationship between the East European leaders and those in the Kremlin. It seems fair to say that ultimately no ruler in Eastern Europe may engage in any "national" manifestation or deviation that would be, in any way, incompatible with Moscow's interests. Technical modifications and the adoption of forms of governance and party organization that stabilize the Communist order in any given state are indeed tolerated, or even encouraged, by the Kremlin, but any deterioration in the power of the Communist parties that may result in a weakening of ties with Moscow or pose a threat to the unity of the Warsaw Pact or of COMECON are deemed intolerable. The Brezhnev Doctrine is by no means dead.

Even in matters related to foreign policy, deviations from Soviet norms are feasible only within well-defined limits. It is noteworthy that all the Communist states of Eastern Europe, with the exception of Yugoslavia, Romania, and, in its own way, Albania, have adhered rigorously to the Moscow line in foreign affairs. The parroting of the Kremlin's pronunciamentos and rhetoric is as evident today as it was thirty years ago and is likely to be during the 1980s and beyond. The argument that support of Soviet foreign policies has allowed greater flexibility in Hungary and Poland in the pursuit of domestic policies, most notably along economic and cultural lines, appears to be unfounded. There is no quid pro quo in the Kremlin. Nor is there any basis for the thesis that internal "Stalinism" in Romania has compensated, in Moscow's eyes, for Ceauşescu's pursuit of an "independent" foreign policy. It is true that Romania, like Yugoslavia and often even more than its Western neighbor, has sought protection against Soviet imperialism through the pursuit of foreign policies frequently at variance with Moscow's since at least the 1960s. It is also true that Romania's foreign relations—political as well as economic—based, as they are, on "friendship with all countries regardless of their political systems," have, on occasion, been upsetting to the Kremlin. However, the Romanian leaders have always been keenly aware of their limits and thus have avoided the implementation of the Brezhnev Doctrine at their expense. On the other hand, the possibility of military intervention by the Soviet Union, threatened as it was during the Czechoslovak crisis of 1968, cannot be discounted altogether. Yugoslavia's independent foreign policy, like Romania's, is designed primarily to protect the nation's independence and has been characterized by prudence and avoidance of direct confrontation with Moscow.

Since the ultimate concerns of Moscow and of the East European Communist states are related to political stability, i.e., to the maintenance of the Communist order, whatever concessions Moscow made to its socialist partners and the national Communist parties made to their peoples have been in the economic sphere. But, the concessions that were made were themselves a function of political considerations and were, more often than not, revocable or subject to alteration also in terms of political desiderata or necessities.

As the 1980s begin, the economic conditions in Eastern Europe are precarious, albeit for different reasons than those affecting East European economies in previous decades. The days of joint Soviet–East European companies, which represented the crudest forms of Soviet economic imperialism, are gone. COMECON, likewise, has lost its monopolistic position, although it continues to operate as an instrumentality of Russian economic controls. The scope of bilateral relations between the USSR and the countries of Eastern Europe has not narrowed, and, in the most crucial area of energy supplies, the dependency of the East Europeans has become more severe. The Kremlin's insistence on receiving payment in convertible currencies for its rapidly rising prices for energy resources has, inter alia, forced large price increases in all commodities available in the member states of COMECON, with resultant adverse effects on internal economic development and foreign trade. It is true that industrial and agricultural productivity have increased, occasionally dramatically, throughout Eastern Europe in the 1970s, but there have been no corresponding increases in the standard of living, at least during the last years of that decade, when inflationary pressures and unfavorable trade balances affected the East European economies even more than those of the Western industrial world. The opportunities for economic development afforded in the 1970s by rapid expansion of bilateral relations with Western Europe, primarily with West Germany, have not borne the expected fruit, largely because of the noncompetitiveness of the East European economies and the resultant inability of most East European countries to repay the large loans for economic development made available to them by the Western industrialized world. The enormous trade deficits speak for themselves in that respect. Similarly, the ever-growing economic relations with the Third World, particularly with the nations of Africa and the Middle East, have brought only limited economic advantages to the member nations of COMECON, although the corollary political advantages have been considerable.

Even such successful socialist economies as those of Yugoslavia and Hungary are retrenching. The high prices of energy have affected them adversely and, in the case of Yugoslavia, the economic instability of Western Europe has lessened both the need for *Gastarbeiters* and these workers' ability to bring Western currencies back to the mother country. Elsewhere, economic prognoses are even more negative. The Polish economy has been beset for years by endless difficulties in both the agricultural and industrial sectors, with little likelihood of its ever attaining viability in the critical 1980s. The Czech economy has been artificially propped up, for political reasons, by the USSR after the tragic events of

1968, but the industrial machinery is antiquated and the workers' lack of incentive and low productivity are painfully evident to the Moscow-installed rulers. Bulgaria, which for a large number of years was able to maintain economic stability through exportation of agricultural products and planned industrialization, is now seeking expanded economic ties with the West to attain its modest economic goals and insure a minimal standard of living for its population. Romania's aggressive economic plans and policies have been unable to insure independence from COMECON, a significant betterment of the inhabitants' standard of living, or an effective utilization of its industrial capacity. The country's natural resources, so plentiful in the 1950s, have become inadequate for the grandiose plans of the 1970s. Short of increased dependency on COMECON and, particularly, on the USSR, Romania is in for difficult times in the 1980s. Similar considerations apply to the German Democratic Republic, whose total dependence on the USSR augurs badly for the attainment of its economic goals at a time of anticipated economic difficulties for the Soviet bloc in the 1980s.

Undaunted by economic realities, however, the countries of Eastern Europe are continuing to emphasize the needs of industrial societies in the all-important area of education. In fact, the educational systems have evolved in a manner more compatible with the needs of advanced rather than of developing industrial states. The de facto abandonment of class warfare at all levels of the educational system may have been inevitable because of the simplification of the social structure some thirty years after the East European revolution. Still, the ever-growing emphasis on technical and scientific education and the maintenance of high standards for admission to specialized institutions have assured the creation and development of very competent professional cadres as well as a pool of well-trained secondary school students. Political propaganda and indoctrination, which remain all-pervasive throughout the educational system, do not materially affect the quality of scientific and technical training. They do, however, have a negative effect in culturally oriented fields, particularly in literature, history, and philosophy. Indeed, history has become the ultimate instrument of "revolutionary and patriotic education," because it is used to legitimize the Communist regimes as the ostensible fulfillers and executors of the historic legacies of the East European countries and of their revolutionary traditions. The misuse of history is indicative of the continuing concern of the Communist rulers with acceptance of their legitimacy by the peoples of Eastern Europe, a concern also expressed in neo-Stalinist, or at least regressive, policies directed against writers and artists.

As the 1970s moved on and the 1980s were ushered in in the spirit of "revolutionary militancy," most of the countries of Eastern Europe moved away from a period of cultural "thaw" to one of controls and confrontation with suspect cultural tendencies. The key issues seem to be those of combatting "bourgeois" influences and attitudes and, above all, dissidence. The very existence of dissident movements in Poland, Czechoslovakia, Yugoslavia, Romania, and even the German Democratic Republic reflects the restlessness and disaffection of members of the intellectual community with the policies of the ruling groups in matters cultural and political. In turn, the direct reactions of the Communist parties to dissent, often quite moderate, reflect the unwillingness to make heroes of the small number of intellectuals who express the muted feelings of the silent majority. The corollary restrictions imposed upon the relative freedom of expression enjoyed by artists and writers in earlier years are evident in the ever-more-primitive forms of expression now prevalent in Bulgaria, Albania, Romania, the German Democratic Republic, and Czechoslovakia. Even in Hungary and Poland retrenchment has become evident at the start of the 1980s.

Thus, as Eastern Europe enters the decade of the 1980s, the expectations of the 1960s for a gradual evolution of socialism in the direction inherent in the early promises of Khrushchevism or Titoism or, for that matter, toward variations of "socialism with a human face" have all but waned. Similarly, the expectations of better economic conditions and of general progress within the framework of the socialist system have been disappointed. Moderate optimism has given way to resignation, and the only consolation is that the crudest forms of Stalinism are not likely to reoccur in the developing industrial societies of Eastern Europe.

To a considerable extent the pessimism of the politically conscious East European is based on a general assessment of the problems of the industrial world at a time of shortages of resources and opportunities for industrial expansion and development. The crisis in the world economy is bound to have repercussions in all industrial societies; it is certain to have repercussions in developing industrial states, such as those of Eastern Europe, whose competitive positions are hampered not only by basic economic, but also, and more relevantly, by basic political factors. Eastern Europe's economic dependency on the industrialized West and, to a lesser degree, on relations with the Third World is ultimately less significant than dependency on the Soviet Union. As emancipation from Moscow is impossible for obvious political reasons, the future of Eastern Europe in the 1980s will continue to be, as it has been in the past decades, a function of Soviet imperialism and of the general international situation. Realistically, global economic conditions are not likely to favor meaningful economic progress in Eastern Europe and these conditions will, in all likelihood, lead to increasingly greater dependence on the USSR. Political prognoses are also on the dark side. The continuing crises in the Middle East, the growing rift among the Western industrial nations, the eroding of the policies of détente and peaceful coexistence between the United States and the Soviet Union, the apparent exacerbation of the Sino-Soviet conflict, in sum, the uncertainties, fears, and apprehensions that are manifest throughout the world are at best likely to assure the maintenance of an uneasy status quo and, in fact, are more likely to bring about a decade of renewed tension between the Soviet Union and its clients and the United States and its reluctant allies, present and future. In this scenario the future of Eastern Europe is at best uncertain. To paraphrase the diagnosis of East European cynics, the 1980s in Eastern Europe should be worse than the 1970s but better than the 1990s.

Index